SAN DIEGO'S NAVY

SAN DIEGO'S
NAVY

AN ILLUSTRATED HISTORY

Bruce Linder

Local Author

NAVAL INSTITUTE PRESS

Annapolis, Maryland

Naval Institute Press

291 Wood Road

Annapolis, MD 21402

Library of Congress Cataloging-in-Publication Data

Linder, Bruce R., 1949-

    San Diego's Navy : an illustrated history / Bruce R. Linder.

        p. cm.

    Includes bibliographical references and index.

    ISBN 1-55750-531-4 (alk. paper)

    1. Navy-yards and naval stations—California—San Diego.

2. San Diego (Calif.)—History, Naval. I. Title.

VA70.S36 L55 2001

359.7'09794'985—dc21

                          00-054907

Printed in the United States of America on acid-free paper ∞

08 07 06 05 04 03 02 01   9 8 7 6 5 4 3 2

First printing

Frontispiece: Vought SU-2 Corsair over North Island, c. 1933.
National Archives

To my parents who had the good sense to lead the family to San Diego and Coronado, then manipulated Navy orders and circumstance to stay much longer than chance would normally allow and, through it all, taught me a thing or two about the Navy.

CONTENTS

FOREWORD

Of all unexpected things, Bruce Linder's important history of a very personal relationship—that between San Diego and the United States Navy—is not just a good local story. It can be read as a social history of migration and transiency, and the rewards of sinking shallow and temporary roots that intertwine until they grow entrenched and stable.

That is also the hopeful theme of the contemporary American West, for its pell-mell growth over the past century may just now begin to be sorted out for its rewards and consequences. In such a context, this story of the United States Navy and its largest civic partner is one that enlightens the regional consciousness. As I read this book, treasuring the author's dutiful scholarship, something struck me that I had missed in fifty years of writing about California and the American West. I came, without planning to, from North Carolina to belong to both the Navy and San Diego, and Linder helps to tell me why. San Diegans and the Navy are much alike. Both came from somewhere else and found a home together in the restless West. Like wagon trains circling for the night, they accommodated each other. They looked after each other. They grew up together. They fought. They came to respect each other. Now it becomes unimaginable to both San Diegans and the Navy that the marriage would ever break up.

The modern Navy's first large civic partner, beginning more than a century ago, was Norfolk. Today, by any measurement, the Navy's presence is largest in San Diego. If San Diego had a Main Street, it would be its harbor, including the twenty miles of it owned by the United States Navy. In the year two thousand, annual military payrolls in San Diego were just under $4 billion, almost twice those of Norfolk and Honolulu. There are more than one hundred thousand Navy personnel and Marines on active duty in San Diego, with twenty-six thousand civilian employees. Most remarkably, perhaps, almost sixty thousand retired Navy people live in San Diego. I remember one year in the 1950s when almost two out of three physicians belonging to the San Diego County Medical Association were former Navy doctors. As civilian San Diegans have often been migrants from the South and Midwest, lines between civilian migrants and military migrants have never amounted to much.

The author, a retired Navy captain now living in San Diego as a civilian consultant, never lapses into a sycophantic view of the Navy or of San Diego. He nicely interprets one of the harbor's compliments—Richard Henry Dana, writing in 1835 of "the security and snugness of San Diego"—as an invitation that was largely overlooked by the Navy until the San Diego Chamber of Commerce began soliciting the Navy with obsessive zeal in the early decades of the twentieth century. Its primary goal was to dredge and convert a backwater, small-town harbor into a Navy port and fend off ever-hovering recession.

As California historian Kevin Starr wrote, "by 'joining the Navy,' San Diego created a sustainable industrial economy that could be kept under control . . . a way to develop its economy while remaining a resort." We are fortunately not spared from hearing of the little wars that have since erupted between Navy and San Diego, nor of the abundant continuing goodwill that overrides them. San Diegans, Linder explains, have always had two mayors: the one they elect, and a Navy "mayor" through whose command the Navy invests much of the diplomacy that has marked this peaceful cohabitation of America's southwest corner.

San Diego and its Navy have had interlocking needs over these past eighty years, and Bruce Linder doesn't flinch from pursuing them. He was well prepared for this quest through family ties. He lived in the San Diego neighborhood of Clairemont when his father, a naval officer, settled his family in San Diego through three tours of duty. He graduated from Coronado High School and went on to the Naval Academy, then managed three tours of duty in San Diego himself before retiring as the penultimate commanding officer of the San Diego Naval Training Center, later decommissioned.

As this pivotal downtown base goes public, more issues of community property lie ahead for San Diego and the Navy. All three major potential sites for a larger San Diego airport—long and critically needed in San Diego—are now owned by the Navy. "Sometimes," the author confides — speaking now like the civilian consultant that he has become—"it might be better for San Diego if the Navy were not so dominant."

Neil Morgan

PREFACE

There are as many stories of the Navy in San Diego as there have been recruits entering the gates of the Naval Training Center, bluejackets standing at deck's edge while entering port, or naval aviators clattering overhead on azure crisp mornings. Millions of individual remembrances, hair-raising tales of valor and misadventure, and crusty sea stories have enriched the San Diego landscape for over 150 years.

This history is but one of many that could be penned in hopes of deciphering the quintessential essence of San Diego's Navy. The Navy's boost to the civic spirit of this sun-splashed corner of the nation has been mammoth; but its presence, indeed its meaning, is redefined each year, propelled by changing national policies, budget cycles, and the ebb and flow of international events.

To gain some insight into the complexities of this unique relationship I invite you to stand by the flagpole on Ingram Plaza at the old Naval Training Center. No glorious flag flies from this flagpole but if you reach out you can still touch halyards imbued with the symbolism of shaping the spirit of Navy men and women across seventy-five years. Now turn slowly in a complete circle and observe small specks of red, white, and blue flying proudly in the distance. There is the tall wooden mast at Old Town, the lofty flagpole at Fort Stockton, the many skyscrapers of an economically robust downtown, the yardarms of cruisers under way in the harbor, the fantail of an aircraft carrier at North Island, the small stanchions on sub-marines at Ballast Point, and the flagpole with the Stars and Stripes at half-mast at Rosecrans National Cemetery. Each flagstaff forms a portion of the San Diego–Navy legacy, each tells a portion of the affinity between city and Service, and each defines a portion of the San Diego landscape that would be dramatically different had the Navy not helped color the San Diego mainstream.

The Navy may not be truly worthy of San Diego. At times the Service has been exploitative and rude—a dominant land-grabber and bureaucrat insensitive to the Southland's environment and ambitions. But however imperfect the partnership, the Navy has remained a persistent and beneficial strand of the DNA code that is San Diego. It has brought financial stability in times of economic travail, excitement and patriotic spirit to an appreciative populace, and a sense of honor, technological sophistication, and genuine national service that transcends the ordinary.

The essence of the San Diego–Navy relationship is at once obvious and subtle, wide-ranging and focused—for the Navy is more alive in San Diego than in any other city in the nation. It is an artist's blend of red, white, blue, haze gray, and sunlit gold, and a conductor's blend of "Stars and Stripes Forever," "Surfin' Safari," and "Proud to be an American." It may be as complex as a description of the intricacies of a nuclear aircraft carrier or as simple as a San Diegan's license plate that matter-of-factly declares "NVY LFE."

ACKNOWLEDGMENTS

No histories of this breadth can ever succeed without the inspiring assistance from a host of friends, confidants, and experts in their field, and this book has benefited immensely from countless individual contributions. I owe a great deal to the enterprising network of Navy public affairs officers in the San Diego area who consistently ensured that I was supplied with the most accurate information available. Although I received friendly and professional support from everyone I turned to, Captain Gregg Hartung, Lieutenant Sean Banks, Mr. Tom LaPuzza, Mr. Doug Sayers, Mr. Fred Wilson, Lieutenant Dawn Cutler, Mr. Clint Duncan, Lieutenant Commander Dave Werner, and Ms. Patricia O'Connor were especially helpful.

I owe a special debt of gratitude to my friend Sharon Nelson of the Fleet Anti-Submarine Warfare Training Center, whose pugnaciousness toward the importance of libraries for our sailors is always inspiring. Susan Ring Keith contributed lavishly with uncompromising insight, an impeccable memory, and unflagging good humor, and generously allowed me access to her extensive family archives. I owe thanks as well to Cindi Malinick and Ms. Irve Charles LeMoyne of the Coronado Historical Association, John Panter of the San Diego Historical Society, Chuck Bencik of the San Diego Maritime Museum, Don Crawford of the Naval Special Warfare Command, Cynthia Scott of the NAS North Island library, and the many fine librarians of the California Room of the San Diego City Library.

The assistance and advice of the following individuals were invaluable: Jeff Weiman, who made the extensive archives of the San Diego Chamber of Commerce available to me; Michael Nash and Marjorie McNich of the Hagley Museum and Library, in Greenville, Delaware; Bill Doty of the National Archives in Laguna; Gay Dearinger, Linn McLaurin, and STCM Bill Donnelly. The oral histories of the U.S. Naval Institute orchestrated by Paul Stillwell and those of the Hotel del Coronado astutely organized by Chris Donovan proved another valuable source.

I am most grateful to Andy Yatsko, Jan Larson, Sigmund Bobczynski, and GMCS Keith Robinson for their special insights on San Clemente Island and the Navy's successful balance of operational training and environmental preservation. Special thanks to Howard Stovall who contributed original PBY Catalina material from his father.

For assistance with photography I could not have gone far without the aid of Doug Siegfried of the Tailhook Association, Mark Stevens of MCAS Miramar, Casey Smith of the San Diego Aerospace Museum, Jerry Mosely of SPAWAR Systems Center, Alex Macensky of the Navy Historical Foundation, Lieutenant Commander Steve Stopler, and PHC Mahlon Miller of the Fleet Imaging Command, Pacific. Commander Tom Twomey and Tank Shireman inspired me with both their breadth of knowledge and with their willingness to donate time and high-impact images to the effort.

At the Naval Institute Press, this book received total support from many people, most notably Ron Chambers, Tom Cutler, Fred Rainbow, Kristin Wye-Rodney, and Dawn Stitzel. Therese Boyd has generously helped with editing and proofing.

SAN DIEGO'S NAVY

PROLOGUE

The story of San Diego's Navy is the story of San Diego Bay.

The United States Navy first came to San Diego to leverage the advantage of a protected anchorage, reappeared years later to establish a supply base along the bay's shores, launched its newborn aviation program into the perfect wind and water of Spanish Bight, and ultimately flourished along a bay shoreline blessedly free from competing development.

The careers of thousands of Navy men and women began within sight and sound of the bay's edge and many thousands more lie at peace high atop Point Loma, overlooking the bay's azure blue expanse. The bay was at first a magnet drawing the Navy's attention, then an engine powering its expansion, and, at all times, a comfort nurturing its vitality. Every time a navyman returned to port, the bay provided its own welcome of placid comfort long before family and friends could provide their own. Every time an underway order was given, the bay subtly assayed a mariner's instincts and seamanship long before he could be challenged by an unforgiving sea.

Viewed from space, San Diego Bay is the singularly most distinctive coastal feature along nearly a thousand miles of California coastline from Punta Eugenia to Monterey Bay. The fishhook curve of San Diego harbor, tucked behind a protec-

tive and prominent headland, is an eye-catching anomaly in the midst of miles of wave-battered western shoreline. To early mariners striking north along the desolate Pacific coast of the old Spanish empire, San Diego Bay represented the only harbor south of San Francisco that could afford a sheltered anchorage from the onslaught of northwesterly storms. Where San Francisco's much grander and deeper harbor hung hidden from view behind cloaks of fog and storm for decades, the harbor of San Diego beaconed warmly on early Spanish charts as a conspicuous navigational keystone.

But much earlier than Spanish cartographers could record, ancient forces of ocean, river, and mountain shaped the destiny of the modern-day bay. At one time in its geologic past Point Loma probably stood as a nearby offshore island like the present-day Coronado Islands.[1] Working slowly over great periods of time, silt and debris from a churning, twisting San Diego River built a wide fan of deposits seaward from the mouth of Mission Valley. Time would shape these river deposits into a broad flat plain, linking Old Town, Point Loma, and Mount Soledad and leaving twin embayments—one to the river's north in the shadow of Mount Soledad, one to the south behind the impressive Point Loma palisade. The river's flow was irregular, meandering left and right across its flood plain to empty capriciously into either San Diego Bay or the lagoons to its north.[2]

1

The rocky jut of La Jolla into the sea and the prominent north-south run of Point Loma kept dominant ocean currents offshore, while nearer to the coast a circular ocean eddy formed in the lee of the Point. This counterclockwise eddy fathered a strong northward current along southern beaches that gently swept silt and sand from the Tijuana River valley toward the Silver Strand and, more substantially, to North Island, Coronado, and Zuniga Shoal at its northern terminus.[3] Then, over eons, the cleansing currents of the San Diego River collaborated with these oceanic forces to scour a single exit channel for the newly formed bay, one that would swirl by a small jut of land that would later be called Ballast Point.

Noble in size and visual appeal, the bay still has shortcomings tied to this complex geologic ancestry. A product of the mudflats and flood plains of multiple rivers, the bay remained universally shallow and dotted with shifting sandbars and shoals. Where it is deep, it is due to the hydraulic actions of swiftly flowing natural currents, such as near the tightly constricted entrance at Ballast Point. Over history, the pristine tempos of the bay's shallow, lagoon-like conditions proved perfectly attuned to the sunning habits of the great gray whale but vastly less hospitable to the ocean-going ships of man.

As the site of the first Spanish settlement in Alta California, the anchor for a long string of Franciscan missions, and the site of California's first military presidio, the bay prodded California's history forward out of the darkness. Beginning with Juan Rodriguez Cabrillo in 1542, the magnificent bay consistently drew voyagers and adventurers San Diego's way. Sebastian Vizcaino stayed within the safe confines of the bay for ten days in 1602, calling it "the best to be found in all the South Seas . . . being protected on all sides and having good anchorage."[4] In 1793 British captain George Vancouver wrote a résumé for the bay that would stand for the next 150 years: "the bay affords excellent anchorage and is capable of containing a great number of vessels but . . . the channel between Point de la Loma and the shoal is the only navigable passage for shipping, [the rest of the bay] with its shallow depth of water renders it ineligible excepting for boats or vessels of very small draught."[5]

No American ship would test the bay's uncertain waters until August 1800 when the brig *Betsy,* late of Boston, loaded wood and water and then sailed for China. A smattering of fur and hide traders would follow, generally looked upon with considerable suspicion and apprehension by protective colonial officials. Although growing in repute among the closed circle of the world's master mariners, the bay had potential, which lay slumbering in midday siesta until a day in 1846 when a small group of naval officers—sons of Boston, New York, and Wilmington—gathered to plan an anticipated military campaign. Unrolling portfolios of nautical charts across a sailing master's teak chest, they studied as one the long unbroken coastline of Alta California while searching for the perfect hospitable harbor for the landing of large amounts of military supplies. Their eyes easily caught the seductive curve of the bay and it did not take them long to recall Richard Henry Dana's prophetic description of the "security and snugness of San Diego" from the widely read *Two Years Before the Mast:* "For landing and taking on board hides, San Diego is decidedly the best place in California. The harbour is small and land-locked, there is no surf, the vessels lie within a cable's length of the beach, and the beach itself is smooth, hard sand without rocks or stones."[6] Dana's popular 1835 description of San Diego harbor and the American Navy's bold inclination to action would merge to send American fighting ships into California waters. And as the bay's waters became American waters, the warships that had been the messengers of change would also begin to shape the destiny of a city.

1846

At present San Diego is, all things considered, perhaps one of the best harbors on the coast from Callao to Pugets' Sound, with a single exception, that of San Francisco. In the opinion of some intelligent naval officers, it is preferable even to this. The harbor of San Francisco has more water, but that of San Diego has a more uniform climate, better anchorage, and perfect security from winds in any direction.

Lt. W. H. Emory, U.S. Topographical Engineers, 1846

The early morning fog above San Diego spread over the dry California mesas like a rumpled bedspread, tightly tucked at the sides by the nearby canyons and arroyos. Although mostly the product of the moist, morning sea air, the haze held a brownish-gray tint, the result of four narrow threads of wood smoke rising lazily from a line of nearby tannery campfires. An early morning calliope blending a blacksmith's clang with a woodsman's chop drifted smoothly seaward across the placid water.

As the small settlement first began to stir in the pale morning light, a single ship approached far to seaward. She was black-hulled and sleek, and sat low in the water. A single row of white-painted gun ports adorned each side. Flags and pennants hung limp. Despite the set of all sails and topgallants, the ship crept only at bare steerageway in the characteristic light air of a California summer morning. Those ashore could not immediately identify the ship's nationality as she plodded southerly along the barren coastline and slowly tacked to wear around Punta de la Loma, the rocky peninsula of land that guarded the harbor mouth.

The date was 29 July 1846. The Californios of the dusty settlement of San Diego numbered barely five hundred—including many seasonal transients following the vagaries of the tannery or whaling trade for their livelihood. The frontier towns and ranchos of Mexico's Alta California were spread thinly, communication was difficult, tempo languid and slow.

But "change," a seemingly lost commodity in the listless pace of the old Spanish empire, was in the dusky dawn air, arriving aboard the black-hulled sloop working its way slowly toward the harbor mouth.

Amid crisply shouted orders and the rustle and pop of freshly sheeted canvas, the U.S. Navy's sloop-of-war *Cyane*, of twenty-two guns, swung in a lazy arc until her bow was pointed into a placid westerly breeze in the lee of the dramatically chiseled headland. The water was flat and a wide semicircle of wake trailed astern, colored in a curious mixture of aquamarine and brown, dotted by broad-leafed tendrils of seaweed and kelp. As all way was finally bled from her momentum, another order from the quarterdeck let fly the ship's quarter-ton black-tarred anchor that found the sandy bottom at $9\frac{1}{2}$ fathoms. "We crossed the bar with six inches to spare and luffed into the harbor in gallant fashion, clewing up the sails and coming to anchor without accident," *Cyane*'s captain, Comdr. Samuel Francis DuPont, wrote later. For the very first time, the U.S. Navy had come to the slumbering Mexican settlement of San Diego.[1]

Cyane crewmembers, many bare-chested or wearing the lightest of frocks in the warm July sunshine, busied in their tasks of pulling a man-of-war into port. Those who might have turned to the quarterdeck to look at their captain saw one of the most respected commanders in the Navy of the day. A member of the well-to-do DuPont family of Delaware, *Cyane*'s captain was described in a contemporary account as

> tall, straight, handsome . . . a commanding figure with a strong clear voice. He is dignified, amiable, exceedingly winning in manners and instructive and agreeable in conversation. Learned without pretension and truly kind-hearted, he is rightly considered in the Navy a perfect model of an officer.[2]

DuPont had first gone to sea as a midshipman in 1815 aboard the ship-of-the-line *Franklin* and had risen to command of the schooner *Grampus* and sloop-of-war *Warren*. He had served with the Navy's Bureau of Ordnance ashore and had helped to establish the U.S. Naval Academy. In 1845 he briefly assumed command of *Congress,* flagship of the Pacific Squadron, and had shifted to command *Cyane* just the month before.

From the quarterdeck, DuPont could easily see the scattered adobes at the head of the broad sweep of inner harbor. They looked dingy and ill-kempt, framed by distant saw-toothed peaks and ridges that tumbled down toward the water. He knew that most on shore would have already heard that the United States and Mexico were at war. Dispatch riders flashing southward along El Camino Real would have brought word that *Cyane* and two other ships of the Pacific Squadron had hoisted the American flag at Monterey earlier in the month, claiming possession of the city and all of upper California.

In July 1846 command of the Pacific Squadron had passed from Commo. John Sloat—beset by ill health and an indecisive nature—to Commo. Robert F. Stockton, an energetic leader skilled in both naval and diplomatic dimensions. His service record was superb from midshipmen aboard frigate *President* during her successful wartime cruises of 1812 to command of ship-of-the-line *Ohio.* With the raising of the American flag in Monterey, Stockton proclaimed himself civil

San Diego's Navy history begins as the first boatloads of California Battalion troops under Maj. John C. Frémont are rowed ashore at La Playa late in the afternoon of 29 July 1846 to relieve sailors and marines at the town square and to garrison the city. Mexican brig *Juanita* lies at anchor behind *Cyane. Naval Historical Center*

governor and military commander in California in concert with his duties commanding the Pacific Squadron.[3]

A drumbeat of rumor and innuendo had slowly built to a crescendo as winter warmed toward summer across Mexico's northern frontier in 1846. Nearly everyone in the West realized that war was inevitable as America reached aggressively westward to complete its Atlantic-to-Pacific destiny while a relatively weaker Mexico struggled simply to communicate with—much less govern—its northern territories.

DuPont's mission was straightforward, the next move in a complex American plan to capture California in the opening days of the Mexican War. *Cyane* had been ordered to sail from Monterey to San Diego, take possession of the town, and raise the American flag. DuPont was also to land a force of troops that would head inland and northward, seeking out the largest remaining concentration of Mexican forces in Alta California. Reports indicated that the Mexican camp was near Pueblo de los Angeles under the command of Gen. José María Castro.

American presence and commercial influence were rising in San Diego, propelled by interests in tanneries, shipping, and whaling. DuPont assumed that the numerous Americans believed to be in the town would welcome the ship and thwart any ensuing attempt at resistance by the local Californios.

The Pacific Squadron had operated near-continuously in the Pacific since 1818 when the frigate *Macedonian* first sailed around Cape Horn to protect American trading interests. By the early 1840s, in the face of rising tensions between Mexico and the United States and broadening American commercial interests in California and Oregon, the squadron had slowly grown in strength and its activities focused on the coasts of Mexico and California. The undisguised colonial aspirations of England and Russia along the Pacific coast had also concerned American naval commanders, and Royal Navy operations were closely scrutinized and shadowed.

By mid-1845 the Pacific Squadron consisted of a frigate, three sloops-of-war, a schooner, and a storeship. Secretary of the Navy George Bancroft envisioned a major role for the Navy in the event of hostilities with Mexico and he dispatched *Cyane* and the largest pure frigate in the Navy—the newly constructed *Congress*—to join the squadron late in the year. During the spring and summer of 1846, two sloops-of-war, the razee *Independence,* and a storeship also sailed for the Pacific, the sloop *Saratoga* was diverted from the Brazil Station, and the ship-of-the-line *Columbus* was ordered to California from Chinese waters.[4] This rapid concentration of naval might by Secretary Bancroft would be the force needed to command the seas during any war with Mexico, block any attempt by En-

Comdr. Samuel Francis DuPont, c. 1848. A member of the fabled DuPont family of chemical and munitions fame, DuPont would rise through a fifty-year career to command fleet actions at Port Royal and Charleston during the Civil War. *U.S. Naval Institute*

gland to lay claim to Pacific territory, and provide a mobile military force that would not be encumbered by the substandard roads and communications of Mexican California.

DuPont's *Cyane* was an efficient man-of-war, a rated second-class sloop, with a size and armament well suited to the California campaign. Her draft of fifteen feet would allow her to stand close to shore or enter nearly all Mexican ports and her twenty-two guns outmatched anything Mexico could throw against her. Versatile as she was, her design was not considered entirely successful by naval officers of her day who rated her a "good sailer" but not handsome.[5]

As *Cyane* lay at anchor near a scruffy line of clapboard tannery buildings at La Playa, only one other vessel was present, the Mexican hermaphrodite brig (part brig, part schooner rig) *Juanita.* The town was quiet. Suspecting that *Juanita* was in port to support General Castro or one of his lieutenants, DuPont quickly ordered a boarding party to check the ship's papers and passed orders for his embarked troops to prepare to go ashore. DuPont's boarding party discovered that *Juanita*'s cargo contained military supplies, including forty thousand percussion caps, and DuPont ordered her seized.[6]

At 1500 that afternoon Lt. Stephen Rowan, *Cyane*'s executive officer, led a small landing party of sailors ashore, augmented by the ship's Marine guard headed by Lt. William Maddox, USMC. Their mission was to proceed ashore in two boats, reconnoiter the town, and test for any opposition. The landing party proceeded unopposed up the rutted dirt path toward the settlement's center near the crumbling remnants of the aging Mexican presidio. There, on a small rise overlooking the confluence of the San Diego River into the northern sweep of San Diego Bay, they raised a naval ensign—the first official United States colors in San Diego. As Rowan wrote later, "Landing with the Marine guard and a few sailors, I marched up to the town a few miles away and, having read the proclamation, hoisted the flag without opposition. The Marines were left to guard the flag." Rowan returned back aboard by 2250.[7]

Earlier that evening, DuPont had landed the first portion of an American force of 160 men, led by the impetuous Maj. John C. Frémont, with orders to relieve the Marines at the town square and establish a defensive camp. The rest would follow the next morning. Counted among the men of Frémont's landing force were frontier scout Kit Carson and eight Delaware Indians.[8]

A noted frontier explorer and soldier (and later governor of California, California's first senator, and the Republican Party's first candidate for president), Frémont had been operating in California since late 1845 as the head of an American topographical survey expedition. In two previous expeditions, he had done much to chart the most favored routes across the West, including surveying new trails to Oregon and northern California. His expedition reports, filled with stirring tales of adventure, scientific observations, heroic exploits, and detailed maps, were widely read in the East. As Frémont's expedition was the only organized American land force operating in Alta California when hostilities began, Commodore Stockton ordered them integrated within the American campaign plan. Frémont's backwoodsmen, augmented by many American settlers—including many who had participated in the Bear Flag Revolt against Mexican rule—were formally renamed the California Battalion of United States Troops.

Walter Colton, a chaplain with the Navy, described members of the battalion as they rode through Monterey to be embarked aboard *Cyane* for the voyage to San Diego: "Their rifles, revolving pistols and long knives glittered over dusky buckskin which enveloped their sinewy limbs, while their untrimmed locks, flowing out from under their foraging caps and their black beards, with white teeth glittering through, gave them a wild savage aspect."[9]

Tough as this band of irregulars appeared, they were still wobbly with seasickness by the time they finally went ashore in San Diego. Frémont had voiced high expectations of the voyage from Monterey:

> My men were all greatly pleased at the novelty of a voyage in a man-of-war, which they anticipated would be very pleasant now when the regular northwest wind belonging to the season was blowing and there was no prospect of storms. But like many prospective enjoyments this one proved to be all in the anticipation. By the time we had been a few hours at sea we were all very low in our minds; and there was none of the expected enjoyment in the sparkling waves and the refreshing breeze and the sail along the mountainous shore as the ship rolled her way down the coast. Carson was among those who were badly worsted by this enemy to landsmen and many were the vows made to the winds that never again would they put trust in the fair-weather promises of the ocean.[10]

DuPont was anxious to pass word of his successes and up-to-date intelligence to Stockton, who had taken *Congress* to San Pedro to seize that port. Fearful that a dispatch rider would be captured on the ride north, DuPont ordered Lt. G. W. Harrison of *Cyane* to take the ship's launch and

> [p]roceed to the Bay of San Pedro and deliver accompanying despatches to Commodore Stockton. . . . A Pilot acquainted with the boat navigation of the coast will embark with you. The present condition of the country must enjoin upon you proper circumspection in approaching the Port. It is unnecessary to endeavor to anticipate contingencies and I rely upon your discretion and intelligence to meet any emergencies and be careful to the health of your men. After reporting to Commodore Stockton, you will of course wait his orders.[11]

DuPont liked what he found in San Diego and wrote to his wife that the settlement was a "much more agreeable place than Monterey," a point undoubtedly influenced by the warm welcome DuPont received from Señor Juan Bandini. "Bandini's house [on Old Town Square] has been thrown open to us and is the resort of the other society of the place they contrive to have music and dancing every night, the sole diversion of California."[12]

Don Juan Bandini was one of San Diego's most prominent and influential citizens in 1846, cutting a striking figure in town in serape and sash. He had been a member of the

National Congress in Mexico City, owned several large California land grants, and was a vigorous supporter of the Americans (seeing their arrival as a stimulus to trade). A "man of decided ability and fine character," Don Juan at sixty was also well known for his dancing and DuPont enjoyed the music, food, and hospitality of his home.[13]

Confident of his position within the town and while awaiting orders from Stockton, DuPont availed himself of San Diego's hospitality, which he described to his wife:

> Until yesterday I have been sleeping in town, coming down to breakfast in the morning and returning before sundown in the evening.... I ride about eight miles if not ten a day and as all riding means a gallop, I have found it delightful and healthy. The road [to the anchorage] lies along the shores of the harbor and estuary. If you were able to see me mounted with my Panama hat, blouse over my uniform coat, rifle across the saddlebow, revolving pistol on one side and my sword on the other, you would not recognize your peaceful husband. The day before yesterday the Doctor and I started a little earlier than usual and extended our ride to the Mission of San Diego some six miles beyond the town. You debouche into a valley, the high hills which enclose it being those that surround the harbor . . . the mission buildings were good, picturesquely situated with a church but now all is in a mournful state of decay. We were received by the old Padre, a Franciscan, a perfect Friar Tuck, who was what sailors term "two sheets in the wind." He sent for some pears . . . and we looked at the dilapidated church and tattered paintings . . . we galloped back as we had come, the air perfectly delicious and the full moon prolonging the twilight.[14]

Frémont's battalion remained in San Diego for ten days, gathering supplies and horses for their campaign northward. On 8 August they broke camp for the march toward Los Angeles. The launch returned to San Diego that same day with orders to get under way immediately for San Pedro to support the second phase of Stockton's campaign. DuPont left a skeleton force in San Diego, comfortable with the city's warm reception. "The very small population, their quiet and orderly character, and their friendly feelings towards us, keep me from apprehending much trouble in consequence," DuPont reported to Stockton.[15] Although DuPont was not worried about the reaction of San Diegans, those in San Diego were quite concerned about the apparent departure of their American protection and approached DuPont "in great terror that they were to be left in a defenseless state." Privately, in letters to his wife, DuPont shared much the same apprehension and later made a forceful plea to Stockton to ensure the protection of the city.[16]

Stockton's string of military successes continued in Los Angeles. By 13 August the city was firmly under American control and the remnants of Castro's militia had surrendered on parole. Stockton, with victory assured, withdrew the bulk of his forces and began to organize them for the next phase of his campaign plan—operations against Mexican ports to the south.

Less than two months later—to Stockton's dismay—most American gains in Alta California, so rapidly garnered, had been lost. Independence-minded Californios and militia remnants had compelled the small American garrison in Los Angeles to surrender. The countryside descended into a state of general revolt and mounted detachments headed toward both Santa Barbara and San Diego to retake the towns from skeleton American garrisons.

In San Diego, Californios loyal to Mexico swept rapidly through town, forcing the small defending garrison of Americans to seek refuge unceremoniously aboard the American whaling ship *Stonington* anchored in the harbor. The American sympathizers were incensed, complaining that "they had gone off again, left [the flag] flying without having anyone to protect it and exposed to insult." The Californios replaced the Stars and Stripes with the Mexican flag on the prominent central flagpole of town. However, a few days later, on 9 October, the Americans on board *Stonington*—led by Ezekial Merritt, a captain in Frémont's California Battalion—returned ashore to restore the American flag above town.[17]

Upon receiving a report from Merritt describing these chaotic events, Commodore Stockton dispatched Lt. George Minor and fifty-two men from the frigate *Savannah* in San Pedro to reinforce the San Diego garrison. In San Diego the sailors moved to fortify a group of barracks west of the presidio with six brass nine-pounder cannons. Minor engaged in daily skirmishes with the surrounding Californios and was greatly relieved when *Congress,* carrying Stockton's flag, appeared at the harbor's mouth on 30 October.

It was obvious that San Diego held a key strategic position in this unanticipated new phase of the war. In Stockton's new operation plan, San Diego would become his central base of operations for a renewal of a campaign to retake Los Angeles. No other harbor south of San Francisco offered better protection to anchored ships or a better site to concentrate war materiel than San Diego. In addition, Stockton realized that San Diego's central location could support campaigns north toward Los Angeles and south against Mexican settlements in Baja.

As *Congress* maneuvered up into the harbor, led by two boats and a pilot for soundings, her deep twenty-three-foot draft "stuck frequently on the bar"—the first of many naval ships to suffer this malady in San Diego. An hour later *Congress* "wore ship and stood out [of harbor], anchoring in 10 fathoms of water." Two cutters of ship's marines, riflemen, and irregulars were sent ashore to reestablish unquestioned American control of the town. Stockton dispatched *Stonington* with a detachment from Frémont's California Battalion under the command of Capt. Samuel Gibson to Ensenada to seize the port and forage for livestock and supplies.[18]

Congress left San Diego for San Pedro on 3 November but returned by 14 November. After sending ashore supplies and "clothing for the California Battalion" and sounding and buoying the channel, *Congress* stood into harbor. In a discouraging replay of her first arrival in harbor, she again ran hard aground. This time she stuck not on the channel bar but inside Ballast Point on the prominent middle ground shoal. As luck would have it, she grounded as the tide was beginning to run out of the bay, and as the tide ebbed further she began to heel over. A force of about a hundred Californios, observing this debacle from shore, took the opportunity offered by American disorder to attack the fortified barracks again. They were beaten back by sailor musketeers after a sharp struggle and, fortunately for the Americans, *Congress* refloated with the tide later that day. She anchored in deep water and trained her formidable guns toward town to discourage further Californio adventurism.

Later that month, still seeking ways to strengthen the American position, Stockton ordered the building of a fort of logs and earthen embankments on the hill above the settlement to be called Fort Stockton. Midshipman Robert Duvall of the *Savannah* recalls construction of the American fort:

> Three hundred whale oil casks [from *Stonington*] full of sand close together, thirty yards by twenty square throwing a bank of earth and small gravel up in front as high as the top of the casks and running a ditch around the whole. In the inside, a ball-proof house was built out of planks, lining the inside with adobes, on top of which a swivel was mounted. The entrance was guarded by a strong gate having a draw bridge in front.

This area of the Mission Hills region of the city still bears the commodore's name.[19]

At the fort Stockton began drilling companies of sailors in the techniques of land warfare, both for the impending advance on Los Angeles and to better defend San Diego against further intrusions threatened by a local force of Californios led by Capt. Andrés Pico. In one bluejacket's view:

> The days were consumed by drills in squads and companies in the morning, exercises, the artillery and firing at targets. Each afternoon the whole command was paraded. . . . [T]hey were taught to march and countermarch to "file right into line," to wheel by platoon and battalion and to form the grand move of the whole campaign, a hollow square to receive the charge of cavalry.[20]

Later in November, to emphasize San Diego's expanding importance as a campaign supply base, *Congress* was joined in harbor by the frigate *Savannah* and the newly commissioned sloop-of-war *Portsmouth*. Sailors from these ships went ashore to join Stockton's burgeoning land force. The scene aboard *Portsmouth* was typical of that repeated aboard every squadron ship in San Diego that week:

> Muskets, carbines, pistols, pikes and ammunition were strewed all over the quarterdeck. In a short time the Marines appeared fully accoutered for landing and different companies [were formed] according to the species of arms they could muster. There were 25 or 26 musketeers and the balance were armed with carbines, pistols and pikes, while each man carried a cutlass. Every officer fore and aft save the Gunner and the First Lieutenant was to go ashore.[21]

Meanwhile, Brig. Gen. Stephen Kearny of the U.S. Army with a hundred dragoons from his grandly titled Army of the West was marching overland from Santa Fe to join forces with Stockton. As he advanced down the San Pasqual River valley, forty miles north of San Diego, he stumbled headlong into Pico's force of mounted Californios. In a carelessly orchestrated battle on 6–7 December, Kearny's small force of largely exhausted Americans was soundly repulsed, suffering twenty-two dead. Alerted to Kearny's distress by couriers who had slipped through the Californio lines (including Kit Carson and Navy lieutenant Edward Beale), Stockton dispatched two companies of sailors in relief. Kearny finally straggled into San Diego on 12 December.

The number of American forces in San Diego now nearly matched the total number of town residents. After allowing Kearny's party several days of rest, Stockton gathered his disparate force together and marched out of town on 28–29 December. The ship's yeoman from *Portsmouth* recounts the scene:

> By 9 a.m. the whole battalion was formed in line of march in [San Diego's] square, every man with a light heart and a tolerable heavy knapsack. The baggage, provision and ammunition carts were got into their proper places, the vaqueros were riding in all directions, shouting and hallooing at the top of their voices to keep the stray cattle in order. Shaking of hands and wishes of success were passing between those who were to go and those who were to stay, the staff and officers were all mounted and their horses were kicking up the very devil in the square. All was noise

Congress spent a great deal of the Mexican War in port in San Diego to coordinate naval operations along the entire Pacific coast. When she was launched in 1841 she was widely seen as the culminating example of successful American sailing frigate designs. In 1862 in Hampton Roads, Virginia, she was attacked by the Confederate ironclad *Virginia*. Unable to bring her guns to bear effectively, she struck her colors after a heavy loss of life and burned to the waterline. *U.S. Naval Institute*

and hubbub outside the line when out pops the Commodore and the General, side by side. They take their station in the center of the square, the band struck up a Quick Step and with a cheer that made the heavens ring again, the command obeyed that well known and so much revered voice [of Commodore Stockton] as it gave the order to Forward, March.[22]

To his credit, Stockton had succeeded in organizing a balanced and disciplined force composed of Kearny's regulars, members from the California Battalion, and detachments of sailors from ships of the Pacific Squadron. Although lacking the mobility of the Californio and Mexican forces with their horse cavalry and dragoons, Stockton's force was easily the strongest in California at the time and featured tightly concentrated musket firepower and artillery that his opposition could not match. *Congress, Savannah,* and *Portsmouth* sailed from San Diego shortly after Stockton's departure to support

the commodore's northward march. *Cyane* arrived back in San Diego on 27 December to protect the harbor but contributed 108 men to Stockton's force, leaving too few to sail the ship. DuPont discovered opportunity in adversity: "it's a glorious chance to paint the ship, which we are doing thoroughly."[23]

Stockton's regiments caught up with the principal Mexican/Californio force under Gen. José María Flores at the San Gabriel River on the Los Angeles plain and defeated them soundly in two battles on 8–9 January 1847. Flores's collapse largely ended organized opposition in Alta California and the focus of the Pacific Squadron shifted again southward to blockade and capture Mexican ports in Baja California and along the Pacific coast.

On the lighter side, the lengthy stays of American men-of-war proved a decided boon to society in San Diego. Every woman of the settlement, it seemed, had a good time dancing with the naval and Marine officers, and Stockton's military band from *Congress* was a popular attraction in the plaza nearly every afternoon or evening. DuPont kept pace with his social responsibilities. "I have invited the Bandinis and all the society (for they are all intermarried) to spend Saturday on board the *Cyane*," he said in a letter to his wife. "I believe the circle of San Diego consists of eight ladies, old and young. They were so kind last summer when we first took possession here, and since our arrival I have long wanted to pay them some civility." The next day, tired from the exertion of his civil responsibilities, DuPont provided another glimpse of San Diego social life: "Rain has set in and cooped up a dozen women in my cabin. I have retreated and left them to the care of the officers and brought my portfolia here to close my letter, for if the weather permits, the [mail] brig will be off tomorrow."[24]

As winter turned to spring in early 1847, *Cyane* again deployed from San Diego to help American forces seize San Blas, La Paz, Guaymas, Lorento, San Jose del Cabo, and Mazatlan. San Diego–based ships of the Pacific Squadron blockaded or captured every Baja California port and defeated all organized resistance. At the end of the war, though, in a move bitterly denounced by American naval officers, Baja California was restored to Mexico by treaty.

After returning *Cyane* to Norfolk, DuPont would serve in the Navy for twenty more years, finishing with a total naval service of nearly half a century. He commanded the South Atlantic Blockading Squadron as a rear admiral during the early years of the Civil War and directed the capture of Port Royal and Beaufort, South Carolina.[25]

Lieutenant Rowan, who had landed the first party in San Diego, was mentioned prominently in dispatches for his heroics in leading several *Cyane* armed landing parties, especially at San Blas and Mazatlan. In commanding the steam sloop *Pawnee* on the Potomac River during the opening days of the Civil War, Rowan was instrumental in protecting Washington, D.C., and was ordered, too late, to relieve beleaguered Fort Sumter. He was active with Union Navy forces off Cape Hatteras and later in the blockade of Charleston, where he commanded the most powerful ironclad of the time, *New Ironsides*, which—by coincidence—was assigned to DuPont's squadron. After the war he rose to the rank of vice admiral and the command of the Asiatic Squadron in Far Eastern waters.

Commo. Robert Stockton returned to the east overland after being relieved in California in March 1847. He would later serve three years as a U.S. senator from New Jersey.

In Stockton, DuPont, and Rowan, the Navy—by happy confluence of destiny—brought together in San Diego three serving or future flag officers who would accumulate 150 total years of naval service among them. In later years, the Navy and the nation would remember their celebrated careers by naming a total of ten different torpedo boats and destroyers after them.

The Mexican War in Alta California was largely a naval campaign and the Navy's use of San Diego as its central support base inevitably proved to be one of the most crucial factors in the success that U.S. forces enjoyed. As in all wars, the ebb and flow of military logistics ruled the tempo of the commanders. The ability to concentrate forces and guarantee an uninterrupted flow of resupply were the key elements in final victory. Without the protected anchorage provided by the harbor of San Diego, the American campaign would have been much more disjointed and perilous.

Lightly defended Mexican ports fell easily to disciplined American crews and no ships of the diminutive Mexican navy could thwart the American command of the seas. By using the mobility offered by their ships, Commodore Stockton and other commanders like Kearny and Frémont were able to concentrate land forces at will or extract them when necessary. As Army forces were largely engaged in other theaters of the war, it fell to armed companies of sailors to provide most of the American forces ashore in California. This they did either in limited amphibious attacks direct from ships' boats, as garrison forces in forts and presidios, or as organized companies of foot soldiers in the midst of swirling land battles.

As one ship's crewmember observed: "It was a splendid and heart warming sight to see these brave men become what a sailor hates most, soldiers, upon Emergency, but it was a proof of what Yankees can do in a pinch."[26] The California campaign of the Mexican War marked the first time in American military history that armed landing parties from American ships had been used in such roles under overall naval command stretching over a large area.

The first U.S. Navy ships to visit San Diego harbor in 1846 went on to distinguish themselves in other battles and in other duty on distant stations. After the Mexican War *Cyane* returned to Norfolk where she was singularly recognized by the secretary of the Navy for her contributions to victory. In 1858 she returned to the Pacific where she served constantly for thirty years before being paid off at Mare Island on 30 July 1887.

The first U.S. navyman to die and be buried in San Diego was Ordinary Seaman John Simpson who, according to the log of the *Congress,* fell to his death from the fore royal mast at 0630 on 5 February 1847. The following day he was interned at La Playa "attended by the top men and his messmates." The sailor graves at La Playa and Ballast Point were later disinterred and moved to Fort Rosecrans Cemetery.

Congress later served as flagship of both the American Mediterranean and Brazil Squadrons, but finally met her doom when she was engaged and sunk by the ironclad CSS *Virginia* (ex-*Merrimack*) on 8 March 1862 in Hampton Roads. Frigate *Savannah* served as flagship for the Pacific Squadron from 1849 to 1852. During the first years of the Civil War she was assigned blockade duty off the shores of Georgia and for many years was the sail training ship at the U.S. Naval Academy. She was sold at Norfolk in September 1883. Sloop *Portsmouth* enjoyed an intensive later career with assignments as varied as suppressing the African slave trade to engaging Chinese warlords. During the Civil War she was a member of the Gulf of Mexico Blockading Squadron and helped capture New Orleans. She remained part of the Navy until sold in April 1915.[27]

After the war with Mexico, a board of Army and Navy officers was formed to examine "the coast of the United States lying upon the Pacific ocean with reference to points of defense and occupation for the security and accommodation of trade and commerce and for military and naval purposes." This Joint Commission arrived in San Diego on 30 September 1850 aboard *Massachusetts,* a wooden auxiliary steampacket assigned to the Pacific Squadron for survey work.[28]

In February 1852 (encouraged in part by Commander DuPont's writings in a national pamphlet that "with reference to fortifying our new coast on the Pacific, [it is] a work which surely ought not to be delayed") the secretary of war recommended to the president that a federal reserve for harbor defenses be established in San Diego on "that portion of the peninsula lying on the west side of the entrance to the harbor. Which shall be included between the southern-most point of the peninsula (Puenta de Loma) and a line drawn across said peninsula from the harbor to the ocean at the distance of one

In Old Town San Diego today, this plaque rests on a prominent rock in the central square. It is the second plaque set in place, as the original erroneously gave prominence to Maj. John C. Frémont instead of Lt. Stephen Rowan for raising the flag. *BRL Photos*

and a half miles above Puenta de Guirarros." President Millard Fillmore approved the recommendation by issuing an executive order on 26 February 1852, the first military land in San Diego.[29]

Other naval surveys would follow, notably that of *Active* in 1856, commanded by noted naval explorer and hydrographer James Alden, which produced some of the first accurate navigational charts of San Diego Bay, False Bay, and the Cortes Bank.[30] In large part, though, San Diego would drop quickly from the Navy's attention after the Mexican War. The port did not have a good reputation among the mariners of the day and most steered clear. The captain of the steampacket *Oregon* stopped in the port in March 1850, calling it "[a] very quiet, dull place said to be desolate and hot in summer and going to ruins."[31] Master C. Forbes of the steamer *California* logged in May 1849 that "this is the meanest place of all, not a morsel of fresh provisions and the town in four miles from anchorage."[32]

It would be forty long years before San Diego Bay would rise from its slumber.

1893

24 July, San Diego. My dear Mother. It is not hot, except in the interior and the nights are always cool. All in all a good climate but I think I should like to hear Pennsylvania thunder just for a change.

Assistant Paymaster Z. Wells Reynolds, USN

A raw sea wind had blown all day, hauling slate-gray clouds from south of the Coronados and slinging them inland laden with silvery threads of drizzle. All morning the normally dusty streets of downtown had thirstily absorbed the rain while San Diegans clutched cloaks and shawls to step carefully between muddied wagon ruts.

This gray February day in 1893 did not diminish the exhilaration of the moment for Ziba Wells Reynolds—universally and sensibly known as Wells—as he stood by the Santa Fe tracks. Most of his worldly possessions surrounded him, crammed into two leather suitcases and a battered cruise chest. The trip south along the coastal railroad spur from Los Angeles had been a marvel to a man of twenty-five who had never before traveled west of the Susquehanna. "My Dear father," he wrote later that day to his family in snowbound Tunkhannock, Pennsylvania, "I arrived safely and the ride was grand. Today it was orange groves with the trees loaded down with great yellow beauties and it was just as pretty as it could be."

Hiring one of the plentiful lorries that seemed to bunch around the infrequent trains like ants on sugar, Reynolds made his way past dirty two- and three-story Victorian-style buildings toward a beckoning forest of wooden masts that crowded the bay shore like so many willow reeds. There, at what is now

Market and Pacific Highway, he waited for a small launch that would take him to the naval steamer *Thetis* at anchor in the bay. He would report on board that afternoon as the ship's assistant paymaster.

Reynolds had been born in northeastern Pennsylvania in 1868, the son of an attorney and member of the Pennsylvania legislature. In 1885 he earned a coveted appointment to the U.S. Naval Academy but his studies were almost immediately interrupted when he contracted typhoid fever and was posted home for convalescence. He never returned to Annapolis but completed his university schooling at George Washington University, graduating in 1890 several weeks ahead of his ex-Annapolis classmates. Family tradition holds that Reynolds's grandfather, no fan of naval duty, had intercepted and destroyed Reynolds's recall orders to the Naval Academy, only admitting the deed after Reynolds was safely established at George Washington. Internal family conspiracies notwithstanding, duty with the fleet still held Reynolds's imagination and he quickly volunteered for the U.S. Navy Pay Corps in 1891.[1]

Reynolds's first orders were to the receiving ship *Franklin* and then, in late 1892, additional orders directed him to travel across the country to join *Thetis*. Reynolds found the steamer swinging at anchor midway between the bustle of the downtown waterfront and the nearly barren and treeless backdrop of Coronado. The afternoon's drizzle could have done nothing to glamorize her sullen, wide-beamed countenance in the eyes of her newest crewmember. *Thetis* was only a third-rate Navy steamer. When she infrequently found herself at anchor near a sleek new steel-sided cruiser, the picture was one of a squatty wrestler—with short stocky legs and a once-broken nose—standing next to the high school quarterback.

Thetis's naval commission was an accident of history. Never included in any Navy budget and never graced at launch with red-white-blue bunting or brassy renditions of "Columbia Rules the Waves," she first entered seafaring life in 1881 as a staunch Scot-built whaler. Her intelligent mix of both sail and auxiliary boilers provided exceptionally long endurance, which meant profit to her owners in the uncertain science of the whale hunt.

When Congress ordered a relief expedition to save an American arctic meteorological expedition led by Lt. A. W. Greely in 1884, the Navy responded by purchasing *Thetis* and rapidly dispatching her northward into the ice. *Thetis*'s successful arctic mission was her last brush with glory. In a navy where a third-rate steam frigate was considered backwater, she was but a third-rate steam *auxiliary*. Her long cruising range, though, favored assignment to distant fleet stations and she had been assigned to the Navy's Pacific Squadron since 1887.

Since the middle of 1892 her primary assignment involved a long-term survey of Baja California coastlines.[2]

Thetis was a relatively happy ship with eight officers, a crew of ninety-five, and one lone howitzer mounted forward to stoke her nascent warship aspirations. Reynolds was excited as he appraised his new home: "I am more than satisfied with the ship and the officers." Backwater as their circumstance was, several members of the *Thetis*'s wardroom from its San Diego days would later be promoted to admiral: Louis deSteiguer would rise to four stars as Commander, Battle Fleet; Miles Stirling would author books on the Navy after his flag officer days; and Roger Welles would return to California as the very first commander of the fledgling San Diego Naval Operating Base.

Ens. S. S. Robinson's entry in *Thetis*'s log of 9 February completed the official formality of Reynolds's arrival on board:

> 4 to 8 (p.m.). Overcast and cloudy. Light airs and breezes from SW. Barometer steady. 5:15: Asst. Paymaster Z. W. Reynolds, USN, reported on board for duty as the relief of Paymaster W. W. Galt.[3]

The position of assistant paymaster was both a rank within the Pay Corps and a billet aboard ship with duties similar to that of a supply officer/disbursing officer aboard a small warship of today. In the months to come, Reynolds would disperse the crew's pay, maintain the ship's strongbox, and contract for all

In this rare undated photo, *Thetis* swings at anchor in San Diego Bay. The first Navy ship to operate regularly from San Diego, she conducted extensive surveys of Lower California, beginning in 1892, which demanded consistent chandlery that San Diego merchants could supply best. *San Diego Historical Society*

nature of ship supplies and foodstuffs. When *Thetis* arrived in a port of call, Reynolds would frequently be the first ashore to barter for coal or to sign for the ship's mail. At sea Reynolds stood deck watches and claimed the large expanse of the ship's holds as his own.

After slipping her anchor on the morning tide on 11 February, *Thetis* made sail for San Ignacio Lagoon in Lower California with a fresh quartering breeze and cooperative weather. Survey work began immediately after anchoring in Pequena Bay five days later. "The survey work was unending," wrote one *Thetis* junior officer. "It was divided between the ship, doing offshore hydrographic work or soundings, and with the parties ashore, erecting and occupying signals, measuring baselines and helping the observation parties with their observations."[4] Reynolds's days were full with uncounted challenges in supply and outfitting. One entry in his ledger read: "Survey expenses: 73 mules (at $1 per mule) + guide for 16 days ($1.60 a day)."

Thetis would typically work three months on station before returning to San Diego for supplies and coal. After this length of time in the handsome but barren frontier of the Baja, the social amenities of even the relatively unexciting San Diego were sure to dazzle a jaunty young man of only twenty-five. In letters to his parents Reynolds wrote of the surveys in a drab, repetitive, unexciting syntax. His descriptions of liberty in San Diego were spiced with mention of "damsels," costume parties, Saturday dances, and Sunday outings. "There are so many nice people at the big hotels here—pretty girls, lots of them," said one letter, and "the daughter of the manager of the Southern Pacific was off to the ship today with a party of girls, every one beautiful," explained another.[5]

Uniformed naval officers were a rarity in San Diego and the city's blossoming social circles soon latched onto their distinctiveness. In fashionable San Diego, matrons and socialites saw natty, well-educated naval officers adding to the status of their events. Naval officers were just as anxious to find relief from the tedium of lengthy cruises. As with many dimensions of the San Diego–Navy relationship in later years, both sides appeared to benefit. Reynolds lost no time in using his uniform's glamour to advantage, but by 1894 his eye consistently fell upon the stunning daughter of William Wallace Stewart, a prominent San Diego merchant and landowner.

Ruth Isabelle "Belle" Stewart was attractive, rich, and accomplished. Once described in the social pages of the *San Diego Union* as "an exceptionally handsome young lady and a social favorite in San Diego," she had been raised in privilege but held her own with beauty and talent. She had led the

Ziba Wells Reynolds as a captain in the U.S. Navy Pay Corps, c. 1915. *Susan Ring Keith*

Grand March to mark the opening of the famed Hotel del Coronado and had appeared in local theatrical productions of *Mikado* and *Loitta*. In 1894 she reportedly was the first woman to swim across San Diego Bay.

Belle had come to San Diego in 1869 at the age of three months with her family aboard the steamer *Orizaba* from Hangtown, California, where her father had pursued his fortune in the Gold Rush country. W. W. Stewart's wealth accumulated rapidly in the boom-and-bust years of land speculation in San Diego. When the first San Diego phone exchange was established in 1881, Stewart's phone number was assigned as number 21 out of thirty-nine subscribers. By 1890 he owned a good portion of downtown San Diego and had helped form the San Diego Philharmonic Society. The local newspaper declared that he was a city "pioneer who believed in the power of music."

Stewart's maritime credentials were also impressive. Once president of the powerful San Diego Chamber of Commerce, he was one of the first civic voices raised in support of coordinated port development. In 1889 he was appointed to the first Board of Harbor Commissioners for the city.[6]

In 1888 Stewart partnered with Capt. William Bell to establish San Diego's first shipyard, the San Diego Marine Railway and Drydock Company, located on the northeasterly point of North Island. The shipyard would serve the San Diego maritime community until the end of World War I when it was displaced by seaplane hangars of the Navy's new air station. The yard's marine railway featured a stationary steam engine, wheels, rails, and a massive hauling chain. Those seeing it from Coronado described it as "an empty skeleton—ribs rearing against the sky that could be rolled down a track and into the water to pick up small vessels to be hauled out for repairs." The first vessel was hauled out on 4 May 1888. The Spreckels Brothers Commercial Company eventually took over and ran the shipyard with Spreckels's tugs and ferries its constant customers.[7]

Wells Reynolds and Belle Stewart were married on 21 August 1895 in "brilliant nuptials for one of the most charming and popular young ladies of San Diego." Belle was described as one "who has been prominent in social and musical circles since her childhood." Dress uniforms, gold braid, and expensive finery were the rule of the day at lavish receptions honoring the couple. The extravagant Stewart-Reynolds ceremony set a high standard as the first large naval wedding in the city's history.[8]

By 1895 the American Navy had suffered through twenty years of neglect following the Civil War, and ships on the Pacific Station inevitably were drawn from the bottom of the Navy's deteriorating barrel. Only rarely did Pacific Squadron ships boast the armor, modern rifled guns, efficient steam engines, or any of the various other improvements introduced into the world's navies since the Civil War. All were built of wood, none were in good condition, and most suffered accelerating rot.[9]

Those few U.S. Navy ships that did sail the Pacific Station rarely visited San Diego. Despite the outward appearance of a perfectly protected harbor, the bay was annoyingly shallow with a reputation for tricky navigation. An outer bar, Zuniga Shoal, sat squarely across the entrance channel in the lee of Point Loma, and inside Ballast Point the channel shoaled to twenty-one feet across a substantial middle-ground bar. A deeper channel, scoured by brisk tidal currents, lay close inshore to Point Loma but could only be navigated with difficulty and was too crooked for safe navigation by larger ships. "An ugly left turn was required to stay in the channel," reported the commanding officer of USS *Ranger,* describing the S-style turn of the deeper water channel near Ballast Point.[10]

To improve the harbor for commerce, the silting of the bay (caused primarily by river deposits and beach sand) would have to be controlled and dredging would be required to cut new deeper channels into the mud. In 1853 Lt. George Derby of the U.S. Corps of Topographical Engineers undertook the first attempt to build a levee to rechannel the San Diego River into False Bay to remove the primary source of river silt from the bay, but the "Derby Dike" of gravel and timber collapsed within two seasons of winter floodwaters. The San Diego River returned to its channel, emptying into San Diego Bay until a second (and ultimately successful) levee was built in 1876.[11]

San Diegans also vigorously petitioned to have the Army Corps of Engineers dredge Zuniga Shoal and build a jetty to combat the longshore flow of harbor-clogging sand up the Silver Strand. Congress approved the bill but President Franklin Pierce vetoed the appropriation, leading the editor of the *San Diego Herald* to support the candidacy of Millard Fillmore: "[W]e cannot conceive how any permanent resident of San Diego can vote for Mr. Pierce who is so uncompromisingly opposed to the system of internal improvements on which the prosperity of our city depends." It took nearly forty years to start the Zuniga Jetty effort and eleven years and half a million dollars to finally complete the jetty to a length of seventy-five hundred feet.[12]

The era of the "New Steel Navy" came to the Pacific Station with the assignment of the protected cruiser *Charleston* to the force in January 1890. Built at Union Iron Works in San Francisco, she was over four thousand tons and armed with two 8-inch and six 6-inch rifles. But in true Pacific Squadron fashion, she was not the top of the line and was viewed as too lightly armored for the fleet's principal battle line in the Atlantic.[13]

In 1891, though, *Charleston* would play the key role in the first defining event of San Diego's modern association with the Navy, an event that had its genesis in the midst of a civil war in faraway Chile. The Chilean navy, one of the world's most modern at the time, had sided with Chilean revolutionists who had risen to depose a stringent nationalist president and virtual dictator. These Chilean revolutionists had purchased arms in the United States and the Chilean navy ordered the iron steamer *Itata* and the modern protected cruiser *Esmeralda* northward to collect them. *Esmeralda* had been built of an advanced British design and her two modern 10-inch guns, six 6-inch guns, and armored sides made her a formidable match for anything in the U.S. Navy.

While *Itata* and *Esmeralda* sailed toward the United States, the illegal arms (two thousand cases of rifle ammunition and fifty thousand rifles) were loaded aboard the American lumber schooner *Robert and Minnie,* which then sailed for Santa Catalina Island. *Itata* arrived in San Diego on 3 May, short of

San Diego harbor about 1895. Already the Navy is "present" with a white-painted cruiser of the New Steel Navy depicted in the channel beyond the site of the Quarantine Station pier. *U.S. Naval Institute*

coal and anxious for information on *Robert and Minnie's* whereabouts. At twelve hundred tons *Itata* was an eye-catcher, the largest passenger steamer ever to visit San Diego—but she was also not totally what she appeared. A good portion of *Esmeralda's* crew had been secretly transferred aboard *Itata* and *Esmeralda's* captain was aboard masquerading as *Itata's* master. On 5 May, while *Itata* replenished provisions and coal, the U.S. government impounded the vessel, placed a U.S. marshal on board, and arrested the captain for violation of neutrality laws.[14]

The press quickly caught wind of the developments and circulated zesty reports of intrigue. A fishing boat claimed seeing *Robert and Minnie* ten miles offshore. The *Itata* was reportedly frantically loading coal despite her seizure. A sinister black-hulled warship, "twice the size of *Itata*," was seen by several observers off Point Loma.

Despite the impediment of "arrest," *Itata* took advantage of a lapse in the marshal's attention, upped anchor, and slipped out of San Diego on 6 May, graciously landing the federal officer as she departed. She rendezvoused near San Clemente Island with *Robert and Minnie*, transferred the contraband arms, and took off at full steam for Chile. With word of the *Itata's* escape, *Charleston*—then at Mare Island—sailed in pursuit.

Newspapers stoked public interest in San Diego with stories of the provocative *Itata* affair. *Charleston* was sighted off Ocean Beach midday on 11 May, heading south at high speed. Word spread quickly around town and soon "house tops of the city were filled with observers with glasses watching her movements."[15]

Esmeralda and *Itata* rendezvoused south of Manzanillo, Mexico, on 15 May, but in a remarkable feat of timing, navigation, and luck *Charleston* appeared on the horizon just as

they prepared to transfer coal and cargo. The Chileans hurriedly broke off the transfer and scattered, and it was not until 0300 the following morning that *Charleston* caught up with *Esmeralda* off Acapulco.

Tensions ran high. When an *Esmeralda* searchlight fell upon *Charleston*, the American captain ordered his crew to quarters and loaded his batteries. The captain of *Esmeralda* later said that had a pistol shot been fired on either side, it would have been a signal for an instant and bloody engagement.[16] When *Itata* finally arrived in the Chilean port of Iquique, she was met by the trained guns of the American Pacific Squadron, who impounded her cargo.

The *Itata* affair proved a bit of a milestone for the fledgling steam navy of the United States. *Charleston's* dash southward at full power approximated what would be called for in wartime. Her captain frequently cleared the ship for action, had stripped the ship of combustibles, and had honed the crew through incessant gunnery exercises.[17]

Itata, escorted by *Charleston* and the Mexican gunboat *Democrata*, arrived back in San Diego on 4 July. *Charleston* anchored a mile off the Hotel del Coronado and *Itata* was directed to a detention anchorage near Spreckels Wharf. The public watched as *Itata* wearily made anchorage: a "huge black iron hull crept slowly up the [bay] like an unwilling guest at a fete."[18]

Throughout the *Itata* affair ships of the Pacific Squadron became increasingly frequent visitors to San Diego. In fact, on the day *Itata* broke arrest and dashed from the harbor, she passed the wooden screw sloop *Omaha* of twelve guns inbound from Far East duty, and the day she returned under the sharp eye of *Charleston*, the steel gunboat *Ranger*—newly constructed but with a outmoded full sail rig—lay at anchor in the harbor.

The arrival of the protected cruisers of the "New Steel Navy" in the early 1890s caused the first serious look at San Diego as a support base by naval planners. As these new cruisers were relatively lightly armed, they maneuvered together in squadrons to increase their effectiveness. Coal-powered engines allowed the tactical advantage of coordinated maneuvering in battle lines that sailing ships could never match. These complex maneuvers and modern tactics required practice—lots of it—and the agreeable weather conditions of Southern California made San Diego an increasingly favored locale for operations.[19]

On 28 September 1892 the Pacific Squadron commander used the occasion of the 350th anniversary of Cabrillo's first landing at San Diego to exercise his ships in coordinated maneuvers before arriving in port. *Charleston* and *Baltimore*, with gleaming white-painted sides and gilded swirls and eagles across each bow in the style of the New Navy, joined the city's festivities. During the celebration three companies of sailors and Marines participated in "the finest parade ever witnessed" and that night the ships performed a dazzling exhibition with their searchlights. "[T]he display continued for over an hour and when the lights were turned on Old Town, over four miles away, the trees and shrubbery on the lawns could be counted." San Diegans were mesmerized with this maiden display of naval might, and when *Baltimore* opened for visitors the following day so many people hired boats that her captain suspended boardings for over an hour.[20]

In 1894 the gunboat *Bennington,* representing a new class of steel warship, arrived for a visit in San Diego shortly after joining the Pacific Squadron. Built to 1,710 tons and mounting six 6-inch rifles, she had been designed as a less expensive adjunct to the more glamorous armored cruisers of the era. Her design favored speed and flexibility to protect the fleet against the new threat posed by rapidly proliferating torpedo boats. San Diego would see much of *Bennington* throughout the next decade.[21]

William McKinley's presidential election in 1896 marked an important turning point in San Diego's naval affairs that no one at the time recognized. Coming into office with McKinley was an energetic assistant secretary of the Navy, Theodore Roosevelt, who quickly became the point man for a whole host of initiatives, including strengthening naval forces in the Pacific.

For the first time in memory, the Navy rotated modern and well-armed vessels to Pacific duty instead of the second- and third-rates that had been the norm. The monitor *Monadnock* and the battleship *Oregon,* nearing completion at Union Iron

Painted in the white and buff style of the 1890s, protected cruiser *Charleston* stood between two eras in warship design. She featured a wood-paneled wheelhouse and 6-inch broadside battery of old balanced by a modern steel hull and breachloading guns of the New Steel Navy. *U.S. Naval Institute*

Works in San Francisco, would be among the first heavily armored ships to patrol the West Coast routinely and would be frequent visitors to San Diego as a result of this new Pacific emphasis.

Roosevelt found resonance in calls for a more balanced naval force in both the Atlantic and the Pacific, forces that could provide immediate naval superiority over Japan in the Pacific and, when combined, could be a powerful naval counter to Germany in the Atlantic. In 1897 he openly lobbied for funds to build six new battleships, four for the Atlantic and two specifically for the Pacific.[22]

In the midst of this growing fervor for a strong Pacific battle line, Rear Adm. Charles Beardsley brought seven ships of his Pacific Squadron to San Diego to celebrate George Washington's birthday, 22 February 1897.[23] What followed was another in a series of increasingly positive fleet visits, with the newspapers ebulliently reporting that the public was entranced with the spectacle. The Navy enjoyed the obvious warmth of the welcome. John Philip Sousa's band played two concerts for over ten thousand spectators, while the fleet dazzled onlookers with electric up-and-over lights and colored rockets that accompanied crewmen singing the "Star Spangled Banner." Spectacle blended with patriotic fervor. The *Union* boasted, "[T]here breathed no man yesterday that felt no exultant patriotism in his breast at the sight of the men in fine uniforms on the street."[24]

Whether San Diego as a whole recognized what these events

were to mean in the long term is unclear. What many did see, though, was a growing familiarity between the Navy and the community, a relationship that would blossom over the years as each used the other to mutual advantage. As if to reinforce this point, the Hotel del Coronado produced a glossy marketing pamphlet that showed how the Navy could support San Diego's great tourist industry. It listed recreational activities for its guests that included such things "as sail on the bay, match games of water polo in the bathhouse, morning quail hunt on North Island . . . and attend weekly receptions on board the US cruisers of the Pacific White Squadron[,] some of which are usually riding at anchor in the harbor."[25]

Through increasingly positive fleet visits such as this, many San Diegans viewed the Navy as a valued member of the community and a positive and trusted contributor to the social fabric of the city. Partly founded in good will, partly in the promise of commercial gain, strong and unflinching public support for the Navy was slowly becoming a hallmark of San Diego, the Navy homeport.

With the *San Diego Union* reporting, "The spirit of war and patriotism pervaded practically the whole city last night," the United States declared war against Spain in April 1898, two months after the battleship *Maine* exploded in Havana harbor.[26] All battleships and armored cruisers in the Pacific Squadron quickly sailed to join either the Atlantic Fleet or Commodore Dewey in the Far East. *Bennington,* under Comdr. E. D. Taussig, sailed westward to the Philippines, claiming Wake Island for the United States on 17 January 1899 while en route.

Rear Adm. Joseph Miller, Pacific Squadron commander, prepared a patchwork plan for the protection of West Coast ports and augmented the only two remaining Navy ships in his squadron with an auxiliary naval force composed of revenue cutters, armed yachts, and other hastily converted vessels, manned in part by the naval militia. The revenue cutter *Corwin* was ordered to San Diego to help protect minefields that were planned for the harbor entrance.[27]

As minefields fell within the overall scheme of harbor defense, the Army assumed their responsibility in San Diego. The mines chosen for San Diego harbor defense were crude, electrically controlled devices triggered from an observation post ashore to detonate under a threatening vessel. The first mines arrived on 28 April from San Francisco aboard steamer *Bonita.* Manually deploying these mines into the channel from a storage magazine at Ballast Point was a difficult and burdensome task, and when Army lieutenant James Meyler was ordered to enlist the services of 120 "patriotic citizens" from

town to help in this hazardous work he could only find 88 willing workers.[28]

On 23 May 1898 Meyler and his men began planting the submarine mines in a fan-shaped array across the harbor mouth. Five triple groups of 32-inch buoyant mines were placed in line across the westerly portion of the main entrance channel. The mines weighed between fifteen hundred and eighteen hundred pounds, including anchor, and contained approximately one hundred pounds of dynamite. To deploy the mines Meyler commandeered the tug *Santa Fe,* the largest steam-powered tug in San Diego. Once the harbor was mined, special navigation regulations went into effect, closing the port every evening from 2000 to 0400 and dousing navigation lights at Ballast Point Lighthouse and on harbor beacons.

The minefield remained in place until 17 August 1898, when orders were received to remove the mines. Again *Santa Fe* was used and Meyler completed the removal over three days, ending 23 September. As the mines were pulled from the water, one mine came aboard the tug with a large dent in its side. An unknown ship (but an obviously lucky one) either entering or leaving port had apparently run into the mine without detonating it.[29]

At the onset of the war in April 1898 the commander of the San Diego Naval Militia was ordered to recruit his Third Division to maximum strength of one hundred men. Only twenty-five of these were mobilized for service and none, apparently, served in combat.[30]

In the wake of the Spanish-American War, the Navy's strategic frontier stretched entirely across the Pacific and the trend toward greater American naval power in the Pacific accelerated, further increasing Navy interest in bases along the West Coast. To extend the Navy's Pacific reach, coaling stations in Guam, Samoa, and the Philippines were proposed and plans were begun for a transoceanic canal route across Central America.[31]

None of these trends were lost on the more astute business and political leaders of San Diego, who had long desired a military presence in the city. The very first annual report of San Diego's Chamber of Commerce appropriately listed "making San Diego the headquarters of this military district" as one of its goals, but progress in reaching this goal had been inconsistent and disorganized.[32]

Army or Navy activity on the Point Loma military reservation had been slow in developing. Point Loma served as little more than a quarantine anchorage and a source of ship's ballast. The Army finally took formal possession of the Point

Gun crew exercises aboard protected cruiser *Charleston*, c. 1893. *Charleston* became one of the first ships of the modern Navy to visit San Diego on a frequent basis. *Naval Historical Center*

Loma Military Reservation in 1873 and evicted a short-lived whaling industry operating from the deserted hide houses of La Playa, at Ballast Point, and across the channel on North Island. With care and not a little forethought, the Army also reserved a single acre of land high atop the Reserve as a post cemetery for its San Diego barracks. The federal government established a quarantine station at La Playa in 1888.[33]

Although the geopolitical realities that were fueling the Navy's increasing interest in the Pacific were well known in San Diego, there was little coordination among city and business officials to capitalize on events and no clear plan to influence Navy officials or members of Congress on the city's behalf. In the first formally published plan for the improvement of San Diego harbor, developed in 1898–99 by state harbor commissioners and city planners, no mention was even made of the Navy. Instead, a grandiose scheme was presented to encircle the harbor with over 170 slips and piers and triple the width of the Silver Strand through dredging and reclamation (presumably turning the Strand into a warehouse and cargo transshipment area). Despite the commissioners' hopes, nothing was ever done to implement the plan and no immediate answer was provided on how deep draft ships would enter the notoriously shallow harbor.[34]

The primary impediment to increased use of the bay remained the shallowness of the harbor entrance and by 1898 this deficiency had reached critical proportions. Commercial ships had grown in length and draft so that by the late 1890s the largest could no longer enter the bay. Ships were forced to anchor in Coronado Roads and lighter their cargoes ashore—a time-consuming and expensive process.

But business leaders such as W. W. Stewart and George Marston also knew that the magnitude of dredging and harbor construction for San Diego was clearly beyond local means and could only be accomplished through projects controlled by the influential U.S. Army Corps of Engineers. There, San Diego faced considerable disadvantages. San Diego had little experience lobbying the Corps and, worse, it had little organized presence in Washington. But with the threat of major disruptions in seaborne commerce, San Diego businessmen rallied to coordinate their voices under the overall aegis of the San Diego Chamber of Commerce, a powerful assemblage of the city's biggest employers, bankers, landlords, philanthropists, and newspaper owners. Their new strategy: to "persuade the Navy Department to make more and more use of the bay." If that happened, they hoped, "the Navy might use its influence to persuade the Corps of Engineers to improve the harbor" and with that would come increased commerce and business prosperity.[35]

This was an astute and credible plan. First-rate warships were being ordered to the Pacific as never before and increases in size and draft of Navy cruisers and battleships matched the same trends that were apparent in larger merchant ships. The Navy would need bases, and those bases would need deepwater anchorage. One would assuredly lead to the other. If San Diego could win Navy bases within the harbor, the Navy would inevitably help deepen the harbor.

But before San Diego could organize a cogent campaign to woo the Navy, the Navy's Bureau of Yards and Docks surprised everyone in 1898 with a report to the secretary of the Navy recommending San Diego as a preferred site in Southern California for a repair base and dockyard for Pacific-based ships.[36] Caught off-guard by this stunningly positive endorsement, San Diego business leaders reacted slowly, and it was not until April 1900 that Chamber of Commerce secretary H. P. Wood sent letters "urging the necessity for establishing a coaling and repair station for the Navy on San Diego Bay." On 7 April 1900 chamber president George Ballou signed a letter to the secretary of the Navy expressing hope that he would give the matter his "careful and favorable consideration," and Sen. George Perkins sent correspondence offering an appropriation for a "commission to examine and locate a proper site for a coaling station in San Diego."[37]

As well meaning but disorganized as San Diego's case appeared, the Navy's plan to meet the demands of its expanding Pacific commitments was little better. Despite the endorsement of Yards and Docks and the first appearance of letters from San Diego political boosters, most in the Navy Department believed that San Diego could, at best, support only smaller classes of ships. Many in the Navy Department preferred San Francisco, San Pedro, or even Magdalena Bay in Mexico for coaling or repair bases.

It was a "Catch-22" before anyone recognized the meaning of the phrase. San Diego needed the Navy in order to make the case for a deeper harbor, but the Navy wouldn't come due to the shallow entrance to the harbor. Typical of the thinking of the time was the Bureau of Equipment's response to the chamber's April 1900 letter that noted: "Should the entrance to San Diego be sufficiently deepened and the middle ground shoal

Santa Fe Wharf in 1905. Monitor *Monterey* and gunboat *Nashville* are present making smoke. *U.S. Naval Institute*

removed, this port would present a favorable place for a coaling station and the Bureau would strongly advocate it."[38]

Views and opinions from a distant Navy Department notwithstanding, the inescapable fact was that Pacific naval forces demanded large amounts of coal from strings of coaling stations along favored transit routes. It fell to the chief of the Bureau of Equipment, Rear Adm. Royal Bradford, to address the issue of West Coast coaling sites. One of his first steps was to resolve the mismatch between the glowing Yards and Docks report of San Diego potential and the negative attitude of his immediate staff. It was known that the commanding officer of the gunboat *Ranger,* Comdr. W. L. Field, had had long service with the Pacific Squadron and Bradford had *Ranger* ordered from duties surveying the Lower California coast to proceed to San Diego to report on the harbor's merits.[39]

On 24 May 1900 Commander Field anchored *Ranger* off La Playa and set vigorously to work sounding and surveying the bay. Each of Field's actions was studiously followed by San Diego newspapers, kept appraised of developments through the efforts of San Diego–elected representatives who were taking indirect credit for "inducing" the Navy's interest. "Survey of Harbor has commenced" read one headline as *Ranger's* survey parties fanned out to several sites in the harbor. The *Union* reported further that "as soon as the orders were received, the work commenced and it will keep the men reasonably busy for almost two weeks."[40]

President Ballou and Secretary Wood called upon Captain Field frequently to "present the condition of the entrance to the harbor in the correct light."[41] By early June 1900 Field had prepared an articulate and compelling report back to Admiral Bradford and the secretary of the Navy. In that report he unabashedly emphasized San Diego harbor's attributes as the "only good harbor south of San Francisco" and the American port "closest to the Isthmus." He emphatically concluded, "After investigating different localities [for a coaling station], I favor the location immediately below the quarantine station wharf. It is on government land, plenty of level land, easy of approach, room to turn in the channel, well defended from attack from seaward."[42]

Bradford took immediate interest in the report, complimenting it as "excellent" and asking for further information, including Field's opinion of an alternative coaling site on the North Island side of the channel. Field replied that the North Island site was satisfactory except for the difficulty in connecting the site by rail.

That summer, as a direct result of *Ranger's* survey and recommendations, Bradford and Secretary of the Navy John Long

Ranger, the last full sail-rigged ship built for the Navy, played a prominent role in increasing San Diego's attractiveness to the predominantly Eastern-based naval establishment. Her surveys of San Diego harbor in 1900, brilliantly articulated by her captain, Comdr. W. L. Field, caught and held the Navy Department's attention. *U.S. Naval Institute*

opened negotiations with the War Department for a bayside parcel of land on the Military Reservation (exactly the site near the quarantine station that Field had recommended).[43] Bradford was the first senior American naval official to argue convincingly of the importance of San Diego harbor to future naval operations. Commander Field also consistently kept San Diego harbor's attributes forefront in the Navy's planning, at one time filing a report that stated, "[T]he strategic importance of San Diego is so great that sooner or later a dry dock and repair shops will be constructed at this port, in which case the quarantine station will have to be moved."[44] A man of action, Bradford scheduled a fact-finding trip to San Diego for December 1900 to survey the situation personally.

News of the impending visit galvanized the San Diego business community into action. The Chamber of Commerce had recognized its past ineffectiveness and by the time Bradford had finished the difficult five-day cross-country train trip, a busy itinerary had been polished for him with equal parts business and entertainment. Bradford would first board the Army's steam launch *General de Russey* for a trip to the quarantine station, then inspect various Point Loma facilities and visit the Harbor Department. Later, he would tour the city by tally-ho and be regaled at a Hotel del Coronado dinner in his honor. The *Union* oozed optimism as it reported these developments. It was said that while Bradford was at the del Coronado he "watched for several minutes the surf breaking in the

Officers and crew of gunboat *Bennington,* photographed in San Diego harbor on 3 March 1906, just four months before the explosion that would kill nearly a third of the crew. *Naval Historical Center*

moonlight on the beach."[45] San Diego boosters may have had trouble within the lobbying circles of Washington, but once operating on home turf they were a potent force.

Perhaps still under the influence of his pampered reception, Bradford uncharacteristically broke standard bureaucratic conservatism to declare boldly the next day that while a Navy coaling station was "assured" for San Diego, the details of a specific location were still under consideration. San Diego business leaders were ecstatic.

On 17 December, after the tiring return trip to his office, Bradford again kept his observations exceedingly positive. He told a delegation of San Diegans that he hoped to procure over two hundred acres of land, including the site of the quarantine station, but added that the quarantine officials were averse to moving.[46]

In the annual report of the Navy Department for 1900, the secretary of the Navy echoed Bradford's sense of progress:

The Bureau is desirous of establishing a naval coal depot at San Diego, Cal. Its location on the extreme southern limits of the Pacific coast of the United States renders it of value in this connection. While the largest ships cannot enter this port, there are sufficiently sheltered waters outside where they can safely anchor and receive coal from barges. Vessels drawing 22 feet or less can freely enter the harbor at high tide. There is a large Government reservation from which it appears, from negotiations with the War Department, a site may be selected suitable for the construction of the necessary storage houses and pier.[47]

Events accelerated in 1901 under Bradford's urging. In April the admiral notified San Diego officials that his department had the necessary funds to begin building at San Diego as soon as the Army land was turned over to the Navy.[48] Several months later "a parcel of land enclosed by the northern boundary of the reservation, the waters of the bay on the east, the waters of the Pacific on the west and a line on the south drawn from the Bay to the Pacific coast parallel to the northern boundary and commencing on the Bay at the northern limiting line (about 2900 feet)" was formally transferred to the Navy Department, completing the deal. The land would be the first in San Diego transferred to the Navy and the coaling station would be the first Navy shore station in San Diego.[49]

In his annual report of 1901, the secretary of the Navy reported these events for the record:

The War Department, at the request of the Navy Department, has transferred to the latter during the past year a section of the Point Loma military reservation at San Diego, Cal. for the purpose of establishing thereon a naval coal depot. The final steps of the transfer have but recently been completed. In the meantime a thorough survey has been made of the locality by the USS *Ranger*. The geographical position of the harbor, its immediate proximity to the frontier of the United States, and the prospect in the near future of extensive harbor improvements make it exceedingly valuable as a coaling station.[50]

By late 1901 business leaders of the Chamber of Commerce could smugly look around San Diego and see their heretofore-chaotic plans suddenly gaining relatively spectacular momentum. On North Island the Corps of Engineers was nearly finished with Zuniga Jetty; on Point Loma the Army planned further harbor defenses; at La Playa the Navy's first base in San Diego appeared to be a reality; and in the harbor plans for further dredging and improvements moved forward. The only hint of trouble, and it seemed minor at the time, was that Congress had failed to act on two proposals for harbor-dredging appropriations in 1900 and 1901.

In the midst of this sense of progress Congress's failure to approve dredging promptly now came to haunt San Diegans and threatened to derail the entire carefully contrived naval development plan. While the Navy Department negotiated with the War Department, the surgeon general of the Marine Hospital Service took things into his own hands. He saw Congress's inaction to approve dredging in 1900 and 1901 as a signal of their indifference and, consequently, an opportunity for the Marine Hospital Service. Keen to expand the quarantine station, he proposed building a new Marine hospital on six acres of land immediately adjoining the quarantine station—exactly the land the Navy had eyed for its coaling station.

Added as a rider to a sundry civil bill passed by Congress, the action suddenly had the power of law and overrode the carefully wrought land deal between the Navy and War Departments. The secretary of the Navy reported these facts dryly in his annual report of 1902: "Recently the Bureau discovered that Congress has transferred 6.5 acres of the most valuable portion of this same land to the Treasury Department as a site for a marine hospital. This matter is at present being considered by the two departments."[51]

The Navy's efforts to resolve the dilemma lost steam through 1902 and little headway was made to resolve this dispute. In 1903 the secretary of the Navy lamented:

No progress has been made during the past year in establishing a naval coal depot at this port . . . as the desirable portion of the land obtained by the Navy Department from the War Department for this purpose having been transferred by act of Congress to the Treasury Department for use as an quarantine station, the entire matter is held in abeyance for further action of Congress.[52]

Having tasted the first fruits of their coordinated strategy to attract the Navy's support to deepen the harbor, the San Diego Chamber of Commerce was reluctant to let the matter lie fallow for long. The chamber voted on a resolution in late 1902 favoring Navy ownership of the land over the Treasury Department and offered to show other sites to Quarantine Service officials. San Diego businessman Ed Fletcher wrote directly to President Theodore Roosevelt in September 1902 calling for a new "first class Naval Station of the interest of San Diego itself and the United States as well, owing to the proximity to foreign territory and the Isthmus."[53] Chamber officers met with the president and the secretary of the Navy to discuss San Diego Bay improvements in May 1903, and the chamber's tireless secretary, H. P. Wood, devoted much of his time and many long train trips to Washington to help resolve the matter. San Diego historian Abraham Shragge called this "the first of many instances in which officers of the San Diego Chamber of Commerce would attempt and succeed at steering the course of naval policy toward their own ends."[54]

Naval interventions in Central and South America finally helped to break the logjam between the Navy and Treasury Departments and Senator Perkins and Rep. M. J. Daniels introduced a bill in Congress during January 1904 to move the quarantine station. News of the Senate ratification of the Hay Herrian (Panama Canal) Treaty on 17 March 1903 was cause for great jubilance in San Diego. George Marston of the Chamber was quoted in the *Union* as saying, "[T]wo great results are bound to follow: the commercial use of the harbor

Greater loss of life was averted aboard *Bennington* when she was heroically pushed onto the city shore by tug *Santa Fe.* Many of the dead were still being removed late in the afternoon of 21 July 1905. *Naval Historical Center*

with an immense expansion of business and the great development of army and navy equipments here."[55]

The secretary of the Navy frequently referred future fleet planning to the Navy's General Board, a respected senior advisory council headed in the early years of the century by the most esteemed officer in the Navy, Adm. George Dewey, victor at Manila Bay and the Navy's first four-star admiral. Admiral Dewey was not unfamiliar with San Diego, having visited the harbor in 1873 as the captain of the screw frigate *Narragansett*.[56]

Although San Diegans could declare that San Diego was the "best site for a dry dock and repair station on the Pacific Coast," few on the General Board agreed. At the request of the secretary of the Navy, the General Board reviewed the case for larger bases in San Diego in October 1904. Admiral Dewey's formal reply was polite but negative. It agreed to the probable need for additional naval facilities in San Diego at some time in the future, but not immediately. It was a theme from the General Board that would be repeated often over the next

decade and one that served as a dampening force for San Diego's enthusiasm.[57]

The chamber tried to rekindle support for base expansion by inviting the first high-level delegation of officers from the Navy Department to visit San Diego on 29–30 November 1904. The president of the Chamber of Commerce accompanied Assistant Secretary of the Navy Charles Darling and Frank Sargent of the California Naval Militia on a harbor tour and an inspection of the La Playa Coaling Depot. Darling called the harbor "one of the most important in the country" and was particularly interested in land north of the coaling station that he thought best suited for a drydock and repair station.[58]

In the wake of Darling's visit, the chamber redoubled efforts to broaden its message to naval officials within the Pacific Squadron and in Washington, D.C. In a 1905 internal memo for the chamber's board of directors, Secretary Wood outlined a detailed plan to capture additional naval facilities:

> The first step in the way of development of the Naval Reservation will probably be the building up of the coaling station, followed by the installation of a wireless telegraph plant, a Marine Hospital will also be constructed, and a Naval Training Station established after which will come the repair station to be followed ultimately by a dry dock and ship-building yards. Petty jealousies and political intrigue may retard matters somewhat, but cannot prevent the harbor of San Diego becoming ultimately one of America's greatest Naval strongholds on the Pacific.[59]

By November 1904 Secretary Wood helped finalize the quarantine station agreement and the Navy assigned Lt. Comdr. J. H. L. Holcombe as the coal depot's first officer-in-charge and set out to construct the first buildings and pier. Even before the quarantine station was out of the way, Holcombe began to clear a large laydown area for coal piles and ordered the construction of a three-story iron loading crane.

City officials never missed a beat in processes now honed through three years of practice. They used the tiny Point Loma coaling station to argue for appropriations to dredge the harbor to hasten commercial development and kept up a steady stream of correspondence and office visits to Washington. Typical of the material prepared was a booklet forwarded to the secretary of the Navy by the Chamber of Commerce in August 1904 entitled, "The Pacific Ocean and Its Shores Are Destined to Be the Theater of the World's Greatest Commercial Activity." "It was therefore incumbent upon the federal government," read the pamphlet, "to finish dredging out the channel, move the quarantine station expand the capacity of the coal depot, establish a naval training station, build a naval hospital and wireless telegraph station and do some additional dredging in order to make available the best site for a dry dock and repair station on the Pacific Coast."[60]

By all accounts San Diego city officials and businessmen were satisfied with their courting of the Navy by mid-1905. But apart from watching a sleek cruiser navigate toward anchorage or viewing companies of bluejackets march proudly in an occasional holiday parade, the citizenry of San Diego had been largely left untouched by the growing naval presence. On a slightly overcast morning in July 1905 a signature event would forever change how San Diego viewed its Navy neighbors.

The Navy's steel gunboat *Bennington,* by 1905 a long veteran of Pacific Squadron duty, had stopped in San Diego harbor for an extended port call during March of that year. Her stay had been long enough for the crew to develop a comfortable shore-liberty routine, frequenting favored entertainments downtown, shopping in a wide variety of stores, and journeying to the country on weekend excursions. Members of the San Diego Naval Militia had been invited to train alongside *Bennington* crewmembers in gunnery and small arms exercises and had raced against a *Bennington* launch in a spirited weekend regatta—high points for the frequently overlooked San Diego irregulars. *Bennington*'s young and dashing captain, Comdr. Lucien Young (widely recognizable for a booming voice, infectious laugh, and a stylish, bushy mustache), was also one of the most highly decorated naval officers of his era.[61]

On Wednesday, 19 July, *Bennington* returned again to San Diego after a rough eleven-day transit from Honolulu where she had been hurriedly ordered on 12 May, cutting short recommended engineering repairs. Although busy all Wednesday and Thursday (first coaling the ship and then laboriously cleaning the soot from *Bennington*'s gleaming sides), the crew was looking forward to renewing old acquaintances in San Diego during promised weekend liberty.

Late in the day on 20 July new orders were received directing *Bennington* under way to escort the disabled monitor *Wyoming* from Port Harford to Mare Island Naval Yard for

On 7 January 1908 San Diego turned out en masse to attend dedication ceremonies for the *Bennington* memorial at Fort Rosecrans cemetery, just as it had done three years previously during actual burial ceremonies. A *St. Louis*–class cruiser, possibly *Charleston,* is entering the channel far below. *Naval Historical Center*

repairs.[62] Commander Young ordered preparations to get under way, planning to leave the harbor by midday on Friday, 21 July.

By Friday morning, *Bennington* was anchored one hundred yards off of what is today Market Street, and Commander Young had taken the launch ashore to "take care of a few last bills" and conduct other ship's business.[63] The Black Gang lit fires, and stokers and coal-passers heaved scoops of coal into the roaring furnaces to slowly raise steam preparatory to testing main engines. The crew of 179 men went about their duties while they awaited the return of their captain. Quartermasters laid out their one-day track up the coast, and deck seamen busied themselves topside maintaining their ship in fighting trim.

At 1033 two dull explosions echoed across the harbor in quick succession, shaking windows, startling horses, and catching the attention of nearly everyone in town. *Bennington* was momentarily lost from view, enveloped in clouds of escaping steam. Teenager Asa Bushnell, rowing a wherry nearby, remembered "a deep muffled roar; steel gratings flew to masthead height and steam and black smoke began pouring from her ventilators."[64] Sailors at La Playa saw clouds of steam rising in the harbor and rushed to the scene to organize care for the crew.

Within minutes *Bennington* established a pronounced list to starboard. Screams mixed with the steady hiss of live steam as many sailors dove overboard to escape the spread of the murderous steam. Dazed and injured crewmembers filled the decks for a breath of fresh air. Hundreds gathered along piers and quays, gawking or trying to assist swimmers make shore. Bushnell himself picked up men in the water and pulled rapidly back to the Rowing Club. A *Bennington* life ring that he recovered that morning hung in the club for years after.

The *Bennington*'s officer of the deck, Ens. Newman K. Perry, was killed instantly by scalding, super-heated steam. His post on the quarterdeck was almost exactly above the explosion. Gunner's Mate J. H. Turpin was blown into the water by the concussion and swam safely to shore unharmed. For Turpin it was a horrific déjà vu as he had been badly injured seven years earlier when *Maine* exploded in Havana harbor—the Navy's largest single peacetime disaster until *Bennington* eclipsed that mark.[65]

Joe Brennan, deckhand of the tug *Santa Fe,* heard the rumbling blast and, not waiting for the tug's master, raced to the scene. Seeing that the gunboat was taking on water, Brennan maneuvered *Santa Fe* alongside. By this time, *Santa Fe*'s skipper, Bob Morris, had arrived on board and began shouting orders to the gunboat's dazed deck crew. Chief Boatswain's

Mate L. J. "Whitey" Gauthier helped secure the tug alongside but quickly realized that *Bennington* could not be towed toward safety without raising its anchor. With the anchor windlass useless without electrical power, Gauthier grabbed a fire axe and disappeared below decks into scalding steam, courageously making his way to the chain locker. There he hacked a manila stopper free from the bitter end of the anchor chain, allowing the chain to carry into the bay. *Santa Fe* pushed *Bennington* into a shallow mud bank along the downtown shore, saving her from sinking and undoubtedly saving additional scores of her crew. Tragically, Gauthier died the next day in a nearby hospital, the victim of severe steam inhalation suffered during his intrepid dash.

With flames advancing toward the ship's magazine, Lt. (jg) Alexander Yates, the senior officer on board, ordered the magazine flooded. Chief Gunner's Mate John Clausey raced below in the face of scalding steam to open the flood valves to prevent an even greater catastrophe. Clausey would be awarded a Congressional Medal of Honor for his heroics, one of eleven Medals of Honor awarded to *Bennington* crewmen. Each of the eleven was also given a "gratuity of one hundred dollars in cash."[66]

The response of San Diegans was instantaneous. Many walked or ran to the waterfront, and boats of all sizes (including the Coronado ferry *Ramona* and the Army tug *General de Russey*) swept the bay for those blown overboard, dead and injured alike. Physicians (and competing undertakers) raced to the scene in horsedrawn buggies and wagons. San Diego hospitals quickly became overloaded and the old Army Barracks on Market was pressed into service as an emergency ward. Citizens carried blankets, pillows, and books to bedside convalescents. Cots and mattresses used by jurors at the downtown courthouse were rushed to the waterfront. The procession of ambulances and wagons with litters was watched by hundreds.[67] Most scheduled events were canceled, and the disaster was the topic of most Sunday sermons.

In all, sixty-four enlisted men and one officer perished in the explosion and only twenty-five of the total two hundred-man crew escaped unharmed. A court of inquiry would later attribute the disaster to defective material in one boiler and a boiler pressure gauge rendered inoperative by an untrained watchstander.[68]

On Sunday, 23 July, San Diego held a mass burial service in the post cemetery at Fort Rosecrans atop Point Loma. A huge crowd turned out for the burial, snaking in long lines up the twisting roads leading to the Point Loma summit. All sixty-four of the sailors killed in the explosion were ultimately interred at the site.[69] Commander Young eulogized his fallen crewmembers: "I want to commit to [Ft. Rosecrans'] care the bodies of our misfortunate shipmates and patriotic dead. May their graves never be forgotten by the hand of affection and may marble slabs rise upon this, their last earthly resting place, and may the morning and evening sun, playing upon the grassy mounds, be symbolic of their shipmates affection." Following the ceremony, as the crowds dispersed, wagons loaded with heaps of floral offerings were brought in and the flowers were arranged on the graves.[70]

The tragedy bonded San Diego to the Navy in a powerful and enduring way. A disaster of this magnitude was unheard-of in a San Diego only the population of today's Coronado. "No incident in the city's history has so stirred the people with profound grief," read one editorial, and "there was such an out-pouring of sympathy, helpfulness and generosity as San Diego may well be proud of and such as may well endear its people to the Naval Service forever," read another account.[71]

Bennington was later refloated and towed to San Francisco Bay. She would never again see active service, her hulk ending its days as a water barge and molasses carrier in the Hawaiian Islands before being scuttled at sea.

Although acquitted of formal charges at his courts martial, Commander Young received a letter of reprimand for the incident but, perhaps, reflecting different perspectives from a different era, the incident would not slow his rise in promotion. Young would retire as a rear admiral in 1910.

Three years after the incident, a soaring granite obelisk seventy-five feet high was raised next to thirty-five *Bennington* headstones still present at Fort Rosecrans Cemetery. In a scene reminiscent of the original burial ceremony, thousands made their way along the difficult road to the crest of Point Loma to attend the dedication. On its sides are inscribed:

To the *Bennington*'s dead, July 21, 1905. Erected by the officers and men of the Pacific Squadron to the memory of those who lost their lives in the Performance of Duty.

1906

The day we are celebrating is beyond all comparison the greatest day in our history. The biggest thing that ever happened to San Diego was the raising of the Stars and Stripes. It revolutionized the character of the region politically, religiously, socially, economically.

William F. Smythe, 29 July 1906 (on the occasion of the sixtieth anniversary of the first raising of the American flag over San Diego)

By the time the dead of *Bennington* had been laid to final rest high above the harbor entrance it had been more than a decade since Ziba Wells Reynolds had called San Diego home. Navy orders of the day planned little for a personal rotation between shore and sea duty. Officers were ordered where the need was greatest and for Wells Reynolds, working his way up the seniority ladder of the Navy Pay Corps, the need was aboard ship.

By 1906, in his fourteenth year of service, Reynolds had already served as paymaster aboard six different warships. During the Spanish American War, he had been caught in the nationwide patriotic whirlwind swirling around the Navy as events marched toward war with Spain. Reynolds received orders to join the battleship *Oregon* off the coast of Cuba and, later, continued on board when she sailed for the Philippine Islands to assist in actions against Filipino insurgents. In the Philippines he joined the monitor *Monterey* and then was ordered to the cruiser *Charleston*. During Reynolds's first month aboard *Charleston* she participated in the capture of the strategic deepwater harbor at Subic Bay, an operation that would impact nearly every San Diego naval officer for the next hundred years.

But Reynolds's assignment aboard the cruiser that had gained nationwide fame during the *Itata* affair ended abruptly on 2 November 1899 when *Charleston* grounded on a reef near Camiguin Island. Reynolds was recognized for his work in safely evacuating the crew to a nearby island and establishing shelter for ten days with salvaged ship's stores.[1]

In 1906 Wells Reynolds received long-anticipated orders ashore and he and wife Belle traveled to San Francisco Bay and to quarters on dank and windy Goat Island where Reynolds assumed the paymaster billet for the Navy's only West Coast training station. In ten years of marriage following her high society wedding in San Diego, Belle had raised three children (son Stewart and daughters Ruth and Eleanor) and had established households in San Diego, San Francisco, Vallejo, and for an extended time with Reynolds's parents in Tunkhannock, Pennsylvania. It was a story that would be told in a hundred thousand ways, with a hundred thousand variations by a hundred thousand Navy wives who would begin their Navy "lives" in the sun-splashed city by glistening San Diego Bay and would see the world through travel fueled by U.S. Navy orders.

San Diego stayed a favorite with Belle, and while Reynolds was serving at sea aboard *Texas* in 1903 and early 1904 she stayed with her parents in their large house overlooking downtown. "Living in such a place and climate just spoils one for anything else. . . . I can't understand people with means living in any other climate than this, it is a perfect paradise."

Daughter Eleanor was less than a year of age when the Reynolds family arrived in San Francisco and so would not remember being shaken awake in the predawn hours of 18 April 1906 with the first tremors of San Francisco's 6.3 earthquake. "The first shock was like a great shove," Reynolds would say later. "It pushed me out of bed and I had Ruth, blankets and all, under one arm and on the way out. I opened Isabelle's door, told her to bring the baby, then went into Stewart's room." Perhaps remembering earthquakes from her Southern California upbringing, Belle weighed the first tremors differently: "Wells was scared to death, but I wasn't and stayed in bed when he insisted I should get up. Well, when I finally got to the door it was all over."

The training station, sitting on the rocky outcroppings of Goat Island (now Yerba Buena Island) and separated from the city's fires by three miles of bay, survived unscathed and intact and was quickly transformed into the perfect staging area for relief parties and troops who streamed into the city. By hap-

penstance, Belle's sister had been in the city visiting friends and Reynolds had searched for her through the burning districts of San Francisco. "He was in his naval uniform and she was happy to see him and he brought her back to safety by the [Goat Island] tug," Belle recounted. For her part Belle "joined several of the ladies to take sandwiches and water to anyone who would need it." Paymaster Reynolds tirelessly shouldered most of the responsibilities to clothe and feed victims and rescuers alike. Among the many groups that he helped outfit was a company from the San Diego Naval Militia that helped enforce the curfew.

For almost three decades the San Diego Naval Militia was an integral part of the community's life. It furnished valuable training and wholesome recreation for its members and it provided no small amount of local color. Militia members were frequent participants in a wide variety of local ceremonies and contributed materially during times of need.

Congress first authorized a naval militia program at the

Lt. Comdr. Don Stewart stands at the head of a detachment of the San Diego Naval Militia at their 28th Street Armory, c. 1914. The armory was built largely by militia members and for a time in 1920 housed the San Diego Yacht Club. *San Diego Maritime Museum*

Rear Adm. Caspar Goodrich, with his staff aboard the protected cruiser *Chicago,* was the Pacific Fleet commander from 1904 to 1906 and an early champion of San Diego for both increased fleet operations and as the site for a West Coast training station. *San Diego Historical Society*

state level in 1891 and one of its first militia companies in California was designated for San Diego. The first mustering-in ceremony took place on 12 September 1891 at the old Armory on Second Street for the company's rolls of ninety-seven men. Thomas Nerney was elected lieutenant by acclamation.[2]

The armored cruiser *San Francisco* arrived in San Diego on 28 December 1891 and offered to train the new company. As members of the naval militia had not yet obtained their uniforms, *San Francisco* performed night searchlight displays and volunteered their band to play at a gala fundraiser to help raise money from the citizenry. The company marched in its first parade up Broadway on 28 September 1892 in a commemoration of the 350th anniversary of Cabrillo's landing in San Diego.[3]

Two training boats were allocated to the militia in 1896: a cutter from *Hartford,* Civil War flagship of Adm. David Farragut, and a ten-oared barge from the monitor *Monadnock.* It was said that the *Hartford* boat never lost a pulling boat race (a

favorite form of recreation of the time that sparked intense competitions with boats from visiting warships). In 1898 the fourth-rate screw steamer *Pinta* of 550 tons was assigned to San Diego—her poor mechanical reliability was legend and she spent most of her San Diego days tied up to Santa Fe wharf. During the Spanish-American War the militia requested that *Pinta*'s inoperative armament (two Civil War howitzers, two Hotchkiss guns, and a ten-barrel Gatling gun) be readied for operation. The Navy denied the request.[4]

Lt. Comdr. Don Stewart took a group of militia volunteers to help suppress a mutiny among 950 Chinese laborers aboard the British steamer *Maiori King* in 1907 and later led the Third Division on patrol duty along the Mexican border from April to May 1914 to protect the city's water supply. As World War I began the secretary of the Navy ordered the naval militia into federal service and on 13 April 1917 156 men (the largest number of naval militiamen from any city in the state) left aboard a special train for Mare Island. Most of the men served aboard

Frederick and *Pueblo,* first in South American waters and then on North Atlantic convoy duty.[5]

A brilliant sun of early morning was still low over Otay Mountain when the new Navy radio station on Point Loma swung into action with the first news of San Francisco's earthquake crackling across the airwaves. Although the station was still a month away from formal commissioning, its chief operator, Chief Petty Officer Robert Stuart, had been testing the new Mossie transmitter for a month with calls primarily to the Navy radio facility on Mare Island. His first test call had set a Navy record for wireless transmission over land (that had previously stood at only 110 miles).[6]

Ships of the Pacific Squadron had just finished a week of maneuvers off Point Loma when word of San Francisco's disaster reached their commander, Rear Adm. Caspar Goodrich. Goodrich had led protected cruisers *Boston* and *Chicago,* gunboat *Princeton,* and revenue cutter *McCulloch* to sea at about

NPL as it appeared in September 1924 with the coaling station below on the bayshore with piles of coal next to a multistory coaling tower. *National Archives*

Steaming in battle divisions, the Great White Fleet approaches Coronado beach in 1908. *San Diego Historical Society*

0500 that morning. At a distance of about twenty miles from the coast his experimental DeForest wireless received: "Earthquake at 5:24 am, San Francisco. Nearly demolished city. Call Building is down and Palace Hotel, both telegraph offices, Wells Fargo Building. All water pipes burst, city fire department helpless. City is in flames." Goodrich immediately ordered cruiser *Marblehead* and collier *Saturn,* who were still in San Diego, to San Francisco at best speed. A second message soon followed from San Diego's mayor confirming the initial report and a continuous stream of news from the earthquake-ravaged Bay area poured into Navy wireless operators in Southern California.[7]

Admiral Goodrich's use of radio communications in San Diego to order urgent fleet operations was the first of its kind in history, underlining San Diego's leadership position in the wireless communications revolution of the early twentieth century. By accident of geography San Diego found itself in a prime position to lead the Navy into new technologies. The Navy had rushed to support the early experiments of DeForest and Marconi and planned a chain of wireless shore stations, one of which was forecast for the far southwesterly corner of the country to provide the furthest arc of southwest radio coverage over the ocean. San Diego fit the bill exactly.

For over a decade San Diego businessmen and the Chamber of Commerce had led spirited campaigns to convince a sometimes reluctant Navy to build a new coaling station, dredge the harbor, and station units of the Pacific Squadron in San Diego. Just the opposite was true of the new Navy radio station on Point Loma. The Navy knew what it wanted and took decisive steps to meet its requirements.

Navy Radio Station, Point Loma was formally established 12 May 1906 in a small frame building on the Point Loma Military Reservation with the comment that "wonderful aerograms can now speed through five hundred or more miles of space as readily as they cross the bay from Point Loma to Granger station."[8] NPL (also the station's radio call letters) would operate at the same site on Point Loma for more than forty years, usually staffed by two radio engineers, two enlisted men, a secretary, and an officer-in-charge.[9]

NPL handled more than three thousand messages during its first year of operation and contributed significantly to early experiments in radio broadcasting. When Dr. Lee DeForest performed his breakthrough experiments in ship-to-shore radio telephone communications, battleship *Connecticut* exchanged messages with NPL at a world distance record of twenty-nine hundred miles. Soon thereafter NPL recorded the first trans-Pacific transmission with a wireless operator in Petropavlosk, Siberia, a long-distance radio record that stood for two years.[10]

But life at the isolated Point Loma site was not all records and disaster relief. During the first few years of operation NPL dependents were not allowed to live on station, but regulations quickly fell victim to matters of the heart. Newly married and only seventeen, Bertha Ginther was determined to be as close to her husband, First Class Electrician O. D. Ginther, as possible. She set up an 18 x 15-foot one-room tenthouse immediately outside the radio station property and stood her ground for eight months. Trips to town included the use of the Army's tug *General de Russey* from Fort Rosecrans and frequently would end with late-night returns with the couple navigating up dark cowpaths to the wireless station and their tenthouse. During her stay Bertha became proficient in shooting rabbits to augment her meager supplies.

At the beginning of Theodore Roosevelt's presidency in 1901 the United States ranked fifth among the world's naval powers with nine first-class battleships in commission and eight more authorized and being built. By 1906 the American Navy had

The Great White Fleet battleline at anchor in Coronado Roads, April 1908. The crew of battleship *Illinois* gathers on the forecastle with *Virginia* and *Ohio* anchored astern. *San Diego Historical Society*

risen to third in the world but vocal Pacific coast communities, citing the rise of the Imperial Japanese Navy and the sudden emergence of colonial German naval power in the central Pacific, pushed for even more naval "protection." Theodore Roosevelt wanted the American Fleet to inspire worldwide respect and impress the American people with its international responsibilities. From these themes grew a plan for a voyage of the American battleline around the world and, with due regard to the public clamor in the West, for a series of splashy naval reviews along the Pacific coast.[11]

Preparations for the world-circling voyage of what was soon to be known as the Great White Fleet began at Atlantic Fleet headquarters in late 1907. A general plan slowly took shape: a voyage down the east coast of South America, a tran-

sit through the Straits of Magellan, visits to West Coast ports (especially San Francisco and Seattle), an emphasis on Japanese and Far Eastern port visits, and a return to the Atlantic through Suez and the Mediterranean.

Now fine-tuned to Navy staff planning, the San Diego Chamber of Commerce was shocked to discover that San Diego did not appear on the earliest drafts of the Great White Fleet's itinerary. With the fleet planning to sail literally right by San Diego's front door, city businessmen and elected officials were jolted into action and a flurry of correspondence flooded the offices of the secretary of the Navy and the Commander in Chief, Atlantic Fleet. Not only did the Chamber want the fleet to stop in San Diego harbor but they wanted the bigger prize of bragging rights as the first American port of call for the fleet

When it was established in 1904 the coaling station at La Playa represented the first permanent naval facility in San Diego. A new fuel-storage tank has just been completed in this 1923 photo, a harbinger of the eventual conversion of the entire fleet to fuel-fired boilers. The Quarantine Station (to right) long stood as a stumbling block to the Navy's plans for coaling station expansion. *SSC San Diego*

Torpedo boat destroyers such as *Whipple* (DD-15) began regularly operating out of San Diego harbor in 1909. Relatively calm Southern California waters aided division and squadron training for the light and fast destroyers. *Naval Historical Center*

after its lengthy cruise around South America.[12] The Fleet Celebration Committee was quickly established and bankrolled to galvanize preparations and a little-known San Diego insurance agent and sometime member of the Chamber, William Kettner, was placed at its head.

By March 1908 the Great White Fleet was well into its cruise, had circled South America, and had arrived at Magdalena Bay for fleet training with still no official confirmation that a stop in San Diego had been ordered. Worried, Kettner chartered a steamer to travel down the Baja coast to meet the fleet's commander. Accompanying him were the mayor, the president and several directors of the Chamber of Commerce, and an able San Diego harbor pilot (brought along to dispel any fears concerning the shallowness of the harbor).

A reluctant Adm. "Fighting Bob" Evans couldn't ignore the obvious sincerity of Kettner's entourage and finally agreed to a compromise: a stop at San Diego, an entry into the harbor by cruisers and destroyers, but all battleships would anchor outside the harbor owing to the shallowness of the entrance. Kettner was ecstatic; surmising that he had clearly saved the day, he quickly energized the Fleet Celebration Committee to new activity. Many in the Chamber (and many San Diego friends within the Navy) viewed the unfolding events more pragmatically as a golden chance to make San Diego's case for harbor improvements. "There can be no stronger argument of the imperative importance of Congress making the necessary appropriations to deepen the entrance to your harbor and establishing a dry dock at your port," one naval officer was quoted as saying.[13]

It had been one of the busiest months—no, the busiest month—of the cruise for Ens. William F. Halsey. But the results had been worth it. His division of *Kansas* boatswain mates and deck seamen stood at attention before him, seasoned by 119 days and thirteen thousand miles since leaving Hampton Roads. The past six weeks of intense fleet exercises in Magdalena Bay had honed instinct and seamanship skills even sharper.

Early that morning the most powerful fleet that had ever sailed under American colors formed into steaming formation twenty miles seaward of the sleepy fishing village of Ensenada. Bill, or "Bull" Halsey as he was known in the wardroom (a moniker earned from exploits as a star halfback on the Annapolis football team), noted proudly that *Kansas* had been selected to lead one of the columns of battleships arrayed into four divisions. Other columns of cruisers hovered nearby and torpedo boats dashed about in nuisance, but Halsey didn't care. He knew all eyes would stay focused on the sixteen behemoths of the American battleline. *Kansas* was the most advanced of the sixteen, displacing over seventeen thousand tons and armed with four 12-inch and eight 8-inch guns. She had been hurried to completion in the spring of 1907 specifically to join the Great White Fleet in Hampton Roads.[14]

The Mexican-American border had been easy to spot from Halsey's station on the starboard side amidships near the ship's boats. From that point northward solid crowds lined the shore to witness the fleet's arrival, and a hundred or so smaller boats reached out from Point Loma. The *San Diego Union* estimated that twenty thousand lined the shores. By 1 P.M. *Kansas* had let go her anchor fifteen hundred yards off the red-roofed turrets of the Hotel del Coronado amid a flotilla of red-white-blue festooned welcoming craft. Local boats delivered thirty-three thousand oranges to the fleet while another boat brought young women bearing armfuls of flowers.[15]

"Never before has San Diego and Coronado been the scene of such a gathering and such enthusiasm," a reporter declared. "Early in the morning the crowds began going to Coronado. The streetcars and ferries were jammed. As the hour for the arrival of the fleet approached, the crowds increased. Thousands ignored the streetcars and walked from the Coronado ferry slip to the beach. Every position of advantage in Coronado was stood upon and soon crowded."

The date was 14 April 1908. Kettner's Fleet Celebration Committee had done a masterful job of mobilizing both city resources and spirit in a tumultuous event that would catch Halsey and the other men of the battlefleet unprepared to absorb its effusive reception. One fleet officer commented: "Every point of entertainment for the officers and men was carefully attended to in detail by the people at that little city."[16]

Officers who went ashore the first day were overwhelmed. A carnival air hung over city streets as celebrants attended balls, guided tours, dinners, luncheons, teas, and theatrical presentations. The fleet released sixteen thousand officers and men into San Diego, most of whom had never seen anything like the reception they were receiving. City theaters such as the Pickwick and the Empire and other places of amusement such as Ansel's Wild West Show and even Bentley's Ostrich Farm offered free admission to sailors in uniform. Lemonade was served to officers and men in uniform at a booth in the Plaza in front of the U.S. Grant Hotel from 9 A.M. to 9 P.M. In honor of the fleet, the Hub Clothing Company on H Street offered "Uncle Sam" suspenders for only 19 cents a pair (warranted for six months). In the evening San Diegans crowded around beach fires to watch the electric lights and searchlight displays from the ships anchored in Coronado Roads.[17]

On 15 April a huge parade was held along San Diego streets wreathed in patriotic bunting. Sailors in "[s]ixty-four companies of men of warsmen in uniform with trousers reefed down in canvas leggings and sixteen companies of Marines, soldierly and straight, formed this notable land display." The *Union* reported that seventy-five thousand people turned out for the two-mile procession from the foot of D Street to the terrace in City Park where the governor of California officially extended the state's welcome. Rear Adm. Charles Thomas followed with words reflecting how taken he was by the courtesy and enthusiasm of the reception. "Your royal welcome has indeed touched our hearts deeply, yes, very deeply." He ended his

Handsome sister ships *St. Louis, Milwaukee,* and *Charleston* were frequent visitors to San Diego during pre–World War I years. A pulling boat in the foreground practices for periodic intership competition while steam-powered launches stand alongside to transport officers ashore and resupply the ship. *San Diego Historical Society*

remarks with a line that could chronicle the San Diego–Navy relationship for the next ninety years: "San Diego appreciates the fleet; the fleet appreciates San Diego."[18]

The visit of the Great White Fleet would have an impact on San Diego far beyond anything originally imagined. Just as Chamber officials had hoped, newspaper reporters flooded the city to signal the arrival of the fleet at its first American port of call on the Pacific. Official cables poured into the Navy Department in Washington, D.C., effusive in praise of San Diego's reception. Politicians and Navy officials waxed eloquent on future expectations.

But, above all, the dazzling reception would make a lasting impact on the then-junior officers who would later form a pantheon of Navy leadership across two world wars and years of rapid naval expansion. Not only was Bull Halsey seeing San Diego for the first time—and seeing it in the best positive light—but present also were Lt. Harry E. Yarnell and Ens. Royal Ingersoll (*Connecticut*); Lts. Henry Mustin, J. K. Taussig, and E. C. Kalbfus (*Kansas*); Ens. H. R. Stark and Midshipman Raymond Spruance (*Minnesota*); Ens. Husband Kimmel (*Georgia*); Midshipman R. S. Edwards (*Stewart*); Midshipman John Towers (*Kentucky*); Ens. D. W. Bagley and Midshipman W. H. Lee (*Rhode Island*); Ens. D. I. Selfridge (*Virginia*); Lt. F. J. Horne (*Illinois*); Midshipman Thomas Kinkaid (*Nebraska*); Midshipman H. K. Hewitt (*Missouri*); Lt. Comdr. E. W. Eberle (*Louisiana*); and Midshipman Isaac Kidd (*New Jersey*).[19] This stunning collection of future four- and five-star admirals, Medal of Honor winners, naval aviation pioneers, and leaders of the great battle fleets of World War II would take from this experience a lasting impression of San Diego's infectious enthusiasm for its Navy.

At 0630 on 18 April the fleet was under way for the ten-hour trip to San Pedro, hugging the coast as close as safe navigation would allow. Despite the early hour, thousands lined the beach and vantage points from Point Loma to La Jolla to see the battleships off.

> The trip up the coast was made slowly at first, the ships steaming at a pace not exceeding ten knots after full headway had been made. It was, perhaps, the greatest naval parade in history of the nation, those vessels steaming northward so close to the shore that the residents of Pacific Beach, La Jolla, Del Mar and Encinitas turned out en masse to witness the marvelous sight. The ships were about two miles from shore at Del Mar but then turned more directly toward the open sea.[20]

It does the visit little justice to describe it simply as a roaring

success. The three-day visit of the Great White Fleet certainly solidified the relationship between a young San Diego and a rapidly modernizing Navy, but it did so in a way that was to align a great collection of forces that would power an engine of change for the next fifty years. In a reprise of the event written two years after the visit, D. C. Collier editorialized: "It was only when the great American armada reached this port—the first American port on the Pacific and the first one since its departure from Hampton Roads—that the people of this country awoke to the fact that San Diego was on the map."[21]

San Diego's persistent lobbying for more ship visits, more Navy investment, and more harbor improvements gained new momentum following the spectacular success of the Great White Fleet's visit. So much correspondence inundated Washington from a battalion of San Diego city officials that one local historian commented that "the efforts of the Chamber in behalf of a great naval drydock, of a coaling station and of a naval training school have been intelligent and persistent."[22]

When the Pacific Squadron merged with the Asiatic Fleet in 1907 to form a new Pacific Fleet, the president of the Chamber wrote to the secretary of the Navy: "We respectively ask your support . . . for establishment in San Diego harbor of a dry dock and naval repair station. You are familiar with the strategic importance of this harbor and its unsurpassed facilities for all naval purposes." In an allusion that would be repeated many times in the upcoming years, John Osborn of the San Diego City Council described San Diego as the "strategic and commercial Gibraltar of the United States on the Pacific coast."[23]

San Diego's perseverance (and, perhaps, the lingering good will from the Great White Fleet cruise) moved the Navy slowly toward the conclusion that San Diego held great promise as a support base. In his 1908 annual report the secretary of the Navy took care to include the comment: "[A] substantial wharf is being built at [San Diego] and will be completed probably in November 1908 and plans are being developed for a modern coal-handling plant for this important point." In a letter dated 26 November 1909 the secretary asked the commander of the Pacific Torpedo Fleet, who was beginning to frequent San Diego with his squadron, to report on "the practicability and advisability of establishing a base for torpedo vessels on Point Loma." The reply enthusiastically recommended either the coaling station or the quarantine station as the best site for improvement for torpedo boat operations, keeping San Diego in the limelight among distant Navy planners.[24]

Nearly everyone was aware that federally sponsored dredging projects through 1909 had made great progress in deepening and straightening the channel. Conservative as always, the Navy took until late 1910 to test the harbor's conditions with a deep-draft ship.

On 4 December 1910 the armored cruiser *California* (ACR-6), fourteen thousand tons, 503 feet long, 69 feet wide, and drawing 27 feet, gingerly entered the harbor under the command of Capt. Henry Mayo. With hundreds watching from rooftops and hundreds more cheering from a flotilla of small craft, *California* anchored in midchannel near the Spreckels Company coal wharf at the foot of G Street, becoming the first modern naval combatant of its size to navigate the channel safely.[25]

Taken in isolation this event should have made only a trifling difference in the flow of daily events. However, in the broader sense, this single event was to prove to be an important cornerstone of the entire San Diego Navy experience. The city had bested the Navy Department's inertia at every turn and responded with its own brand of rousing enthusiasm. Every time the Navy showed any inkling of interest in basing forces in the harbor, the city responded with eagerness and spirit. It had pried a coaling station from a grudging Navy Department, had avidly welcomed the construction of an experimental wireless station, had shown itself as a spectacular liberty port and logistics port for the Pacific Fleet, had provided unmatched offshore training conditions, had proven to be an acceptable base for the small ships of the Pacific Torpedo Fleet, and could now welcome capital ships in its newly improved channel. *California* showed that San Diego had arrived.

Now, two final parts of the equation would have to come together to finally lock the Navy and San Diego unquestionably in place: the coming of the naval airplane and the arrival of a San Diego booster par excellence, Congressman William Kettner.

1911

North Island, occupying the center stage of the harbor, is a body of land completely surrounded by planes and submerged under planes. A condensed history of flying was enacted there, is still being enacted there, and the patron saint of North Island is Glenn Curtiss.

Max Miller, "Harbor of the Sun"

Great possibilities rode with aviation pioneer Glenn Curtiss as he cast off from the shallows of the beach and urged the sputtering eight-cylinder engine of his newfangled floating biplane to smoothness. It had been only seven years and one month since the Wright Brothers had briefly soared skyward at Kitty Hawk. The waters of Spanish Bight were glass smooth, the afternoon breeze light but steady off the ocean.

Pointing into the wind toward the low sand spit that joined North Island and Coronado at low tide, Curtiss threw the throttles wide open and stretched as far as he could out of the cockpit to watch the pontoon—newly redesigned—float on the water. As the plane gathered speed and bounced lightly on puffs of ocean breeze, the pontoon skipped higher and higher on the water (an earlier version of the pontoon had actually dived underwater when speed was increased) until it barely skimmed the surface. The strings-and-percussion sounds of wind ricocheting through wing stays and frame supports mixed with the resolute throbbing of the plucky engine. "So intent was I in watching the water," Curtiss later wrote, "that I did not notice that I was approaching the shore and to avoid running aground, I tilted the horizontal control and the machine seemed to leap into the air like a frightened gull."[1]

Curtiss bounced several times into the air for brief spurts, then flew for half a mile, turned, and landed lightly back onto the water—a flight of barely half a minute. Men of his company hollered from the shore and threw hats into the air in their enthusiasm. Later that afternoon Curtiss coolly repositioned the craft, gunned the engine, and rose once again into the air, this time aiming in the direction of San Diego. Men on the naval repair ship *Iris* ran up on deck as Curtiss passed at masthead height and saluted the ungainly flying machine with blasts of the ship's whistle that soon had the attention of everyone near the bay.

The date was 26 January 1911. The public picked up their newspapers the next morning to read, "Chapter One in the history of North Island as an aviation center has been duly set down." Curtiss had accomplished the world's first practical waterborne takeoff and landing and his new "hydroaeroplane" was the talk of the town—the seaplane had been born.[2]

Curtiss's timing was perfect, the mark of the consummate showman that he was. The San Diego Aero Club had advertised for an air meet the coming weekend at Coronado's Polo Grounds. Word of Curtiss's exploits spread like wildfire before a Santa Ana wind. Headlines such as "Biplane Conquers Air and Sea. Curtiss Machine Rises from Bay; Alights with Ease of Water Bird" fanned tremendous interest.

The hype brought nearly twelve thousand San Diegans across the bay for the two-day event, each paying a ticket price of sixty-five cents. Curtiss pilot Eugene Ely opened the meet with a dramatic high-level spiraling flight of one of Curtiss's landplanes, taking off from North Island, following the beach line, turning over Spanish Bight, circling over the Polo Grounds, and landing in front of the grandstands. Curtiss and his corps of trained pilots then looped, rolled, and spiraled over the thrilled crowds, making low, slow passes over the Polo Grounds or landing on its broad playing field.

Naval aviation was then to log its first minutes aloft—although quite by accident and with a degree of inelegance. Navy lieutenant Theodore G. Ellyson (in the Curtiss camp barely two weeks) had only been asked to drive a low-powered Curtiss training plane—used mostly for ground instruction—around the Polo Grounds in front of the crowd. During one long straightaway, his engine accidentally throttled up. Ellyson hit a bump and fell back in his seat. The action elevated the plane's front control. To his surprise, Ellyson found himself some fifteen feet in the air in front of an approving crowd. Unfortunately, fame and elation were short-lived as seconds later the skittish machine came abruptly back to earth, breaking one wing.[3]

North Island was an experimental airman's dream. The weather was perfect; the wind consistent, and the flat, unremarkable landscape boasted a number of potential landing areas. Spanish Bight, separating North Island from Coronado, offered a straightaway of flat water that was ideal for hydroaeroplane operations. Above all, North Island was private, isolated from the main activities of the city and from the crush of potential sightseers.

Curtiss liked what he saw.

Our San Diego, Cal. Aviation Training Grounds situated on North Island, San Diego Harbor, are the finest in America, if not the world. North Island is leased by us exclusively for Aviation purposes and comprises one thousand acres of flat, level sand unobstructed by rock, tree or building; thus offering every advantage as a flying course. The island is entirely private, yet within a few minutes of San Diego, one of the most progressive and attractive cities on the Pacific Coast.[4]

The military had first come to the John D. Spreckels–owned expanse of North Island in 1901 when Fort Pio Pico was established on 38.56 acres of land near Zuniga Point. A battery of seacoast guns, calibrated to cover the harbor entrance and christened Battery Mead, was installed in 1903–4. By 1911 only

Glenn Curtiss (or his assistant Roberts) rises from San Diego Bay in the first successful design of his hydroaeroplane. *San Diego Aerospace Museum*

two or three caretakers remained at the fort, with soldiers crossing the channel from Fort Rosecrans when needed.[5]

When Glenn Curtiss came to San Diego in 1911 he was a modest, slim thirty-two-year-old with a rapidly expanding reputation as an expert pilot, aircraft experimenter, and tinkerer of any kind of machine. In 1903 he had won the first American motorcycle championship and had established several world land-speed records to cement an unofficial title as the "Fastest Man in the World" in 1907. Starting in earnest in 1908 he designed and flew aircraft in Hammondsport, New York, and first experimented with a hydroaeroplane design in 1909.

Curtiss, who had established his fledgling Flying School and Exhibition Company in Hammondsport by 1910, needed a winter flying site near a calm body of water to continue both his school efforts and his hydroaeroplane experiments. He knew of Coronado and North Island from one of his flight students, Charles K. Hamilton, who had thrilled crowds at one of the West's first aero meets at Coronado in 1910 with six short flights in a Curtiss Reims Racer, including the first flight across the Mexican border.[6]

The Aero Club of San Diego knew of Curtiss's desire to establish an aviation school in San Diego and helped negotiate with the owners of North Island (the Spreckels-owned Coronado Beach Company) for a three-year no-cost lease. Buried in the lease was a little-noticed clause that allowed Curtiss to invite the War and Navy Departments to share the field's use for flying instruction.

Curtiss, ever the astute businessman and clever promoter, had had his eyes on Navy and Army aviation business for two years. Realizing that a cadre of trained military aviators would generate sales of military aircraft, Curtiss wrote Secretary of the Navy George von Meyer on 20 November 1910, offering free flight instruction for one naval officer:

> That [my experience] may be of some practical value to the [Navy] department, I am prepared to instruct an officer of the Navy in the operation and construction of the Curtiss aeroplane. As I am fully aware that the Navy Department has no funds available for aviation purposes, I am making this offer with the understanding that it involves no expense for the Navy Department other than the cost of detailing an officer to the aviation grounds in Southern California. The officer so detailed would be in a position to conduct many experiments himself as well as to suggest such tests as will involve problems that the navy department would have a special interest in solving.[7]

The Navy accepted the offer and on 23 December 1910 ordered a ramrod-straight Lt. Theodore Ellyson to the Curtiss Aviation Camp on North Island. The twenty-five-year-old

Ellyson was a tall, freckle-faced, redheaded submariner known to his friends as "Spuds," ostensibly for his fancy for potatoes. Ellyson had graduated from the Naval Academy with Chester Nimitz in the class of 1905 and already had command of two submarines under his belt. His service reputation was long on engineering and dependability and as a veteran submariner he was seen as the right fit for the unconventional world of aviation.

Ellyson started quickly. Even before his flight instruction began, he assisted Curtiss by designing sandbag arresting wires used by Curtiss pilot Eugene Ely in his first-ever landing aboard armored cruiser *Pennsylvania* in San Francisco Bay on 18 January 1911.

Curtiss knew that one of the Navy's early priorities was for a plane that could take off and land on water. Capt. W. I. Chambers, in charge of naval aviation affairs for the secretary of the Navy, had pressed for such an aircraft "that would simplify the aerodrome problem for us" and not disrupt the accepted superstructure of ships with large new flat decks. If Curtiss could develop a plane that could operate from water and be hauled aboard ship by crane, the Navy might be interested.

San Diego Aero Club members pitched in quickly to prepare North Island for Curtiss by clearing brush from the area to be used as an airfield. The central area of the island was saved for landplane operations while the northern shoreline was utilized for launching and recovering Curtiss's hydroaeroplanes. From 1911 to 1914 the Curtiss camp devoted a small section of the central area of the island to flight instruction.[8]

The only structures Curtiss found on the barren island were an old farmhouse and hay barn. He quickly converted the hay barn into a hangar and built a small machine shop nearby. The San Diego Aero Club added two more hangars, covered only with canvas and tarpaper. For his seaplanes Curtiss built a hangar on the beach of Spanish Bight and a small pier by the Spreckels Marineways on the northeast corner of the island to ferry people and supplies. Ellyson took accommodation at 320 First Street in Coronado, within sight of Curtiss's hydroaeroplane hangar, and commuted to North Island by boat. For a time Curtiss owned a home in Coronado on Alameda Boulevard between Third and Fourth Streets, rumored to cost the outrageous sum of $7,000.[9]

Curtiss's instruction of his new aviation students (Ellyson, three Army lieutenants, and two civilians) began in earnest after the January Coronado Aero Meet. Ellyson learned "the details of the aeroplane, the construction, wiring, bracing and engine details." He then progressed to the "grasscutter," a purposely underpowered four-cylinder machine for moving

Lt. (jg) Jack Towers (*left*), Naval Aviator no. 3, receiving flying training from Lt. T. G. Ellyson, Naval Aviator no. 1, on the twin-seat Curtiss A-1 hydroaeroplane. *San Diego Aerospace Museum*

around an open field or low-level simple flights. As the grasscutter had but one seat, Curtiss instructed from the ground.

Typically, a day began at 0400, preparing aircraft for the day's first work. During the early morning hours, while there was little wind, Curtiss's students would fly the machines down the runways and go through endless hours of practicing. Later in the day, when the wind became too gusty for the fledgling pilots, they would don bathing suits to help Curtiss with the hydroplane experiments. Later, when the wind subsided, the students launched again, keeping roughly to a one-mile closed course.

Ellyson's work with the grasscutter progressed to short jumps, longer jumps, and straightaway flights of up to a mile and a half. Soon he was making extended runs and turns and finally, on 31 March, reported to Captain Chambers that "in my opinion and that of Mr. Curtiss, I have qualified in practical aviation under favorable weather conditions."

During all this time, Curtiss continued an unbroken wooing of Navy attention for his inventions. He encouraged Ellyson's almost daily reports back to Captain Chambers and peppered Washington with his own steady correspondence proudly announcing each new advance. Chambers, in turn, asked

Ellyson to encourage Curtiss to develop a machine that could operate from both land and water and helped write the secretary of the Navy's response to Curtiss after his 26 January flight:

> Before you can convince us that the aeroplane is a weapon in which the Navy Department could officially interest itself, you will have to show us that you can land your plane, not on any interfering platform on a fighting ship, but on the sea alongside. When you have invented an aeroplane which can be picked up by a boat crane and hoisted aboard a battleship without any false deck to receive it, well then I shall be ready to say that the Navy Department is convinced.[10]

Curtiss, with Ellyson's assistance, set out to meet each of those goals.

On 17 February 1911 Lieutenant Ellyson and Charley Witmer, a Curtiss civilian student, rowed out to the cruiser *Pennsylvania* anchored off the Spreckels Marineways in San Diego Bay to request permission from Capt. Charles Pond for Curtiss to land alongside. Pond, a senior naval officer who recognized the potential of the naval aircraft, needed little convincing and ordered a ship's boat lowered to provide sufficient room to handle the aircraft. Curtiss took off from Spanish Bight, barely rising off the water surface before landing alongside *Pennsylvania* and taxiing up under the forward starboard boat crane. The crane hooked onto a sling mounted on the upper wing of the plane and Curtiss and machine were hoisted aboard the cruiser while sailors packed the rail to observe. After Curtiss had a short visit with Pond, the plane was lowered back over the side and Curtiss flew it back to North Island.

Curtiss's flight was a nice blend of showmanship, timing, and practicality. The hydroaeroplane had flown less than a quarter mile to reach *Pennsylvania* and the raising of an aircraft by a reliable boat crane from smooth water held no particular challenge. But Curtiss had cleverly contrived an aviation "first," specifically orchestrated to catch the imagination of an approving media. The *San Diego Union* captured the moment:

> The entire program required less than half an hour to carry out. There was no hitch and not the least difficulty was experienced in hoisting the plane on board or lowering it over the side. The officers were enthusiastic over the ease with which the landing was accomplished. "We now know," Captain Pond said, "that a machine can rise from the water, fly alongside and be picked up, then go over the side and sail away."[11]

Ellyson wired Chambers: "In hydroplane, Curtiss flew to *Pennsylvania* this morning. Came alongside, was hoisted aboard by boat crane, landed superstructure deck forward starboard side.

Experiment proved aeroplane adaptable use Navy."[12] Curtiss added in his own correspondence that "[i]t demonstrates to the Navy Department that the use of the aeroplane, or rather the hydroplane, for warships at sea is practical. . . . [T]he naval officers appeared more [than] satisfied with it, when I was welcomed on board the cruiser after my arrival."[13]

Six days later Curtiss conducted the first seaplane flight with a passenger on board by converting his standard hydroaeroplane to fit a third wing and fashioning a passenger seat low on the pontoon. No word survives on how wet Lieutenant Ellyson, the designated passenger, became during takeoff and landing.

Inspired by this unbroken string of successes, Curtiss now set out to demonstrate the first truly amphibian airplane. He designed a "retractable" landing gear with wheels that were mounted on jointed braces under the wing. These wheels could fold up under the wing during water operations or could be dropped down on either side of the pontoon for landing on the ground. On 26 February Curtiss took off from Spanish Bight, circled twice over the bay, and, in carefully staged choreography, landed on the beach next to the Hotel del Coronado. "He arrived at the grounds in time for luncheon and was the guest of Manager Ross at the midday meal while attachés of the hotel guarded the machine on the beach." After lunch Curtiss calmly took off from the beach, witnessed by three thousand spectators on the nearby rocks, rose into the air, and landed back in the protected waters of Spanish Bight.[14] Curtiss

Glenn Curtiss stands atop the wing of his hydroaeroplane as it is lifted aboard armored cruiser *Pennsylvania* anchored in San Diego Bay while its crew packs the side. Curtiss's feat was the first time that an aircraft had landed next to and then had been hoisted aboard a warship, proving the utility of aircraft for use aboard ships without the need for constructing a large flat flying deck. *San Diego Aerospace Museum*

named his land-sea-air machine the Triad, the model for the Navy's first airplane, the A-1.

The Navy was convinced. In one remarkable month Curtiss had met or exceeded every Navy requirement and, as one historian observed, "The connection had been made between seapower and the airplane."[15] On 4 March 1911 Congress approved the sum of $25,000 for naval experiments in aeronautics, and on 8 May Captain Chambers used these funds to requisition the Navy's first three aircraft. Two were landplanes, one to be built by the Wrights and one by Curtiss, and the third was a seaplane of Curtiss's Triad design. A clause in the contract required the builder to train a pilot and a mechanic for each plane. The pilot chosen for the Curtiss aircraft was Lt. (jg) John Towers.[16]

The Navy placed its A-1 in service 1 July 1911 at the Curtiss plant in Hammondsport. Both Curtiss and Ellyson flew A-1, and on the next day Ellyson qualified for his aviation pilot's license and his designation as Naval Aviator No. 1.

The first naval aviation unit was formed that summer at Greenbury Point, near Annapolis, Maryland, and quarters were sought for the following winter season. Guantanamo Bay, Cuba, was initially considered, but Ellyson favored North Island, where "we can work with the ships and they always have the time and have shown interest in the work, whereas the Atlantic Fleet is always busy and rushed."[17]

San Diego greeted the returning aviators warmly during the winter of 1912, hopeful of another spate of "firsts." Ellyson established his flying camp near the Spreckels Marineways, about three-quarters of a mile away from the Curtiss Aviation Camp. Between 15 January and 24 April 1912 the entire flying Navy—three aircraft, four pilots, and seven enlisted men—was stationed at North Island.

The Curtiss A-1 was the first of the aircraft uncrated and brought to flying readiness and San Diego reporters were quick to mark the event: "The first flights here this winter by Lieutenants Ellyson and Towers were made yesterday to the delight of Coronado people and particularly the guests at Hotel del Coronado as the aviators flew over the hotel several times."[18]

Lt. (jg) Jack Towers had been designated Naval Aviator No. 3 in September 1911 after instruction by Ellyson and Curtiss at Hammondsport. A 1906 graduate of the Naval Academy, Towers had at first been assigned to the gunnery divisions of battleships *Kentucky* and *Michigan* and volunteered for aviation duty as he thought such a capability in the Navy would be advantageous for gun spotting. A bachelor of twenty-eight, strikingly handsome, modest, friendly, and dapper, Towers quickly became the object of affection for any number of San Diego ladies.

Days were busy with experiments. The two landplanes, the Curtiss A-2 and a Wright B-1, were soon converted to hydro-aeroplanes and the aviators worked with ships in the harbor and with some of the first tests of wireless radio from the air. The repair ship *Iris*, sent to San Diego as a tender for the Navy's torpedo flotilla, provided Ellyson with a motor launch and supplies. In a tongue-in-cheek reference to the capriciousness of the early aircraft designs, the struggles of experimentation with cutting-edge technology, and a spate of crashes, the Navy camp picked up the unofficial nickname "Camp Trouble." On 28 February 1912 Ens. Victor Herbster, the youngest of Ellyson's cadre of pilots, qualified for his pilot's license and designation as Naval Aviator No. 4, the first naval aviator to officially qualify at North Island.[19]

On 3 May 1912 Ellyson's Aviation Detachment broke camp, crated all aircraft, and departed North Island for Annapolis. The Navy would not return to San Diego in the winter of 1913, transferring its aviation camp from Annapolis to Guantanamo Bay.

By the time the Curtiss school closed after the season, North Island was already recognized as one of the nation's outstanding aviation fields, thanks to Curtiss's extensive advertising and the Navy's high-profile activities. Typical of the nationwide publicity being generated for the Navy and San Diego was a piece of marketing derring-do penned by Curtiss for a 1912 aviation book:

> Flying an aeroplane is a thrilling sport, but flying a hydroaeroplane is something to arouse the jaded senses of the most blasé. It fascinates, exhilarates, vivifies. It is like a yacht with horizontal sails that support it on the breezes. To see it skim the water like a swooping gull and then rise into the air, circle and soar to great heights, and finally drop gracefully down upon the water again, furnishes a thrill and inspires a wonder that does not come with any other sport on earth.[20]

It was an element of pride to San Diegans that they stood at the leading edge of early aviation, a civic attribute that would circulate again and again in stories, brochures, and glitzy marketing features as San Diego told its story across the country. Beginning in 1913 the Empress Theater captured this enthusiasm in one of the most popular vaudeville revues in San Diego by featuring the Aeroplane Ladies—lovely damsels who entered stage while strung by wires in midair.[21]

The expiration of the Curtiss lease and the departure of naval aviators did not signal the end of military aviation on North Island. By mid-1913, the Army Signal Corps, acting within the bounds of the original Curtiss lease, had established

Curtiss A-1 with Ellyson and Towers aboard being steadied by two enlisted crewmen off the beach of North Island during the winter of 1912. *U.S. Navy*

a burgeoning military camp, rent-free. By December of that year North Island was designated as the "Signal Corps Aviation School" with twenty officers assigned.

In January 1914 the Coronado Beach Company granted the Army permission for new construction of "temporary" buildings with the stipulation that this permission was not to be interpreted as conferring any permanent right to the land. The Signal Corps quickly established twenty-two notably nontemporary buildings for its flying activities along the northern edge of the island and eight months later organized its first tactical flying squadron at North Island. The First Aero Squadron was destined to be the first American flying unit ordered to France, and in the years leading to World War I operational and tactical training rapidly expanded at North Island. Knowing that these operations would put a greater strain on the "temporary" nature of the Army's facilities, Lt. Col. Samuel Reber, head of the Aviation Section of the Signal Corps, conferred with Coronado Beach Company officials on 23 October 1914. After stiff discussions, he came away with only an agreement that the Army could continue operations for an additional eighteen months.[22]

Army officials, increasingly worried that they would lose their largest aviation training and operating base, began to work closely with newly elected San Diego congressman

William Kettner. With Kettner's sponsorship, Congress passed an act on 4 March 1915 directing the secretary of war to establish a commission to study the feasibility of acquiring land "near the Bay of San Diego" and elsewhere for an aviation school and training grounds for the Signal Corps. On 31 March, to no surprise, Colonel Reber was appointed as the commission's senior member.

The commission inspected sites throughout San Diego. Colonel Reber approached the Coronado Beach Company on 13 July seeking a fair purchase price for the property. Reber's request was bluntly refused and, upon returning to Washington, a frustrated Reber approached the Judge Advocate General in order to attack the validity of the Spreckels title—a legacy of Spanish land grants before California statehood.

On 1 December, clearly startled by the Reber legal offensive, the Coronado Beach Company attempted to regain possession of the island by sending a letter to the commanding officer restating its policy and pointing out that prior to Curtiss occupancy the island "had been surveyed and plotted in lots and blocks, it being the intention of the company to put North Island on the market as a high-class residential property." They asked the Army to vacate "as soon after March 31, 1916 as is possible."[23]

Reber's report, dated 29 December 1915, provided detailed information on five potential sites around San Diego Bay for Signal Corps aviation operations: "the terrain in the vicinity of San Diego Bay fulfills aviation requirements better than any other section of the United States." Reber then clearly recommended "North Island as the best possible site for the location of an aviation school."[24]

Other military activities on North Island further complicated Spreckels's attempts to regain ownership. As early as March 1911, during the time of increased border tensions during the Mexican Revolution, the provisional 4th Marine Regiment used North Island as a temporary support site named Camp Thomas. A portion of the regiment was disbanded in June of that year and the camp abandoned in July.[25]

On 3 July 1914 the 4th Marine Regiment, fresh from duty aboard warships patrolling the west coast of Mexico, again landed at North Island. Initially with Spreckels's permission, Col. Joseph Pendleton established a new and larger camp, Camp Howard, along Spanish Bight. At its height Camp

Howard was home to over 1,100 Marines, housed in row upon row of canvas field tents, and included a rifle range by the ocean near Fort Pio Pico. In December 1914 the regiment was ordered to duty supporting the San Francisco and San Diego expositions with only two corporals and twenty-seven privates remaining to patrol North Island.[26]

As 1916 progressed, a debate raged in Washington, D.C., and across the country on the nation's preparedness to enter the European war and the Navy's plans for fleet expansion. The secretary of the Navy appointed Rear Adm. James Helm to head a five-officer commission to conduct an exhaustive survey of potential base sites on the Pacific Coast. Its six full reports were completed over a period of eighteen months with a preliminary report delivered to Congress on 17 January 1917.[27]

Although San Diego advocates had pressed the commission hard for new bases, the commission largely rejected San Diego's appeals by recommending major new naval bases at Alameda, Pearl Harbor, and San Francisco, as well as a sub-

Glenn Curtiss's first demonstration (widely publicized in advance to ensure a large crowd) of his Triad amphibian aircraft design. He took off from Spanish Bight, landed on the sand by the Hotel del Coronado, had a gentlemanly lunch with the hotel manager, and then flew back to a water landing. *San Diego Aerospace Museum*

marine base for Los Angeles (San Pedro). The commission did favor North Island as a site for aviation training, citing its "outdoor, all-year lifestyle" and other attributes, and strongly recommended that the Navy be immediately "authorized to acquire by purchase, through condemnation or otherwise, for aviation purposes, all or any portion of the land on San Diego Bay known as North Island" for its major air base on the Pacific coast.[28]

By January 1917 the cards were quickly falling in place for a return of naval aviation to North Island. With war at hand there was little lingering doubt as to the government's intentions for North Island. Within two weeks of receiving the Helm Report the Navy Department began drawing plans for eleven new bases nationwide, with North Island capturing a lion's share of available appropriations.[29]

Following America's formal declaration of war, Congressman Kettner introduced a bill authorizing "the President to take possession, on behalf of the U.S. for use as sites for permanent aviation stations for the Army and the Navy . . . the whole of North Island in the Harbor of San Diego." As finally approved on 27 July 1917, this bill condemned the entire tract of North Island and the government assumed control by executive order on 7 August with compensation to be finalized following hostilities.[30]

In the years following the First World War, the question of fair compensation for North Island played out in a series of courts leading up to the U.S. Supreme Court. Congressman Kettner served as mediator between the two parties and lobbied to set the value of compensation from findings of a San Diego jury—a value very favorable to Spreckels, a friend and important constituent. Once the value was set, Kettner then persuaded Congress to ratify this agreement with appropriate legislation. On 30 December 1921 Spreckels happily appeared before the Federal Court in Los Angeles where he was handed a check for $5 million for the land plus over a million dollars in accumulated interest, an average cost of about $2,400 per acre. In 1891 the Coronado Beach Company had originally offered all of North Island to the government for the bargain price of about $300 per acre, including extra provisions for water and ferry service.[31]

At the time of America's entry into World War I, the Signal Corps Aviation School on North Island, by then named Rockwell Field, had grown quickly in importance and stood as the largest of six Army schools in the United States. The Army had also been active, with the assistance of the Chamber of Commerce, in identifying other aviation facilities in San Diego County. On 7 April 1918 the Army obtained a lease to a flat open area of 650 acres on Otay Mesa for use as an auxiliary landing field that would first be called East Field and ultimately Brown Field. When negotiations stumbled over residents' reluctance to surrender a schoolhouse and church, the Army major coordinating the transfer was told "to leave everything in the hands of the Chamber of Commerce."[32]

Also in 1918, the Army moved to expand its cavalry base at Camp Hearn in Imperial Beach to act as a second auxiliary airfield, which they would call Oneonta Flying Field and later Ream Field. The chamber stepped in to help pay the initial $674 needed for the lease.[33] Army troops had camped in the area since 1910 as one of many Mexican Revolution–era military posts erected along the border. Camp Hearn was officially named on 11 July 1916 and Oneonta Field was established on 1 June 1918 on a portion of its parade ground. When Jimmy Doolittle reported there in 1918 for flight training, he found two dirt strips, several long, one-story barracks and administration buildings, and several large packing-crate-looking hangars with canvas curtains for doors. "The requirements of a good pursuit and gunnery school," he wrote later, "were plenty of level ground, large expanses of water or unoccupied country for aerial gunnery and still water for placing targets to be fired at from the air. These features were obtained at Rockwell, Ream, and Otay Mesa Fields; the last was used for formation and aerobatic flying."[34]

With the impetus of advancing hostilities and with the recommendations of the Helm Board in hand, the Navy moved quickly to reestablish itself at North Island. On 8 September 1917 it entered into a rushed agreement with the War Department dividing North Island into two parts. The Army would administratively retain the south and west side of North Island fronting the ocean; the Navy gained the north and east half of the island along the bay. Both services agreed that aviators could use the whole of the island for actual aircraft operations.

From the start, the Navy had big plans for North Island and was not looking at it merely as a stopgap wartime training site. In his 1917 annual report the secretary of the Navy referred to North Island as "undoubtedly the largest and most important naval aviation station on the west coast."[35]

On 25 September the Navy hurriedly dispatched orders to Lt. Earl Winfield Spencer Jr., then serving as the head of a small naval aviation training detachment at Squantum, Massachusetts, to "proceed for duty in command of the Naval Air Station, San Diego, Cal." Win Spencer, twenty-nine years of age and the son of a Chicago stockbroker, had graduated from the Naval Academy in 1910 where he was remembered as a popular but rowdy midshipman not particularly fond of studies.

Naval Air Station, San Diego was the first naval operating base in the city and Lt. Comdr. Win Spencer was its first commanding officer. Spencer's historic claim to fame, though, was much more closely aligned with his marriage to Wallis Warfield, later Duchess of Windsor. *U.S. Navy*

He received flight training from Curtiss at Hammondsport in 1914 and his designation as Naval Aviator No. 20 was dated 27 September 1915.

Spencer arrived in Coronado on 8 November 1917 with his wife, Wallis Warfield Spencer, and took up residence for a time in the Hotel del Coronado, where many San Diego–based naval officers were then billeted. The Spencers had been married exactly one year, having been introduced in Pensacola by Lt. Comdr. Henry Mustin, the station's commandant. Mustin, an icon of early naval aviation, had married Wallis's distant cousin Corinne.

Most who met the young couple immediately saw contradictory differences in character. Lieutenant Spencer was coarse, gruff, and task-oriented, with piercing eyes, a sharp nose, and a firm jutting jaw that radiated a certain degree of quiet arrogance. Jaunty and gay one minute, he would frequently lapse into quiet, sullen moods.[36] Wallis was a statuesque beauty, attractive but not striking, with a degree of sophistication that reflected her exclusive girls' school upbringing in Baltimore society.

People remember Spencer as a complex man with a hard-to-pigeonhole personality. Widely regarded as a martinet and more than infrequently as a moody drunk, he still impressed many as an able administrator and "an efficient naval officer."

He was recognized as a naval aviation pioneer, but also as one with subpar flying skills. He vigorously guarded the Navy's interests in early tête-à-têtes with the Army on North Island and personally penned one of the first comprehensive guides for naval flight instruction, but was never seen as an up-and-comer in the profession. Even in Wallis Spencer's memoirs, a book soaked with sentiment, Win Spencer comes across as brooding and bitter.

Wallis had been fatally attracted to the swashbuckling young aviator when they had first met in Pensacola. She was a favorite of many pioneer naval aviators, had a self-admitted penchant for men in "starched whites and gold," and once described Spencer as "the world's most fascinating aviator." Her social elegance was a good match for the del Coronado and she floated easily between the Navy's budding social circles and those of the established Coronado and San Diego elite. Years later, one of Spencer's junior officers recalled Wallis's style at a reception at the Spencer home on Coronado where Mrs. Spencer served highballs with each guest's initials frosted in the glass.[37]

The flickering Spencer marriage, ill matched from the start, began to falter almost immediately. Used to Eastern social climes, Wallis considered San Diego a backwater. Increasingly affronted with Spencer's drunken capers "with the boys," she turned to drink herself and, after Spencer's transfer from North Island, both were driven to affairs. The Spencers divorced in 1927. Wallis remarried for a brief time to Ernest Simpson, but soon became locked into the storybook romance with Britain's Prince of Wales that would capture the world's imagination and result in the king of England surrendering his crown. She would lead her later life with the title Duchess of Windsor.[38]

By far the most telling slap against Spencer in the eyes of the service was his substandard flying skill. "We didn't think much of his flying ability," said one naval officer, continuing uncourteously; "all the flying he did was to take short monthly pay hops." At a time when most early aviators were rapidly expanding the horizon of flying, Spencer's career never marched forward. He was well known in San Diego, returning to North Island—surprisingly—as the station's executive officer from 1927 to 1930 and continuing on duty aboard carriers *Saratoga* (as Air Department head) and *Ranger* (as executive officer) in the 1930s. He retired as a commander in 1939 and died while visiting Coronado in May 1950.[39]

Spencer's orders upon arriving in North Island in 1917 were to establish a flight school for student flight officers, a school for aviation mechanics, and a coast patrol department for aerial patrols of California waters, and to prepare architectural plans in conjunction with an assigned public works officer for a permanent air station. This complex mix of responsibilities spanned operations, training, and construction, all against a backdrop of the expanding European war. To establish a Navy toehold, Spencer immediately directed the occupation of two old buildings and the Curtiss hangar on the North Island's eastern shoreline, but the Army would not vacate even their temporary buildings on North Island until new ones were constructed on their side of the divide.[40]

With Navy personnel arriving for mechanics training and no room on North Island, Spencer quartered and schooled his students at temporary Naval Training Station buildings within vacant Panama-California Exposition buildings in Balboa Park. By late November 1917 two hundred air station personnel were housed at the park, but by the following summer most had moved back on base. Donald Bates, an early Navy pilot, remembered arriving for duty at North Island to find three or four unpainted woodsheds, all looking like former barns. One shed became the mess hall, one the bunkhouse, and the remainder one-plane hangars.[41]

During 1918 separate design bureaus within both the Army and the Navy developed independent plans for permanent buildings across North Island. The noted industrial architect Albert Kahn orchestrated the Army's plan for the development of Rockwell Field. Kahn's plan, dated 25 August 1917, grouped noncommissioned officers' quarters and the hospital together along Spanish Bight with officers' quarters along the ocean. A broad main avenue, Quentin Roosevelt Boulevard, extended from the Navy's dock by the old Marineways south across the entire breadth of the island to the new officers' quarters. On 1 June 1918 a wooden bridge was completed across Spanish Bight while work began on the first three permanent buildings in Kahn's plan, two hangars, and a sentry gate/gauge reading building at the foot of the Spanish Bight bridge. Only a portion of the total Kahn plan was ever completed.[42]

The Navy's Bureau of Yards and Docks ordered Comdr. Leonard Cox of the Civil Engineer Corps to San Diego in October 1917 to assume responsibility as public works officer for the region. Famed New York architect Bertram Grosvenor Goodhue agreed to consult with the bureau on the air station design and he grouped the principal buildings into a quadrangle along an east/west axis with a "signature" administration building and control tower at the eastern end, two arcaded blocks of barracks flanking the northern and southern sides, and student officers' quarters to the west.[43]

The Spanish Colonial Revival design of Goodhue's Exposition buildings enjoyed enormous popularity and Goodhue quickly became a local and regional favorite for architecture that was seen as authentic to regional style, climate, quality of life, and heritage of Southern California. The impact on a San Diego busily redefining itself during a turbulent period of transition from quiet Pacific border town to California metropolis was immense. Many San Diegans felt that the Balboa Park Exposition architecture *was* San Diego.

To its undying credit, the Navy realized early that North Island would form an important vista from the San Diego bayfront and unusual care was taken in building design to ensure that the base (and thus the Navy) would "blend into" the community. Key to this masterstroke was the involvement of Goodhue with the North Island designers. Although both sides of the Goodhue-Navy partnership chaffed at what each perceived as unreasonable restrictions (the bureau pressed for austere designs to meet tight wartime budget and time constraints; Goodhue consistently fought for architectural merit in designs that would bear his name), Goodhue met Commander Cox face to face in 1918 and they quickly arrived at a plan that satisfied the architect's aesthetic intent but resulted in sparer and more utilitarian building designs than graced Balboa Park.[44]

The principal historic buildings of the naval air station have concrete foundations framed with reinforced concrete and accented with hollow terracotta tile. Red clay tile adorns the sloping roofs and the floors are hardwood in the officers' quarters. Although Goodhue moved away from a pure focus on his ornate Spanish Colonial Revival design later in his career, it is in San Diego that his legacy is the strongest, for his genius helped form an indelible image associated with the Navy's presence in the city.

Navy planning and construction quickly began to outpace that of the Army as Cox and Spencer worked feverishly while wartime funds were relatively plentiful. Permanent hangars for seaplanes and landplanes began to dot the field and plans were finalized at Spencer's urging for the largest structure on the island, an imposing dirigible hangar. Spencer had pressed for lighter-than-air craft operating from North Island and hangar 17 was designed so it could handle a dirigible 250 feet long and 140 feet wide. The Spencers hosted a grand fête attended by civic officials and even a sprinkling of Hollywood elite to mark the hangar's opening on 13 April 1919. Spencer had the longest open car anyone had ever seen (a Winton, as some recall) and the festivities again proved that the best job on the station was to be his driver. Late in 1919 the airship C-6 arrived, marking the beginning of naval lighter-than-air activities in San Diego.[45]

The first Navy hangars on North Island were built along the island's bayshore. *U.S. Naval Institute*

By the end of World War I the Navy had trained 892 aviation mechanics and 206 officers from its flight school on North Island. Army activities were even more extensive and, notably, the venerable military "dogtag" was invented at North Island. Following a midair collision that claimed the lives of two Army cadets in September 1917 (leaving their bodies almost unrecognizable), Col. Alexander Dade required all flyers to wear aluminum identification tags around their necks inside their shirts. The tags were stamped with their name and squadron or company. American servicemen were not required to wear dogtags until 1918.[46]

On 27 November 1918, to "commemorate the achievements of American aviators during the Great War," 212 military planes (141 Army and 71 Navy) staged a dramatic flight over San Diego. The planes took off from Rockwell, Ream, and East Fields, and each formation was guided by radio from the ground at Rockwell Field. Under a canopy of thick gray clouds, the viewing was perfect and thousands stopped what they were doing to look skyward at what the *Union* described as the "sight of a lifetime." Although mass flyovers had been staged on 16 October and early November, none equaled the spectacle of the 27 November demonstration.[47]

During the summer of 1919 the U.S. Fleet was realigned into separate Atlantic and Pacific Fleets, and on 17 October 1919

Air Detachment, U.S. Pacific Fleet was established with Capt. J. Harvey Tomb, commanding the aircraft tender *Aroostook* (CM-3), designated as detachment commander. The original Air Detachment organization included twenty-seven regular and reserve officers and about eighty enlisted and were divided into three divisions: Landplane, Shipplane, and Seaplane, which would later evolve into Fighting, Spotting, and Patrol Squadrons respectively.[48]

Establishing the Air Detachment at North Island brought the era's top naval aviators to San Diego, causing the *Union* to comment, "San Diego's importance as a Naval Aviation Base is shown by the officer personnel assigned here."[49] Capt. Henry Mustin assumed command of *Aroostook* and the Air Detachment on 7 December 1919 and a day later Tomb relieved Spencer as commanding officer of the Naval Air Station. By that time, Lt. Comdr. Jack Towers had also received orders to return to San Diego as aviation officer of the new Pacific Fleet air detachment and was busy arranging the transfer to NAS San Diego of eighteen seaplanes, two airships, and six kite balloons. Also present at North Island was Lt. Comdr. Marc Mitscher, who headed the original Landplane division and then Spotting Squadron 4 that operated seaplanes from *Aroostook*. Mitscher had been in San Diego before, assigned to the destroyers *Whipple* and *Stewart*. Academy classmate John "Stumps" Edgerly, who had left the Navy to enter Army aviation and rose to be an Air Force general, remembered many conversations with Mitscher at the bar of the New Palace Hotel discussing the military value of aircraft. Interestingly, Mitscher told Edgerly that aviation might work for the Army but that planes would never successfully operate with the fleet.[50]

Capt. William Moffett would also soon become a frequent visitor in San Diego while in command of the new battleship *Mississippi.* Moffett had first come to San Diego as executive officer of cruiser *Maryland* in 1908–9. On 6 February 1920, not long after Moffett arrived on the West Coast, Mustin paid him a call that soon grew into a fast friendship. In the ensuing months Mustin and Moffett often dined together in San Diego to discuss at length the potential of naval aviation and its operation with the fleet, particularly the exciting new idea of a ship devoted solely to carrying aircraft. Moffett transferred his two spotting planes to North Island to develop aerial spotting tactics for *Mississippi*'s 14-inch guns under Mustin's direction. He also later experimented with a flying-off ramp erected over a *Mississippi* gun turret in tests off the coast of San Diego.[51]

Life was gay for young naval officers in San Diego during 1919 and 1920. Jack Towers had married Lily Carstairs, the daughter of a socially prominent London art dealer in 1915, and the Towerses, Mustins, and Spencers soon were at the center of the social whirl. One conspicuous masquerade party hosted by Jack and Lily made the society pages in August 1920. The couple also attended receptions for the visiting prince of Wales. Mitscher, on the other hand, only reluctantly went to parties on North Island to please his wife, Frances. He didn't dance and hadn't cultivated a taste for polite cocktail party conversation.[52]

Mitscher would relieve Mustin for a time as Commander, Air Detachment, Pacific Fleet on 29 June 1920. On 10 December Towers, who had served as the executive officer of *Aroostook,* was given command of Seaplane Division Two and the newly converted seaplane tender *Mugford.*[53] Mustin left San Diego in October 1921 for duty as assistant chief of the new Bureau of Aeronautics.

As the decade of the Great War turned toward that of the Roaring Twenties, San Diego found itself at the fortunate nexus of intertwining factors that would establish the foundation for everything that was to follow in its relations with the Navy. Concern for the nation's new responsibilities in the Pacific in the face of the expanding Japanese empire had brought a growing fleet of warships to the Pacific coast; the work of a little-known but spirited congressman by the name of Kettner had driven San Diego to the top tier in Navy planning; and the airplane was dramatically redefining, in ways inconceivable to a prior generation, how San Diego would be seen in the national limelight.

1912

When history is written fifty years from now, the establishment of Army and Navy units in San Diego between 1914 and 1920 will be cited as the starting point of San Diego's real permanent growth and stabilized prosperity.

Congressman William Kettner

LANDSLIDE FOR WILSON, VICTORY FOR KETTNER
"BRUDER BILL" SURPRISES SUPPORTERS

The headlines that swept San Diego newspapers in November 1912 signaled the culmination of one of the most celebrated elections in San Diego history. At the national level, four memorable candidates—President William H. Taft, Theodore Roosevelt, Woodrow Wilson, and Socialist Eugene Debs—had fought a rousing campaign for the presidency. Locally, an engaging San Diegan had scrambled from behind to defeat a cross-state rival. For San Diego the rise of this team of new political personalities at both the national and local level would redefine forever the fundamental San Diego–Navy relationship.

With Woodrow Wilson's election to the White House, new vibrant leadership came to the Navy Department in the unlikely form of a party loyalist and editor of the *Raleigh News and Observer.* Josephus Daniels, a secretary of the Navy with no particular maritime experience, energized a moribund bureaucracy with a carefully cultivated homespun persona, taut administrative abilities, and firm—even radical—views. Daniels would be the first Navy secretary to fly in an airplane and the first to witness battleship gunnery practice at sea. Not at all out of character, Daniels would be remembered for

decades within the Navy as the prohibitionist who first restricted liquor aboard ship.[1]

For assistant secretary of the Navy, Daniels chose a handsome and energetic New York aristocrat, Franklin Delano Roosevelt. Roosevelt fancied himself as cut from a navalist bolt of cloth and, not surprisingly, "the admirals considered Franklin a sympathetic soul and cultivated him enthusiastically." He had coveted the assistant secretaryship, the same position his "uncle" Theodore had held during the McKinley administration.[2]

In San Diego, when the incumbent declined a run for reelection in the largely Republican Eleventh Congressional District that spanned seven counties across Southern California, local businessmen identified San Diego candidates for both the Republican and Democratic nominations. When the San Diego Republican hopeful lost in the primary, the gentlemen in their stiff collars around the San Diego Chamber of Commerce board table rallied behind their remaining hope for San Diego representation, Democratic nominee William Kettner, a popular local insurance broker. On election day any Republican advantage in the district was largely negated by the Bull Moose candidacy of Theodore Roosevelt and, in the final tally, Kettner won only three of the district's seven counties but carried San Diego County by nearly a three to one majority to garner overall victory.

Kettner was the city's perfect booster: charming, soft-spoken, modest. His wide covey of friends and associates were comfortable with calling him Bill, even "Bruder Bill" ("Bruder" being German for "brother"). Throughout his tenure he traveled easily in the Chamber of Commerce slipstream and astutely maneuvered local politics to advantage. His balance of a stylish wit, a focused pugnaciousness, and, above all, a single-minded devotion to San Diego won him respect and cooperation from the nation's capital to the Southland. Many remembered his leadership of the Fleet Celebration Committee for the 1908 visit of the Great White Fleet, a point that solidified his reputation with the navalists of the day.

A few days after the election the San Diego City Council asked Kettner and Rufus Choate of the Chamber of Commerce to go immediately to Washington to present the pressing needs for harbor development to the Army Corps of Engineers. No single issue held a greater priority for San Diego businessmen. As the nearest West Coast port to the Isthmus, San Diego businesses stood poised to reap significant profits if only their harbor could be improved to accommodate the large steam freighters that would soon be transiting the canal. In editorializing on the election two days after Kettner's victory, the *San Diego Union* cut right to the importance of the harbor: "Representative-elect Kettner will be the first San Diego man in the House in many years.... [T]here is every reason to believe that [San Diego's] interests, notably those of the harbor, will be furthered by Mr. Kettner with energy and success."[3]

Improved commerce was not the only reason to seek new federal funding for harbor development. In May 1911 San Diego had finally wrestled jurisdiction of its bayfront tidelands from the state on condition that the city spend a million dollars of its own within five years to develop the waterfront. Two local bond issues were passed in 1912–13 approving $1.4 million for land reclamation of about sixty acres of downtown tidelands west of the railroad depot from D Street (now Broadway) to Date Street and to build a new municipal pier eight hundred feet in length—Broadway Pier.[4]

Everyone agreed that these expensive improvements would exhaust nearly all local resources available for other harbor improvements and that more financing would have to be found to deepen the harbor to thirty-three to thirty-eight feet and to remove the middle-ground shoal between Point Loma and North Island. All of this would cost money—big money—but winning federal support, especially on short notice, was not a simple matter. The Army's Corps of Engineers would have to be convinced to reprioritize planned projects and both houses of Congress would have to approve appropriations. To

William Kettner (*right, in Panama hat*) and Navy Secretary Josephus Daniels (*center*) made a formidable team that consistently favored San Diego for increased Navy investment in the years around World War I. Here they are seen with San Diego's mayor, Louis J. Wilde, aboard the battleship *New Mexico* in San Diego harbor, 19 September 1919. *Naval Historical Center*

prevail, San Diego would need Washington influence, insider skill, and (as always in Congress) a reservoir of IOUs and favors—all commodities that Kettner had, admittedly, in short supply.[5]

Upon his arrival in Washington, Kettner first met with the Corps of Engineers and the Senate Commerce Committee, which resulted in polite interest but, exactly conforming to script, not a penny of appropriations. Sen. John Works of California urged Kettner to seek out either Adm. George Dewey, president of the Navy's General Board, or the secretary of the Navy. Not forgotten was the key role the Navy had played ten years before when San Diego had first won federal appropriations for deepening its harbor channel to thirty feet.

But gaining Dewey's support was a long shot. Since 1906 Dewey and the General Board had consistently rebuked San Diego's concerted efforts to win a large naval station. Although the General Board had begrudgingly supported a coaling station and possibly a naval training station in San Diego, they consistently favored San Francisco as the primary site for a naval operating base, not San Diego or San Pedro. Correspondence from the board varied little in content from 1906 to 1912: "Referring to the proposed establishment of a naval station at San Diego, the General Board believes that this place is not naturally well adapted for the purpose and that its strategic value as a supplement to other stations now existing in the same area would be small as compared with that of stations in areas where we are now."[6]

So it was with no small amount of trepidation, perhaps offset by freshman enthusiasm, that Kettner first approached the commanding figure of the victor of Manila Bay, Admiral of the Navy George Dewey. Dewey was polite to Kettner but firm. The Navy had already invested fifty years and millions of dollars in facilities in San Francisco Bay and it "was not good policy, economical, or desirable, from a naval standpoint, to establish a naval station on the coast of California south of San Francisco."[7] Moreover, with no naval station, there would be no need for Navy-financed harbor improvements.

Kettner called on Dewey a second time and was similarly rebuked. The next day Kettner dined with three officers attached to the General Board at Washington's Army-Navy Club. They suggested that Kettner meet Dewey again the following Monday. At first thinking that perhaps they "might be trying to have more amusement at my expense," Kettner ultimately took their advice and approached Dewey a third time. Finally surrendering to persistence and no small amount of Kettner charm, Dewey reluctantly agree to compose a letter

that Kettner could take to the Senate Commerce Committee that, while carefully not endorsing San Diego as a major operating base, did state that "it was probable that the naval use of [San Diego] will increase in the future," and that "it was desirable that a depth of 35 feet over the middle ground and 40 feet over the bar be provided to permit the entrance at all times to the inner harbor of capital ships of the Navy."[8]

Half-hearted as Dewey's qualified response was, Kettner quickly accentuated the positive and hurried to pass the Navy's "requirements" to various members of Congress, especially to members of the powerful House Committee on Rivers and Harbors, the one committee in Congress that held the greatest influence in harbor appropriations and the one that Kettner had cleverly maneuvered the House leadership to allow him to join. Appropriations for $249,000 for dredging and engineering surveys were quickly found and Kettner had his first victory for San Diego.

As William Kettner was sworn into the 63rd Congress early in 1913, only two permanent naval facilities existed in San Diego, the modest La Playa coaling station and the small collection of

La Playa Fuel Depot, 1925. *Naval Historical Center*

wood clapboard huts and lofty antennas high on the Point that called itself Navy Radio Point Loma. However, everyone in town remembered the two just-completed seasons of pioneering hydroaeroplane flights from North Island and were dazzled with the sleek new destroyers and torpedo boats that were beginning to operate out of the harbor on training exercises.

The Navy had discovered that its relatively diminutive torpedo boats and destroyers handled better in the protected reaches of San Diego Bay and the benign waters of Southern California and frequently ordered its Pacific Fleet Torpedo Flotilla to San Diego from Mare Island and Puget Sound. These low, swift craft were catchy to the eye, with a sleek silhouette of four stacks raked jauntily as if for added speed, a high turtleback forecastle accenting a low amidships freeboard, and a paint scheme of dark bottle green. They were relatively heavily armed with guns and torpedo tubes and could reach sprint speeds of twenty-eight knots. In late December 1909 the supply steamer *Iris* had been ordered to San Diego to serve as a tender for the 1st, 2nd, and 3rd Torpedo Boat Flotillas, who would operate out of San Diego during winter months.[9]

Warship visits to San Diego were steadily increasing. During 1914–15 armored cruisers (including *South Dakota, Pittsburgh, Chattanooga,* and *Maryland*) maintained neutrality patrols off western Mexican ports with San Diego serving as their coaling and supply base.[10] Bluejackets on liberty became a common sight at downtown shops and, not quite as positively in the eyes of local merchants, in the Stingaree red-light district. *Chattanooga*'s commanding officer, Comdr. Thomas Senn, would later command San Diego's Eleventh Naval District as a rear admiral in the 1930s. As late as 1914 the San Diego Naval Militia mobilized to protect the city's water supply near the Mexican border.

With the coaling station playing a prominent role in naval operations, Kettner astutely set out early in his term to expand and rejuvenate the station. La Playa had formally opened in 1904, but by 1913 operations were inconsistent, and, occasionally, the Navy had even temporarily abandoned the station. A 1909 appropriation to improve the station had become sidetracked in Congress despite the fact that Rear Adm. Henry Manney, former chief of the Navy's Bureau of Equipment, had been brought out of retirement and sent to San Diego to oversee construction. But on his first attempt Kettner helped pass a bill early in 1914 that won $95,000 for the station—$45,000 to complete coal-handling structures, including a steel tower and $50,000, foresightedly, for new fuel-oil tanks and piping.[11]

The first La Playa fuel-oil tanks were reported completed in the 1915 annual report of the secretary of the Navy, and Kettner won new appropriations later that year to dredge in front of the coaling station and in the approaches to San Diego's Municipal Pier. Even crusty Admiral Dewey was beginning to see the value in San Diego as a means to defend the western approaches to the Panama Canal. In 1916 Dewey recommended further increases for the La Playa fuel depot, saying, "During the recent disturbances in Mexico, and previously in Central America, San Diego has been used to a considerable extent as a position in readiness for concentrating naval forces and as a base of supplies including fuel for the forces employed in those waters. San Diego is used as a liberty port with fleet drill grounds and target practice grounds near by."[12]

From the start Kettner wooed Secretary Daniels, playing up San Diego's advantages and urging Daniels to visit the city. On Daniels's first West Coast inspection tour of naval facilities, Kettner successfully squeezed a day's visit into the secretary's itinerary between "more important" politicking in Los Angeles and San Francisco. San Diego officials were ready with an impressive reception that they hoped would outdazzle what other Pacific coast cities may have mustered in political clout. Daniels and his wife were met in Los Angeles and escorted to San Diego by the president of the chamber and now-retired Rear Admiral Manney. "At San Diego our reception had a cordiality all its own," Daniels wrote. "Its representative in Congress, Bill Kettner, had talked to me in Washington of the advantages of San Diego as a Naval Base, and the whole population was united to convince the new Secretary that San Diego was by far the best site for naval bases on the Pacific."[13]

In San Diego a motorcade whisked the secretary and Mrs. Daniels to an elegant seaside suite at the Hotel del Coronado. Dressed in porkpie hat and string tie and armed with country editor pleasantries, Daniels was in his element. That evening "one of the most elaborate affairs ever held in San Diego" was organized in his honor, featuring a table of honor and speaker's podium mounted on a replica of a stern portion of an imaginary battleship, the USS *Daniels.* The secretary, warming to the overplayed welcome, stoked the fires of anticipation further when he rose to announce, "It is my ambition and purpose, when the Panama Canal is opened, to come through the canal with that fleet, bringing every ship in our Navy to San Diego."[14] San Diego collectively beamed.

Comfortable as he was with politicians and banquets, Daniels in 1913 was still somewhat the novice navalist who depended on reasoned professional advice to set Navy policy. To support the secretary's visit to San Diego the armored cruiser *South Dakota* had been ordered to the port. Her commanding officer, Capt. Charles Plunkett, was an enthusiastic

The Chollas Heights radio transmitter site represented the first place in San Diego that the Navy procured for its use. Its landmark six hundred-foot towers graced the hills behind the city from the time of the station's activation in 1917. The reservoir at the bottom of the picture was built to cool the site's high-power transmitters. *National Archives*

advocate of San Diego's attributes. "I have traveled much and anchored in many of the harbors of the world, but in no harbor to equal San Diego," he was quoted as saying and "the natural advantages of San Diego are bound to win out."[15]

Daniels rose early the morning following his banquet to inspect the Point Loma wireless station. Captain Plunkett hung constantly at his side, pointing out the harbor's advantages with a keen mariner's viewpoint that generated instant credibility. Later that morning, the Daniels entourage boarded *Venetia*, John D. Spreckels's opulent personal steam yacht, for a voyage up the coast to San Pedro. With Daniels standing at *Venetia*'s rail, Plunkett's *South Dakota* fired a nineteen-gun salute and North Island Army airmen made a low pass in an experimental Curtiss landplane. *South Dakota* left later on the

tide to convoy the *Venetia* northward and Daniels commented approvingly in his diary, "Had a very pleasant day on the ocean."[16]

The visit proved to be a crucial episode in San Diego–Navy history. Throughout his tenure as secretary, Daniels, who had never visited San Diego before 1913, was mesmerized by the city and by the positive picture painted by the chamber and Captain Plunkett: "I have often said that I regarded San Diego as a second home."[17]

Reflecting the city's keen interest in attracting the Navy, the morning paper lavishly covered Daniels's visit on page 1. Coincidentally, the back pages of the paper featured a small, barely noticed article headlined, "To Begin Dredging Harbor Entrance to 33 Feet; US Army Engineer Calls for Bids," referring to Kettner's hard-won $249,000 dredging appropriation.[18] Without even realizing its significance, the *Union* had brilliantly bookended a discerning perspective of the different threads of influence that Kettner was already pulling for San Diego's benefit.

One of San Diego's goals for the Daniels visit had been to press for further expansion of the Navy wireless station on Point Loma. City officials knew that the Navy had planned for a new high-powered worldwide wireless telegraphy network with stations in northern Virginia, the Canal Zone, Manila, Honolulu, and Southern California.[19] The specific site in California had not yet been identified, and Kettner had cleverly planned for the secretary to visit the spectacular vistas of NPL to not-so-subtly advertise San Diego's attributes as an established wireless site.

By September 1913 a Navy survey panel had investigated several promising sites in San Diego and Los Angeles for the new powerful transmitters and accompanying tall transmitting antennas. The most favored sites in San Diego included Linda Vista, Grossmont, and a 73.5-acre site at Chollas Heights.[20]

The General Board recommended the Chollas Heights site as first priority with a site at Whittier near Los Angeles as a second option, due to "the probability of naval vessels being in port because of a naval fuel station [in San Diego], in time of war naval vessels may not be expected to be in the vicinity of Los Angeles."[21] But the Chollas Heights parcel was owned by Henry Carling, who resided in New Jersey and was not inclined to surrender the land cheaply. A year-long multisided negotiation ensued, involving a Navy Department feigning lack of money, a Chamber of Commerce anxious to solidify another Navy success (and containing members who themselves owned several of the competing land sites), flinty Carling, and Congressman Kettner, who worked tirelessly to resolve the matter favorably for San Diego. All nature of negotiation tactics were used during the acrimonious haggling, including threats of outright property condemnation, but Kettner's adroit balancing act kept the chamber in line and convinced the Navy to increase its offer. With the help of Rear Adm. Robert Griffin, chief of the Bureau of Steam Engineering, the Navy finalized what would be its very first land purchase in San Diego on 21 July 1914 by paying Carling $15,000 for the tract (with an additional $1,000 thrown in by the chamber).

Construction at Chollas Heights continued through 1916, with the Navy spending $278,700 on structures and equipment. Three large antenna towers were constructed (the largest 625 feet high), a small lake was built to help cool the giant two

Armored cruiser *San Diego* (originally christened *California*) became the first deep-draft warship to enter San Diego harbor and was flagship of the Pacific Fleet. She sank during World War I when she struck a mine that had been deployed by a German U-boat off Fire Island, the only large warship loss of the war for the United States. *Naval Historical Center*

hundred–kilowatt Poulsen-arc transmitters, and ancillary buildings were built for the over fifty officers and operators who would man the site. When finally in operation, keyed remotely from Point Loma, Chollas Heights was described as the most powerful radio station in the world. In his 1917 annual report Secretary Daniels noted, "On May 1, 1917, the high-power station at San Diego was placed in commission and after a short period of test was placed in regular service as one of the chain of naval radio stations. This station is equipped with the latest apparatus and reliable communication over the ranges for which it was designed is assured."[22]

In 1914, just as the Chollas Heights dealmaking was at its height, Kettner identified yet another opportunity to solidify San Diego–Navy ties. The Navy had changed the naming convention for its capital ships and announced that its powerful new super-dreadnought battleships would thereafter be named after states of the Union. Older armored cruisers that had carried the names of states would be renamed. Congressman Kettner, quick as always to seize the initiative, noted that a new battleship had been tentatively assigned the name *California*, requiring that armored cruiser *California* (AC-6) be renamed. He contacted many of his growing list of friends within the Navy Department and lobbied for the name "San Diego," despite the fact that other cities in California such as San Francisco or Los Angeles were more prominent or commanded greater Navy resources.

With undisguised glee, Kettner opened Secretary Daniels's letter on 1 August that began: "I have the honor to inform you that the name of the United States armored cruiser *California* will be changed to the U.S.S. *San Diego.*" On 16 September the rechristening took place in a gala ceremony at anchor in San Diego harbor. The mayor declared the day a holiday, three thousand were treated to a barbecue in Balboa Park, and the manager of the U.S. Grant Hotel threw a banquet and ball in honor of the officers and their ladies at his personal expense.[23]

San Diego had been a frequent visitor to its now-namesake city beginning in 1910 when she became the first Navy deep-draft combatant to enter the harbor. Often in 1914 this spit-and-polish cruiser would serve as flagship of the Pacific Fleet and was a popular visit ship during the Panama-California Exposition of 1915–16.

The Panama-California Exposition in Balboa Park was both a celebration of the opening of the Panama Canal—in August 1914—and a commercial and marketing tour de force that for San Diego became the defining event of pre-1920 society. The exposition was never planned as a means to necessarily promote the Navy in general or its expanding relationship with San Diego in particular, but the ensuing tight alignment between the Navy and the exposition remain one of the enduring outcomes of its two-year play. The exposition also allowed Kettner to champion San Diego, and a steady stream of cross-country Washington dignitaries heard San Diego described as a budding naval base, training site, and deep-water port.

On 12 April 1914 Navy Secretary Daniels sent Assistant Secretary and Mrs. Roosevelt as an advance party to the San Diego exposition and to evaluate the La Playa coaling station land as a potential site for either a repair or training station. The ranking naval officer in San Diego, Comdr. Clelland Davis, escorted the Roosevelts on a tour of harbor facilities aboard Spreckels's *Venetia* and took them in a touring car to the Naval Radio Station—with a short detour for golf at the Point Loma Country Club—and to the new radio site at Chollas Heights.

"A magnificent harbor with more magnificent possibilities," said Roosevelt, understating what for him would be a lifelong love affair with the city. According to a *San Diego Union* reporter, when Roosevelt was pressed to comment on the Navy's future role in San Diego, he "let it be inferred" that the Navy might permanently transfer a few torpedo boats to San Diego after the canal was open. Boisterous as always, the *Union* headlined the story: "San Diego to Be Great Naval Base, Says Roosevelt."[24]

During March 1915 Roosevelt again visited the exposition, this time accompanying Vice President Thomas Marshal.[25] When Roosevelt stepped off the destroyer *Paul Jones,* which had carried him down from San Pedro, he was greeted by adoring directors of the chamber and members of the press. Roosevelt boosted expectations still higher by announcing plans for a West Coast dirigible base (that would "probably" be in San Diego) and promising that San Diego would be the first port of call for a new battleship force that would soon pass through the Panama Canal.[26]

So stark was the Naval Hospital when first constructed that local politicians rose in opposition, one claiming, "The Navy Department pledged itself to the construction of a most beautiful and artistic building. . . . I can hardly imagine a more severe, plain and unattractive structure than the one they have erected on the most prominent spot in Balboa Park." In response the commanding officer hired an English gardener, William H. Crofts, to brighten the premises. This photo was taken 1 February 1922. *National Archives*

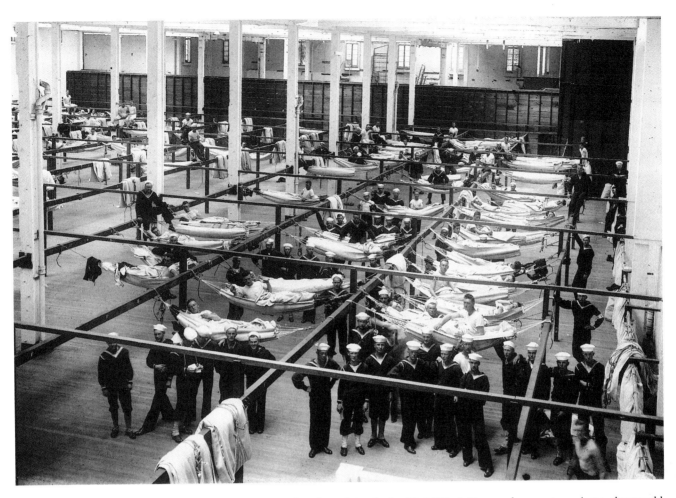

A San Diego Exposition building turned barracks houses sailors for training during World War I. Hammocks were strung just as they would be aboard the warships of the era to give the recruits experience in that mode of sleeping before reporting aboard their first ship. *San Diego Historical Society*

The immensely popular Navy exhibit at the exposition included a 900-pound projectile from a 12-inch naval gun, a model of the newly commissioned battleship *North Dakota,* and a model of the armored cruiser *San Diego* assembled by sailors from both the coaling station and radio station. Throughout the exposition, the Navy was fully incorporated within its daily events, providing continuous spectacles of sailors, Marines, parades, and band concerts. On 28 July 1915, true to Roosevelt's promise, the Naval Academy Practice Squadron, composed of battleships *Missouri, Ohio,* and *Wisconsin,* entered harbor after transiting the canal. The battleships were open to streams of visitors and the midshipmen paraded through Plaza de Panama for former president Theodore Roosevelt.[27]

As disappointing as the 1917 Helm Report had been to San Diego by recommending new bases for other sites in California and Hawaii, it only proved a temporary setback. As involve-ment in the First World War loomed, naval operations increased at North Island, the coal depot, and the radio station. Not wanting to lose this accelerating momentum but suspecting that he could not directly pursue a naval station due to the wording of the Helm Report, Kettner began to beat the drum for an installation not mentioned in the report—a naval training station.

The San Diego Chamber of Commerce had established a special committee on a naval training school as far back as the 1890s. On 5 January 1894 George Marston, chairman of that committee, reported "progress" to the chamber but a month later discovered that the Navy favored existing facilities at Mare Island, north of San Francisco, for establishment of its first Western training site. The chamber quickly countered by convincing Hotel del Coronado owner Elisha S. Babcock Jr. to offer land on North Island for the school, an offer that was ultimately ignored.

A bigger prize loomed later when the Navy proposed a fundamental shift in its entire training philosophy in 1901. The Navy had always trained its apprentice seamen aboard ship, first on sailing ships during long voyages, then in training squadrons, and then aboard specific training vessels tied up at bases. At the turn of the century the Navy found that training its increasing numbers of apprentice seamen could be accomplished more cheaply at shore training stations. Despite critics' charges that training *seamen* on *land* was clear folly, the Navy established its first three training stations at Newport (Rhode Island), Norfolk, and San Francisco—moving its fledgling trade school at Mare Island to permanent facilities on Goat Island.[28]

But San Diego still hoped to capture a training station even after the Navy was established in San Francisco. The chamber knew that San Diego had been recommended favorably in 1904 as the site for a training station by a special commission of naval officers. They also knew that the commander of the Pacific Squadron, Rear Adm. Caspar Goodrich, had responded favorably to the chamber in 1905 with this thought: "Why not try to bring the Naval Training Station from San Francisco to San Diego, where everything necessary in the way of climate, harbor, places and opportunity for drill and exercise has been prodigally lavished by a generous nature? In that you may count upon my voice."[29]

On 24 February 1906 the chamber followed up with Rear Admiral Goodrich, offering the idea of North Island as a training site. Goodrich thought North Island an ideal place for the station and agreed to meet with John D. Spreckels to discuss its potential use. The meetings fizzled when it became apparent that the ever-cagey Spreckels was more interested in reserving North Island for residential development or, at least, a substantially higher sales price than the Navy was offering.[30]

During the exposition years, San Diego officials increasingly

Recruits and Naval Training Station staff spell out "NAVY" in Plaza de Panama, c. 1918. *San Diego Historical Society*

pressed visiting Navy officials for a major new Navy training station in San Diego. Secretary Daniels was known to be distressed at the poor training conditions at Goat Island and Kettner discovered that Roosevelt felt that the island's cold and damp weather was responsible for a high incidence of sickness among the recruits.[31]

The third strike against Goat Island came early in 1917. With the nation heading toward war, each of the Navy's training stations was ordered to expand in anticipation of a flood of new recruits. Goat Island had already reached the physical limits of the island and could not meet the growing demand. The Navy officially began to consider other alternatives.

Glimpsing the possibilities of finally capturing the Navy's fluctuating interest for a permanent San Diego training station, San Diego Park commissioners proposed a lease of the exposition areas in Balboa Park to the Navy for a temporary training camp at a dollar a year. In a rush indicative of wartime exigencies, the Navy accepted that proposal on 1 May 1917, issued orders to Capt. Arthur MacArthur as commanding officer, and placed Naval Training Station, Balboa Park, into commission on 20 May.[32]

Two "detention camps" were established, one near the zoo and one near the site of the Organ Pavilion. The "boot camp" for the youngest recruits was across the street from the lions' cages as Yeoman Seaman Arthur C. Campbell remembers. Nearly four thousand sailors passed through boot camp in Balboa Park during the four years of its existence with many thousands more attending other training classes.

During October 1918 Captain MacArthur received instructions from the Navy Department to inspect different sites in San Diego suitable for a new training station. Kettner and several members of the chamber joined MacArthur during inspections to "assist" and the search quickly concentrated on three sites at Coronado Heights (just north of Imperial Beach on the Silver Strand), the southeast corner of False Bay, and a site partially on tidelands at Loma Portal. MacArthur reported his strong preference for the Point Loma site, land that was owned in large measure by the San Diego Securities Company, whose directors included several friends of Kettner.[33]

After the Chollas Heights deal, the chamber increasingly and confidently found itself in the position of "middleman" for a string of land arrangements with the Navy. It was a natural outgrowth of events and one that would establish the dominant chemistry between city and Navy during these crucial years. Washington officials were comfortable with the personalities that they had worked with in San Diego, and San Diegans were growing experienced in the ways of influence and

barter among the committees of Congress. As they marshaled support for a permanent training station, it was obvious that beginning with Chollas Heights, "the Chamber had created a special position for itself as the Navy's exclusive broker in San Diego while doing a much better job of promoting the interests of its members [especially the directors]. This in turn would ensure that future real estate transactions involving the Navy would be amicable and mutually advantageous."[34]

The chamber's go-between with Washington was Rufus Choate, a whirlwind of activity and Kettner's right-hand man in dealing with both Washington and the city. Choate's expertise at corresponding, telegraphing, cajoling, or explaining became legendary.

Kettner's growing prestige in Washington had a profound effect on how Congress perceived the priorities of the once-backwater port of San Diego. As one Washington official concluded, "During the war and subsequent thereto, San Diego had one of the most active representatives in Congress. He was backed to the limit by a Chamber of Commerce that left nothing undone to help him, no matter what the cost. Together they worked so successfully that San Diego's functions as a naval base will probably increase."[35]

The proposed Loma Portal site for a naval training station was an unpolished jewel. Located at the most commanding spot along the northern curve of San Diego Bay, the site stood at the juxtaposition of sight lines that flew down the harbor's entrance toward Old Spanish Light on one side and soared toward the commercial bustle of downtown on the other. The comfortable rise of Point Loma flanked its western edge, the placid waters of the bay lay to the south, and the adobes of Old Town and the crest of old Fort Stockton reflected its historical bonds to the north and east.

Once the Navy's preferences for Loma Portal were known, the chamber and the city council swung into action. Kettner pressed the chamber for immediate support: "If we want the Naval Training Station to stay here, action must be taken quickly. . . . [T]his means more to us than five or six shipbuilding yards."[36]

By letter and telegram to the secretary of the Navy on 18 and 22 November 1918, the city of San Diego made offers to present to the government a tract of land to be used as a naval training station that could accommodate five thousand to ten thousand men. The city council promised to raise $280,000 by public subscription to purchase 135 acres of privately owned land along Rosecrans Street and would donate an additional 142 acres of tidelands, for a total of 277 acres. Of the 135 acres, about 120 acres were owned by the San Diego Securities

Company (for which a sales price of $200,000 was agreed upon) and the remaining 15 acres held by small landowners. Kettner worked closely with the city council to place a bond issue on the ballot to cover sales expenses. In Washington, he handed the secretary of the Navy the city's offers. In parallel, Kettner worked the Hill to pass an authorization on 11 July 1919 to formally accept the land and then sponsored the first appropriation for construction—appropriations that by 1923 would total $2.3 million.[37]

Plans for a naval training station and a new large naval hospital were always linked in Kettner's mind as he knew that some medical facilities would have to be present to serve the thousands of recruits at the training station. Kettner also shrewdly knew that, just as with the training station, nothing in the Helm Report precluded the active pursuit of hospitals.

In the summer of 1914 a simple field hospital, accompanying the 4th Marine Regiment but manned by Navy personnel, had been established at North Island when the regiment encamped there following duties in Mexican waters. On 9 December 1914 the regiment and its field hospital were moved to Balboa Park to support the Panama-California Exposition and remained there until the exposition closed.

A medical department, named the War Dispensary, soon grew out of the basic field hospital when the exposition grounds were turned over to the Navy in the spring of 1917 for use as a training camp. "It was rough going," said Lt. (jg) Alma Smith. "The commander at the Balboa Training Camp had nearly 2,000 boots on hand and no medical department. He told me to open a dispensary. I borrowed a truck and the Marines gave me 35 beds, some tents, sheets, bandages, one electric sterilizer, and first aid tools. Now that's a shoestring budget."[38] The dispensary was housed in the headquarters building of the Park Police in May 1917 and ultimately consisted of two wards of twenty-five beds each.

The dispensary expanded in sync with the rest of the camp until, at the end of the war, it had reached a capacity of eight hundred patients in tent camps. The first senior medical officer of the War Dispensary was Comdr. Ammen Farenholt, who was assigned to the dispensary on 4 May 1917.[39]

The Balboa training camp was abandoned in early May 1919, but on 20 May Secretary Daniels designated the camp's War Dispensary as a naval hospital in its own right, a formality that assisted ongoing talks between the city and Washington on land grants and federal appropriations. The newly designated "hospital" remained in full operation throughout the 1919 worldwide influenza epidemic, while Navy architects began planning for a permanent hospital structure.[40]

The Navy wished to build the new permanent hospital in its wartime location, but after long negotiations both the Navy and the city agreed to move the hospital to an undeveloped site on the fringe of the park called Inspiration Point. Although Congressman Kettner recalled that City Councilman Walter Moore first suggested the site, Secretary Daniels also took credit:

Upon my next visit to San Diego, Bill [Kettner] and the city fathers and leading citizens showed me half a dozen sites for a Naval Hospital. All the time my heart was set on an elevation in Balboa Park for a Naval Hospital, but the committee showed me every other possible location. I was not impressed with any of them. I finally said, "Let us drive through Balboa Park." When we reached the eminence I had in my mind picked out for the hospital I asked Bill to stop so that we could stand upon the hill and get a view of the Pacific Ocean and beautiful Point Loma in the distance. "If you will deed this site," I said to Bill and the committee, "I will recommend to Congress the erection of a modern hospital at San Diego." They were not eager to give that particular site. Riding back to the hotel, I told Bill that unless he could induce the city fathers to donate the site I had picked out, the Navy would not be interested in the proposition. He and the other public-spirited citizens convinced them and one of the best Naval hospitals in the country crowns that location and convalescent sailors can sit on the lawns and look far beyond Point Loma and see the ships that ply up and down the Pacific.[41]

Kettner quickly aligned with Daniels's proposition and when many opposed the surrender of a prime tract of parkland, he deftly turned it aside, saying that such a site would reflect "the handsome way in which the Navy takes care of its unfortunates."[42]

On 3 September 1919 the city of San Diego deeded land to the federal government for the training center and 17.35 acres of Inspiration Point in Balboa Park for a permanent naval hospital. The Navy accepted these offers on 10 October and the acting secretary of the Navy later lauded San Diego "for the patriotic action of the city in placing this property at the disposal of the Navy."[43]

As soon as the vote ratifying the donations of city lands was official, Kettner did what he did best, corralling $500,000 in unobligated funds to begin immediate hospital construction and steered an additional $1,975,000 through the next naval appropriation bill for the hospital's first phase.[44]

Secretary Daniels insisted that the hospital design match other Southern California styles and the chamber told the San Diego public that the hospital design would "conform to the general character of the other buildings in the park the same as the Marine Base and the Naval Air Station." Although Goodhue was no longer a consultant to the Navy, his Spanish Colonial Revival style (even modulated by austere postwar budgets that minimized ornamental details) clearly guided the hands of Navy draftsmen as the hospital's design matured.[45]

The final hospital design produced by the Bureau of Yards and Docks favored lushly planted interior courtyards and symmetric two- and four-story buildings laid out along an axis of arcaded walkways and courts—exactly as the Marine Base, North Island, and the Naval Training Station had been designed. As it was anticipated that most of the hospital's personnel would come by trolley, a new hospital trolley station was constructed (with little or no parking provided for automobiles). On 22 August 1922 the initial 250-bed, $1.1-million phase of the complex was commissioned and the complete plan was built out in several stages extending until 1937.[46]

During the years of the First World War, most of the principal units of the Pacific Fleet and their commander in chief, Adm. William Caperton, were ordered to the South Atlantic on extended patrol. Armored cruisers *San Diego* and *Saratoga*, the fleet's destroyers, and newer submarines were all sent to the European war zone. Remaining on the Pacific coast was a polyglot group of reserves loosely organized into Patrol Force, Pacific Fleet, commanded by Rear Adm. William Fullam, whose flag flew from the aging battleship *Oregon*.

Fullam's few ships, such as gunboats *Yorktown*, *Annapolis* (PG-10), and *Vicksburg* (PG-11), new classes of submarine chasers, and old supply ships armed as auxiliary cruisers, were concentrated on patrols along the Mexican west coast. These patrols were to deter any German infiltration along the coast and included vessel registration checks, stops in Baja California inlets in search of enemy supplies, and searches for rumored German U-boats, surface raiders, or radio stations. Submarine tenders *Alert* and *Beaver*, which had been bought by the Navy from the North Pacific Steam Line, shepherded older F- and H-type boats used for training crews for new West Coast–built submarines.[47] With San Diego close to the primary area of Pacific Fleet operations in Mexico, flagship *Oregon* was a frequent visitor at Municipal Pier.

The operational tempo was slow, the results nearly nonexistent. Illustrative of what San Diego's Navy faced was the case of the *Alexander Agassiz*, a seventy-five-foot schooner from San Diego but of questionable registry. She was detained off the Mexican coast by the auxiliary cruiser *Brutus*, patrol boat *Vicksburg*, and submarine chaser *SC-302* in early 1918. Of vanishingly little threat to anyone, she was nonetheless interred due to the dubious discovery of German flags, several small

In 1911 two Navy submarines, *Grampus* (SS-4) and *Pike* (SS-6), visited San Diego and conducted diving exercises within the bay, much to the consternation of local ferry captains. San Diego's early attraction for submarine operations did not prevent the Navy, though, from awarding the West Coast's primary submarine base to San Pedro after World War I. *Naval Historical Center*

arms, and German-speaking passengers. Some made a big case of the successful thwarting of a German plot, but the *San Diego Sun* responded with perhaps a more accurate headline: "Five Naughty Pirates Are Taken by U.S."[48]

The most serious war loss in the Pacific occurred off San Diego on 17 December 1917 when submarine *F-1* sank following a collision. Submarines *F-1*, *F-2*, and *F-3* were operating on the surface at nine knots heading for an operations area off Point Loma when they entered a wall of heavy fog. In maneuvering to steer free of the mist, *F-3* rammed *F-1* just abaft her bridge, tearing a three-foot hole in her pressure hull and rupturing her main ballast tanks. Cold ocean water poured into the tight confines of the submarine and as the crew of *F-3* watched in horror *F-1* disappeared below the waves in less than ten seconds. Nineteen sailors lost their lives while Lt. Comdr. Alfred Montgomery and four men on the bridge escaped.[49]

By 1918 and 1919 American naval planners were turning their full attention to their service's role in the postwar world and were ready to give their full attention to the Pacific. "Yellow Peril" and the "Japanese Menace" were increasingly heard in the commentary of the day, and naval men, almost without exception, viewed the ambitious Japanese naval program and the Japanese seizure of German possessions in the Pacific with alarm. Key naval planners called for a two-ocean Navy with two battleship forces (each composed of sixteen battleships) and new bases in the Pacific. Increasingly their sights turned toward San Diego, where Kettner's naval infrastructure was reaching self-sustaining critical mass and where San Diego was recognized as the Pacific Fleet's primary operation base during World War I.[50]

As the Atlantic and Pacific Fleets were sorted out after the war, destroyers were among the first forces ordered west, playing directly to San Diego's advantage in its fight for predominance among other West Coast cities. As light forces began to gather in San Diego harbor, a squadron of eight subchasers arrived in San Diego on 12 April from "war duty," to be welcomed by front-page coverage of their exploits. They nested four abreast at Municipal Pier but two days later further front-page coverage (this time not quite so laudatory) related the accidental gasoline explosion aboard subchaser *SC-297* that burned her superstructure to the deck edge.[51]

In June 1919 Secretary Daniels formally ordered the new Atlantic and Pacific Fleets and Adm. Hugh Rodman assumed duties as Commander in Chief, Pacific Fleet. On 7 August the new Pacific Fleet commander brought his battleline northward from Panama. San Diego, as the American port closest to the Canal, was a natural location to conduct a grand naval review to celebrate the new fleet's formation. Secretary Daniels reviewed the fleet from armored cruiser *Montana* while "[t]hirty-one American fighting ships comprising the main battle squadrons of the new Pacific Fleet with battle flags flying from fore and main truck and from the gaff passed in impressive review in the Coronado roadstead."[52]

The entire length of Point Loma was lined with automobiles as San Diegans flocked to see the impressive array of the Navy's most formidable warships. A Navy seaplane flew overhead to capture the event on "moving pictures." Battleships *Vermont* and *Georgia* and cruiser *Birmingham* later anchored in the bay, destroyers spread out to the Coronado docks, and the larger battleships anchored off the Hotel del Coronado.

That evening thousands of sailors flocked ashore to share in the city's celebratory mood. The city decorated its downtown, the *Union* issued a special edition, and the Marston Department Store prepared a souvenir booklet labeled "The Harbor of Opportunity," with pictures of warships at anchor and details on the city's climate and real estate. Festivals for officers and enlisted were held and Daniels again grabbed the limelight, telling an enthusiastic audience that "he would never be satisfied until Congress had created sufficient appropriations to make San Diego Harbor one of the great harbors of the world."[53]

Not surprisingly, the arrival of Rodman's forces in 1919 quickly overtaxed the West Coast facilities required to service

them. Secretary Daniels tapped Rear Adm. J. S. McKean to dust off the Helm Report and to further study Pacific base requirements. Although still endorsing main fleet operating bases at only San Francisco, Puget Sound, and Pearl Harbor, McKean was "further of the opinion that the operations of the fleet on the west coast will require additional facilities in San Diego Harbor, consisting of a supply base, repair base for all but capital ships and a large addition to the Fuel Supply Base as planned." Rear Admiral McKean further praised the clearly popular support of San Diegans for the Navy that could make it "the third naval base on the coast" after Bremerton and San Francisco.[54]

By 1919 the important weight of the Navy's General Board was also swinging solidly behind San Diego. Not only did the General Board favorably endorse McKean's findings, but it published its own policy paper on 23 June 1919 that urged an expansion of aviation at North Island and added a recommendation for a new naval air station across the harbor at Dutch Flats.[55]

During the immediate postwar years, San Diego faced an economic depression. Tourism generated by the Panama-California Exposition had fallen off, any wartime industrial stimulus had already bypassed San Diego, more than one hundred thousand jobs on the Pacific Coast disappeared in the wake of peacetime cutbacks, and hundreds of thousands of returning former servicemen reentered the job market.[56]

San Diego voters felt the pinch. Bond issues failed, citizens grumbled, and most realized that to develop the harbor—the absolute key to San Diego's economic future—would require a huge infusion of outside funds. "Smokestacks versus geraniums" was the key watchword in local elections and political oration separating those favoring economic growth stimulated by vigorous industrialization from those favoring San Diego as an aesthetic resort enclave.

In this divisive, volatile debate the Navy stood as a shining star for all sides, promising both an infusion of federal spending for the harbor and a continuous stream of revenue generated from naval salaries, infrastructure growth, and the relatively "clean" industries of supplying, repairing, and operating its forces. It offered a means to stimulate industrial and economic recovery without the sins of industrialization and it promised economic stability well into the future. "By 'joining the Navy,'" historian Kevin Starr wrote later, "San Diego created a sustainable industrial economy that could be kept under control . . . and found a way to develop its economy while remaining a resort."[57]

But attracting the attention of the Navy could have its downside as well. The Navy was interested in bargains and was

A SEAL unit crosses a Coronado beach during ingress training. *U.S. Navy*

BUD/S candidates learn to act as a team through weeks of physically demanding activity all with the enthusiastic support and encouragement of a nearby instructor. *U.S. Navy*

Opened in 1905 as a foundry, National Steel and Shipbuilding Company (NASSCO) is one of several shipbuilding and repair companies that densely pack the San Diego industrial waterfront. Here, the forty thousand-ton amphibious assault ship *Essex* (LHD-2) rides comfortably within a NASSCO drydock.
National Steel and Shipbuilding Company

Right: The Navy's legacy in San Diego is reflected even in some of its homes. This stained-glass window of carrier *Lexington* is found at the Kipperman residence in Coronado. *BRL Photos*

Facing page: Two symbols of the San Diego waterfront share the limelight: an aircraft carrier at North Island and the *Star of India* under sail for the Coronado Bridge. *Carl "Tank" Shireman*

Below: The Miramar Fightertown hangars were a San Diego landmark for years while the base operated as a naval air station and homebase for the Pacific Fleet's fighter squadrons and wings. *U.S. Navy*

A C-2 utility aircraft departs North Island enroute to a carrier operating off the coast. *Carl "Tank" Shireman*

Much of the original architecture of the Naval Training Station is to be restored within a ninety-acre historic district as part of the city's redevelopment plan for the land returned by the Navy in 1999. *BRL Photos*

A symbol of the Navy legacy for San Diegans at the Naval Training Center. *BRL Photos*

Although significantly reduced in numbers from their Cold War height, submarines still sail regularly from Ballast Point for the excellent underwater operating areas offshore and on extended deployments to distant patrol stations. *Carl "Tank" Shireman*

A *Ticonderoga*-class Aegis cruiser
maneuvers in front of the city's skyline.
Carl "Tank" Shireman

The Navy has always enjoyed thrilling San Diegans with spectacular fleet displays. Fleet Week, an annual celebration of San Diego's Navy begun in the 1990s, featured this launch of a S-3 Viking from aircraft carrier *Nimitz* sailing inside San Diego Bay while thousands cheered from along the bayshore. *Tom Twomey*

The sophisticated E-2 airborne early warning aircraft was based at Miramar and provided carrier battlegroups with long-range radar coverage and fighter interception control. *U.S. Navy*

Blue Angel pilots "take the walk" as they man their F/A-18 aircraft for the aerial demonstrations that are always the highlight of the popular annual Miramar Air Show. *Tom Twomey*

The TOPGUN Fighter Weapons School, a Miramar mainstay for years, operated several different types of aircraft painted in different paint schemes to make its aerial training as realistic as possible. *U.S. Navy*

A Navy F-16 "aggressor" aircraft attached to TOPGUN flies over Mission Bay in 1990 *Tom Twomey*

Two Tomcats from VF-124 over Coronado. *Tom Twomey*

Commissioned in December 1995, *John C. Stennis* (CVN-74) was
the first of several nuclear-powered carriers to be homeported
in San Diego. To support her arrival, a huge new berth was
constructed at North Island on land once favored as a floatplane
anchorage near some of the original hangars built for the air
station. *U.S. Navy*

Below: Boxer (LHD-4) returns from deployment and sails under the Coronado Bridge. *U.S. Navy*

Overleaf: During the holiday months the entire waterfront takes on a festive air at the Naval Station as ships return from distant cruises and rig up-and-over lights in celebration of the season. *U.S. Navy*

Ship classes may change but Point Loma looms as it always has, marking the point of departure for generations of navymen who trade the warmth and comfort of the city for the challenge and excitement of the sea. *U.S. Navy*

The evening inport watch is set at 32nd Street. *Carl "Tank" Shireman*

USS *John Paul Jones* (DDG-53) moors in a drydock at
Naval Station San Diego on a moonlit fall evening. *U.S. Navy*

Members of Special Boat Unit TWELVE exercise at high speed in a thirty-three–foot Rigid Inflatable Boat (RIB) on the smooth waters of San Diego Bay. *U.S. Navy*

Facing page: Two Navy SEAL parachutists thrill Fourth of July crowds during their annual demonstration in Glorietta Bay. *Carl "Tank" Shireman*

The standard jet departure from Miramar took fighters directly toward the ocean over the Torrey Pines cliffs. *Tom Twomey*

Officers and men of protected cruiser *Saratoga* pose c. 1914 around the ship's 8-inch main battery. Assigned to the Pacific Fleet throughout 1917, *Saratoga* took part in Mexican neutrality patrols returning to San Diego for supplies and fuel. *San Diego Historical Society*

well aware of its strong negotiating position—many other West Coast communities were lobbying vigorously for naval bases of their own. To attract the Navy's attention—and with it the promise of economic stability—San Diegans would have to give up important rights to many of the most precious areas of the city, including its waterfront and portions of its vast city park.

By city charter, land donations such as those proposed for the training station and naval hospital had to be ratified by the voters, and such an election was held on 3 August 1920. The election culminated decades of good will between the Navy and the city and stood to validate a mountain of work by Congressman Kettner and San Diego businessmen and civic offi-

cials. It boiled down to a matter of economic policy and social choice with the promise of a "naval industry" without the offending "smokestacks." "All the government asks of San Diego is the concession of a few acres of tidelands and a site for a hospital in Balboa Park," spoke the editors of the *Union*. "[I]n return, it gives San Diego one of the finest naval establishments in the world."[58]

The vote was overwhelmingly in favor of the Navy, the loss of the use of prime city property never a serious consideration. "Never in the history of the city has such a sweeping vote been polled at any election," related the *Union*'s cover story. Four separate ballot measures were voted on for four separate donations of land to the Navy. The vote for the hospital land in Balboa Park was the "closest," passing in favor of the Navy, 9,341–134. The Roseville district of Point Loma, closest to the training station land, voted 160–0 in favor of the Navy.[59]

Even the Navy was overwhelmed: "Dear Mr. Kettner," wrote the secretary of the Navy, "My heartiest congratulations to you and to the citizens of San Diego on the gratifying result of the election to ratify the grant by the City of San Diego to the Navy of lands for the site of the Naval Training Station, and also the grant for the Naval Hospital at Balboa Park. As you will see by the enclosures, the Navy will begin active operations immediately."[60]

Once a broad citywide consensus was reached, it continued unabated for decades to come. Kettner's mastery of what years later would be called "pork-barrel politics" had primed the pump of federal resources that would guarantee the uninterrupted flow of federal largess even to the present day. No city in America focused as single-mindedly on the Navy as did San Diego nor became as dependent on the vagaries of the federal government to augment its local economy.[61]

Secretary Daniels and Congressman Kettner would both recede from the stage after the 1920 elections, Daniels to return to North Carolina with the end of the Wilson presidency, Kettner to return to his insurance business. Neither would soon forget the successes they had wrought for the good of San Diego's Navy. Writing some two decades later in 1944, Josephus Daniels reminisced:

As a result of (my 1913) visit and my knowledge of the climate and the fact that San Diego was the nearest port on the Pacific to the Panama Canal, before my term of office expired there had been established at San Diego a Training Station for young sailors replacing the one on Goat Island in San Francisco harbor, an aviation base on North Island, where during the World War it was largely expanded, a Marine Headquarters with training facilities, large supply buildings, repair shops and in fact it has since become one of the greatest Naval bases in the country.[62]

1920

Sleek in its sunny days, perhaps a bit smug in its moonlit evenings, San Diego sauntered in the [1920s and '30s] with the nonchalance of a future star ready to be discovered. The First World War was won, but the Navy, its big payroll, and its handsome officer uniforms would stick around.

Welton Jones

The naval base at San Diego, Calif., is hereby established and shall consist of the naval air station, the naval fuel depot, the naval hospital, the marine barracks, the radio stations and such other naval activities as are now or may be established in San Diego or in the immediate vicinity.

Navy General Order no. 514, dated 31 December 1919

With naval operations in San Diego expanding at a rapid clip by early 1920, the Navy recognized the need to bring a flag officer to San Diego to coordinate its widespread and suddenly very diverse activities. During modest ceremonies at North Island on 26 January, Rear Adm. Roger Welles formally assumed duties as the first commandant of the newly recognized Naval Base, San Diego.

Barely three months prior, Welles, stocky yet patrician with a full head of white hair and a neatly trimmed white moustache, had been walking the teak decks of his flagship at the head of an Atlantic Fleet battleship division. Shortly after attending the 1919 Army-Navy game he had been asked by CNO Adm. Robert Coontz to consider a transfer to San Diego. Welles had been initially cool to the idea, but when his wife suffered a sudden bout of appendicitis forcing an operation, Welles began to think of the potential assignment in terms of her recuperation. "She is very weak and Southern California will be just the place in which for her to convalesce," he wrote. But devoted as he was to his accomplished wife of many years, he was also quick to emphasize other priorities easily recognizable by career navymen: "I would be glad to accept the detail solely on account of Mrs. Welles' health," he wrote Adm.

Henry B. Wilson, "but I want you to know that had there been the slightest chance of getting to sea in the near future, I should never have given my consent to be detached from the fleet."[1]

As soon as his orders had been confirmed, Welles wrote the senior San Diego base commander, Capt. J. Harvey Tomb, inquiring about quarters. Tomb steered Welles toward a suite at the Grant Hotel, "the best hotel in San Diego and one that caters to the Army and Navy. Due to the fact that so many naval officers are here, all bungalows are taken and only the more expensive houses can be obtained. By expensive houses, I mean from $150.00 to $250.00 per month. Bungalows occupied by naval officers rent from $50.00 to $90.00 per month."[2] Tomb's honesty and thoroughness were to cost him, as Welles decided to claim Tomb's comfortable and newly built quarters on North Island as his own.

Welles knew San Diego, having visited in 1887 as a junior officer aboard *Thetis,* and was determined to make a rapid and determined start. From his very first public address to a luncheon meeting of the San Diego–California Club he assiduously assumed the duties of guardian of the Navy's public image: "That the Navy Department is back of San Diegans," Welles was quoted, "in their ambition to make this the greatest naval base on this side of the continent is not only because

Rear Adm. Roger Welles, the first "Navy mayor" of San Diego, 1920. *Naval Historical Center*

her citizens want it, but because it will benefit the entire United States Navy."[3] To the Rotary Club Welles emphasized business and economics: "the Navy's payroll is already large here but in a very short time it will be doubled and tripled, and it behooves us to see that the men of the Navy who are with us and will make their homes here are treated right and made to feel that they are wanted."[4]

Welles set out immediately to solidify the Navy's position while he could depend on the CNO's support. "In order to make the position of Commandant Naval Base, San Diego at all possible," Welles wrote to Coontz,

it seems to me there are several things that should be done at once. . . . First, [Southern] California should be made a separate Naval District with the Commandant of the Naval Base as commandant of that naval district and it is recommended that this District be made No. 11. . . . [A]t present everything concerning policy etc must be referred to the commandant of the 12th district. This causes delays and the commandant of the 12th district is not in a position to judge of what is needed in Southern California. Second, there should be a receiving ship stationed at San Diego. There are at present 53 vessels of all kinds in this harbor, but there is no receiving ship. Third, as it

is proposed to make this an operating base, I am soon to recommend that a storehouse be built at the foot of Broadway which shall act as the storehouse for supplies for the fleet as well as offices for the Commandant. Fourth, the Commandant should have a house built for him.[5]

Beyond the rapidly expanding naval facilities at North Island, the Naval Training Station, and the Naval Hospital, Welles also set his sights on the need for a large naval repair base. In a study dated 11 December 1919 that Welles carried with him across country, the CNO's Plans Division cited that "operations of the fleet on the west coast required additional facilities in San Diego including a supply base, a repair base for all but capital ships and a large addition to the fuel supply base."[6]

In May 1918 owners of Philadelphia's Scofield Engineering Company had approached Congressman Kettner, asking to gain a contract with the U.S. Shipping Board Emergency Fleet Corporation to build concrete ships at a new shipyard in San Diego. Kettner helped find several local investors to join the venture that ultimately incorporated as the Pacific Marine & Construction Company.

By September 1918 an agreement had been struck between the city and the Emergency Fleet Corporation allowing a lease of 77.2 acres of land and 21 acres of water and marsh at the foot of 32nd Street. Scofield immediately reclaimed six hundred feet of tidelands behind a quay wall with dredge material, provided for railway access to the site, and began construction. Concrete ships *Cuyamaca* and *San Pascual* were completed in the spring of 1920.[7]

During this same time Kettner helped pass a bill of $175,000 for a marine railway in San Diego large enough to handle vessels of twenty-five hundred tons and three hundred feet in length. The marine railway would replace the long-time Spreckels Marineways on North Island that had been dismantled in favor of seaplane ramps and hangars. Work began in early 1919 at a site long anticipated for the marine railway adjacent to the La Playa fueling station, but it soon became clear that Kettner had bigger plans. Thwarted at every turn to gain support for a major new naval base, Kettner envisioned a "repair base" as a means to his desired end. "The Marine Railway is practically a Naval Base," he told the chamber's board of directors. "Admiral Fullman is figuring on doing all [his] repair work there, except for battleships."[8]

Central to Kettner's strategies for increasing naval investment in San Diego during 1912–20 was his conviction that one facility would quickly lead to a second, and two facilities would expand to three, and so on, until a substantial infrastructure would result. In a surprisingly candid address to the Cham-

Welles reading his orders establishing Naval Base San Diego on 30 January 1920. *U.S. Navy*

ber of Commerce board of directors, Kettner laid out his thinking: "As soon as we start [on the quay wall for the marine railway] we can add to it every year. As soon as we open an account with the government, it is easy to do business, but first we must open an account. Every new officer that comes to a place wants to do good work and improve things. It is the same way with the Marine Ways, if we can get them started, it is only a question of time until we have a nice crowd of men over there."[9]

By the middle of 1919 the separate fortunes of the new marine railway and the 32nd Street emergency ship plant would be joined. Knowing that the La Playa site was cramped and concerned that resources for new bases would dry up after the war, Kettner rushed to have the railway moved to the emergency ship plant and to have the site formally deeded to the Navy. Again, as with so many other Navy projects of this decade, the plan was a perfect match for all parties. The government would protect a $3-million investment in plant equipment and would receive important harbor property for no cost, the city would increase Navy investment and would be assured of continued industrial work at 32nd Street, and Kettner would have the Navy established on a site ideal for further growth into a "real" base.

The donation of ninety-eight acres to the Navy was approved by the city council, the deed presented in escrow to

the secretary of the Navy in September 1919 and approved by the voters on 3 August 1920. Secretary Daniels joined with Kettner in calling for $750,000 in the 1920 Naval Appropriations Bill for site improvements to "take over as soon as possible this property and put it in shape for repair of destroyers and other craft."[10]

On 7 February 1921 Kettner telegraphed the chamber that "Shipping Board instructs their western representative to turn over plant immediately. Admiral Welles should be notified." A week later, on 15 February, Welles took formal custody of the yard, buildings, and machinery.[11] The transfer of the marine railway from La Playa to 32nd Street was completed in February 1922.

If the newly constituted Pacific Fleet had provided the foundation for Kettner's strategy to bring a major new naval base to San Diego, it was the presence of the mass-produced destroyer that provided the catalyst for the ultimate breakthrough. The World War I U-boat threat had driven the need for large numbers of convoy escorts, construction that caused a massive glut of destroyers by war's end. In the four years from 1913 through 1916, the U.S. Navy had commissioned barely twenty-four destroyers; in the four years from 1917 through 1920, ten times that number were commissioned. When the Pacific Fleet came westward after the war, its rolls included 170 destroyers but demobilization meant that only a fraction of this number could be operated. The remaining destroyers were remanded into reserve where long-term berthing was needed.[12]

With its inactive destroyers moored helter-skelter around the harbor, the Navy moved quickly to consolidate. On 10 June 1921 Comdr. H. N. Jenson, commanding officer of *Prairie* (AD-5), was ordered to moor at 32nd Street and on 23 February 1922 U.S. Destroyer Base, San Diego was officially established by Secretary of the Navy General Order no. 78 with Commander Jenson designated as the base's first commanding officer. After dredging and the installation of mooring dolphins, sixty-nine destroyers were ordered to the new base by September and one month later another fifteen destroyers arrived. Tender *Buffalo* (AD-8) replaced *Prairie,* and *Buffalo,* in turn, was replaced by the newly commissioned tender *Rigel* (AD-13) on 3 January 1923 on which date Capt. H. L. Brinser of *Rigel* relieved Jenson of command of the base.[13]

Long, graceful destroyer hulls nested in groups of three or more and anchored in mid-harbor became the dominant fea-

ture of the harbor. The entire bay resonated to an exhilarating new tempo: destroyers dashed seaward singly at flank speed with "bones in their teeth" or sortied in formation as straight as if they were drawn on a string. Signal flags snapped in the breeze. The distinctive "whoop-whoop" of the siren and the deep-throated rumble of the ship's whistle blended in calliope precision. Small launches darted everywhere, dashing from fleet landing to quarterdeck, and then back again across the choppy harbor. At night, dark shadows moved silently in the harbor, invisible except for the twinkle of red and green sidelights or the occasional flash-flash of signal lamps.

Those who commanded these twelve hundred–ton greyhounds were a unique lot. Generally the products of the Naval Academy classes of the century's first decade, they had already witnessed tremendous advances in naval weaponry, tactics, and engineering and were not afraid to think broadly about new breakthroughs in naval aviation or wireless communications. They had cut their teeth combating the new threat of the submarine in the North Atlantic and favored the destroyer's independence, speed, and effective gunnery. They reveled in

After World War I Navy destroyers flooded the harbor and tied up at any convenient location. Reclamation of land to the west of Pacific Highway is well under way in this picture, c. 1919. *National Archives*

The first batch of reserve destroyers takes up residence at the newly designated destroyer base in 1922. Tenders *Prairie* (AD-5) and *Buffalo* (AD-8) oversee their brood. Thirty-second Street prominently connected the base with the rest of the city, forever earmarking the site to generations of San Diego sailors. *Naval Historical Center*

intricate, flank-speed maneuvers off Point Loma, gracefully pirouetting in unison, rooster tails churning astern and green water shaking from their forecastles. Once seasoned through the rigor of fast-paced destroyer exercises off San Diego they would rise to reach flag rank just when America would need their talents most in the furious battles that lay ahead during the Second World War.

On 1 November 1920 Capt. William Pratt assumed duties as Commander, Destroyer Force, Pacific Fleet and broke his broad pennant in *Brooklyn*. Plagued as it was by shortages in manpower and maintenance funds, the force could only keep 54 of over 150 destroyers operating. To meet operational requirements Pratt devised a "rotating reserve" system where one-third of the force would lie at the pier with only a bare maintenance crew; one-third would lie in the stream with 50 percent complement; and one-third would operate with a full complement. A surprisingly high state of readiness ensued

with all vessels moving from one group to another and crews many times assigned to different hulls.[14]

Pratt's star division was led by the flashy young commander of *Wickes* (DD-75), Lt. Comdr. William F. "Bull" Halsey. Halsey had the good fortune to have another top performer within his division, Lt. Comdr. Raymond Spruance, skipper of destroyer *Aaron Ward* (DD-132). It was during this period in San Diego that Halsey and Spruance established a lifelong friendship. Halsey "extolled Spruance in fitness reports for his skill as a destroyerman as well as for his character and brains. Spruance, in turn, admired Halsey's seamanship, his daring and his fighting spirit."[15]

Destroyer division officers and their wives were a close-knit, gregarious group with a reputation for weekend socializing fully as effusive as their aviator brethren. Many times, according to biographer Thomas Buell, Spruance and his wife were the only ones sober enough to keep things organized. "But

Capt. William V. Pratt (*center, with pipe*) and his staff while serving as Commander, Destroyer Force, Pacific Fleet in 1922. The small, quick destroyer became the predominant ship homeported in San Diego after World War I and its officers quickly gained a reputation for élan and dash. Pratt, who would later rise to Chief of Naval Operations, believed in close and informal relations among his staff members. *Naval Historical Center*

once in a while Spruance unwisely joined in their drinking. One Sunday morning he awoke with a hangover and a realization that his cherished Panama hat was missing. He had worn it the day before at a beach party and later that night when the group had caroused at a popular Coronado tavern. His wife went to retrieve it and it was returned with an explanation that it had been found atop a palm tree."[16]

At dawn on 8 September 1923, fourteen ships of Destroyer Squadron 11 under Capt. Edward Watson sortied from San Francisco and turned south toward their homeport of San Diego. By that evening, Captain Watson had arrayed his ships in a Form 18 steaming formation with ships in a column by divisions astern of flagship *Delphy* (DD-261). Spacing between ships was a mere 250 yards. A high-speed engineering trial at twenty knots was ordered along an intended track that took them straight down the central California coast within sight of land, then through the Santa Barbara Channel between the Channel Islands and the mainland, then west of Santa Catalina and finally to San Diego where they were scheduled to see Point Loma light at sunrise.

Watson was just shy of fifty, with graying hair, a bristly mustache, and an air of authority. He was a second-generation graduate of Annapolis; his father was a retired rear admiral who had served with Farragut at the Battle of Mobile Bay. Watson's excellent service record included command of the battleship *Alabama* and naval attaché to Japan.[17]

At about 2100, well after dark, *Delphy* reached her intended turn point and with two blasts of her whistle she led the squadron in a corpen turn to a new course of 095 to take them down the middle of the Santa Barbara Channel. The ships of Destroyer Division 33, following in line directly astern of *Delphy*, turned one by one—each conning officer carefully eying the "knuckle" of disturbed wake ahead that marked the turn point of the ship directly ahead to gauge his turn. First was *S. P. Lee* (DD-310), then *Young* (DD-312), *Woodbury* (DD-309), and *Nicholas* (DD-311). Astern of them nine more destroyers of Divisions 31 and 32 followed.

The squadron was acting exactly the way that destroyermen

By 1915 the tempo of Navy operations in the harbor was increasing markedly. Here a swift torpedo boat passes cruiser *Raleigh* in the stream as its officer of the deck observes from the foredeck. *San Diego Historical Society*

The doomed ships of Destroyer Squadron 11 lie among the rocks at Point Honda. From the top they include: *Nicholas, S. P. Lee, Delphy, Young, Chauncey, Woodbury,* and *Fuller. U.S. Naval Institute*

enjoyed—tight maneuvering, close disciplined formations at high speed, exacting response to maneuvering signals—the ships stayed rigidly in station despite darkness, despite a lack of radar, despite rudimentary navigation.

Within minutes of turning, *Delphy* disappeared from view into thick coastal fog and, minutes later, disaster struck. Going at nearly twenty knots, *Delphy* ran hard aground at Point Pedernales, known locally as Point Honda, just south of Point Arguello Light. Through faulty navigation, the formation had turned early, missing Santa Barbara Channel and striking a rocky outcropping of the California coast ten miles north.

All of the ships of Division 33 were quickly among the rocks. Whistles and sirens split the heavy night air in a vain attempt to warn others away from danger and searchlights tried to pierce the foggy murk. In all, seven destroyers were wrecked among the unforgiving rocks of Honda, and two others barely escaped, scraping bottom but extracting themselves before foundering. In the carnage of that evening, twenty-three would die and the loss of personnel and equipment at Honda would stand as the greatest American peacetime naval disaster to that time.[18]

At noon the following day, Rear Admiral Pratt, then serving as commander of Battleship Division 4, was playing golf at a San Francisco course during a short fleet visit when an orderly brought orders to proceed at once to Honda. He then traveled

on to San Diego to lead an immediate Court of Inquiry conducted at the administration building on North Island.

News of the disaster struck the tight-knit San Diego waterfront hard, as literally everyone knew someone in the crews involved. The press had a field day with stories of catastrophe and heroism. The tone of San Diego editorials was distinctly supportive, tending to focus on the relatively low loss of life and the heroism, teamwork, and patriotism that soon rose as the silver lining in the Navy's cloud: "Another high tradition has been added to pages already glorious. The destroyermen have shown generations of service men to come how those who go down to the sea in ships can meet disaster and turn it into victory."[19]

On 23 September more than ten thousand attended a memorial service at North Island with Adm. Robert Coontz,

Vice Adm. William L. Calhoun commanded *Young* during the disaster at Honda but was exonerated of blame at the ensuing courts martial. He later rose to command the Pacific Fleet's Service Force during World War II. Here in 1949, while sixty-five years of age, he holds his daughter Rosalie in Coronado.
Rosalie Calhoun

Destroyermen from ships of the West Coast Sound Training Squadron moored in a nest at 32nd Street, c. 1935. *Rathburne* (*left*) was one of the first ships permanently assigned as a schoolship for highly classified sonar training. *Naval Historical Center*

With the first buildings of the new Naval Training Station rising behind him, Rear Adm. Roger Welles dedicates the station with a brief ceremony on 1 June 1923. So rushed was the planning for the ceremony to meet Admiral Welles's departure date, that the station's prospective commanding officer, Capt. David Sellers, was not in attendance. *Naval Historical Center*

Commander in Chief of the U.S. Fleet, speaking. Shortly before noon, Destroyer Division 32 with *Kennedy, Thompson, Stoddert,* and *Paul Hamilton* stood out to sea. Survivors from *Young* and *Delphy* stood on the ship's fantails next to mountains of flowers. Once in Coronado Roads, with North Island's towers in sight, *Kennedy*'s rudder was put over into a tight turn and the formation swept into a circle at high speed. The flowers were then thrown astern into turbulent wakes to form "a wreath of color on the tossing seas." As one historian put it: "Their shipmates had lived in racing four-stackers, they had died in crashing surf. It was fitting that the gay flowers given the waters in their memory would toss in foaming wakes."[20]

Pratt had a tough assignment. Despite the generally sympathetic San Diego press that blamed bad luck and emphasized the heroic efforts of the crews, many chastised the Navy for faulty navigation and a flawed "follow the leader" mentality. "This is the worst job I ever had," Pratt described in a letter to his wife. "Most of these men are my friends. I commanded the force, am looked upon as a destroyer man and a friend of the organization. Yet I have to give it the biggest knock it ever had. . . . I have got to do this for the good of the Navy and because it is so."[21]

Pratt's conclusions were masterful, not citing fog or unusual circumstances as the accident's cause but emphasizing the time-honored responsibility of every commander to ensure the safety of his command and to practice sound seamanship, navigation, and shiphandling. "The traditions of the sea are strong, the ideals high, and the rules which seafaring men set for themselves are rigid and hard," Pratt carefully said. "Each Captain who loses his ship must bear a responsibility due to

that loss. Only by maintaining this standard can the high ideals and traditions of the Navy be preserved."[22]

Watson ultimately was found negligent at court-martial, was reduced 150 numbers on the captain's list, and was sent ashore. Several survivors, though, rose to flag rank, including Ens. Charles Hartman of *Farragut*, who would serve as commandant of the Eleventh Naval District in the 1950s.

The commanding officer of the *Young*, Comdr. William Calhoun, received a letter of commendation from the secretary of the Navy for "Coolness, intelligence and seaman-like ability. . . . Every member of the crew who reached the beach owed his life to Commander Calhoun." Calhoun would later command destroyer *Melville* and Destroyer Division 31 in San Diego and would serve for three years on the staff of the Eleventh Naval District. During World War II he commanded Service Force, Pacific Fleet, placing him in charge of all the fleet's logistics and naval shore-based establishments. He retired in Coronado as a full admiral.

Sixty years after the Honda disaster, the waters of Point Honda surrendered a final surprise for a Coronado family. A recreational diver amid the rocks and mire of the bottom discovered a 1906 Academy ring. The eighteen-carat-gold ring, crowned with flowing mermaids and graceful sailing ships, held a simple inscription on the inside: "William Loundes Calhoun, U.S. Navy." The ring was returned to Calhoun's widow in 1985. "When Mrs. Calhoun put it on, tears swelled up in her eyes," and it has stayed with the family since, a symbol of the history and tradition that are alive in San Diego.[23]

Pratt's rotating scheme of destroyer maintenance at the destroyer base proved its value after Honda when reserve destroyers quickly replaced those lost to the rocks. In mid-1923, the destroyer base was caring for eighty-four decommissioned destroyers; during 1924 seventy-seven destroyers were decommissioned and seven recommissioned. Destroyers were hauled up on the marine railway, their hulls cleaned of marine growth and rust and painted (many times with an orange-red paint undercoat that led to the public's nickname of "Red Lead Row" for San Diego's reserve ships). All machinery was opened, dried, and treated with oils or heavy coats of grease. Piping connections were blanked off to prevent flooding and fuel, and water tanks were drained and cleaned. When the Navy closed its submarine base in San Pedro during 1923–25, it transferred repair and upkeep responsibility of fleet submarines to San Diego.[24]

The destroyer base was also beginning to serve as the central Navy school site in San Diego for both trade instruction (for reduced-complement ships) and tactical training. A "Destroyer Staff College" was established to improve destroyer operations. Torpedo officers were trained at the Destroyer Force's Torpedo School beginning in 1923, and enlisted wireless operators received instruction at the Radio School there in 1924.[25]

With a flag officer in charge, San Diego enjoyed increased funding—good for the harbor but not, as it turned out, good for Rear Adm. Roger Welles. He quickly gained a reputation, wrongly, within the Navy Department for extravagant spending, causing the CNO to caution: "What I must impress upon you, Welles, is the necessity for economy in the district and the not asking for any money or anything of that character that is not absolutely necessary."[26]

The Naval Training Station's Main Gate. *U.S. Naval Institute*

Welles's call for a separate naval district designation for San Diego came to fruition on 26 January 1921 with the establishment of the Eleventh Naval District, with Welles remaining as commandant. The new Naval District stretched from New Mexico to the Pacific coast and included the six southern counties of California. Welles's first staff numbered only seven officers.[27]

Welles had maintained offices in North Island's administration building but planned to move to the new naval warehouse building under construction at the foot of Broadway. The original naval supply department in San Diego occupied office space at the destroyer base in early 1921. On 5 July 1921 the department moved to the third floor of Municipal Pier in downtown San Diego. Two weeks later, on 16 July 1921, the Naval Fuel Depot at La Playa was formally placed under the cognizance of a renamed San Diego Naval Supply Depot. The naval supply depot moved to the Fleet Supply Storehouse on 5 June 1922 on land donated to the Navy in 1920 by the city. The depot was formally commissioned as Naval Supply Depot, Naval Base, San Diego on 8 August 1922.[28]

Naval stores shipments quickly intensified during the 1920s, overwhelming the capacity of existing downtown piers. The Navy had entered into a "gentleman's agreement" with the city that allowed use of Municipal (Broadway) Pier until a new pier could be constructed. It took Congress over two years to act on the Navy's requirement (all the time allowing the Navy free use of Municipal Pier), causing a "considerable discontent over the present arrangement," and it was not until 1929 that Navy Pier was finally completed. Demand continued to outstrip planning and the Navy was to

The Naval Training Station in October 1928. Tent camps dot the station as barracks construction has not yet caught up to demand. *U.S. Naval Institute*

The regular weekly review of recruits at the Naval Training Station became a San Diego staple for over seventy-five years. *U.S. Naval Institute*

lease back Broadway Pier from the city in 1938. By 1942 the Navy had three piers available for the transshipment of wartime cargo through San Diego—Navy, Broadway, and the newly completed NSD Pier.[29]

In mid-1923 Welles received orders to relieve as commandant of the Fifth Naval District in Norfolk, Virginia—an assignment he bitterly opposed. "I feel that the remainder of my active duty should be at a station which Mrs. Welles prefers. As you know, she writes short stories and, as you may not know, she is an artist, having had many of her pictures in different exhibitions. At Norfolk, there is no art, no music, or no literature worthy of the name. In view of the above I should much prefer Boston to Norfolk."[30] In the end, reflecting his difficult relations with those back in Washington, Welles was peddled to Norfolk with his orders stamped: "this employment on shore duty is required by the public interests."

San Diego immediately recognized its loss. A lead *Union* editorial summarized the thoughts of many: "Because the Navy's business in the 11th Naval District was well carried on, the harbor of San Diego with its wide and safe shelter and its strategic importance was brought increasingly to the attention of the Navy Department. . . . Since Admiral Welles came here, the Navy has spent millions of dollars in this port—and more important than that—has signified its large purpose to develop one of America's great naval bases at San Diego. In all of this Admiral Welles has had his part."[31]

Welles missed by just two months the formal dedication of one of the jewels of his tenure—the new Naval Training Station. Bertram Grosvenor Goodhue's successful Spanish Colonial Revival style heavily influenced the design of the training station just as at North Island and the Naval Hospital. The Navy's original station design was arrayed along two axes, an east-west axis that would contain most of the barracks and instructional buildings, and a north-south axis featuring a large administration building tower facing the bay, in the same spirit as the Goodhue tower at North Island. Although the tower was never built, due to lack of funds, the other themes of simple arcades, red-tiled roofs, broad exterior surfaces of rough stucco, and breezy outdoor courtyards tie all of the Navy architectural designs of the period together.[32]

Rear Admiral Welles pressed for some nature of ceremony at the training station prior to his departure. At that small commissioning ceremony on 1 June 1923 Welles spoke before ordering that the station's first flag be raised. The formal dedication ceremony was a much more stylish affair, scheduled on Navy Day, 27 October 1923. Capt. David Sellers, the new commanding officer of the station, hosted the ceremony and retired congressman William Kettner delivered the dedication address. Sellers pointed to the donation of land that made the station possible: "it is particularly gratifying to me that the land came to us in this manner as it showed conclusively that we were wanted."[33]

Navy crews march in formation up Broadway past the YMCA on 7 November 1924 with their battleships anchored in midchannel behind them. Navy and civic reviewing officials would routinely stand on a narrow porch immediately above the building's front entrance. *San Diego Historical Society*

Sellers set out immediately to establish an efficient training institution even in the face of continued construction. His initial staff consisted of ten officers and fifty enlisted and, with the formal closure of the Goat Island training station in August, more than fifteen hundred sailors descended on San Diego for training. An additional 350 students were assigned to the Service School Command in courses that included preliminary radio, yeoman, bugler, and musician, and in 1924 the Navy's only Electrical School was moved to San Diego from the Boston Navy Yard. Sellers's first goal was to establish an efficient recruit-training program of sixteen weeks' duration— "boot camp"—that would begin by a three-week period for new sailors in a "detention camp" of canvas-covered tented barracks.[34]

One of Sellers's early priorities was to improve and beautify the grounds. Names such as John Paul Jones, Decatur, Truxtun, Preble, Chauncey, Dewey, Porter, and Lawrence soon differentiated streets, fields, and courtyards and helped the station reflect a distinct naval heritage that was unique in California for its breadth. John Morley, the long-time superintendent of Balboa Park, prepared detailed landscaping plans and a citywide Naval Training Station Tree Committee gathered small trees and scrubs for donation. By 1925 landscaping activity also included a small but notable golf course on the station's northeast corner that would ultimately be named "Sail Ho." Years later, future golfing legend Sam Sneed would help administer the course when he was assigned to the station as a specialist second class during the Second World War.[35]

The Naval Training Station would prove to be one of the great magnets of the San Diego naval culture, drawing to it all nature of farmboy, mechanic, workingman, and adventurer and introducing them to the delights of Southern California. To experience the training station was to encounter a mixed ambiance of heritage and purpose, wholesomeness and nurturing. One station commander described its mission as nothing less than "molding the best of American youth to the highest standards of manhood."[36] More than one veteran, now living comfortably in Pacific Beach, Coronado, or El Cajon, can nostalgically point to their days at the training station as the single event that would successfully shape their careers and form the starting point of dreams that would bring them back to the city in later years.

Among the cadre of young Navy destroyer officers who poured into San Diego for duty in the early 1920s was one already thoroughly familiar with the city. Although San Diego's population had tripled in the twenty years since he had first lived in San Diego as a boy, Ens. Stewart Reynolds found San Diego and Coronado comfortable and familiar in 1921 when he stepped down from the train at Santa Fe Station ready to report to destroyer *Stoddert* (DD-302). It was a picture remarkably similar to that of his father, Assistant Paymaster Wells Reynolds, in 1892.

Stewart had attended Lafayette and Yale, but when America entered the First World War he volunteered for naval training and was ordered to a minelayer. After the war he completed his degree at Yale, sought a naval officer's commission, and specifically asked for duty with the flashy destroyer force in San Diego.

His mother, Belle Reynolds, returned to Coronado herself in 1923, a widow. Wells Reynolds's naval career had been spec-

tacular, as he rose steadily in the Pay Corps until he was named inspector general with the rank of pay director, one of the three top positions in the Corps, in 1915. The Reynolds family (Wells and Belle, son Stewart and daughters Ruth and Eleanor) had moved to a large house outside Washington, D.C., and Wells was thrust into the hectic job of overseeing the pay concerns of a rapidly expanding Navy. Tragically, in 1917 Wells contracted cancer and passed away while still on active duty.

Stewart helped Belle and sister Eleanor settle in Coronado and one evening introduced his mother to a young daughter of a well-to-do Coronado family who had caught his fancy. Four years later, outfitted in dress blues, complete with long coat, epaulets, and sword, Lieutenant Reynolds and Miss Jane Keck would marry in Coronado's Christ Church.

Eleanor Reynolds had attended four different high schools, finally graduating from Coronado High School in 1924. As accomplished in many ways as her mother, Eleanor excelled in sports and enjoyed the extroverted gaiety of the 1920s, with its bobbed hair, rising hems, flapper slang, convertible cars, and the knock-kneed flailing of the Charleston. Dances at the Hotel del Coronado were a regular Saturday event, where many a young naval officer could be found in attendance, although Belle refused for a time to allow Eleanor to attend on consecutive weeks with the same beau.

Belle's protective nature notwithstanding, Eleanor enjoyed the flash and daring of the nearby North Island pilots and made friends with many at the field. Eleanor married a naval aviator in 1925 and years later enjoyed pointing to a 1928 group photo of North Island aviators. The air was one of jaunty confidence with aviators standing in front of their aircraft, arms crossed, some with leather helmets, some with slightly lumpy uniform hats. With a twinkle in her eye, Eleanor would say, "All three of my husbands are in this picture."

1924

The next morning we launched from *Lexington's* deck and headed for Point Loma, sticking out in the distance. Alex led us around the Point over the lighthouse and out across the strand below Coronado. We made a wide sweep, closed up in a tight formation, and roared back low over North Island. As we flew over the island, you could see the officers' and enlisted men's families standing out along the edge of the mat, waving and watching. We spread out in a V formation, slid back into sections, and turned back across the field to break up into three-plane groups and get down into the landing circle when our turn came. Those cars down there that lined the roads to the air station were full of families waiting for "daddy" to come home. We were back home!

Boone T. Guyton, *Air Base*

On 29 November 1924 the look of San Diego's waterfront changed forever with the arrival of what the San Diego media dubbed the "Deadliest Ship Afloat."[1] Deadly she might have been, but to the eye *Langley* (CV-1) invoked other less complimentary descriptions. Aptly and universally known as the "Covered Wagon" and later described as "unpopular, unlovely, unusual and ugly," the nation's first aircraft carrier was ungainly and top-heavy with a girder-supported aviation deck built high above a traditional superstructure. But as she took her place smoothly alongside North Island's dock, a new era for San Diego began.

Many of the Navy's impacts on San Diego have been either subtle in their execution or economic in their measure. The arrival of the aircraft carrier was neither. Carrier aviation boldly influenced the city's sense of self in a way that no mere measurement of dollars and cents can attest. In nearly every aerial photograph of San Diego harbor since 1924, at least one aircraft carrier can be seen. Every city event on the waterfront has for its backdrop the imposing gray-slab sides of an aircraft carrier; every harbor tour includes their description; every visitor arriving into Lindbergh Field spies a carrier even before touching down. The carrier is to San Diego as San Diego is to the Navy: prominent and inseparable.

The aircraft carrier boldly propelled San Diego to the highest tier of American naval bases. Beginning with *Langley,* most of the Navy's prewar carriers developed their airpower tactics—which would prove so dominant during the Second World War—in waters off San Diego. The San Diego Aerospace Museum estimates that over 114 different aircraft carriers have moored or anchored in San Diego since the arrival of *Langley.* No other naval base has been so central to carrier aviation; no other American city can take as much pride in its accomplishments as can San Diego.

During the interwar period naval aviation became the hub of the naval experience in San Diego, just as North Island is the focus point in any high-altitude photo of metropolitan San Diego. Pioneer aviators had been among the first to capture the public's fascination with the Navy and, in the 1920s and '30s, the aircraft carrier helped consolidate that appeal.

In 1920 the U.S. Navy identified the large collier *Jupiter* for conversion into the "experimental" aircraft carrier *Langley.* No one was exactly sure what aviators wanted—except that there had to be a deck that planes could land on. As a result, *Langley* represented a hodgepodge of ideas and designs. *Langley's* bridge was underneath the flying deck. The stack ultimately was hinged to bend away from the deck during flying operations. No hangar deck existed but aircraft would be assembled on the upper deck and lifted to the flying deck by a single rickety elevator. Cranes were installed to service floatplanes alongside.[2]

After two years of trials in the Atlantic, *Langley* was ordered to the West Coast and assumed flagship duties for Commander, Aircraft Squadrons, Battle Fleet at North Island.[3] For the next decade both she and San Diego would share nearly every advance in carrier operating doctrine that American naval aviation would employ. As important, the flower of young naval aviation would walk her decks or plan her operations. Marc Mitscher would be *Langley*'s air operations officer and later her executive officer; Jack Towers would act as executive officer and later commanding officer. Jerry Bogan, Duke Ramsey, Arthur Radford, Wu Duncan, Miles Browning, Put Storrs, Thomas Sprague, Jock Clark, and Frank McCrary would all help perfect aircraft operations from her deck.

Langley's operating tempo soon became comfortably familiar with San Diegans. In the haze of early morning she would cast off from North Island and head down the channel at a languid five to nine knots, hardly leaving a wake in the still water of dawn. Those on Point Loma would look up from morning tea to gauge her lazy progress and the occasional fisherman or harbor boatman would raise a leisurely wave of "good morning" to those on deck. Aircraft were rarely spotted aboard and her precarious lines spoke a degree of awkwardness that was in many ways disarming. A flashy destroyer or potent battleship might evoke visions of strength and authority, but *Langley* was less "deadly" than she was plodding, less "cutting edge" than eccentric.

Once clear of the channel, she would begin a busy day of pilot qualifications, usually within sight of Coronado Beach or the crest of Point Loma. By late afternoon she would be back in the channel, the lengthening shadows cast by the loom of the Point nipping at her stern.

"Firsts" came quickly for *Langley* in 1925. On 22 January VF-2 commenced landing practice off the coast, the first squadron trained to operate from a carrier.[4] On 2 April Lt. Comdr. Charles Mason catapulted off her deck while she lay at her North Island berth, demonstrating the first-ever flush-deck catapult launch of a wheeled landplane.[5] A week later Lt. John Price made the U.S. Navy's first night landing aiming for the tiny square of lights that outlined her deck.[6]

In 1921 the entire Pacific Fleet air force was based on North Island—consisting of thirty-six aircraft, an assortment of seaplanes and torpedo planes, and one lonesome bomber.[7] North Island was prized by the Navy as "the only place in Southern

Langley steaming slowly up channel, returning from flight operations off the coast in November 1924. *National Archives*

Langley preparing for flight operations off Point Loma, October 1927. *National Archives*

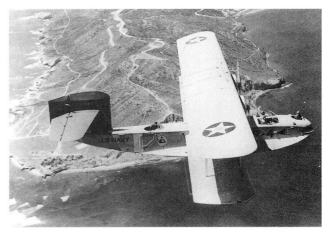

A Douglas PD-1 flying boat from VP-7B over the Point during October 1934. *National Archives*

A Curtiss R-6L floatplane uses the bay as a testing ground during September 1920. *Naval Historical Center*

California where level ground exists close enough to a deep water harbor to permit the direct interchange of aircraft, stores and personnel between ships and air base, and where seaplanes and landplanes can operate from the same base."[8] In anticipation of *Langley*'s arrival, a practice carrier-landing platform was constructed in the center of an open field on North Island in 1921. This three-inch-thick wooden deck served as an important element in an aviator's carrier qualifications and remained on the airfield until approximately 1927.[9]

Floatplanes were everywhere in evidence, "anchored" off their hangars or scooting like waterbugs in their takeoff runs. Innovative but fragile, they quickly caught the rancor of surface sailors. Arleigh Burke once commented: "No deck officer liked airplanes, because they got oil all over the damn decks and were always in the road."[10] By 1924 the first practice catapult for cruiser/battleship forces was installed at North Island pointing out over the bay, presenting new hazards for unwary San Diego Bay mariners.[11]

Before *Langley*, long-range patrol seaplanes were the pacing technology in naval aviation. In 1919 Jack Towers had commanded a flight of three Navy Curtiss NC flying boats in a historic first transatlantic flight. On 30 December 1920 twelve F-5-L and two NC flying boats left San Diego on a seven thousand-mile round-trip flight to Panama, the longest flight

ever made by a squadron of seaplanes. Capt. Henry Mustin had overall command, with the NC portion of the flight directed by Jack Towers from tender *Mugford*.[12] Beginning with the eye-catching newspaper headline, "Dash into Uncharted Airlanes between Here and Panama Set to Begin at 8am Today," San Diegans carefully followed the squadron's progress as it beach-hopped down the Mexican and Central American coasts, stopping for rest, fuel, and supplies in several protected bays en route.[13] The F-5-Ls arrived in Panama on 17 January 1921. Towers's NC boats didn't fare as well; both were damaged and abandoned during the lengthy flight.

San Diego was the national focus of another aviation breakthrough on 10 October 1924 when the massive *Shenandoah* (ZR-1), the first Zeppelin-sized airship built in America and the first rigid airship ever seen on the West Coast, reached North Island after a transcontinental trip from Lakehurst, New Jersey. *Shenandoah* arrived over North Island at 2248—a spectacular sight, looming in the floodlights as large as a battleship. Unluckily, an inexperienced mooring crew took over two hours to secure her and, in the jumbled process, allowed the airship's rear gondola to hit the ground, buckling a vertical girder.

The delay for repairs was an unexpected plus for San Diego as crowds of sightseers swarmed to North Island to observe the huge silver zeppelin. Six days later, on a raw and hazy morning, *Shenandoah* cast off, rounded Point Loma, and headed northward to rendezvous with the Battle Fleet on maneuvers off San Pedro.[14]

Shenandoah would return to San Diego on 21 October, approaching her mooring at 0500 atop fog that hid everything but the wireless towers at Chollas Heights and delayed final mooring until 1140. She refueled, reprovisioned, loaded 150,000 cubic feet of helium, and departed a day later for Fort Worth, flying eastward over Sweetwater Lake, Jacumba, and Yuma.[15]

As the twenties progressed, a flurry of aerial "firsts" titillated San Diegans: the first nonstop coast-to-coast flight terminated at Rockwell Field, the first midair refueling occurred between two Army planes over San Diego Bay, and the first regularly scheduled year-round airline route linked Los Angeles and San Diego. On 16 August 1927 a Navy crew in a PN-10 seaplane set a world flight endurance record of 1,569 miles and 20 hours 45 minutes by circling a course 101 times that had been laid out between Coronado Heights, the Chollas Heights radio towers, and the San Diego Brewery.[16]

In the midst of this concentration of aviation talent stepped a tall, bashful, young airmail pilot from Minnesota by the name of Charles Lindbergh, who came in 1927 to oversee the

Curtiss TS-2 floatplanes from VF-1 flying above *Langley* and North Island about 1926. *Naval Historical Center*

design and construction of the *Spirit of St. Louis* at the Ryan factory near Dutch Flats. During his stay Lindbergh developed a close working relationship with several naval aviators to learn more about cross-ocean navigation: "the naval officers are as fine a group of men as I've ever met," Lindbergh penned, "courteous, genial, intelligent."[17] When first completed, his aircraft was tested on the muddy parade field at old Camp Kearny and then was brought to North Island's bumpy, grass-covered field for final preparations. On 10 May the *Spirit of St. Louis* departed North Island on the first eastward leg of Lindbergh's historic flight.

In July 1926 naval aviation leaped forward with a congressional authorization of the first installment of a five-year, one thousand–aircraft program. American senior officers, such as Joseph Reeves, Ernest King, and Towers, were shaping this

breakout technology, and younger generations of swashbuckling naval aviators, aptly represented by Put Storrs, D. W. Tomlinson, Stan Ring, and Frank Wagner, were adding to the sophistication.

Opposite in career background, Rear Adm. Joseph Reeves and Comdr. Jack Towers were of surprisingly like energy when it came to accelerating the practical employment of aviation within the fleet. The intersection of their energies occurred aboard *Langley,* where Reeves used the carrier as a centerpiece of his operational experiments and where Towers served as executive officer and later commanding officer. It was an exciting time of new inventions and new discoveries at sea, and for four years Reeves and Towers involved *Langley* in every challenge, gradually making a fighting ship out of the heretofore "experimental" platform.

To most San Diegans, he was "Bull" Reeves, a nickname

In a photo that originally appeared in *National Geographic*, *Shenandoah* departs North Island to head northward on the morning of 16 October 1924. *Naval Historical Center*

surviving from Academy football days. Photographs show an aristocratic naval officer, thin as a rail, with a strikingly white, precisely trimmed Van Dyke beard and sleeves striped in gold braid. In the fleet he was a demanding man of action who had risen steadily on competence and was at ease with the rapid technological advancements of the day. His renown as a superb and knowledgeable speaker served him well and for years he was the most sought-after Navy spokesman in San Diego.

In October 1925 Reeves took command of the Battle Fleet's aircraft and broke his flag in *Langley*. He set diligently to work, due in part to his familiarization with *Langley*, a vessel he had commanded before her conversion from collier *Jupiter*. His first take on *Langley* air operations was not positive. The carrier was operating only eight aircraft when authorized to handle twelve. Reeves had his sights on thirty or more and started to press the pilots for more, despite protests of handling and operating safety.

With Towers's help, Reeves organized the deck-handling crews into small groups of specialists wearing specifically colored shirts: blue for plane pushers, brown for crew chiefs, purple for fuelers. He fine-tuned cyclic operations to discover the optimum tempo for landings and takeoffs and experimented with bombing tactics against a host of different targets and fighter tactics against opposing aircraft. During January 1926 *Langley* exercised as a convoy escort off Point Loma and six of its fighters, under Lt. Frank "Spig" Wead, successfully intercepted an incoming bombing strike, catching fleet commander Adm. C. F. Hughes's eye.[18]

Commander Towers was of like popularity with the press and frequently served as both the official and unofficial spokesman of the deckplate naval aviator. Despite his designation as Naval Aviator No. 3, Towers had to first qualify as a carrier pilot aboard *Langley*. Qualification in a single-engine Vought fighter, practice landings on North Island's wooden deck, and then familiarization bounces at sea consumed his days. After the requisite ten landings and takeoffs Towers proudly proclaimed himself "a qualified carrier pilot, the oldest and most senior in the world."[19]

Activities ashore on North Island had grown to match the increased tempo of carrier operations off the coast. "A typical North Island day for the whole station is long and noisy," spoke a contemporary account.

At about eight each morning, planes start taxiing down the line to the take off area and from then on an unceasing procession of take offs and landings is made. All day long the fighters, scouts and bombers roar up and away to their practice areas or to any of the numerous auxiliary fields. Planes circle the island, towing sleeve gunnery targets behind them. On the bay, seaplanes and flying boats dodge shipping as they take off and land amid wallowing tugs, maneuvering destroyers and anchored cruisers. From sunset until ten the roar of powerful Cyclones and Wasps abounds in the air as planes practice formation flying or make night-practice carrier landings on the field. One by one around ten o'clock their twinkling red and green running lights would round the edge of

Rear Adm. William A. Moffett, chief of the Bureau of Aeronautics, is welcomed to San Diego after *Shenandoah* is secured to the mast at North Island in October 1924. *U.S. Naval Institute*

Langley demonstrating her ability to launch a Douglas DT-2 aircraft while moored pierside at North Island in 1925. For a time, *Langley* was equipped with the Navy's first carrier deck catapult. *U.S. Naval Institute*

the golf course on the Coronado side of Spanish Bight to swing in over the patrol hangars and settle down on the field. Then it would be quiet again for the townsfolk.[20]

For every tale of experimental tactics or breakthrough firsts, there were other more interesting tales of derring-do that seemed to follow aviators of the period like frosty contrails. In 1925 Lt. Daniel Tomlinson was flying a Hispano Jenny over Coronado at fifteen hundred feet when his engine quit. Diving under telephone wires he flared with his last ounce of lift and landed squarely in the middle of a convenient city street. "When I came to an intersection there came a milk truck. I was going pretty fast, really charging down Olive Avenue. I just hopped over the milk truck and landed again on the other side."[21]

Donald Bates remembered downdrafts along the crest of Point Loma that "always created great interest" as the under-powered biplanes banked toward the ocean when departing

North Island. Higher on his interest list were the purposely low flights over the Deni-Shawn Dancing School for Girls near La Jolla that "produced minor heart murmurs" among the pupils.[22]

Lt. Stanhope Ring became a member of the tongue-in-cheek "Caterpillar Club" when he had to "hit the silk," bailing out of a burning aircraft over San Diego. Thousands on the ground watched as the pilotless plane circled over East San Diego for a further half-hour before crashing into a chicken coop. The next morning, the front page of the *San Diego Union* declared, "Wild Navy Plane Endangers Lives, Pilot Bails Out," but noted that not one of the three dozen residents of the coop had been lost.[23] Ring sustained second-degree burns that etched a faint outline of his aviation goggles on his face that stayed with him for the rest of his life. What control he was able to exert over his burning aircraft he attributed to a pair of

Three different types of lighter-than-air craft operated from the newly completed dirigible hangar at North Island in February 1921. For years the hangar was the largest structure on the station and the officer assigned to observe field operations stood his post on the building's roof. *National Archives*

thick leather gloves. Shortly after he reported this to the Bureau of Aeronautics, gloves became mandatory flight equipment for naval aviators.

During the fall of 1927 Tomlinson decided the Navy needed an aerial exhibition team. He picked Lts. (jg) Bill Davis and Put Storrs as his wingmen and began practicing over level open ground around Ramona and Escondido, where he hoped they would not be seen, as his activities were somewhat lacking in enthusiastic official endorsement. The result was the formation of the Navy's first aerobatic team, the precursor of today's Blue Angels. Storrs supplied a fitting name, the "Three Seahawks." Tomlinson led the team during its two-year history at fleet aerial parades, air shows, and the National Air Races.[24]

At the dedication ceremony for Lindbergh Field on 16 August 1928, 222 Army and fleet aircraft flew in precision formations over the field while Admiral Reeves broadcasted the show's commentary over the Pacific Radio Network. Mission Hills filled with cars, dignitaries crammed the reviewing stand, and fifty thousand San Diegans watched in person. At the end of the exhibition the Three Seahawks swooped in from the

This 1927 photo clearly shows the location of the practice wooden landing deck that was built in 1921. *U.S. Navy*

northeast. "We came in five to ten feet apart. Right in front of the grandstand, we did three successive loops and then our inverted stuff."[25] In articles effusive with spectacular adjectives, reporters anointed the stunt as "*the* real thriller of the day."

Hollywood enthusiastically recognized this newfound fervor for the naval aviator and many production companies journeyed to San Diego to collect film footage for upscale movies. San Diegans flocked to theaters to see movies such as *The Flying Fleet, Gold Braid, Hell Divers, Sea Eagles, Wings of the Navy,* and *Dive Bomber,* partially to thrill at the spectacle, partially to see their backyard from five thousand feet. During the filming of *The Flying Fleet,* Lt. Put Storrs was aloft when an aerial camera ignited the fabric of his F2B, nearly burning off his tail before he completed an emergency landing on North Island.[26]

By the early 1930s naval aircraft operations had become so important that the Bureau of Aeronautics was reporting that "the Fleet has been operating at San Diego a total of 219 land-planes and 150 seaplanes. San Diego is now the center of a far more intensive air activity than any other similar area in the world."[27]

Flying safety for this large number of aircraft proved to be a continuing challenge near the field. Not all aircraft were equipped with radios until well into the 1930s, and the air station itself did not have a radio-equipped control tower until 1939. A primitive control platform stood on the roof of the large balloon hangar. "By use of the wind sock and black diamonds, pilots could tell which way the wind was blowing.

There was a man on duty to report by telephone if crashes occurred. He was also equipped with a Very Pistol to signal an airplane *not* to land. The usual procedure was that the pilot made his landing approach and if all looked clear, he landed."[28]

No more important tactical advance would take place during this period than the perfection of the aerial dive-bombing attack. Dive-bombing tactics that would play so vital a role in the effectiveness of American naval air power in the skies of the Pacific during the coming war were, in large part, perfected in and around San Diego.

Adm. William V. Pratt, then Commander, Battle Fleet; Rear Adm. "Bull" Reeves; and Capt. Frank McCrary share a moment at NAS San Diego on 27 December 1928. *Naval Historical Center*

Many who would don a Navy uniform and be ordered to duty in San Diego during the 1920s and 1930s, such as these from VS-3, might never have come had it not been for Navy orders. Once introduced to San Diego's lifestyle and climate, many stayed, and many more began a drumbeat of positive word of mouth advertising that would soon spread San Diego's naval reputation worldwide. *U.S. Navy*

Aircraft line up for inspection in May 1932. *National Archives*

Lt. Stanhope Ring flying a Curtiss F6C-2 over San Diego in the early 1930s. *Susan Ring Keith*

Aerial attacks on ships at first featured low-level bombing runs that most pilots considered risky and inaccurate. During the summer of 1925 Lt. Comdr. Frank Wagner, hoping to improve on the dismal strafing accuracy of his squadron, pressed his pilots to approach their targets from successively higher altitudes. Soon, dives were being performed nearly vertical to the target with dramatically improved results.

Wagner invited Commodore Reeves to stand in the middle of the field on North Island and witness his squadron's evolving new tactics. One after another Wagner's aircraft swept down on the small party as Reeves carefully stroked his beard in thoughtful conjecture. Finally confident that Wagner was onto something, Reeves arranged for the squadron to demon-strate its new tactics on the Battle Fleet at sea. On 22 October Wagner's section spotted flagship *California* (BB-44) under way from San Pedro. Roaring down from twelve thousand feet Wagner came in so swiftly that the battleship could neither maneuver out of the way nor man its battle stations.[29] It was a moment of clear theater as battleship officers looked skyward, arms folded in futility and disgust, while gun crews scrambled for helmets and jackets. As the screams of each succeeding aircraft overcame the clang of the ship's gong, a moment in history was passing—in one sense totally unexpected, in another totally predictable. By the time Wagner had again reached the field, a dramatically new and powerful weapon had been added to the fleet's arsenal, honed to perfection in San Diego.

Later in 1927 Wagner's squadron continued to perfect new tactics by screaming down in near-vertical dives at Ream Field, much to the displeasure of a few nearby neighbors. In the 1930s dive-bombing was practiced against the radio-controlled target battleship ex-*Utah* in the waters between North Island and the Coronado Islands.[30]

The Navy's next aircraft carriers, the regal *Lexington* (CV-2) and *Saratoga* (CV-3), boasted displacements of thirty-six thousand tons, speeds in excess of thirty-four knots, twin-mount eight-inch guns, flight decks twice as wide as and one-third longer than *Langley,* and an aircraft complement double that of the nation's first carrier.[31] As converted battle-cruisers they were the largest and most powerful warships in the world.

Lexington sailed first to the West Coast to join the Battle Fleet in June 1928, and by January 1929 both carriers were actively engaged in rewriting naval tactical doctrine. Due to their size *Saratoga* and *Lexington* were both based with the fleet's battleline in San Pedro, but their striking silhouettes soon became familiar sights at anchor in Coronado Roads and each carrier's "air group commander would [regularly] lead their group in a salute over Coronado just prior to departing for the ship. It is sort of a parade gesture."[32]

On 7 November 1931, with San Diego's channel newly dredged, *Saratoga* gingerly made her way into harbor for the first time, becoming the largest vessel ever to enter San Diego Bay. *Saratoga*'s commanding officer, Capt. Frank McCrary, was the quintessential choice for this delicate task, as he may have known San Diego Bay better than any other naval officer of his era. By the time McCrary sat in his cabin while *Saratoga* swung at anchor in the turning basin off Municipal Pier, he had already spent a decade directing the Navy's fortunes in San Diego. First arriving with his family in June 1921, McCrary was named as NAS San Diego's third commander, relieving Capt. J. Harvey Tomb. Orders commanding tender *Canopus* and carrier *Langley* followed, as did a second tour commanding North Island from September 1927 to August 1930 (where he was credited as having been the first to employ asphalt on hereto-fore dirt or grassy aviation runways). Throughout this entire time the McCrary family lived almost exclusively in Coronado and North Island, except for a brief stint to Lakehurst when McCrary commanded both the air base and the dirigible *Shenandoah*. He retired to Coronado in 1935 and became active in local civic affairs but was recalled to active duty during World War II to command NAS Alameda. Three generations of McCrarys were naval officers who called Coronado home. Both of his sons became Navy officers, his daughter married one, and his grandson Capt. M. Shannon McCrary was a top Navy SEAL.[33]

With *Saratoga*'s toe in San Diego's door, knowledgeable naval officers began to argue the merits of basing large carriers in San Diego where they would be closer to their squadrons and to the headquarters of Aircraft, Battle Force. Since coming to the Pacific, the fleet's key ships, their admirals, and staffs had been based in San Pedro, with lighter forces based in San Diego. Los Angeles and Long Beach had relished the distinction, and rivalries that had always been palatable between San Diego and its neighbor metropolis had taken on a distinctive tint of blue and gold.

Rear Adm. Harry E. Yarnell and other members of the staff of Aircraft Squadrons, Battle Fleet in February 1932. Capt. Jack Towers, Yarnell's chief of staff, stands at his right; Lt. Put Storrs stands second from the right in the back row. *U.S. Naval Institute*

The Three Seahawks, established in San Diego as the Navy's first flight demonstration team—and precursor to the "Blue Angels"—swoop down on Lindbergh Field during an aerobatics display in August 1928. *National Archives*

The *San Diego Union* took up the call: "The bigger they come, the better San Diego likes them." The question of where to base carriers quickly ignited passions up and down the California coast. Chambers of Commerce, city leaders, congressmen, and naval officers all entered an intensifying battle of correspondence and rhetoric.[34]

In the end, Commander in Chief, U.S. Fleet, Adm. Frank Schofield recommended in favor of San Diego, setting an important precedent.[35] San Diego had long eclipsed San Pedro in its dedication to the aeroplane and now could capture the distinctive vessels that would carry them. Although *Lexington* and *Saratoga* would continue to call San Pedro home and that port would continue as the base of the heart of the American battleline, it was a "heart" already in tactical decline. As important (and in stark contrast to the support that San Diego had shown the Navy), Los Angeles commercial and oil interests were beginning to oppose Navy facilities on Terminal Island.[36]

Beginning in 1932 the intertwined naval trend lines of San Pedro and San Diego would begin to diverge, with San Diego continuing in ascendancy.

The first U.S. carrier built as such from the keel up, *Ranger* (CV-4), arrived in San Diego on 15 April 1935 and remained based at North Island until January 1939. Although smaller than the *Lexingtons*—a deficiency that would ultimately limit her operational usefulness—she radiated a distinguished air when viewed across the harbor at the Air Station dock. "Her great length was what you saw first, tied up with smaller ships all around," said retired Vice Adm. Lloyd Mustin. "Hundreds of portholes dotted her sides, she was quite a sight." After 1939 *Ranger* did not return to San Diego until July 1944, when she acted as a training ship for carrier qualifications and night fighter tactics.[37] "She had a particularly bad reputation for night landings," remembered Lt. (jg) Milton L. "Bud" Reynolds; "you couldn't see the deck until you had turned up-wind, tiny running lights, severe turbulence from the vortex of hot stack gasses."

During the 1930s Jack Towers stayed close to San Diego. After his tours aboard *Langley,* he assumed duties as chief of staff to Commander, Aircraft Squadrons, Battle Force; then on 30 June 1934 he was named to command NAS San Diego. It was a critical time for the station. With the arrival of the *Ranger*'s air wing in late 1934, North Island was packed to the gills with over a thousand aircraft, yellow wings and silver fuselages shining in the sun. Towers looked for innovative ways to support these burgeoning requirements with tight Depression-era budgets. Chefs from the El Cortez and Coronado hotels were invited to instruct Navy cooks and he prodded Navy wives, including Eleanor Ring, to raise pennies to build a new pool for the officers' club.

Towers's toughest challenge involved his relationship with the Army, which still operated the western half of North Island. As the Navy had expanded their operations on North Island,

so too had the Army. Congestion was endemic both on the field and in the air, especially during the summer fleet concentrations in Southern California waters.[38]

Both the Army and the Navy chaffed at joint ownership of North Island. J. L. Locke remembered that the Navy always scheduled full dress personnel inspections on Saturday morning, and inevitably Army planes would purposely come in for landings close enough to the inspection party to cover the entire group with clouds of sand.

Prodded by congressional hearings on the issue, the Joint Army/Navy Board recommended that the Army reestablish its California flying operations elsewhere. The secretary of war would have none of it. "The War Department is not agreeable to a transfer to the Navy Department of that part of North Island upon which Rockwell Field is located," he said bluntly and then funded a five-year $1.6-million development plan for Rockwell, including runway, roads, and officer quarters improvements.[39]

North Island in 1931, cruiser *Detroit* (CL-8) at anchor. *San Diego Historical Society*

Another in a long series of accomplishments for San Diego occurred during the morning of 7 November 1931 when *Saratoga* gingerly entered port and anchored off Broadway Pier, proving that large aircraft carriers could enter the harbor and be based close to their aircraft instead of at San Pedro. *National Archives*

Ranger (CV-4), the first American ship built from the keel up as an aircraft carrier, moors at North Island. Her handsome "modern" lines did little to offset her relatively small size, which quickly reduced her to limited roles. *U.S. Naval Institute*

Naval officers argued that the Army could move its Rockwell squadrons to March Field, fifty miles east of Los Angeles. Land in Alameda and Marin Counties was offered to the Army, as well as 769 acres of Chula Vista bayfront (offered in 1930) and a tract of land in El Cajon Valley (in 1934). All were turned down.[40]

The Navy argument was clear: "North Island is the only place in Southern California possessing landplane and sea-

plane facilities adjacent to a good harbor where aircraft, stores and personnel may be readily transferred from ship to shore and vice versa. There is no place to which the Navy can move, while the Army has several excellent fields in California."[41]

The impasse was finally broken when Rear Adm. Ernest King coordinated a land swap where three Army/Navy shared bases (including North Island) would go to the Navy in exchange for the transfer of NAS Sunnyvale (near Santa Clara) to the Army. President Franklin Roosevelt approved the concept on 26 September 1935 and issued an executive order a month later. At noon on 25 October 1935 Captain Towers formally took possession of all of North Island at a ceremony punctuated by the landing of twenty-eight *Langley* planes on the Army-built circular mat.[42]

Another Army-Navy quandary was playing out on Kearny Mesa that was to have equal impact on naval aviation in San Diego. In 1890 a large and generally flat area of scrub brush and gullies on Kearny Mesa had been purchased as a 2,130-acre ranch site by San Diego pioneer Edward Scripps and named Miramar.[43] During the First World War, with the help of Congressman William Kettner and local businessmen, the War Department purchased the ranch and established Camp Kearny as an Army Infantry Training Center that boasted a capacity of thirty-two thousand men. Its parade field was occasionally used as an Army aviation field, but by December 1918 the camp had been relegated to a demobilization center and would be closed on 31 October 1920, with most of its buildings dismantled and reused for local housing.[44]

As early as December 1920 the Navy's General Board had advocated the establishment of a lighter-than-air naval base in the vicinity of San Diego. In 1921 a special joint congressional committee went on record in favor of the Camp Kearny site for Navy airship operations. On 22 September 1926 enthusiasm began to build for a San Diego dirigible base when Rear Adm. William Moffett and Assistant Secretary of the Navy Edward Warner (accompanied like a shadow by a delegation from San Diego's Chamber of Commerce) inspected four promising sites. No recommendations were immediately forthcoming, but Moffett asked that weather instruments be placed at Linda Vista and Kearny Mesa.[45]

The attributes of Kearny Mesa for a dirigible base were obvious, and city officials and members of the Chamber floated a plan in September 1928 to provide a thousand acres for a shared municipal and military operating base, naval aviation buildings, and a Goodyear dirigible factory.[46] Rear Admiral Moffett applauded the city's zeal and the Chamber led a

Large squadron and air group formations were a common sight in the 1930s. Here F2F fighters from VF-3B of *Ranger* swing over Point Loma headed for the ship. *Naval Historical Center*

campaign to approve the necessary bonds by public vote. The nation was enthusiastic over the promise of long-range dirigible flights and San Diego was angling to capture the West Coast terminus for all nationwide airship operations.

On 2 April 1929 bonds for the dirigible base were passed by a stunning vote of nearly 5 to 1. "The voters recognized the value of making an effort to bring this new and profitable development to San Diego and they said so with an avalanche of votes."[47] During the spring and summer of 1929, a special West Coast Naval Air Ship Base Board was established to study ninety-seven potential sites from Puget Sound to the Mexican border for a new lighter-than-air station for the West Coast. The board was led by Rear Admiral Moffett and, on 29 July, arrived in San Diego to inspect Camp Kearny, Otay Mesa, and Ream Field "which had impressed them favorably."[48]

The competition was fierce, but the choice quickly narrowed to two sites for final consideration: Camp Kearny and seventeen hundred undeveloped acres in the Santa Clara valley near the small town of Sunnyvale. San Diego considered the

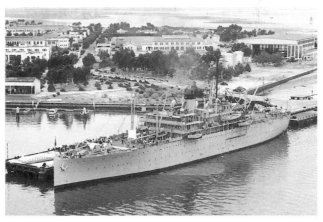

The unique seaplane tender *Wright* (AV-1) operated from North Island from 1932 to 1939 and became a mainstay for Pacific seaplane operations. Commanded by a long line of distinguished naval aviators including John Rodgers, Ernest J. King, Aubrey Fitch, P. N. L. Bellinger, and Marc Mitscher, she played a much more important role in the furtherance of naval aviation than her inglorious classification would indicate. *Wright* was renamed *San Clemente* in 1945. *U.S. Naval Institute*

The Army built its eye-catching circular landing pad and the Navy followed by blacktopping a portion of its ramp, but large portions of North Island still were open to "every man for himself" dirt and grass landings in this 1933 photograph. *U.S. Naval Institute*

Akron jumps upward out of control on 11 May 1932 while attempting to moor at Camp Kearny. Three enlisted linehandlers failed to let go of their lines in time to escape and two fell to their deaths. *U.S. Naval Institute*

decision "in the bag" and was stunned when the board voted for Sunnyvale. The vote had swung on Sunnyvale's supposed better meteorological conditions (Kearny was thought to have severe temperature inversions) and a desire to establish a naval aviation base in the San Francisco operating area, which lacked one. Rear Admiral Reeves had voted for Kearny, citing its strategic location and ability to support nearby fleet operations.[49] In deference to Reeves, the board ultimately recommended that Kearny be purchased as a *secondary* aircraft and airship facility.

The waters were further muddied when both the Navy's General Board and the secretary of the Navy publicly favored Camp Kearny in their written endorsements to the report, setting off a spirited civic fight between San Diego and San Francisco. San Franciscans accused Reeves of being influenced by personal interests, while those in San Diego pointed out that Kearny had fewer fog days than Sunnyvale and was closer to the strategic Panama Canal by 450 miles.[50] San Diego congressman Phil Swing introduced a bill on 6 December 1929 authorizing the Navy to accept a donation of one thousand acres at Kearny while Santa Clara's congressman introduced an opposition bill. Even William Kettner (in failing health) went

The huge *Macon*, moored at Camp Kearny's mast in May 1932. *Macon* had great success operating with fleet units off the Southern California coast (until her untimely crash off Point Sur), proving San Diego's contention that naval aviation should be based in close proximity to ships of the fleet. *National Archives*

The first of the famous Consolidated PBYs flies over the new Consolidated plant at Lindbergh Field, where thousands more would be made. *U.S. Naval Institute*

PBYs in squadron formation during January 1938. *U.S. Naval Institute*

to Washington to lobby for Kearny. In the end, the decision was for Sunnyvale, and a huge dirigible hangar was soon built on the saltflats of South San Francisco Bay with only temporary "expeditionary" masts planned for Kearny.

During the spring of 1932 the first of a new class of giant Navy airships, *Akron* (ZRS-4), a 785-foot dirigible specifically designed for fleet operations, flew to the West Coast to operate with the Scouting Force. At 0800 on the morning of 11 May *Akron* reached Kearny's mast. No rigid airship had visited the West Coast since *Shenandoah* in 1924 and ground-crew members (including many raw recruits from the Naval Training Station) were again slow and inexperienced. Just when it seemed that the mooring was finally under control, *Akron,* its helium heated during the long wait in the morning sun, lunged upward with a sudden accidental loss of five tons of water ballast. The ship's captain yelled to the mooring team to let everything go but three young sailors were carried aloft still clinging to the cables. Thousands on the ground gasped and newsreel cameras rolled. One sailor lost his grip and fell to his death from two hundred feet; a second plummeted from three hundred feet. The third sailor clung to the rope for an hour and a half before being pulled into the dirigible's cabin and safety.[51] It was not until 1900 that evening that *Akron* completed mooring. Her West Coast operations never recovered from the debacle and she never returned to San Diego.

On 16 November 1933 and again on 8 February 1934, *Akron*'s sister ship *Macon* (ZRS-5) flew over San Diego "and stopped traffic across town."[52] During the latter half of 1934 she frequently visited Kearny while engaged in fleet operations off San Clemente Island and as far south as Guadalupe Island. North Island squadrons operating from *Saratoga* took advantage of her nearby basing to develop scouting tactics with the giant airship. Tragically *Macon,* the last of the Navy's giant dirigibles, was lost during February 1935 in an accident off California's Point Sur.

Ironically, it was only after the death of the giant airships that the Navy's original interest in Camp Kearny was vindicated. Kearny had lost to Sunnyvale, in part due to the desire for a new naval air station near San Francisco. Now with no airships, the Navy surrendered Sunnyvale to the Army to concentrate its air operations at North Island due to its nearness to fleet units, exactly the argument Reeves had used in support of Kearny as a lighter-than-air station. A light covering of asphalt was applied at Kearny in 1936 to form a small landing strip on the old Army parade grounds. Three years later the Navy acquired a further 423.52 adjacent acres of land and began construction of a larger general-purpose runway that would open in late 1940.[53]

During the 1920s the cream of America's burgeoning aviation industry—military and civilian, engineer and pilot, mechanic and draftsman—flocked to San Diego. "[T]the very density of such talent helped establish a distinctive urban culture that would eventually render San Diego highly receptive to science and technology at its most innovative."[54]

The Navy was doing its part to develop the aviation trades in San Diego. Beginning in July 1919, the Assembly and Repair Department of the Naval Air Station began repairing fleet aircraft, an operation that would some day rank as the largest single aerospace employer in San Diego County. When Lt. J. Wilson, Construction Corps USN, first came to North Island to establish the department, the department's mission was to overhaul Liberty and Curtiss engines and repair Sopwith Camels and Hanroit Scouts. The 1923 annual report for the department listed overhauls of forty-nine aircraft for the year.[55] The Assembly and Repair Department would ultimately become the Overhaul and Repair Department in July 1948, the Naval Air Rework Facility in April 1967, and the Naval Aviation Depot in May 1987.[56]

Although men such as George H. Prudden, Edmund T. Price, Claude Ryan, and Fred Rohr would found fledgling San Diego aircraft companies, no name was to play a bigger role in the boosting of a San Diego aerospace industry than Maj. Reuben

H. Fleet. It would be the Navy that would play the most prominent role in bringing Fleet's dreams to fruition.

Rather than a scientist or inventor Fleet fancied himself a hard-nosed businessman with a history of developing practical and solid aircraft. While he was ambitious and aggressive (most competitors considered him ruthless), most navymen enjoyed his patriotism and well-designed aircraft.

Fleet had come to San Diego briefly in 1911 as a member of a National Guard unit patrolling the Mexican border, and in 1917 he returned to undergo flight training with the Army at North Island. During his San Diego flying days he once ditched in San Diego Bay next to an anchored cruiser and landed at the deserted parade field at Camp Kearny. After World War I he left the service to found Consolidated Aircraft in Buffalo, New York, and rose to prominence by providing front-line military trainers and by diversifying into the largely untested market of the long-range flying boat.

In 1929 Fleet's experimental long-range Admiral flying boat caught the Navy's attention. The improved Commodore, a commercial flying boat adaptation for luxury long-range routes flown by Pan American Airways, followed. The Navy, interested in the Admiral's potential and the Commodore's success, pressed Fleet to design a naval flying boat of increased

Yorktown (CV-5) at North Island, May 1940. *U.S. Naval Institute*

range sufficient to fly from the Canal Zone to San Francisco or from San Diego to Hawaii. Fleet named the resulting design Ranger (P2Y-1) and twenty-three Ranger flying boats were ordered by the Navy in an initial contract.[57]

In 1933, shortly after the first Rangers had been delivered, six aircraft were ordered to Pearl Harbor. Flying from the East Coast via Panama, these aircraft stayed in San Diego for three months preparing for the lengthy nonstop flight to Honolulu. On 10 January 1934 the squadron, under Lt. Comdr. Soc McGinnis (with assistant pilot Commander Marc Mitscher on board), took off from San Francisco Bay, formed into a dual chevron formation, and headed toward the empty ocean. For 24 hours and 35 minutes, the steady Wright engines propelled the six VP-10 flying boats along a cordon of six support ships until, late the following morning, Diamond Head could be seen in the distance. Fleet's Rangers had made the first successful nonstop squadron flight to Hawaii from the mainland, ushering in a new era of both naval mass flights to the islands and regular Pan American commercial service.[58]

Now flush with new seaplane orders, Buffalo's vexing weather became an ever-increasing problem for Consolidated. "The climate made it the most ungodly place you could possibly have from which to deliver flying boats," Fleet had said of Buffalo. So Consolidated began inspecting plant sites from Florida to Southern California, "for a publicly owned waterfront on a good, but not congested, harbor. And it needed to be in a city large enough to furnish a reasonable supply of labor and materials and of course with all-year flying weather."[59]

Thomas Bomar of the San Diego Chamber of Commerce became Fleet's constant correspondent, constantly reminding Fleet of San Diego's advantages in weather, location near water, and presence close to Fleet's principal customer—the Navy.[60] The match was, indeed, perfect, and during the summer of 1935 four hundred employees, their families, and 157 freight cars full of machinery relocated to California. Consolidated became San Diego's first major industry and, instantly, the city's single largest industrial employer.

Consolidated ramped up rapidly to full plant operations with a large new contract for Army pursuit planes and a new Navy contract for sixty new long-range flying boats built to a new design.[61] This new Navy patrol aircraft was the culmination of everything Fleet had learned in flying boat design and ultimately became the most successful flying boat ever built— the famed PBY Catalina.

On 20 October 1935 Fleet dedicated Consolidated's new 275,000-square-foot plant on the edge of Lindbergh Field. A prototype Catalina, flown to San Diego by Lieutenant Commander McGinnis, served as the ceremonial centerpiece and as a reminder of the link Consolidated had forged with the Navy. The first PBY-1 rolled off the San Diego assembly line in September 1936, only eleven months after plant dedication. The plane was towed across Lindbergh Field and launched into San Diego Bay for its maiden flight. VP-11 on North Island accepted the first PBY on 5 October.[62]

With PBYs steadily coming off Consolidated's lines, a flying boat training program was opened at North Island under Lt. Comdr. William McDade. The program concentrated on the unique complexities associated with the Catalina, including startup, taxiing, and takeoff procedures and the many tasks of its relatively large crew.[63] The plot of *Wings of the Navy,* a 1938 Warner Brothers film starring Olivia de Havilland and George Brent, concentrated on North Island's Catalinas, bringing the Navy, PBYs, and San Diego nationwide attention.

Several mass-formation flights of patrol aircraft to Alaska, Hawaii, and the Canal Zone took off from San Diego Bay beginning in January 1937, demonstrating—particularly to the Japanese—the long-range capabilities of the Navy's new patrol planes. Radioman Second Class Joel C. Stovall of VP-10 logged one of these flights as 20.7 hours San Diego to Honolulu on 18–19 January 1938.[64]

The revolutionary impact of long-range seaplanes on naval operations during World War II cannot be understated, and there was no site more central to the PBY's success than San Diego. The sudden increase in the range and dependability of the "Eyes of the Fleet" was fueled almost exclusively by Consolidated Aircraft products developed in San Diego. These aircraft became key ingredients in global strategies to thwart the Japanese advance across the mid-Pacific and to counter the German U-boat in the Atlantic. San Diego–built PBYs set the stage for the American victory during the Battle of Midway with their early discovery of the Japanese carrier force and relocated the German pocket battleship *Bismarck* in the mid-Atlantic, allowing Royal Navy units to surround and sink her. Across a decade ending in September 1945 2,387 Catalinas were delivered by Consolidated to the United States and other Allied navies.[65]

During the 1920s and '30s tens of thousands arrived in San Diego with families in tow and Navy orders in their back pocket. New systems of paved roads, such as the Lee Highway and Routes 80 and 90, guided them to San Diego. Once in San Diego they settled in homes that seemed to curl up comfortably around the bay from Point Loma to Bankers Hill. Navy

P2Y Rangers of VP-10 trained in San Diego for six months before their first-ever mass squadron flight from the mainland to Hawaii on 10 January 1934. *San Diego Aerospace Museum*

families stayed in close touch, sharing the bonds of common experience. There was even a directory, published like a phone book, listing all active duty and retired officers in San Diego by name, address, phone number, and ship.

The community of Coronado seemed particularly attuned to the tempo of Navy life. Many young naval aviators or fleet officers shared trim rental flats or established family homes in order to commute either to North Island or to ships at anchor from handy fleet landings. They shared the sociality of the island with glamorous resort-goers and found the mix a winning one, with most tourists curious about the sleek warships anchored in the harbor or the daring airmen above, and most naval officers and their ladies frequently sharing in the pomp and luxury of high society.

"You can board a ferryboat, cross the bay between hurrying destroyers and cruisers, and drive out into the little town of Coronado," read one account of the day. "More than seven-tenths of this quiet little resort is taken up with the homes of the naval officers from the air station, who have only to drive across Spanish Bight, a backwash from the bay, in order to be on base. Here, along palm-bordered streets, Navy wives stop to chat and discuss the affairs of Navy life as only Navy wives can. Along the sand beaches and on the tennis courts, Navy juniors romp amid the roar of 'daddy's squadron coming up the Strand.'"[66]

Coronado's popularity as an attractive residential area for Navy families swelled in the early 1920s with the arrival of many aviation and destroyer officers. Midshipman Ralph C. Alexander (USNA '18) had first met his wife-to-be, the daughter of Coronado's mayor, when the midshipmen practice squadron stopped in San Diego during 1915. By 1922 Alexander (now a lieutenant and flag secretary on an admiral's staff) had settled with his wife on Encino Row in Coronado and the couple was expecting their first child. With the ferries closing down at about 11 P.M. and no hospitals on the island, expectant Navy wives would normally move across the bay for the last few days to be sure of making the hospital. As fate would have it, Alexander's wife went into labor unexpectedly early and in the middle of the night. Alexander frantically phoned the flagship moored in the bay and a Naval Academy classmate dispatched the admiral's barge to the officers' landing on Coronado. Richard G. "Dick" Alexander was born aboard the barge in midchannel shortly after his mother stepped aboard. Dick Alexander would later enter the Navy himself, serving in seven destroyers and rising to captain, but always tried to keep the story a secret to avoid a feared notoriety.[67]

In 1930 Coronado had a population of 5,424 and the local *Coronado Journal* kept everyone appraised of bridge parties, polo results, new residents to the island, and the vacation voy-

Rosarito Beach, south of the border, was a favorite destination for naval aviators, their friends and wives in the 1920s and '30s, partly to avoid the restrictions of Prohibition. Eleanor Reynolds Ring stands at right. *Susan Ring Keith*

ages of the social elite on outings and voyages. While Navy couples could depend for their own entertainment on beach parties, costume socials, uniformed balls, and even the occasional sojourn to Rosarito for sun and cocktails, young naval officers could be counted at Sunday afternoon tea dances at the Hotel del Coronado. "Almost all naval officers in residence in San Diego had at least the opportunity to become instant socialites, representing as they did the cream of the city's population."[68]

San Diego's vibrant connections with aviation as the "City of Wings" have been long chronicled but it has been naval aviation that has provided the city the centerpiece of this heritage.

Across eras portrayed by hydroaeroplanes, long-range seaplanes, and jet fighters, one consistent image continues to inspire and connect the city with the glamour and might of maritime airpower, and that is the aircraft carrier. San Diego's memorial to this most powerful weapon in naval history stands today fittingly at the old Fleet Landing along Harbor Drive, where a solemn gray obelisk stands with both the names of every flattop that has sailed under the Stars and Stripes etched on its sides and the noble words: "Powered by the human soul, these ships changed the course of history."

1935

We of this naval harbor cannot help but notice how the popularity of the officers and men, the popularity of the navy in general, rises and falls, rises and falls, in exact proportion to the rise and fall of the tumultuous conditions on earth. And right now, of course, the navy is most popular indeed.

Max Miller, *Harbor of the Sun*

President and Mrs. Franklin Roosevelt, like so many others, journeyed to San Diego in 1935 to visit the California Pacific International Exposition in Balboa Park. But as Mrs. Roosevelt headed toward the Exposition, the president escaped to tour every corner of the Navy's rapidly expanding presence in San Diego. Roosevelt's fondness for the Navy during his whirlwind visit of 2 October showcased much of the sense of what the Navy represented in San Diego before the war. Everywhere he went he saw signs of the robust "urban partnership" between Service and city that had flourished in the twenty years since his visit as assistant secretary of the Navy. The Navy had clearly consolidated its gains in the city and expanded its infrastructure around the harbor—and San Diego had reaped the benefits.

Leaving the Hotel del Coronado that morning, the president headed for North Island in an open car along Coronado streets packed with well-wishers. There, Jack Towers, rigged to the nines in dress blues and ceremonial cocked hat, warmly greeted the president, continuing a familiarity that had begun in 1913 when Towers had taken Roosevelt aloft for his first military aircraft ride. Planes were parked wingtip to wingtip and sailors hung from every window, emphasizing for all the cramped conditions that had led to the Navy's acquisition of Rockwell Field from the Army. Roosevelt then crossed the bay,

crowded with anchored destroyers, visited the Marine Base, and finally arrived at the Naval Training Station to review recruits at calisthenics.[1]

At noon the president attended a private luncheon with city and military officials, including Admiral Reeves, and that afternoon addressed fifty thousand at Balboa Stadium. Later, the president boarded *Houston* (CA-30) at Broadway Pier and conducted a dazzling naval review of 129 ships and over four hundred aircraft off Point Loma. "There was no mistaking the keen interest displayed by President Roosevelt who stood out in the full force of the wind as the *Houston* plowed across the seas," commented one observer.[2] The high-powered visit proved to be both a naval and a San Diego tour de force that emphasized the genuine link between Navy and city at every turn. Stirring as it was, the visit also addressed the practical, with historian Kenneth Starr speculating that "Roosevelt's delight in his San Diego visit together with his concern for the ongoing well-being of the Navy in that town, had a strong connection with the $6 million in WPA projects that subsequently flowed into the city."[3]

The theme of the 1920s and '30s was clearly "consolidation," as the Navy built upon two decades of gains won from a city ready and willing to accommodate. By the time that President Roosevelt inspected San Diego's cluster of naval facilities, the city had already surrendered one-third of its waterfront and an important sector of its large city park to the Navy. In return, San Diego could regally claim the distinction as the second largest naval base in the country and the main Navy home base on the West Coast. More than just bragging rights over San Diego's rivals in Los Angeles and San Francisco, Navy ships and personnel were also bringing San Diego important economic stability during the years of nationwide Depression.

The Navy's concentration in San Diego had occurred neither overnight nor by accident. Once it had a beachhead, the Navy expanded in slow, measured, and purposeful steps, slowly tightening its hold, ship by ship, square mile by square mile. During the mid-twenties, the Navy transferred its submarine base from Los Angeles to San Diego, and a part of the fleet's cruiser force soon followed after a storm battered ships at anchor inside the Los Angeles breakwater. Fleet aircraft operations swelled at North Island while being abandoned in San Francisco. Fleet communications and supply operations followed the fleet's ships and aircraft and began buildups of their own in San Diego. The Navy of the 1920s and '30s was con-

solidating its forces to reap benefits of efficiency and cost savings, reversing a trend of two decades to spread its largess equally along the Pacific Coast.

Three broad international features of the 1920s and '30s influenced the face of the U.S. Navy, and each played to San Diego's advantage. First, to contain Japanese ambitions, the United States routinely assigned its newest and most powerful ships to Pacific coast bases.[4]

Second, in the wake of the First World War, a host of international naval agreements restricted unfettered naval buildups. But treaty limits on warships tended to concentrate on capital ships (battleships and aircraft carriers) of the world's largest naval powers, and not the cruisers, destroyers, and smaller warships in the fleet that called San Diego home.

Finally, as the era of treaty limitations ended and with Franklin Roosevelt in the presidency, Navy appropriations showed a solid up-trend every year from 1934 to 1939. Thus, naval forces assigned to San Diego held their own during lean treaty years and increased proportionately during years of better appropriations. More planes and ships meant larger bases

Three *Omaha*-class light cruisers at anchor in midchannel, December 1934. *National Archives*

Ships of the combined Atlantic and Pacific Fleets anchor in Coronado Roads in the mid-1930s following a fleet problem. *San Diego Historical Society*

and airfields, and by 1935 the Navy had already signed leases on eleven different satellite airfields in San Diego County.[5]

New naval installations generally require large and inexpensive tracts of land; access to protected anchorage; flat, open water for seaplanes; and unencumbered airspace for air training operations. In San Diego, still a relatively undeveloped city along an untouched bay, these attributes were abundantly available. As these facts, long grasped by local officials, became increasingly understood by distant naval planners in the 1920s and '30s, an unwritten "partnership" developed where city fathers generously traded protected anchorages and waterfront installations for protected economic growth and cultural stability.

The Navy held up its part of the bargain and, in short order, "transformed San Diego politically, economically, and socially within a decade after World War I, and in the process elevated a small, struggling town in a remote location with precious few natural assets to cityhood and ultimately metropolitanism."[6] The Navy provided San Diego with an economic foundation against the worst of the Great Depression, populated the city with a positive paycheck-every-payday population, and helped prime the pump of technological growth that was to serve San Diego so well in the years to come.

San Diego navymen and their families would fan out to the four corners of the world and give San Diego that most precious of all commodities, a worldwide reputation for agreeable weather and a healthful and salubrious lifestyle. And Navy servicemen would remember what they saw in San Diego and come back to stay.

San Diegans never avoided their association with the Navy. Here, in the 1938 Rose Parade, the city proudly linked its identity to "Our Navy," with Mayor Percy Benbough riding escort astern. *San Diego Historical Society*

James Brown joined the Navy in 1916, a time when African Americans could serve only as cooks or stewards. During World War I he served aboard the gunboat *Wheeling,* the cruiser *Des Moines,* and the hospital ship *Comfort.* In 1920 the Navy brought him to San Diego, where he bought a house on Webster Avenue. Brown retired from the Navy in 1936 and, comfortable with his surroundings and with the trade the Navy had taught him, launched a concession at the local Navy

A U.S. Geological Survey chart of San Diego Bay in 1930 showing the expanding naval presence from Oneonta near Imperial Beach to La Playa and the Naval Training Station. North Island has not yet benefited from the harbor dredging that would fill Whaler's Bight and Spanish Bight and round out its northern shore. *San Diego Historical Society*

Dredging fill is already starting to round out the shores of the bay by June 1932 and in the distance the open area that would someday be called Miramar can be seen. *U.S. Navy*

commissary. Within a year, he opened a fish market and, later, he added a grocery store, meat market, and café. By the turn of the century his twenty years in the Navy stood as not even a fifth of his 105 years, but his contributions to the community, his San Diego roots of eighty years longstanding, and his twenty grandchildren, thirty-one great-grandchildren, and sixteen great-great-grandchildren spoke volumes of the type of sustained impact the Navy could wield in a locale.[7]

The glue of this Navy-city partnership was a firm determination to be "best of friends"—a goal that both sides worked resolutely to uphold. "The history of the establishment and development of the Naval Base at San Diego has been a continued story of pleasant relations between federal and municipal governments and civilian and military citizens," a senior naval commander said in 1930. "The Navy's greatest need is friends," Rear Adm. W. T. Tarrant added during the 1935 Expo-

sition, "and we have them in the citizens of San Diego, who realize the permanent asset represented in the naval training station, marine base and all the other activities that make up the establishment."[8]

The Navy looked to ceremony and circumstance and played public relations spectacles to the hilt, nearly always well received by appreciative San Diegans. On 4 August 1923 command of the entire U.S. Fleet was transferred at San Diego in a glittering ceremony on the cruiser *Seattle*. On 12 March 1925 the Navy poured a never-before-seen 160 ships and seventeen thousand bluejackets into San Diego for a Fleet Review, winning headlines that read, "Greatest Battle Fleet Ever Seen in Pacific Anchors Here."[9]

When the Zoological Society of San Diego needed assistance in July 1927 to bring the old sailing ship *Star of India* to San Diego for display, the Navy dispatched a group of naval

By the mid-1920s the bay was deep enough to allow entry by heavy battleships. *California* (BB-44), flagship of Commander, Battle Fleet, maneuvers past the harbor fortifications at Ballast Point. *Naval Historical Center*

reservists (including maritime historian Jerry MacMullen), an NC flying boat, and the minesweeper *Tern* to assist, bringing the city's most famous maritime symbol around Point Loma at the end of a Navy towline.[10]

On 10 June 1935 Navy Day at the exposition brought forty-eight warships and fifty thousand bluejackets to the city. Crowds from La Jolla to Point Loma watched the fleet's arrival and a flyover by massed aircraft from four different carriers. Two months later 115 warships of the Pacific Fleet, returning from a cruise off Alaska, passed off San Diego in a column fifteen miles long.

The Navy scheduled a visit by the celebrated sailing frigate *Constitution,* "Old Ironsides," between 21 January and 16 February 1933, to wide enthusiasm and acclaim. "They lined Broadway Pier for a chance to board the massive oaken relic. Trainloads of school children and other visitors came from inland towns to see the legendary ship, bands played spirited marching music on the dock, a dirigible floated overhead and flags flew in the spanking breeze."[11]

With over one-third of its citizens on the Navy's payroll by 1930 San Diego's elected representatives became some of the Navy's best Washington allies. Lobbying strenuously for more resources and a larger fleet, all in the name of national security, San Diegans helped the Navy fight for adequate budgets in the lean 1920s and '30s, further tightening the bonds of the Navy-city partnership.[12]

The interlocking nature of Navy and city goals was vividly

demonstrated by a continuing string of dredging and harbor improvement projects. Dredging project followed dredging project with regularity as comforting as the seasons. Aerial photos recorded the march of progress, year after year, as fresh deposits of fill slowly rounded the edges of North Island, reclaimed the marshlands along the harbor's northern curve, and added to Coronado's beaches. In 1921–23 the federal government dredged an approach to Municipal (Broadway) Pier in exchange for land on Dutch Flats. During 1923–24 six million cubic yards were dredged to deepen shipping channels, including a sixteen-foot channel for the destroyer base.[13] In 1928 a $650,000 city bond issue helped reclaim tidelands for a downtown airport site.

The pace accelerated in the 1930s, with over $6 million earmarked for dredging. In 1931 the turning basin opposite Broadway Pier was deepened to thirty-five feet for the Navy's new classes of aircraft carriers and, not by accident, for large new classes of commercial vessels. More dredge material was deposited along the north and western shorelines of North Island during 1933 to 1936, including the filling of Whaler's Bight.[14]

Robust as federal investment was, appropriations for harbor improvements were only the most visible peak of a remarkable infusion of investment into San Diego during the 1920s and '30s that influenced the city economically and culturally. In 1925 an average of fifteen thousand servicemen were based in San Diego drawing an annual payroll of between $18

The Public Works Administration (PWA) and other Depression-era programs funneled millions of dollars into San Diego naval bases on projects such as this mess hall and barracks built at 32nd Street. *National Archives*

Four pipers moored in San Diego Bay, a common sight during the 1930s: *Barry* (DD-248), *Bainbridge* (DD-246), *Reuben James* (DD-245), *Williamson* (DD-244), *Fox* (DD-234), *Lawrence* (DD-250), and *Hovey* (DD-208). *U.S. Naval Institute*

and $21 million, with expenditures for food and naval supplies adding an additional $18 million. By 1934 total Navy capital investment in San Diego had risen to $28 million, with an annual naval payroll of $30 million.[15]

The clearly visible economic dislocations of the Great Depression magnified the importance of naval investment. With relatively little manufacturing, naval investment in San Diego loomed large in its relative importance—helping to buttress the local economy against the worst of the Depression. Still more federal spending headed San Diego's way as part of Depression programs to stimulate business. During 1935–37 $252,000 in WPA funds was earmarked for the destroyer base. Further improvements surfaced at the Naval Training Station and improved floodlighting, hangars, living quarters, and shops were targeted for North Island.[16]

Blue-and-gold dollars fed a broad spectrum from repair and victualing contracts to out-of-pocket money spent by sailors at shops along Broadway and Rosecrans. The number of tailor shops exploded. Every sailor knew that tailor-made uniforms were the preferred alternative to the baggy-looking regulation uniforms of the period and many a bluejacket

would lay out a hard-earned paycheck on nautical finery.[17]

The fleet's annual training routine cycled the fleet in and out of San Diego, and ships coming and going for maneuvers became an increasingly common sight. "At seven the destroyers and cruisers started to slip quietly out of the bay. They filed out Indian fashion in a long unbroken line, through the narrow channel and out around the Old Spanish lighthouse toward the open sea. Crowds of wives, families and relations lined Ocean Beach in the damp, gray early-morning mist, straining to see 'papa's' ship as it stole out around the breakwater, freshly painted and in top shape for the war games."[18]

Beginning in November 1930 fleet "type" commanders were named, including a Commander of Destroyers and a Commander of Cruisers for both the Battle Force and the Scouting Force. With San Diego the site of both the destroyer base and most of the destroyers in the Pacific, the type commander's staff spent most of their time in San Diego and established a variety of new schools in San Diego such as Gunnery School, Sound School, and Battle Force Torpedo School. By establishing type commanders in San Diego, a practice that continues to the present day, a continuing influx of resources

Destroyer divisions return to port and swing around Whaler's Bight across from Ballast Point in April 1923. *U.S. Naval Institute*

was guaranteed to support the ships under the type commander's administration.[19]

Each of these events helped sustain an already solid Navy–San Diego partnership and helped San Diego see itself, in the positive sense of the word, as a company town—a "Navy town." The Navy had grown to be a constant force in nearly every facet of everyday San Diego life. Large gray ships sat regally in the harbor, sailors browsed downtown entertainment districts, morning brought the "whoop, whoop, whoop" from destroyer whistles, and afternoon drew the powerful clatter from military warplanes overhead.

Beyond the tremendous economic and physical growth wrought by its presence in San Diego, the Navy was also changing the social character of the city. "The Navy is integrated into this community more completely here than in any other American port," the *Union* was able to say.[20] In an accelerating trend during the 1920s and '30s, former navymen began appearing at all levels of government or entered important local businesses and significant organizations such as the Chamber of Commerce, charity boards, or arts associations.

The tone of the citizenry was nearly always positive toward the Navy. Many correctly considered the Navy an economic savior and far more looked at the bluejacket downtown or the Navy family next door as a feature of the community that helped make San Diego unique and appealing. Nearly everyone could agree with the editors of San Diego newspapers that "[e]very San Diegan can . . . subscribe to that fair and courte-

ous attitude toward men of the Navy which has already made San Diego a pleasant home city to thousands of man o' warsmen who are permanently stationed here. . . . [T]he nation's defense depends finally upon the men who man the ships and it is a privilege to make them welcome."[21]

In return, Navy officials were nearly universally appreciative. Adm. "Bull" Reeves emphasized the obvious when he said, "I know of no city [other than San Diego] where the people are more intelligently appreciative of the service of the Navy to our country. I know of no city where the Navy in its work has received greater moral and material assistance."[22]

But as San Diego and Coronado became major bedroom communities for the officers of Navy ships and aircraft squadrons, similar trends among the crews of these same ships and squadrons were still many years in the future. During the 1930s the vast majority of bluejackets were unmarried and lived aboard ship or station. There, they frequently slept in hammocks, washed, dried, and ironed their own laundry, and ate in the same compartment as they slept. The majority of enlisted were assigned to a single ship for lengthy periods of time. "Without wives to encourage them to seek shore duty from time to time such men were comfortable on board, especially when they had become senior enough to live in the ship's chief petty officers quarters. They liked what they were doing and the ship and the Navy was delighted to have men who were content to stay where they were."[23] One example was Chief Watertender Clem "Maw" House, who reported aboard *Ari-*

zona in September 1921, served a while, left briefly, and returned aboard in June 1925. He then served continuously in *Arizona* until killed in action on 7 December 1941.

To the enlisted crew, San Diego was not as much "home" as it was a liberty town—a place for relaxation, fun, or a touch of excitement. Streetcars provided ready transportation to the zoo or the beach. The YMCA, which sat squarely on Broadway two blocks from Fleet Landing, served as an important portal to the attractions of downtown. There, bluejackets rendezvoused to concoct evening plans or study announcements of the city's happenings. Coffee and doughnuts were the YMCA's main commodity, and reading, games, cards, or sing-alongs its main pastime—all officiated by battalions of pretty young girls.

The Chamber of Commerce—that, of course, had a hand in bringing so many navymen to San Diego in the first place—was also a major sponsor of their entertainment. During 1936 Chamber records listed twenty-five "entertainments" for military men attended by 16,672 people. In 1937 the Chamber staged forty-seven social events for the Navy attended by 20,439.[24]

By walking up Broadway, accompanied each step of the way by chants of "Hey, Sailor" or "Have a book of matches," sailors on liberty could sample bowling, shopping, movies, or Big Band dance clubs all within a few blocks. Sodas were a nickel and mugs of beer could be captured for between ten and twenty cents. San Diegans mingled easily with sailors. Said one bluejacket, "When we were with civilians it was very fine, cafés, dance halls, and that sort of thing. I didn't notice any negative feeling."[25]

The Stingaree red-light district provided a constant, if relatively expensive, offering that did little to alleviate the stereotype image of the late-night "drunken sailor." Although the worst of the bawdy houses of the district had been demolished in 1912 in a city-ordered cleanup—including such establishments as the Pacific Squadron Hall, Yankee Doodle, the Dewey, and the Red-White & Blue, which suggested a connection with, or at least an attraction for, naval personnel—the district's entertainment reputation survived for decades, sustained by word of mouth around the fleet.[26]

Inevitably, crowds of "shipwrecked sailors" would make their way gingerly back to Fleet Landing in the morning's wee

The American battleline in review off Point Loma during September 1935. *National Archives*

The most powerful ship of the early U.S. Navy enters the channel while the most powerful ships of the prewar Navy lie at anchor in Coronado Roads. *Naval Historical Center*

hours. Shore Patrol would variously assist or enforce. Groups would be "singing the usual Navy songs that seemed to go with almost any party: Bell bottom trousers, coats of Navy blue / He wants to climb the riggin' like his daddy used to do . . ." Variations in lyrics would multiply in direct proportion to the lateness of the hour.[27]

In 1926, for the first time in its long-range city planning, San Diego began to take note of how the Navy would influence city services. "The navy has recognized San Diego as a splendid port and a point of strategic importance," said one editorial. "It is up to us to keep pace with the navy's vision to develop here a real harborage and a city of commercial importance."[28] John Nolen, acting as city planner, prepared a "Comprehensive

Crowds of San Diegans on hand to greet *Constitution* on 21 January 1933. *San Diego Historical Society*

City Plan for San Diego," with ample mention of the presence of the Naval Air Station, Destroyer Base, and Naval Training Station, and a bold recommendation to construct a Harbor Drive from South Bay around the curve of the bay, across Dutch Flats to the boundary of the Naval Reservation at La Playa. By 1940 the Navy was thinking of the as-yet-unfinished Harbor Drive in defense terms: a highway "around the water-front suitable for the defense forces and the artillery that would be required for anti-aircraft defense. In an emergency it could be taken over and used exclusively for defense purposes." During the war the Navy would help fund Harbor Drive's construction.[29]

Lacking in Nolen's work was advance planning for the impact that the Navy would begin to make on city utilities and public works. As early as 1922 the head naval public works officer in San Diego noted that the Navy had become the largest consumer of water in the district. The Navy also had common consent to dump untreated sewage from both ships and stations directly into the bay. By 1937 one estimate found the Navy emptying 750,000 gallons of sewage each day.[30] Glossed over as they were in the 1920s, these factors would overwhelm city services in the rush of war preparations in the late 1930s.

The San Diego Naval Training Station was going through its own years of expansion in the late 1920s and 1930s. The large "tent city" of permanent tent barracks at Camp Ingram on the western edge of the station had been replaced by permanent buildings in the early 1930s, and a consistent infusion of construction money and New Deal recovery funds allowed for new facilities, streets, lawns, and tennis courts. During 1934 a "music reproducer" amplifier and five portable long-distance horns were added for the playing of marches during recruit reviews.[31]

Although many naval training stations closed during the 1930s for economic reasons, San Diego stayed in operation due to its excellent training weather and its nearness to the Pacific Fleet. The spartan training routine of the 1930s could easily be recognized by many who would train at the training station even decades later. "We drilled a lot. We slept in hammocks and we lashed them up every morning with seven marlin hitches," remembered one recruit.

> Every Thursday we had a review. All the companies would line up in formation on a big grinder that was used just for these reviews. They had VIPs on a reviewing stand all the time, politicians and lots of times, movie people. We'd come onto the field and then stop. Then we opened ranks for calisthenics. After calisthenics, we laid our rifles down and pulled little sig-

The Naval Hospital's administration building, May 1926. *U.S. Naval Institute*

nal flags out of our leggings and went through the alphabet in semaphore. Then we closed ranks, reported, and passed in review. The band was playing all of this shipping-over music. The greatest was "Anchors Away"; I used to get chills up my spine.[32]

By 1939, facilities carefully improved during the 1930s stood ready to accept a sudden flood of new recruits who were being authorized to help fill a rapidly expanding fleet. By the end of the decade the training station could accommodate five thousand recruits, with room for another one thousand trade-school men in a series of schools as diverse as Radio Operator, Cooks and Bakers, Musician, and Electrical.[33]

The initial contract for construction of the Naval Hospital in Balboa Park was let in October 1920 and called for a central administration building flanked by three wards on either end. Four smaller buildings, including a surgical suite and mess hall, were placed nearby, all at a cost of slightly more than a million dollars. On 22 August 1922, with the work completed, Capt. F. W. F. Weiber placed the institution into commission.[34]

The hospital was the last of the four major facilities the Navy would build during the Kettner era and it was the most austere. To meet tight construction budgets, the Navy combed out many of the ornamental details from the plans while maintaining a general Mission style.

This immediately raised the ire of the Chamber of Commerce. One member protested: "I was on the committee that recommended the giving of the present site to the Government. The Navy Department pledged itself to the construction

The Naval Hospital, c. 1940, showing why the hospital site was known as Inspiration Point. *San Diego Historical Society*

of a most beautiful and artistic building. . . . I can hardly imagine a more severe, plain and unattractive structure than the one they have erected on the most prominent spot in Balboa Park." The Chamber forwarded this view to Washington, noting that "the lack of harmony of the Hospital buildings with the exposition buildings and their lack of beauty was expressed by quite a number."[35]

Although at one point grumbling that it was "impossible for the people in San Diego, at such a great distance from Washington, to grasp the necessity for economy in Governmental expenditures," the Navy relented and began directing resources into ornamental niceties and landscaping that would soften the hospital's spartan visual effect. As one first step in these efforts Captain Weiber hired an English gardener to tend to the landscaping around the hospital; the cumulative effect

over many years was an ultimate nomination of the hospital for the U.S. Register of Historic Places as much on the basis of its landscaping as on the basis of its architectural design.[36]

The original 1919 hospital plan was expanded in several phases through 1937. In 1923 a half-million-dollar contract was let for three additional buildings, including a medical and surgical department of three wards and 172 beds, expanding total bed capacity to 618. Another contract, let after public approval of additional land for hospital expansion in 1925, added additional wards, laboratory, X ray, nurses' quarters, and an incinerator building, and increased capacity to 822 beds. San Diego voters would later approve additional land in both 1937 and 1939.[37]

From the beginning the hospital served active duty officers and enlisted as well as many ex-servicemen on behalf of the

Veterans' Bureau. In the 1920s and '30s, on average, a fifth of the hospital's beds were filled by ex-servicemen, including veterans of World War I, the Spanish-American War, and even the Civil War. The hospital also began a strong tradition as a teaching facility during the 1920s and the Navy's only Hospital Corps School moved to San Diego in September 1928.[38]

With its Marine Railway in operation and with scores of decommissioned destroyers crowding its roadstead, the destroyer base near 32nd Street quickly became the hub of the maritime industry in San Diego. For years the city had lagged behind others along the West Coast in fostering sustainable shipbuilding and repair industry. Navy ship repair requirements now stimulated demand. Operating ships had to be periodically repaired and the Navy's scheme of rotating destroyers between commissioned and reserve status demanded a concentration of ship repair trades in San Diego and a consistent flow of money into the city, causing Rear Adm. Luke McNamee, commander of Destroyer Force, to comment in 1927 that "what helps the destroyers helps San Diego."[39]

During 1929 the Navy discovered severe material defects in the boilers of 60 out of 103 active fleet destroyers. With its large force of reserve destroyers, the Navy decided to forgo expensive boiler repairs and replace defective destroyers with reserve warships (some were practically new, having been steamed only a few thousand miles). This decision, however logical it appeared to budgeters in faraway Washington, caused immense and immediate disruption across San Diego. Starting in September 1929 leave was canceled and "all normal operations and training ceased. In the place of such operations was substituted the functions of a seagoing navy yard in modernizing and recommissioning thirty-four destroyers from reserve."[40]

Each destroyer to be discarded was assigned a mate from Red Lead Row. "Each active destroyer got under way under their own steam to get their mate out of the graveyard and to transfer all that was good to it before being put themselves on the dump for disposition and sale. The active destroyer, a shipshape man-of-war with commission pennant flying, was a thing of beauty. The new mate from reserve was dirty and unkempt, spotted like a leopard with daubs of red lead, paint cracked, faded and weathered by years of the action of the elements."[41]

The biggest jobs facing the destroyermen were torpedo- and fire-control rewiring and condenser-tube replacement under the boilers. When the switch was at its height, only eight Pacific destroyers remained in commission. The first of the

Rigel (AD-13), long a stalwart at the destroyer base tending its fleet of reserve destroyers, was also home to Capt. Chester Nimitz and his family during his years when he commanded the tender, the base, and all the destroyers lying in reserve. *U.S. Naval Institute*

Framed between the county administration building and the El Cortez Hotel, *Case* (DD-370) is under way for sea in March 1938. Present at Pearl Harbor during the 7 December attack, *Case* would later earn seven battle stars in World War II. *National Archives*

new destroyers raised her commissioning pennant on 8 January 1930, the last on 4 June 1930.[42]

By 1930 one-third of the Navy's total submarine tonnage was at the destroyer base accompanied by the submarine tender *Argonne* (AS-10), flagship of Submarine Division 20. Division 20 was commanded by one of the Navy's rising stars, Capt. Chester Nimitz. In February 1931 the CNO placed the administration of the San Diego Destroyer Base under the Commander in Chief, U.S. Fleet, and in June 1931 Captain Nimitz took command of the destroyer base and of the thirty-five-odd deactivated destroyers still tied up at its docks. The Nimitz family moved from an apartment in San Diego to living quarters aboard *Rigel* moored alongside the deactivated

A common site throughout the 1930s, destroyers are moored by divisions to a double line of buoys throughout the middle bay. *San Diego Historical Society*

destroyers. Living aboard were Captain and Mrs. Nimitz, two teenage children, an infant daughter, an aging bulldog, and a stray cat by the name Curio, who lived for chasing rats around the ship.[43]

The *Rigel* provided a comfortable residence in a novel setting where the children would frequently lead expeditions over the decks of the nearby destroyers or would make friends with the sailors in the *Rigel*'s machine or carpentry shops. A small staff that included a cook, steward, and two messboys served the family. The children slept in built-in bunks with curtains; *Rigel*'s charthouse became one bedroom.[44]

A favorite Nimitz hiking companion was Capt. Raymond Spruance, who had returned to San Diego as chief of staff of Commander, Destroyers, Scouting Force. Spruance had maintained a close association with San Diego since his initial assignment commanding a destroyer in Halsey's division. He frequently visited San Diego while serving as executive officer of battleship *Mississippi* in late 1929 and after a time at the Naval War College his family settled in a small Coronado apartment where Spruance would walk to Fleet Landing in the morning to take a launch across the bay.[45]

In April 1935 117 naval vessels were then calling San Diego home, a number that demanded expanded base support. Congress had authorized an exchange of nine acres of inland property for six acres of city waterfront land adjacent to the destroyer base late in the 1920s. In 1934 the Navy's first all-steel floating drydock, ARD-1, was towed through the Panama Canal and assigned to the destroyer base. During 1935–37 nearly $2 mil-

lion in development projects were funneled through New Deal agencies to extend the quaywall up to Pier One, build Pier Two, and construct several additional buildings.[46]

Two additional tracts of land were added in 1937 and National City residents voted to sell ninety-seven acres of waterfront property to the Navy in 1939.[47] In July 1940 the city deeded 14.5 acres east of 28th Street and north of Chollas Creek to the Navy for base expansion. In November a further lease of ninety acres of submerged tidelands was approved for use as an anchorage.

On 5 September 1939, in response to the accelerating tempo of hostilities in Europe, President Roosevelt established neutrality patrols of the coasts, and in San Diego twenty-two reserve destroyers were quickly activated for duty. Fourteen of these World War I–vintage vessels would see service throughout World War II as high-speed transports, minelayers, or convoy escorts. Eight of these destroyers (together with forty-two others commissioned in early 1940) would trade sunny San Diego days for the icy spray of the North Atlantic when transferred to Britain as part of the 1940 Lend-Lease agreement.[48]

Those who clambered aboard the old destroyers found faded gray paint, rust-streaked fittings, and weather decks liberally coated with guano. Teams were rotated from ship to ship for "assembly-line" repairs while newly reporting crews self-trained, as best they could, on the ship's equipment. Junior officers who had just reported to the Operating Engineering and Applied Communications courses at the Naval Postgraduate School were turned around and ordered back to sea duty aboard these destroyers. With dark humor these junior officers called themselves the "Seven-Seventy Club"—seven years at sea and seventy days ashore. Little did they realize that it would be another seven years before most would see shore duty again.[49]

Ward (DD-139) was a story in herself. Built in a "world record" thirty days at Mare Island Naval Shipyard in 1918, she served briefly in the European war before transiting back through the Panama Canal in July 1919, never to leave the Pacific again. Operating out of San Diego for two years, she was finally decommissioned and assigned to Red Lead Row in June 1921, forlorn and forgotten. When the call came to reactivate San Diego's destroyers, *Ward* was the very last to be recommissioned. On 10 February 1941 she rounded Point Loma with a crew of nearly all naval reservists and headed into long slow Pacific swells for the first time in twenty years.

Barely ten months later she would enter the pages of history off the entrance channel to Pearl Harbor where she would fire the first shots of the war against the Japanese by sinking a midget submarine an hour before the air attack began on 7 December.[50]

War rumors and war preparations were everywhere in evidence as the 1930s came to an end. Increasing numbers of servicemen began arriving and training, both afloat and in the air, training that increased in seriousness by the day. In the waters off Point Loma, *Saratoga* experimented with oiler *Kanawha* on 12 June 1939 in what would be the first underway refueling of a carrier, testing the feasibility of underway replenishment, which would prove vital in World War II.[51]

In a reflection of the times, Naval Intelligence considered San Diego to be "the very hub of the wheel of Japanese espionage" on the West Coast and posted extra intelligence officers in San Diego, operating from the Eleventh Naval District headquarters building. There they paid attention to Japanese immigrants and to the many Japanese aboard San Diego fishing boats and traced every rumor of American sailors giving up secrets.[52]

As tensions rose and security tightened, so too did rumor. During March 1935 a Japanese "spy" was reported arrested on Point Loma with "detailed drawings of the fort plan." During December 1937 the fleet was placed on special alert and one destroyer was ordered to patrol offshore with a second destroyer anchored athwart the harbor entrance at Ballast Point to check all vessels coming into the harbor. In October 1940 a rumor spread that Japanese suicide planes would attack American ships in harbor, which brought both ships and planes to alert status.[53]

Even when the bulk of the fleet was ordered forward deployed to Hawaii from San Diego and San Pedro, tensions stayed high in San Diego. Security restrictions began to tighten and many navymen in the know looked to the future with an edge of anxiety that easily overwhelmed any feeling of excitement.

1941

From beach palisades, great guns belch their hog-sized projectiles at red targets riding Pacific swells miles out at sea. Every day more, and yet more, Army and Navy recruits pour from incoming trains and buses. High up in the morning skies training planes roll, loop and dive, or flock in wild-goose V-formation to fade behind fleecy cloudbanks. Still more planes, brand new and fresh from finishing lines, roll in ever-growing fleets from gigantic shops—shops so vast and still building feverishly vaster, that in themselves they are veritable cities.

Frederick Simpich, *National Geographic*

The mid-watch had flown by remarkably quickly. The glow of lights to port that marked Los Angeles had fallen slowly astern and only a meager assortment of pinpricks still traced the line of a distant dark shoreline. The comfortable air—surprisingly warm for December—barely rustled the inky water or impeded *Sara*'s southerly pace. It was a good night to flake out on the flag bag's canvas tarp, draw that peacoat closer, and gaze skyward as a million crystal stars rolled left and right to a mesmerizing tempo.

Point Loma's light was raised off the port bow at 0315 and dutifully logged with the help of a red-lensed flashlight. By 0530, with the eastern horizon etched with the slightest blush of gunmetal blue, plane crews began to materialize magically, sifting around the shadowed flight deck in twos and threes, seeking the comfortable familiarity of a particular aircraft. As the shipboard tempo quickened with the steady approach of dawn, the peace was slowly traded for the realities of an aircraft carrier preparing to enter port. At 0700 the few aircraft on deck had been spotted for launch, by 0730 engines were turning over, and at 0819 the first plane lifted skyward for the brief hop ashore.

Ninety minutes later *Saratoga* hove to midway between Point Loma and the Coronados and waited for the steel submarine nets to be pulled from the channel at Ballast Point. The crew stared as one at the warm, relaxing panorama—the radiant white beaches, the stately Hotel Del, the glitter of sunlight off downtown windows—it was all so different from the drizzly environs of Bremerton, *Sara*'s most recent port-of-call. The planned stay in "Dago" was looking brighter and brighter. More than one thought turned to escaping the ship for a warm, relaxing day in a vacationland of beaches, palm trees, and December warmth.

At 1132 *Saratoga*'s log recorded the first line secured at her North Island berth. Only twelve minutes later an excited announcement on the ship's public address system suddenly rippled through the ship, riveting everyone in place: "War has been declared with Japan—air raid on Pearl Harbor."[1]

At 0800 that morning, all personnel assigned to the *Saratoga* Air Group at North Island had been mustered in their hangars ashore for a rare Sunday work session. Squadron baggage, administrative files, and spare parts had to be organized, packed, and loaded aboard trucks for transfer to *Saratoga*. More important, over a hundred planes waited to "waddle" in a long line across base to dockside for hoisting aboard. When word reached the hangars of the attack, *Saratoga*'s fighter squadron, VF-3, was immediately loaded with fuel and ammunition and dispersed around the field. VF-3 pilots and their wives gravitated to their ready room on base, a hushed and awkward gathering that did little to relieve the shock of dramatically changed personal circumstance. Later, two Army pursuit squadrons went on alert to cover North Island while VF-3 loaded.[2]

Lt. Paul Stroop, aide and tactical officer on the Carrier Division 1 staff, was playing golf on the Coronado course next to Spanish Bight when the division commander, Rear Adm. Jake Fitch, ran toward him, cutting right across the course, "The Japs are bombing Pearl Harbor. We're at war. Come with me." Stroop got in the car with the admiral and went straight to the office, remaining in his golf shoes all day.[3]

Navy Radio Point Loma was the first on the mainland to receive word of the Pearl Harbor attack. Radio Pearl Harbor had been engaged in servicing its giant VLF transmitter and NPL was rebroadcasting Pearl Harbor messages using receivers at San Francisco. San Diego radio operators quickly relayed the first message of the attack to Washington and then awaited further news from Hawaii. NPL would be the sole communications link between Hawaii and the continental United States for the next sixty hours and quickly shouldered all Pacific Fleet communications responsibilities.[4]

Radioman Joel Stovall lived on Point Loma. When word came of the attack, he rushed to report in for duty at his North

Saratoga off Point Loma. *U.S. Naval Institute*

Island PBY squadron in blues still soaking wet—his wife had risen early that Sunday morning to wash them. Later that day his son, Howard, walked down to the Naval Training Station to see recruits who had been ordered to man the entire perimeter five or six feet apart.[5]

Capt. Reuben Smith, the Eleventh Naval District Plans Officer, and his wife were having a late breakfast in their sunny Coronado home when the phone rang. With Rear Adm. Charles Blakely spending a few days in the Naval Hospital, the chief of

Two guard ships tend antisubmarine nets that were strung across the harbor's mouth in 1942. *U.S. Navy*

staff out of town, and the operations officer off hunting, Smith was the district's most senior officer and it was his duty to assist acting commandant Capt. Byron McCandless. "I'm going to the office," Smith told his surprised wife after hanging up the phone; "sit by your radio." Shortly thereafter, Smith and McCandless issued orders for military personnel to return to their ships or stations and to wear uniforms at all times. At 0300 the following morning an exhausted Smith finally returned to Coronado. "How bad was it?" his wife asked. "I can't tell you," Smith answered haltingly, then turned away and began to weep.

It was a few minutes before noon Pacific time when radios first hurled word of the attack to a stunned San Diego populace. With the Navy so intertwined within the community, San Diegans intuitively sensed what the newspapers could not say about the attack. "The navy, always having been a part of San Diego, has worked a psychological influence upon the people of this city. For the constant presence of those floating guns and the constant presence of the uniforms have remained a permanent reminder that anything can happen anywhere, that world peace is a myth and that we must not be too surprised each time mankind is obliged to lapse back to the jungle."[6]

Soon, trucks with loudspeakers were crawling down Broadway, blaring news that one had to listen to over and over for the import to sink in—war had come. Sailors at Tijuana's Agua Caliente got the news and streamed back across the border. Within four hours of the first reports forty-seven thousand copies of newspaper extras with headlines like "Japan at War

Photography regulations were in place even before the commencement of World War II. This sign stood at the Naval Supply Depot on Broadway in September 1940. *San Diego Historical Society*

with U.S." and "Coast on Alert for Sneak Blow" were being snapped up by San Diegans. City government went on wartime footing; the shoreline near the commercial Embarcadero was placed off limits.[7]

Reuben H. Fleet of Consolidated Aircraft wired President Roosevelt: "We are on the job and at your command, sir." Sixty-five posts of the San Diego and Imperial County civilian airplane spotter system were manned. Soon, antiaircraft guns would be manned at North Island and on the roof of Consolidated Aircraft, and a sandbagged machine-gun emplacement manned by soldiers with steel helmets, fixed bayonets, and side arms appeared by the city's power station across from Santa Fe Terminal.[8]

"San Diego was listening," said the *Union*.

In hotel lobbies, in the bars, in the restaurants, in the streets. Each new bulletin had special significance for the 300,000 who listened: "A friend of my wife's sister is stationed in Hawaii," "My son is in business in Manila," "My boy may have to go in the next draft." . . . San Diego listened intently. In hotel lobbies, radios that customarily whisper blared forth. On the streets, passersby strained to catch each shouted word of hoarse-throated newspaper boys. Extra editions that followed one after the other throughout the day were snapped up as they hit the street. And yet it wasn't enough. You could still feel the city tense, listening, greedy for more news, exact news, news that was revolting, yet news that you had to listen to.[9]

Rumors flew thick and fast. The Navy had been wiped out, said one; a Japanese air group was preparing to take off from some place in Baja, shouted another. Nearly everyone believed that enemy ships had been seen off the coast. Various blackouts were tried during the next several nights and during these periods of darkness enemy bombers were seen and heard. Flashes of gunfire—later proven to be lightning—were reported from seaward.[10]

Saratoga personnel and those of the Carrier Division 1 staff worked ceaselessly throughout the afternoon and night to ready the carrier for an early morning sortie on 8 December. With the fleet's battleline in shambles, its main striking power now consisted of but three task forces built around carriers *Enterprise, Lexington,* and *Saratoga.* Every crewman felt the urgency of getting *Sara* ready for sea. Large floodlights lit the dock as men, equipment, and airplanes flooded aboard. The air group was assigned an additional fourteen Marine aircraft from VMF-221 and -222 and preliminary orders were received to head directly for Wake Island.[11]

At 0958 the next morning *Saratoga* solemnly cast off her lines with Rear Admiral Fitch in tactical command. With

The newly constructed Plant 2 for Consolidated Aircraft stands at Harbor Drive and Barnett Avenue in January 1942. Fuselage parts and wing assemblies were constructed at Plant 2, painted, and then shipped by a direct rail line to Consolidated's main plant a mile away at Lindbergh Field for final assembly. *San Diego Aerospace Museum*

rumors of Japanese submarines sitting in wait off the coast, Fitch ordered four of the few remaining destroyers in San Diego to accompany the carrier—old four-piper destroyers that had been assigned to the Sound School as training ships.[12] *Saratoga* arrived safely in Pearl Harbor on 14 December.

Chester Nimitz arrived back in San Diego by cross-country train on 22 December and was met by Comdr. E. Robert Anderson, the Naval District's public information officer. En route to Pearl Harbor to take command of the devastated Pacific Fleet, Nimitz stayed overnight at the home of Rear Adm. Ernest Gunther and had the use of Mayor Percy Benbough's official sedan. The next day Nimitz boarded a Catalina flying boat for the long trip to Hawaii, but the tip of the plane's wing hit water on takeoff, forcing the pilot to abort departure. Nimitz was finally airborne at 4 P.M. on 24 December and arrived over Molokai at dawn on Christmas morning after a chilly all-night flight that allowed little rest.[13]

The Navy's concern for the antisubmarine protection of their aircraft carriers was well founded. In late November 1941 the Japanese had dispatched nine long-range submarines to patrol locations off the American West Coast. *I-19* arrived in position off Los Angeles and *I-10* off San Diego in mid-December. Their orders were to shell key naval radio stations and navigation stations—including those on Point Loma—commencing on the night of Christmas Eve, 1941. Just as the submarines were making final preparations, and possibly as Admiral Nimitz's Catalina was overhead, Combined Fleet Headquarters in Tokyo canceled the operation and ordered a return to base for fear of a "very severe" American antisubmarine reaction.[14]

With the rash of false submarine sightings that rose in the hectic days after Pearl Harbor, no one can tell for sure, but *I-10* was probably spotted in mid-December as she cautiously moved into position off San Diego. An Army B-26 on antisubmarine patrol some five hundred miles off the coast was returning to base under a drizzly cloud layer at two thousand feet. Suddenly, both the pilot and the bomber's naval liaison officer spotted what they reported as a large fleet submarine among the white caps eight miles south of San Clemente

Pilot's-eye view of North Island and the harbor in 1943. The Naval Training Station has expanded onto newly reclaimed land, the ASW base stands ready for development near Shelter Island, and sand is shoaling around the North Island causeway. *U.S. Navy*

Island. The pilot bore down on the target in a clean, unopposed bomb run. However, at the last minute, with the submarine already diving, the bombardier aborted the bomb drop as he had been taught during peacetime never to release under five thousand feet. By the time the pilot circled for another attack with a now-persuaded bombardier, the target had disappeared.[15]

A second Japanese submarine, *I-17,* made landfall on Point Loma during the night of 19 February 1942 after a nonstop transit from Kwajalein. After verifying her position on the easily identifiable Point Loma, she turned north. Staying submerged during daylight, she arrived off Santa Barbara at dusk on 23 February where she shelled oil refineries near Goleta and later sank two merchant vessels further up the coast.[16]

In the early days of the war, the Navy rushed its carriers to San Diego and the Pacific to cover the sudden gap in its defenses left by the destruction of the battleline. *Yorktown* (CV-5) arrived on 30 December from Norfolk and left on 16 January as flagship of Task Force 17 (Rear Adm. Frank Jack Fletcher) bound for Samoa. Two months later the Navy's newest carrier, *Hornet* (CV-8), arrived at North Island impatient for action after a rushed shakedown in the Atlantic. Aboard was Lt. Comdr. Stan-

hope Ring, who had advanced rapidly since his days at North Island in the mid-1920s and was broadly seen as one of the Navy's rising stars. Between assignments in San Diego with Fighting Squadron 3 and on the staff of Aircraft Battle Force, he had married Eleanor Reynolds. After tours in command of Patrol Squadron 17 and as a naval observer aboard the British aircraft carrier *Ark Royal,* Ring won the most coveted billet in naval aviation, air group commander in *Hornet.* Shortly after leaving San Diego, *Hornet* rendezvoused with destiny, loading Doolittle's B-25 bombers and then heading westward directly toward Tokyo. Following the raid—*Hornet*'s first combat action—Ring rapidly reconstituted his air group in time for the Battle of Midway, where he would win the Navy Cross. He later would command three aircraft carriers, two of them—*Siboney* (CVE-112) and *Boxer* (CV-21)—based in San Diego.

By 1942 Stanhope and Eleanor had three children, Stewart Andrew, William Reynolds, and Susan. During *Hornet*'s brief stop at North Island, eight-year-old Stewart met the tall and charismatic Lt. Comdr. John Waldron, who would tragically lead *Hornet*'s Torpedo Squadron 8 into the pages of history three months later at Midway.

Eleanor Ring had been at the Family Hospital at North Island on the day of the Pearl Harbor attack, recovering from the birth of her third child, Susan. In an all-too-familiar Navy story husband Stan was not present for the birth but away working with *Hornet*'s new air group in Norfolk. Within days of Pearl Harbor (and with husband Comdr. Stewart Reynolds en route to the front), Jane Keck Reynolds had taken charge of the Ring and Reynolds families and, like many in San Diego who were fearful of attack, had moved them away from the coast to the family ranch in Alpine. Many who remained profited from an unplanned windfall as real estate values plunged. Capt. Frank Van Valkenburg's family was able to obtain a home with an exclusive Star Park address in Coronado "for a song because people were afraid to live on the coast and near a military establishment like North Island."[17] With *Hornet*'s departure, Eleanor moved the family to Pennsylvania, where they spent much of the war, like most American families, glued to daily war bulletins or expectantly waiting for infrequent letters from the distant front.

The men of the Ring and Reynolds families would be at the center of the action during the war. After the Battle of Midway Stan Ring would see action in the Solomons and would serve as the director of Naval Aviation Training in the Navy Department. Stewart Reynolds, after commanding *Truxtun* (DD-229) and serving as repair officer of tender *Altair* (AD-11) in San Diego during the late thirties, would command a destroyer and

nia retained in San Diego. These forces were coordinated from a Joint Operations Center at Naval District headquarters at Broadway Pier.[18]

The Naval Air Control Center (located on the third deck of district headquarters) ordered Sea Frontier air patrols, using Navy PBYs and Army B-24s and B-26s flying from North Island and blimps from Del Mar. During the later phases of the war old fishermen flew as part of blimp crews to spot schools of fish in an effort "highly important to the national food supply."[19]

Wooden schooner yachts, such as *Ramona*, were taken into naval service to augment surface patrols off the coast and the Navy chartered ten tuna clippers for patrols off the harbor mouth and fifty large clippers (with six hundred fisherman volunteers) for submarine patrols along sealanes leading toward the Panama Canal. Naval officers in the control room of the Surface Task Group, Southern Sector at the Joint Operations Center coordinated these patrols.[20]

In July 1941 a Harbor Defense Control Post was established in the Old Spanish Lighthouse on Point Loma with an Army officer, Navy officer, and enlisted assistants managing the defenses of the harbor twenty-four hours a day. A year later the Army and Navy moved into new bombproof facilities on the

Stan Abele (with date and dogtags) was one of many naval officers who were billeted at the Hotel del Coronado during World War II. Treated as regular guests by the terms of the Navy's lease, officers stayed two and three to a room and were transported to North Island or the Amphibious Base by a regular bus service but could enjoy maid service, the hotel's dining rooms, and the swimming pool. *Stan Abele*

By May 1949 Coronado Heights boasted a large communications and cryptologic training facility in addition to its communications and signals intelligence activities, some still located within Fort Emory's underground bunkers. *National Archives*

an attack transport during the war, seeing action from North Africa to Okinawa. Stan's brother Morton would serve in the Logistics Division of the Pacific Fleet staff and would ultimately rise to rear admiral.

The commandant of San Diego's Eleventh Naval District shouldered duties as Commander, Pacific Naval Coastal Frontier for the waters off Southern California beginning in January 1941. In January 1942 a complicated administrative organization was established for coastal defense headed by the commandant of the Twelfth Naval District in San Francisco with command of Local Defense Forces in Southern Califor-

northern boundary of Fort Rosecrans Cemetery and established a joint Harbor Defense Command Post–Harbor Entrance Control Post.[21] They stayed there until 13 August 1945 when the Harbor Defense Command Post was closed; the Harbor Entrance Control Post was disestablished a month later.

At the beginning of the war Navy signalmen stationed atop the lighthouse tower challenged all vessels approaching the harbor by use of a blinker light, twelve-inch signal light, or twenty-four-inch carbon arc lamp. The signalmen would flash "INT" to challenge and would then telephone coded replies to the Harbor Entrance Control Post. "We didn't know what the correct challenge was," said one veteran. "We challenged the ships and reported the reply to the command post and they would tell us whether or not it was correct." Assuming a correct response, submarine nets at Ballast Point would be drawn away from the channel. Eventually, signaling operations were relocated to a forty-foot tower 250 feet south of the Old Spanish Lighthouse that contained a yardarm, blinkers, and canvas flag bag, with a sonar station at its base that could monitor sound buoys off the entrance.[22]

San Diego's reputation during the thirties was that of a quiet residential community of retired Midwesterners and not a few naval officers. Its slow-moving, sunny economy had been built on tourism, real estate, and steady naval expenditures, with little need for industrialization and manufacturing. With almost

Navy WAVES became a dominant portion of the administrative rates by the middle of World War II. Here two WAVES collect streams of teletype copy to construct individual naval messages. *San Diego Historical Society*

a third of the Navy's entire force assigned to San Diego, the percentage of San Diego workers employed by government was double the national average while those engaged in manufacturing was half that across the nation.[23]

However, with the coming of the "defense boom" everything changed. Fifty thousand immigrants from other parts of the country immediately arrived, many attracted by nationwide advertisements for work in defense plants. Consolidated Aircraft held the distinction as the city's largest employer, and by the fall of 1941 its employment exceeded twenty-five thousand workers (and would rise another twenty thousand in the next nine months). Under Reuben Fleet's huge plant sign, "Nothing Short of Right Is Right," 6,724 B-24 Liberator bombers (including its navalized sister, the PB-4Y Privateer) and many thousand PBY Catalina and PB-2Y Coronado flying boats rolled down local assembly lines.[24]

San Diego was ill prepared for the sudden onslaught of added population. Housing quickly filled and city services, depleted by the Depression, neared the point of collapse. Car trailers donated by the federal government crowded vacant lots in Mission Valley and old city trolley cars became makeshift homes for $30 a month. Reuben Fleet helped orchestrate a federal-assisted plan to build new homes for three thousand families in a master-planned community in Linda Vista.

Almost overnight between 1939 and 1943, San Diego's rank as an industrial center rose from seventy-ninth in the nation to twenty-eighth as a sleepy border town morphed into a teaming wartime metropolis. *Life* magazine caught the city's measure in an 1941 article entitled "Boom Town: San Diego":

> A year ago San Diego was a quiet, slow-moving town. But no longer. The defense boom has hit it . . . changing the look of the town. With the boom has come housing projects, trailer camps, traffic snarls, bigger red light districts. But it isn't these things so much that worry the old San Diegans. What makes them fret is the change in the tempo of their town. Until a year ago people walked leisurely down Broadway or drove quietly through Balboa Park. Now they stride hurriedly, drive like mad. Nice old ladies a year ago sat on the waterfront painting pictures of ships coming and going. Now the ships coming and going are Army and Navy transports and nice old ladies are barred from the docks.[25]

Few American cities were more totally dedicated to the war effort than San Diego. Thousands of Navy hospital beds and training facilities moved into former Balboa Park museums, with priceless collections moved to basements. Commercial harbor traffic came to a virtual standstill as the Navy operated the port for the shipping of vast war supplies to the Pacific the-

The first buildings of the Navy Radio and Sound Laboratory in 1942, next to the Point Loma radio station. The buildings' "exposed" position on Point Loma and nearness to the operational radio station drove a requirement for a camouflage paint scheme. *U.S. Navy*

ater. "The roar of B-24's or PBY's being tested filled the air day and night. The harbor was choked with gray ships and the great coastal guns of Point Loma were exercised often."[26]

A new (and suddenly youthful) population brought to the city by Navy orders and war-industry salaries dramatically altered the pace of life and leisure in the city. Men in navy blue packed city buses and trolleys. Eddie's Bar, the Bomber Cafe, penny arcades, tattoo parlors, and peep shows sprang up along Broadway. Tailors and laundries fitted and cleaned a never-ending supply of uniforms. Dance halls, such as the Pacific Square Ballroom on Pacific Highway, featured Glenn Miller, Benny Goodman, and Artie Shaw often in shows that lasted until dawn for those in round-the-clock factory shifts.

"Ashore in San Diego" surveyed the landscape for the visiting navyman:

> Don't let that salty guy tell you there's nothing doing in this port. There's plenty cookin'—a fellow just has to know where to go, that's all. Liberty aboard the station (five theaters, USO Camp show once a month, national radio broadcast of "Anchors Aweigh" every Sunday afternoon, six libraries, sports, bowling). Around San Diego: zoo, museums (take the No. 7 or 11 streetcar). Rancho Santa Fe golf offers free green fees for servicemen in uniform, one dollar in civilian clothes. Padres tickets: 80 cent grandstand seats discounted for servicemen to 30 cents. YMCA: everything from dancing and checkers to

church services. Pacific Square—largest dance hall in SD—has big name bands Friday, Saturday and Sunday; admission 55 cents. See Buckner's for "old time" dancing Saturday night from 2030 to 2400 for 55 cents. Tennis at Morley Field in Balboa Park, Navy Field and in La Jolla, all free.[27]

When *Saratoga* sailed from San Diego into an unknown that no one could forecast, she carried on board a still-secret tactical advantage that no one had ever heard of. Beginning with matchsticks spread across the kitchen table of his Coronado home, Comdr. John Thach (commanding officer of VF-3) evolved a defensive fighter doctrine that replaced traditional three-plane sections with two pairs of fighters that flew abreast to watch each other's tails. The configuration permitted naval fighters to evade and counterattack enemy fighters no matter how they came in. With the help of Lt. Butch O'Hare leading a second section, Thach perfected the tactic in the skies over San Diego. He first called this maneuver the "beam defense position." As it gained fame in the early months of the war, offsetting the advantage of the technically superior Japanese Zero fighter, the fighter tactic quickly gained a more familiar name, the "Thach weave."[28]

Thach's experimental tactics were but one example of how naval aviation prepared for war, all within sight of San Diegans involved in their daily business. "Civilians, in glancing across the bay at North Island today," read one account, "see a baffling land of hangars, shops, factories, runways, landing fields. All is complicated, all is secret, and all is beyond a lone man's comprehension. Records perhaps are being broken, but we know nothing about them, and are not supposed to know anything about them." Although North Island security was tight—as would be expected—every PBY takeoff, every carrier sortie, every mistake, every massed formation whetted San Diego's natural fascination for the Navy and its sense of civic pride.[29]

Throughout the war, air groups for the Navy's frontline carriers would form and reform at North Island. Many thousands of airmen and their aircraft funneled through San Diego either for final training or en route to forward areas. One example of San Diego's value came in the spring of 1942. *Lexington* had been lost at the Battle of the Coral Sea and the remnants of *Lexington*'s Air Group 2 were ordered to North Island to reform as Air Group 11. About 35 percent of the pilots would be brand-new and had to be integrated within the group to make it a cohesive fighting unit. They occupied hangar space at West Beach and stepped through various phases of training using San Diego's outlying airfields.[30]

In July 1940 the CNO formally assigned San Diego the requirement to support four carrier air groups, six patrol squadrons, and one Marine air group. In 1941 this requirement was raised to five carrier air groups, six patrol squadrons, and two utility squadrons, and in 1942 increased yet again to six carrier air groups, one Marine air group, and ninety VP aircraft.[31]

Aircraft were everywhere in wartime San Diego. In one description, "It was a fine clear day, and all you could hear and see were planes. The B-24s rose constantly from the Consolidated field. Two sections of TBFs were out over Point Loma. The field was lined with SBDs, SNJs, Grumman Ducks and P38s. A big 4-engine job, a PB2Y, roared out of the bay below the seaplane tower. A K-3 blimp was nosing lazily towards the destroyer base, presenting a picture of lighter-than-air grace in sharp contrast to the floppy barrage balloons that guarded the city."[32]

Increasing requirements drove the need for larger bases. At North Island two projects dominated its expansion, the building of the station's first concrete runways—runways 29-11 and 18-36—and the reclamation of Spanish Bight.

The need to fill Spanish Bight became a priority when demands for bigger warehouses and more housing began to outstrip the space available. The Navy's first answer was to expand into nearby Coronado. Land on the Coronado side of Spanish Bight was leased for new aviation warehouses and barracks. Then officers from overflowing bachelor officers' quarters were billeted at the Hotel del Coronado, government housing rose at Coronado Flats, and a WAVES barracks was built on Coronado's First Street near the Ferry Landing. However, when other enlisted barracks were proposed on land to be taken over at the city's golf course, city residents finally objected. Exasperated, the Eleventh Naval District Commandant quipped: "Without any apparent knowledge or consideration of the

The first CIC School buildings atop Point Loma along Catalina Boulevard in 1946. *U.S. Navy*

over-all necessity for the area in question in order to prosecute the war in the Pacific, and interested primarily in the preservation of a peacetime way of living in the City, the civic-minded Coronadoans called on California Representatives and Senators to stop the acquisition." Later, he relented and concentrated expansion on Navy-owned land rather than city land.[33]

The Navy's alternatives were few—either expand on Navy-owned property on Silver Strand or reclaim three hundred acres of land in Spanish Bight. With no evident restraint—a byproduct of the exigencies of wartime—the Navy chose not one but both options. Warehouses would be located on reclaimed land on Spanish Bight to alleviate the need to drive trucks of materiel through Coronado and Navy holdings on Silver Strand would be expanded, leading ultimately to the building of the Naval Amphibious Base. The Spanish Bight contract was awarded on 1 March 1944 for fill work and was completed in late July 1944, with the adjacent quay wall completed in October.[34]

The government formally took over many of the nation's Victorian-era hotels for war duties, but not the Hotel del Coronado. Sections of the hotel were routinely reserved for Navy billeting, including a hundred rooms reserved through 1944 for "emergency quarters ashore for two hundred officers when quarters are not available on their ships," and additional rooms set aside "to be used as rest facilities for rehabilitation and recuperation of naval personnel returned from war service at sea or shore duty beyond the limits of the United States" and "including all privileges that go with the regular guests: use of grounds, tennis courts, swimming pool and other facilities."[35]

Naval aviators (sometimes entire squadrons) were billeted at the Del during training, and area officers and their families were posted at the hotel to help ease the burden of finding available housing in town. "When my brother [who was recuperating from war wounds] came to visit me," remembered one veteran, "he couldn't believe it. Here I was at the Hotel Del with maid service. That was not his idea of the military!"[36]

The hotel clearly suffered from wartime shortages of building materials and laborers. "We heard the Navy was supporting the hotel to keep it running," commented local resident Elwood Meyer. "Since the Navy brass liked the hotel facilities for food and drink as well as rooms, they did what they could to help the hotel survive."[37]

Not only were the hotel's rooms utilized for the war effort, but it also became a memorable entertainment mecca. "It would get loaded up at night with military who'd come in to party," recalled Meyer. Buses ran every fifteen minutes from

The bustling Naval Repair Base, c. 1944. *U.S. Naval Institute*

North Island to the hotel and parties and dances were the order of the day. "On Friday afternoons we used to congregate comfortably in rockers on the porch near the hotel entrance to see which female guests arrived unaccompanied," remembered Coronado resident Warren Goodman. "The hotel was the party place. It was girls galore!" remarked another Coronado resident, Stan Abele. "It was the best war I ever fought, that six months at the Del."[38]

The hotel also became a centerpiece of war volunteerism where local ladies could be seen rolling bandages or issuing ration books. The American Women's Voluntary Services (AWVS) sponsored Tuesday afternoon dances for enlisted personnel and Sunday tea dances for officers. It was said that in four years more than two hundred thousand men and girls attended dances on Tuesdays. Room rates for Navy-leased rooms were surprisingly low, certainly less expensive than had been the norm during prewar tourist seasons. "A patriotic gesture," said some. "We make it up with the Navy's business at the Casino Bar," said Steve Royce, the hotel's general manager.[39]

Expansion on North Island inevitably brought increased traffic and, in 1944, the Navy pressed the San Diego and Coronado Ferry Company to add a fourth ferry to their system. When the ferry company demurred, hoping undoubtedly for greater recompense, the Navy countered by threatening to establish its own Navy-owned ferry system. Its bluff called, the ferry company begrudgingly agreed to purchase a fourth ferry

President Roosevelt shakes hands with a bluejacket while visiting the Naval Hospital in 1942. *Naval Historical Center*

(aided by a Navy certification as "essential to the war effort"). The Navy added additional personnel ferries and a parking lot on the San Diego side of the bay.[40]

Coronado hosted the original WAVES barracks in the San Diego area. From the early years of the war, WAVES played a large role in maintaining Navy administration in the city. The first WAVE to report to the Eleventh Naval District was Lt. (jg) Frances Shoup, and the first group of WAVES arrived at the Naval Training Station for training on 17 May 1943. When she arrived, Shoup found some commands that doubted the ability of WAVES to stand night watches and WAVES were assigned only to ratings found "suitable" for women. As the program developed under the direct auspices of the commandant, "everyone wanted WAVES. All the men wanted to play Mr. Roberts at sea and couldn't stand a mere desk job," recollected Marguerite Clakis, who stayed in Coronado during the war.[41]

On 12 October 1942 the secretary of the Navy ordered a streamlined organizational structure by naming North Island as one of four Naval Air Centers. Each center consisted of at least one naval air station and from two to eight auxiliary air stations. North Island's cluster of surrounding airfields included Camp Kearny Field, Otay Mesa Field, Ream Field, the San Diego Coast Guard Air Station, and landing fields at Holtville, Del Mar, San Clemente Island, Huntington Beach, and near the Salton Sea.[42] On 31 August 1944 this organization

changed again to place air base administration directly under naval district commanders, with Rear Adm. Elliott Buckmaster assuming Commander, Naval Air Bases—Eleventh Naval District, overseeing twenty-three naval air stations and auxiliary fields from Santa Barbara to Arizona.

Camp Kearny's old parade ground had been used since 1936 as an emergency Navy landing field. Additional auxiliary runways were installed in late 1940 and 1941, and two five thousand–foot runways were planned to meet the specifications for Army pursuit aircraft. With the completion of these runways Naval Auxiliary Air Station, Camp Kearny was established officially on 20 February 1943.[43]

The Marines leased 324 acres on the north side of the field and for a short time called the site Camp Miramar. This base was reorganized as Marine Corps Air Base, Kearny Mesa on 1 March 1943 with the first elements of the Marine services group living under canvas. On 2 September 1943 the base was redesignated as the Marine Corps Air Depot, Miramar to reduce name confusion with the nearby naval air station.

By the end of the war the shared Navy and Marine facilities at Miramar supported over ten thousand personnel and boasted two concrete six thousand–foot runways. On 22 May 1945 the Marine Fleet Air West Coast headquarters moved to Miramar from North Island and on 8 April 1946 the Naval Auxiliary Air Station, Camp Kearny and the Marine Corps Air Depot were disestablished and their facilities combined and redesignated on 1 May as Marine Corps Air Station, Miramar.[44]

Just before Pearl Harbor, Ream Field stood as an unimproved field used to train pilots in carrier landings. By 1942 Ream's runways had been paved and on 17 July 1943 the site was commissioned as Naval Auxiliary Air Station, Ream Field. By war's end, Ream boasted seventy-eight buildings and four airstrips.

The Army's old East Field on Otay Mesa also acted as a convenient site for carrier landing practice. Commissioned in March 1943 as Naval Auxiliary Air Station, Otay Mesa, the field's name was changed three months later to honor Comdr. Melville Brown. With three runways and over a hundred buildings, Brown Field was prized for its expansion potential and was tapped as the test site for a planned Consolidated heavy bomber near the end of the war.[45] Carrier Landing Strip Sweetwater (located along the north side of Paradise Valley Road) was used for touch-and-go landings.

The open area north of the border and south of the Tijuana River had been used since World War I as a machine-gun range and airborne gunnery range. The Navy assumed control of these ninety-nine acres during World War II as an additional outlying landing field named Border Field. Thirty-five buildings, one barracks, a galley for forty men, and a machine-gun range defined the field. Pilot gunnery training used steam-driven targets that dashed among the dunes on rails called "rabbit tracks." Jack Chilton recalls becoming quite good at carrier landings at the field as there was but a single guy wire to hook. Others remembered a circle target of white stones laid out at one end of the base that was used for dive-bombing practice.[46]

After the war Border Field continued to be used for touch-and-go landings and as a site for the launching of drones. In 1961 the field was deactivated and assigned to the Navy Electronics Laboratory for experimental work, and on 18 August 1971 Border Field's acreage was added to Border Field State Park.[47]

Late in the thirties the Navy used an open area south of Del Mar Racetrack as an emergency outlying airfield for North Island, naming the site Naval Auxiliary Air Station, San Dieguito. In 1941 a one thousand–foot unimproved runway site was established on land originally cleared by MGM for a motion picture featuring blimps.[48] The new runway site was named Naval Auxiliary Air Station, Del Mar and, during October 1942, was selected as an auxiliary field for lighter-than-air operations. Two airship mooring masts arrived by the summer

of 1943 to support two K-type airships from squadron ZP-31 while racetrack buildings were used as barracks, galleys, and offices.

Blimps operating from Del Mar patrolled Southern California waters for submarines as far south as Ensenada, Mexico. In 1944 K-111 crashed into a mountain peak on Santa Catalina Island in dense fog after lifting off from Del Mar. Gasoline and depth charges exploded, killing six. NAAS Del Mar was deactivated in September 1945 and returned to the county, which operated the site as the Del Mar Airport for fourteen years.[49]

To further alleviate crowding at North Island, a new auxiliary air station was constructed near Holtville in Imperial Valley in late 1942, with its two runways completed in 1943. Naval Operational Training Station, Salton Sea was established in 1942 on the southwest shore as a base and practice bombing area for Navy PBY seaplanes. The site was selected as it was "the only area outside *the potential combat zone* that seaplanes could use." The facility was redesignated as a Naval Auxiliary Air Station in 1944.[50]

"We practiced torpedo runs over the Salton Sea," said Tony DeSisto, a TBF Avenger aircrewman, "especially at night," where crews practiced locating, illuminating, and attacking waterborne targets. The training was strenuous: pitch-black nights, glass-flat water, chance winds, unexpected thermals. At least ten Avengers and twenty-three other Navy aircraft were

Amphibious sailors practice boat semaphore signals in 1944 on the flat open fill area of the amphibious base. *Naval Historical Center*

The Naval Amphibious Training Base in April 1944. The landfill was finished in just six months using dredged material from the bay and construction of barracks and amphibious force classrooms continued at a fever pitch during the last two years of the war. *U.S. Navy*

recorded as lost in overwater accidents in the Salton Sea during or shortly after World War II.

Numerous other fields blossomed around the county to meet aviation training requirements. A naval auxiliary field was established on the center plateau of San Clemente Island that grew out of an earthen landing strip used by the Marines as early as 1937. Carrier Landing Strip Ramona was constructed in 1943 with a single paved four thousand–foot runway. The Navy first used Halfhill Dry Lake Landing Field, four miles southeast of Ocotillo Wells, in the late thirties. Jacumba Hot Springs Auxiliary Air Field was used jointly for training by the Army and Navy and Rosedale Field/Bootlegger Field, a mile west of Montgomery Field, was used occasionally. To further augment intensive aviation training, the Navy's first escort carrier, *Long Island* (ACV-1), was ordered to San Diego in September 1942 for carrier landing pilot services, staying through 1943.[51]

The shadowy world of radio intelligence, cryptology, and radio direction finding was for many years the primary—albeit top secret—activity of the naval communications sites that stood at the foot of the Silver Strand at Coronado Heights. The Navy

had first come to Coronado Heights on 20 May 1920 when it established Navy Radio Compass Station, Imperial Beach on 1.91 acres of land that had been part of the Army's Camp Hearn.[52] The site served ships at sea, helping them obtain accurate navigational fixes by reporting the bearings of ship radio signals back to the ship. If two stations were involved, a cross fix could be obtained; if only one, the ship's navigator would obtain a line of bearing.[53]

As radio equipment became ever more sophisticated and sensitive by the end of the thirties, shore stations could "direction find" (DF) high-frequency signals for hundreds (in some cases, thousands) of miles, greatly aiding efforts by Naval Intelligence to track enemy fleet movements.

In 1939 the CNO directed construction of a new strategic high-frequency direction-finding station on the Army's Silver Strand military reservation south of Coronado's Tent City with quarters for a radioman-in-charge and nine men.[54] Closure of the Imperial Beach radio compass station was anticipated, but when the Army erected a high spotting tower nearby the Navy decided instead to enlarge the existing Imperial Beach site that was under lease from the Spreckels estate. Wary of a lease clause that would allow Spreckels to reclaim the Imperial

Beach land on six months' notice, the Navy moved to condemn the property. On 18 October 1941 the first nineteen-acre parcel was condemned at a cost of $8,556, with a later 126-acre parcel condemned on 9 July 1943 for $46,500.[55]

Just five weeks after the attack on Pearl Harbor, the Army established Battery Imperial adjacent to the Navy communications site and in October 1942 took over 412 acres of Coronado Heights, designating the site Fort Emory on 14 December 1942. A huge structure of reinforced concrete was constructed between 1943 and 1944 to support two 16-inch guns that were never installed.

A significant Marine guard of twenty-three enlisted was ordered to the Navy land in January 1942 as the station "was located in a peculiarly vulnerable site, being close to the Mexican border and near a frequently traveled highway, on land where sabotage operations could be conducted quickly and effectively."[56] In December 1942 site plans were forwarded to the Bureau of Ships to transform Imperial Beach from a purely DF site to one that could conduct radio intelligence activities. The endorsement of this plan by the Bureau of Ships ended by saying: "In handling further necessary correspondence relating to direction finders alone at this station, it is suggested that matters may be expedited by hereafter divorcing 'confidential' direction finding activities from 'secret' radio intelligence intercept activities in order to permit the direction finder installation to proceed under its original classification of 'confidential' status."[57]

Japanese diplomatic and naval messages were intercepted throughout World War II by listening posts throughout the Pacific and along the West Coast. The radio intelligence intercept cell at Imperial Beach was known as Station ITEM (ITEM was the phonetic letter for *I*) and cryptographic channels handling communications intelligence intercepts ran between ITEM and OP-20-G in Washington, D.C. Part of the station's wartime activities involved "radio fingerprinting" of Japanese transmitter characteristics with call-letter changes and monitoring of U.S. naval frequencies within the Eleventh Naval District. Station ITEM's location was particularly valuable because it was one of the flank stations of the Pacific net and possessed excellent electrical characteristics.[58]

Large numbers of WAVE communications personnel were assigned to the station beginning in 1944, including many as intercept operators in 1945. Of the three hundred radio personnel assigned to Imperial Beach in August 1944, 148 were women. WAVES were originally billeted at the Coronado WAVE barracks, but later many barracks were reserved for their use at the beach.

On 4 May 1944 one hundred acres of Fort Emory were declared "in standby" by the Army, and arrangements were made to transfer the land to the Navy. At the end of the war, the Navy fell heir to Fort Emory—empty, half-buried concrete gun emplacements and all—and the entire land area was transferred to the Navy in 1950.[59]

Naval Communications Training Center, Imperial Beach evolved from the wartime cryptologic mission of Coronado Heights to become the primary training site in the Navy for cryptologic specialties. When that training was later moved to Florida, the site became better known as Naval Radio Receiving Facility, Imperial Beach. For anyone driving past the facility it was easily remembered for its huge Wullenweber direction-finding antenna, whose 120 antenna elements (organized in a large circular array of a thousand-foot diameter) were universally known as the "dinosaur cage." The site's mission revolved around long-range DF, ELINT (electronic intelligence collection), communications support, and fleet vulnerability assessments.

Beginning in the mid-1930s San Diego began to take center stage in the development of another new technology, the use of underwater sound to detect submarines. First-generation submarine detection equipment was known by its British Navy acronym, ASDIC, but later was more familiarly called SONAR for "sound navigation and ranging." In 1935 Destroyer Division 60 developed the Navy's first *standard* underwater sound tactics in waters off San Diego and conducted the Navy's first-ever formal training in the use of underwater sound equipment.[60]

From 1936 through 1939 Destroyer Division 19 joined with the Scripps Institute of Oceanography in studies of underwater thermal gradients, and in May 1938 *Porter* (DD-356) and two submarines began regular training of new sound operators in the waters between San Diego and San Clemente Island. This led to the establishment of the Navy's first Sound School at the destroyer base on 15 June 1939. The Sound School was directed by Comdr. Arthur Burhans, commander of DesDiv 19, and was designed to teach "the best soundman from each destroyer" for two weeks of shore training and five weeks at sea.[61]

During the next four years Burhans would become one of the most important voices in antisubmarine warfare within the Navy as he led the Sound School (redesignated the West Coast Sound School in 1942) and a training squadron of school ships and submarines, the West Coast Sound Training Squadron. In December 1941 the Sound School was operating with seven destroyers and six submarines and was turning out about seventy-five enlisted sound operators and fifteen sound officers every five weeks.[62]

Keying in on the need for more research in underwater acoustics, the chief of the Navy's Bureau of Engineering had recommended in May 1939 that a radio laboratory be established near NPL on Point Loma to coordinate the Navy's research in communications and radio propagation. On 1 June 1940 the secretary of the Navy formally established the U.S. Navy Radio and Sound Laboratory (NRSL), the Navy's first laboratory on the West Coast.[63]

The first headquarters building for NRSL (today's Building 4) began construction in 1940 and, in the face of surprising German U-boat successes, NRSL's first priority quickly became underwater sound research. The University of California, under contract, established a Division of War Research (UCDWR) on 26 April 1941 to administer a new underwater research laboratory on the grounds of NRSL and leverage the advantages of Scripps and existing Navy sound training to their needs. Although the Navy owned the facilities, the University of California employed most of the staff. At its wartime peak NRSL had a staff of about 150 civilians, while the UCDWR staff numbered approximately 575.[64]

One member of the UCDWR staff was a young, lanky, and hard-to-ignore oceanographer by the name of Roger Revelle.

Revelle's standing in the relatively fresh science of oceanography was already as prominent as his towering six-feet-four frame and had been further enhanced by a carefully cultivated association with the Navy. Shortly after gaining his doctorate in 1936 Revelle had volunteered to take hydrographic measurements during a Navy summer training cruise to the Gulf of Alaska aboard the submarine tender *Bushnell*. "It was Revelle's first glimpse of the Navy at work and he quickly sensed that the new science of oceanography might be of lasting interest to the Navy."[65] At the urging of *Bushnell*'s captain, Revelle joined the Naval Reserve and over the next several years helped develop strong links between Scripps and the Navy's Hydrographic Office.

In February 1941 Lieutenant (junior grade) Revelle trained aboard one of the Sound School ships, *Rathburne* (DD-113), and was called to active duty in July. Revelle quickly became immersed with underwater sound research, sonar design, and radar operator instruction at UCDWR and "was near the core of the liaison that developed in wartime between academic research and the military."[66]

UCDWR designed sonar transducers, acoustic-homing torpedoes, and the QLA, a high-definition sonar system that enabled American submarines to safely penetrate heavily mined straits. Sea and swell forecasting played an important

The perfect training conditions of the Silver Strand were a boon to generations of "gator sailors" who could learn small boat and large ship maneuvers either along the Strand's oceanside or in protected bay waters. Landing craft practice south of the Hotel del Coronado in 1944. *Naval Historical Center*

Crammed to the gills with replacement naval aircraft for the front, an *Essex*-class carrier glides out of harbor in January 1945. *National Archives*

role in amphibious operations. NAC and NAD sound decoys that allowed American submarines to evade detection from sonar-equipped destroyers were developed at UCDWR, and a few UCDWR scientists accompanied submariners on war patrols, wearing uniforms similar to naval officers but with a small insignia on the collar denoting civilian status.[67]

During the 1940s the people who seemed to know the most about electrical recording and the projection of sound were from the movie industry. Several people at UCDWR were recruited directly from Hollywood, including Arthur Roshon from Walt Disney Studios who was a key figure in the development of both the QLA mine-avoidance sonar and the first ice-piloting sonars.[68]

Originally the laboratory calibrated experimental sound transducers from a barge anchored in San Diego Bay, but sound from passing ships forced the lab to move the barge to Sweetwater Reservoir in 1943. The site was deep, relatively remote, and free of background noise. Later a similar test platform was set up at El Capitan Lake to test NAD beacons.[69]

UCDWR cooperated with the Navy's West Coast Sound School and the Sound Training Squadron in several projects, including development of sound-recognition training programs, training curriculum, ordnance delivery instruction, development of group trainers, development of a range-bearing plotter, and the attack-course indicator.[70]

In August 1942 Captain Burhans of the Sound School sought larger facilities for his rapidly expanding training and arranged for the transfer to newly reclaimed bayside land adjacent to the Naval Training Station by 29 March 1943. Eight

buildings and three piers were originally built, including space for the UCDWR Training Aids Division in bayside buildings that years later would house the Admiral Kidd Club.[71]

In May 1944 the Sound School expanded further, taking control of the tip of nearby Shelter Island as a land firing range for the training of depth-charge crews. From December 1941 to June 1945 the Sound School graduated a total of 4,020 officers and 10,854 enlisted men, and on 21 September 1945 the West Coast Sound School was officially redesignated as the U.S. Fleet Sonar School, San Diego.

On 9 August 1948 Navy officials signed a fifty-year lease with the Harbor Commission of the City of San Diego for the Fleet Sonar School land with provision for a fifty-year renewal. The Navy occupied the land during the lease period without payment of rent but surrendered permanent title to other land along the bay (including 244 acres of Lindbergh Field) in compensation.[72]

NRSL helped test the Navy's first closely guarded radar and helped perfect early forms of IFF to aid radar operators distinguishing between friendly and enemy aircraft. NRSL helped train fighter interceptor controllers at North Island and, beginning in October 1941, trained radar operators at a school that Roger Revelle helped establish in temporary buildings across Catalina Boulevard from NPL.[73]

With the rapid expansion of fleet training in San Diego, the Fleet Operational Training Command, Pacific (OTCPAC) was established on 9 January 1943. Originally, OTCPAC maintained offices at the 32nd Street Repair Base, then for a brief

Sailors enjoy the moment. *U.S. Navy*

period at the Eleventh Naval District headquarters building, and finally to permanent quarters adjacent to the West Coast Sound School.[74]

OTCPAC sponsored shakedown and refresher training, with shakedown training ranging from nine weeks for battleships and aircraft carriers to three weeks for patrol and mine vessels. There was little refresher training early in the war, but by 1945, with ships regularly returning from battle zones for routine overhauls and battle damage repair, the requirement for training increased. Refresher training included underway training in gunnery, damage control, Combat Information Center (CIC), and antisubmarine warfare (ASW). A Battle Problem conducted in waters off Point Loma included air attacks, jamming, dummy mines, navigation, and communications challenges. Most of the shakedown and refresher training became the responsibility of the San Diego Shakedown Group, Task Group 14.1, that was established on 10 May 1944, the precursor to the later Fleet Training Group and today's Afloat Training Group–Pacific. On 3 August 1945 OTCPAC was renamed Training Command, Pacific Fleet.[75]

Antiaircraft warfare became one of the first important priorities for Navy training early in the war to blunt the successes of Japanese air attacks. In early 1942 the Navy cleared land on bluffs overlooking the sea south of La Jolla and began construction of the Naval Anti-Aircraft Training Center, Pacific Beach, that would be commissioned on 2 September 1942. Gun mounts were installed—40mm, .30- and .50-caliber, 3-inch and 5-inch, all with their accompanying directors—and firing was directed to seaward against drones, sleeves, star shells, or rockets. There was even a hand-made tilting platform

for 20mm and 40mm firings to simulate the rolling and pitching of a destroyer deck.[76]

> For over three years the citizens of nearby San Diego and La Jolla have heard the firing of the guns, watched during the evenings the long arcs of the tracers, felt—sometimes a bit nervously—the varying concussions from the guns. At times they have lined up in their cars along the highway paralleling the station and watched with interest the maneuvering of the drone as it simulated a bombing or torpedo run, a strafer or one of the short-lived kamikazes. Occasionally a woman has called the station and complained that the noise keeps her children from sleeping or another has told of watching the plaster drop from the walls or the dishes fall from the shelves.[77]

Over 292,000 officers and men were trained at Pacific Beach (and an estimated twenty million rounds were fired) before antiaircraft training centers were closed at the end of the war in favor of training aboard light cruiser *Tucson* (CL-98).[78]

Training for those watch officers and operators associated with the new shipboard concept of centralized command and control from a CIC also became a pressing need as the war progressed. Beginning in August 1943 training was conducted by OTCPAC officers and included a series of informal lectures given by Lt. Comdr. Frank Johnson and, later, courses for prospective commanding officers and CIC teams. Training aligned with courses at NRSL's Radar Operator's School and included a single day's training on board *Moosehead* (IX-98). CIC group training facilities were also established at NAAS San Clemente in mid-1943 for the training of CIC radar fighter directors.[79]

A CIC Indoctrination School was officially established on 9 February 1945 as an outgrowth of these efforts in a portion of existing CIC training facilities (including a mockup of a destroyer CIC) at the West Coast Sound School. The school rapidly outgrew its facilities by the bay and in 1946 moved to the ninety-five-acre location of the Radar Operator's School on the top of Point Loma, absorbing its equipment.[80]

By 1949 a CIC Team Training Center existed at the site and, in 1954, the center was redesignated as the Fleet Air Defense Training Center. In 1960 it was redesignated again as the Fleet Anti-Air Warfare Training Center, and in 1976 the school's name changed to Fleet Combat Training Center, Pacific.[81]

At the beginning of World War II, Destroyer Base commander Capt. Byron McCandless's domain consisted of 124 acres (of which 82 were water) and 41 buildings. By May 1946 the base had expanded to 294 buildings and 921 acres (659 land) and held within its boundaries sixteen miles of railway. Both before and after the war the base stood as a storage site for hundreds of reserve ships and as a home base for destroyers and submarines that came and went in silent rhythms swayed by training tempos. During the war the base's reserve fleets vanished and operational destroyers and submarines were shunted to forward areas, many not returning to San Diego for the entire duration. The base evolved to become a purely industrial center, with a repair and ship modernization mission. As such, the secretary of the Navy formally redesignated the base as the U.S. Naval Repair Base, San Diego on 7 October 1943 and all repair activities were concentrated within an Industrial Command. Between 1943 and 1945 the repair base performed conversion, overhaul, maintenance, and battle-damage repair for 5,117 ships (2,190 of which were drydocked).[82]

Before the war Captain McCandless was so strapped for operating funds that he had to recycle the ceiling beams from the Coronado Tent City ballroom and a thousand seats and the organ from the downtown Savoy Theater in order to build the base's auditorium. During the war the base was flush with upgrades and at one time boasted eight floating drydocks engaged in round-the-clock repairs.

Destroyer type commander schools and certain repair specialty schools had been established at the destroyer base in the thirties and a new $120,000 central fleet school building was approved in 1935. By January 1941 eight specialties were under training at the base: torpedo, radio, fire control, diesel engine, welders, visual signaling, music, and sound (sonar). In June 1943, in tandem with a streamlined reorganization of the repair base, all nonship repair training was placed under the repair base's Schools and Training Command. On 20 February 1946 this command was subsumed within the Fleet Training Center, a command that exists to this day.[83]

Late afternoon on 14 August 1945, as *everyone* swarms toward Broadway to celebrate. *National Archives*

Pleasure boats, ferries, and small landing craft surround light cruiser *San Diego* (CL-53) as it enters the harbor to begin a city-wide cele-bration on 27 October 1945. All returning Navy ships had their names painted in large white letters on their side as much for the public's use as it was a new style of identification. Rows and rows of now-surplus planes pack North Island behind her. *National Archives*

The number of people assigned to the repair base surged and by war's end would number over twenty-eight thousand. Temporary housing blossomed on newly designated Navy land across Harbor Drive in the "Brooklyn Annex." For a time the repair base also stood as the central receiving station in San Diego, processing all nature of naval personnel en route to and from naval units. That assignment would be transferred to the Naval Training and Distribution Center at Camp Elliott outside Miramar in 1944.

The problem of safely handling naval ammunition in and around San Diego rose in importance with the approach of war. Beyond the storage afforded by ships' magazines, the only other ordnance storage in the area amounted to several small stowage sites at North Island and thirteen magazines associated with the fuel annex on Point Loma. The entire supply of Southern California naval ordnance was dependent on rail shipments from ammunition depots near Mare Island or Hawthorne, Nevada—shipments that could be adversely affected by wartime shortages of rolling stock or by congestion at wartime shipping sites, not to mention the inherent safety concerns of long-range transport of explosives.

Four sites in Southern California were inspected as poten-tial depot sites, with a final site selected on 9,148 sprawling acres of Rancho Santa Margarita Las Flores, midway between San Diego and San Pedro—an isolated area "of no particular agricultural value," with ready access to both rail and highway.

Construction began in early September 1941, and on 2 Febru-ary 1942 Naval Ammunition Depot, Fallbrook was commis-sioned. It began its operations with twenty-six high-explosive magazines and a few key officers, civilians, and Marine guards. By war's end Fallbrook contained 163 magazines with a com-plement of 45 officers and 709 enlisted plus a Marine guard.[84] Shipments from Fallbrook were directed by rail to ships in San Diego Bay or by truck for loading aboard barges within the Oceanside boat basin. Later, shipments aboard large freighters and ammunition ships would be directed to the new Navy ammunition wharf at Seal Beach.

By the middle of 1944 approximately three thousand tons of ammunition to over two hundred vessels per month were being loaded in the highly congested waters of San Diego Bay, causing no small amount of concern to the captain of the port and civilian authorities. To address these issues, the comman-dant proposed a site for a bayside naval ammunition depot south of the repair base on land contiguous to Chula Vista and with sufficient mandated open land surrounding the site for safety. Plans for a quay wall, finger pier, temporary storage areas, and dredging were drawn, but the end of the war ter-minated the project.[85]

According to noted strategist Frank Uhling of the Naval War College, the two greatest naval innovations of the Second World War were the rise in the power projection capability of the car-rier task force and the perfection of the doctrine of amphibious assault. San Diego's association with the fledgling tactics of amphibious warfare in the thirties had been peripheral to its long-standing interest in carrier aviation, but that would change quickly midway through 1942. In February 1942, in the face of a rising need for amphibious training to support landings in Europe and the island-hopping campaign of the Pacific, the CNO directed that amphibious type commanders be named for both the Pacific and Atlantic Fleets, and in September he authorized the establishment of a landing craft detachment of two hundred men and thirty second-hand boats to be formed at the destroyer base. Within six months the detachment had outgrown its quarters and other suitable sites for amphibious training were surveyed. Recognizing that the Silver Strand held obvious advantages with the quiet waters of the bay on one side and rough ocean waters on the other (ideal training conditions for every type of landing craft the Navy used), the secretary of the Navy authorized the establishment of an amphibious training base at Coronado on 12 June 1943.[86]

Beginning in July 1943 a crash program transplanted material from the bottom of San Diego Bay to create a 134-acre landfill perpendicular to the Silver Strand just south of the Hotel del Coronado. This main base site was then augmented by a second site three miles further south as an advance base conditioning area.

Literally out of nowhere, a teaming amphibious training base was formed with property from a variety of sources: leased beach and landfill area from the City of Coronado, beach land from a State of California park, thirteen acres of ocean beach leased from the Spreckels Company, a leased right-of-way from the San Diego and Arizona Eastern Railroad Company, and land ultimately taken over from the Army at Fort Emory and Battery Cortez.[87] A portion of the construction force for the many Landing Force training buildings and barracks was said to have been made up of approximately five hundred German prisoners of war who were transported to Coronado in 1944 and 1945 and who lived in a stockade in the middle of the base.[88]

Naval Amphibious Training Base, Coronado was formally commissioned on 15 January 1944, and the Landing School was consolidated as a department of the training base on 23 June 1945. The base was redesignated as Naval Amphibious Base, Coronado on 7 January 1946.[89]

By the end of the war the base had trained 4,600 officers and an incredible 60,000 enlisted in the art of amphibious assault in a vigorous training regimen that included seamanship, boat navigation, beach landings and retractions, beach marking, flashing light communications, gunnery, and boat

engine repair. It was home to 117 separate barracks buildings, two mess halls, and eleven bachelor officers' quarters buildings. Famed boxer Comdr. Gene Tunney was the base's physical fitness officer. The amphibious base also had cognizance of the Fort Emory Detachment of the Landing Craft School that had set up shop on the grounds of Fort Emory on Coronado Heights in 1944 just north of the Naval Communications Station. Seven thousand enlisted and four hundred officers were assigned to the site, housed in 284 Quonset huts.[90]

The Naval Training Station had benefited from a foresighted decision in 1939 for a major expansion program that in three years had increased its training capacity fourfold. By September 1942 the station had already reached its wartime peak of forty thousand sailors, including twenty-five thousand recruits, and training was humming along on nine-hour workday schedules, seven days a week.

For the first time since its founding in 1923 the Naval Training Station was a closed base. The station commander kept security tight, gates were closed, and civilians were not permitted access to training events or even graduation ceremonies. A permanent Naval Landing Force was organized to provide protection against enemy attack. Sailors were equipped with rifles, pistols, knives, bayonets, and full field packs. On Preble Field 5-inch and 3-inch guns were kept in working order with live ammunition nearby.[91]

From 1940 to 1944 more than one hundred acres of additional land was reclaimed for the station from dredging, adding four new self-contained training camps: Decatur, Luce, Mahan, Farragut. Each camp contained its own medical and dental dispensary, auditorium, gymnasium, swimming pool, recreation center, canteen, and grinder. Entertainment was dispensed across the station by individual camp, so that it was not unusual to have four movies or multiple sporting events running nightly.

A new annex to the Naval Training Station was established in Balboa Park. Just as in World War I, recruits lived in tents and marched to classes along wide exhibition thoroughfares. The annex was opened on 22 December 1941 and was later named Camp Kidd after Rear Adm. Isaac Kidd.

The training station's proximity to Los Angeles made it a favorite of Hollywood stars. Hardly a week passed when there were not shows in either the boxing ring or in Luce Auditorium. So many wartime broadcasts originated from Luce that a radio control booth was build backstage. Stars that appeared in the Center's newspaper, the *Hoist*, included Broderick Crawford, Marilyn Maxwell, Henry Fonda, Betty Grable, Harpo

Marx, Gene Kelly, Jimmy Durante, the Andrews Sisters, Pat O'Brien, Sophie Tucker, and Tyrone Power.

Another "celebrity" who frequented the training station was Abe Hollandersky, better known as "Abe the Newsboy." Abe was as colorful as they come. A prizefighter mentioned in "Ripley's Believe It or Not" for fighting 1,043 fights, he once sold President Theodore Roosevelt a newspaper aboard the presidential yacht *Mayflower* and from that point was recognized as the "only person given the right by presidential proclamation to sell newspapers on any naval station or ship."

While peddling papers to ships and at stations in San Diego and San Pedro, he was also busy boosting the Navy. He was on friendly terms with a wide array of admirals and captains and in 1943 received an Award of Merit from Navy recruiters in Southern California for helping to recruit seventeen hundred men and women. He was a legend at the Naval Training Center "where I have always been welcomed and felt among shipmates."[92]

In April 1944 the secretary of the Navy upgraded the station to Group Command status and redesignated it as Naval Training Center, San Diego. Three primary subordinate commands (Recruit Training, Service School, and Naval Administration Command) were established under a center commander.

The war also dramatically changed Balboa Naval Hospital. In 1941 the hospital was caring for roughly 1,200 patients in 1,424 beds with a staff of 93 medical officers, 92 nurses, and 517 hospital corpsmen. By August 1945 the hospital was caring for over 8,000 patients in 10,499 beds with a staff of 159 medical officers and interns, 530 nurses, and 2,297 hospital corpsmen.[93] Between 1941 and 1945 172,000 patients had been treated with the highest daily census of around 12,000 late in 1944.

Hospital facilities were stretched to the limit, covered walkways became open-air wards, and the central hospital soon expanded into six separate units. Unit One consisted of the buildings at the main Balboa Hospital. Unit Two included twenty-five Exposition buildings in Balboa Park taken over in 1941 for added ward and storage space. This unit contained a tent city of 239 canvas-covered tents sitting on raised wood foundations. The California Building, Fine Arts Gallery, and Museum of Natural History were used as hospital wards. The House of Hospitality became the nurses' quarters. The Japanese Tea Garden became a Red Cross servicemen's center. The lily pond that had been used for seamanship training during the First World War was converted to a swimming pool.[94]

Unit Three, Camp Kidd, was transferred to the hospital in 1944 from the Army and became the site of the Hospital Corps

School. It was made up of thirty-three converted Army barracks near the site of the present Aerospace Museum. Unit Four was made up of twenty-eight Army barracks in the southwestern section of the park and Unit Five was composed of eleven buildings used for storage also in Balboa Park.[95]

Unit Six was the convalescent branch of the hospital and was established in early 1943 on the grounds of the John Burnham house in Rancho Santa Fe. The home included many acres of fruit orchards, a swimming pool, tennis court, archery range, putting green, and a chapel and was reserved for patients who were fully ambulatory but not yet ready to return to active duty. In return for the use of city-owned property during the war the Navy paid $790,000 to the city and, after the war, donated surplus military buildings and equipment.[96]

At four on a hazy mid-summer afternoon, Lt. (jg) Bud Reynolds was piloting his TBM Avenger through tight low-level figure-8s while practicing ASW bombing on smoke floats in glassy waters north of the Coronado Islands. After finishing his carrier qualifications aboard *Ranger*, Reynolds had only a few final training requirements to meet before being ordered to an escort carrier's air group en route to the war zone. "The war zone" in August 1945 meant only one thing—the anticipated invasion of Japan.

Abruptly over "Guard" came the unusual transmission: "General Recall, all aircraft return to base." With a sizable number of aircraft aloft, the order caused an immediate frenzy of congestion as planes approached North Island from every point of the compass. Larger aircraft entered the pattern for the runways; smaller carrier aircraft aimed for the mat, some landing in formation.[97] The air traffic ordeal was now supplanted by a melee of taxiing aircraft all heading for a parking spot on the apron. By the time Reynolds cut his powerful Wright engine, the reason for the unusual recall was clearly obvious—all of North Island was caught in one outrageously out-of-control celebration. Hostilities had ceased with Japan. V-J Day had come to San Diego.

Downtown, buildings and offices emptied quickly and people dashed into the streets. Broadway was ankle-deep in confetti and paper. Kissing was epidemic. A slow line of cars snaked down Broadway, each carrying its own band of revelers. A barefoot Marine scaled a palm tree in Horton Square to plant a flag atop it and was rewarded for his bravado by "women and girls who fought for the privilege of kissing him." At the Hotel del Coronado, the end of the war was announced over the loudspeaker, remembers Melody Morgan, a Coronado teenager. "Then you could hear sirens and church bells."[98]

San Diego makes her approach on Broadway Pier as thousands wait to greet her. *San Diego Historical Society*

Within weeks, Operation Magic Carpet would be under way in earnest, with Navy ships returning to the States jammed to the gills with soldiers, sailors, and Marines. The transport *Grundy* was the first of hundreds of these ships to pull into San Diego.

> Hours before landfall we were all up on the flight deck, our eyes straining at the horizon. Then, the hazy, low lump of hills rose above the morning sea and then the first structures and finally the whole wonderful patchwork, like a Cezanne canvas. There were shouts of "There she is!" and "Home!" or simple, speechless exultant outcries. There was a band waiting on the wharf and that cherished symbol of what we had been fighting for, a majorette, her blonde curls bouncing, and her plump legs flashing in the San Diego sun. As we filed down the gangway, every man of us imagined himself a hero, and some were.[99]

On 27 October, the antiaircraft cruiser *San Diego* (CL-53)—which held the distinction as the first major Allied warship to enter Tokyo Bay—returned to San Diego for a spectacular Navy Day fete. "Thousands Greet Cruiser San Diego on Arrival Here," sang the headlines describing her triumphant transit up the channel, surrounded every yard by fireboats and well-wishers. Ceremonies continued at Balboa Stadium and that evening, for the first time since the war began, ships in the harbor dazzled the city with powerful searchlight displays.

San Diego's only previous visit to her namesake city had been on 17 May 1942 where she arrived for hurried training shortly after being commissioned. As all harbor movements were veiled in official secrecy, there was no formal celebration or official recognition by the city of her presence. During her

stay the story was told of an anonymous sailor from the Engineering Department who was ashore on liberty, liberally inebriated. A local policeman offered to assist him and, as the hour was late, asked, "Where are you from, sailor?" Sailor: "*San Diego*." Policeman: "What part of San Diego?" Sailor: "The forward boiler room." The sailor was led off to a local drying-out tank, the policeman convinced that no such ship existed. *San Diego* deployed on 1 June as part of the *Saratoga* task force that was sprinting to either aid the forces at the Battle of Midway or be in position to protect Hawaii if the Japanese had broken through. That was the first of three years of nonstop action for the cruiser that would steam over three hundred thousand miles in the Pacific theater and would earn eighteen battle stars from Guadalcanal to Okinawa, all without losing a single crewmember.[100]

A month later, to celebrate the end of the war in its own manner, the Naval Training Center opened its gates to the citizens of the city, with an invitation to attend a two-day celebration. San Diego's response was beyond all expectation, with over three hundred thousand taking advantage of planned tours of the station for the first time since it was closed as a security measure in 1941.[101] In one sense this spectacular turnout surprised everyone as those who toured the Naval Training Center reflected fully half of San Diego's population. In another sense, though, it wasn't surprising at all, merely representing the final act in the stunning devotion of the city's energy and enthusiasm that had spanned the total four years of the war effort.

1953

The sheltered harbor and the absence of bad weather during most of the year eliminate the discomforts of boating which destroyermen suffer in most other American ports. San Diego's mild, yet invigorating climate promotes good health and enjoyment of out-of-door activities which naval men love and for which adequate facilities exist locally.

Rear Adm. Luke McNamee, Commander, Destroyer Force, U.S. Pacific Fleet

In early 1953 Bob Wilson went triumphantly to Washington. The new Republican representative of the Thirtieth Congressional District of California had been elected by effective use of the new medium of television advertising and a cachet "for outstanding young leadership" but no clear vision of how best to shape the San Diego–Navy relationship to advantage. Although a distant descendent of a former secretary of the Navy, Wilson had remarkably skimpy military credentials for a representative of a "Navy town," and his campaign themes had not emphasized Defense despite the looming presence of Korea.[1] But through luck and the sanguine advice of retired Rear Adm. Leslie Gehres, Wilson would soon ignite a dynamic growth cycle in San Diego's Navy, fully as conspicuous as that masterminded by William Kettner forty years previous.

In 1952 the Navy spent a respectable $76 million on projects in San Diego County, but most work was scheduled for completion by 1953 with little planned thereafter—a definite red flag for practicing politicians. Soon after the election, Gehres pointedly urged Wilson to seek the single open seat on the House Armed Services Committee—an audacious move for a mere freshman representative. Starting with little more than the intuitive sense that any increase in Navy investment was good for San Diego, Wilson set out to encourage an entire

spectrum of Navy growth, setting in motion efforts that would become so successful between 1952 and 1960 that Navy spending in the county would grow nearly eightfold.[2]

Bob Wilson's San Diego was only eight years removed from the Second World War. As the vast campaigns in the Pacific drew to a close, the United States emerged a superpower; San Diego emerged crowded, dusty, and even a bit drab, its image indelibly forged as a "Navy town." At war's end San Diego was, for all intents, a two-industry town—Navy and aircraft construction—with both industries facing demobilization and a severe postwar correction. In San Diego County wartime airstrips would be decommissioned and ships mothballed. The Naval Supply Center would reduce its workforce by over 50 percent and the Naval Training Center's population would reach a twenty-year low. Aircraft contracts would be canceled en masse and fifty thousand war workers and their families would leave the city as the county's overall population declined by almost eighty thousand by 1950.[3]

Still, all across the West, the war had sown the seeds for a new era of promising economic and population growth. More than ten million servicemen and women were stationed in the West during the war and three million more would pass through western states on their way home after the war. More than any other single city San Diego capitalized on this trend

After the war, the Naval Station again returned to its prewar mission of laying up and caring for hundreds of ships of the reserve fleet.
San Diego Historical Society

and became a favorite destination of many postwar families with its newly built housing, new sewage and water systems, and new city airport.[4]

Famed editor Neil Morgan was one of many offspring of the "defense boom" who came to San Diego in the forties, immediately recognized the region's unique attractiveness, and stayed:

> On my first visit to San Diego, the train snaked down from Los Angeles beside the most exotic coastline I'd ever seen, a voluptuous collision of round green hills and hammering surf, and those snug, unexpected lagoons. Splashing over everything, on that late afternoon in summer, the rich gold sun of California. I [crossed] to North Island . . . on the waterfront nickel-snatcher. There were Navy seaplanes practicing landings on the harbor, old PBY Catalinas and the big new PB2Y-3 Coronados. We dodged our way across the bay while that sun sank low off Point Loma, making amber dazzles on the bay and a sweet ocean breeze kept it cool.
>
> There was a class of ten of us fresh ensigns headed for the Pacific, and the COMAIRPAC captain gave us a brief moment the next day to choose among ten duty stations. . . . [A]fter he'd sent nine others to commands in the Western Pacific, he turned to me with a wicked grin, "There's nothing left for you but Headquarters Squadron of Fleet Air Wing 14-2."
>
> "Yes, sir!" I said, without a clue.
>
> "You'll be helping brief the crews ferrying Convair's PB4Y-2s out to WestPac," he said. "That's out here at Kearny Mesa. You'll be stuck in San Diego."

As would happen again years later after the Cold War, San Diego would be buffered from the worst of the military drawdown by the Navy's desire to concentrate within key fleet operations areas. Although naval forces would shrink everywhere, many far-flung activities across the Pacific would relocate to San Diego, helping to bring the city's economic correction to a "soft landing" in the years before defense spending would again increase to meet the Korean War.

Again as before the war, San Diego's fundamental equation for growth relied heavily upon its close ties to the Navy. In the throes of family relocation, water shortages, economic correction, and canceled contracts, the Navy would provide a certain permanence as a reliable and comforting anchor to windward during the worst of times. "Despite the postwar turndown, it was the Navy, backed by the strong support of the Chamber of Commerce that remained the outstanding pillar of the economy and the community. In 1947 the Navy's forty-five thousand active-duty personnel stationed in San Diego plus its fifteen thousand civilian workers comprised 41 percent of the city's labor force and poured $105 million in wages into San Diego's merchants' tills."[5]

The Navy's first spur to San Diego's postwar economy came not with payroll revenue or fleet contracts but with that most precious of California commodities—water. Over the years San Diego's efficient water planning had paced the demands of a slowly increasing population. When the San Vicente Dam was opened in 1941, its water was planned sufficient for an estimated 1950 population of 260,000. But the "defense boom" drove San Diego's population through the 260,000 target only a year later and to 362,000 by 1946. Worse, water demands at military bases had skyrocketed, with water use among federal agencies in San Diego County increasing from 11 percent of total water consumption in 1941 to 41 percent of consumption by 1945.[6]

By 1943 Navy leadership in both San Diego and Washington had recognized that declining water reserves threatened the war effort and advanced two new plans for obtaining additional water. The first involved building a new aqueduct from the north that would tap Colorado River water destined for Los Angeles; the second plan would build a new aqueduct and pumping system from the east to bring water across the Laguna Mountains from Imperial Valley.[7]

In October 1944 a presidential committee reported: "That an emergency did indeed impend the water supply of San Diego that the aqueduct of the Metropolitan Water District

Naval Training Center showing the effects of its wartime expansion in 1949. *National Archives*

Valley Forge (CV-45) slowly makes her way into harbor on 1 December 1950 after a grueling combat tour at the beginning of the Korean War. She never had the opportunity to enjoy a heartfelt San Diego welcome, though, as she turned around within the week for a second wartime deployment to the Korean war zone. *National Archives*

of Southern California was preferable to extension of the All-American Canal [of Imperial Valley] due to the use of gravity system with a minimum of expensive pumping and that the project should be financed 100 percent by the federal government."[8]

Roosevelt wrote House Speaker Sam Rayburn in November 1944, "An impending emergency in the water supply of San Diego County, California has been called to my attention. Owing to the very large naval, other military, war industrial and war housing installations in the area, the situation is of emergency importance to the federal government." That same day Roosevelt endorsed the committee's findings and ordered the Navy's Bureau of Yards and Docks to build a pipeline to connect San Diego's water system with the Colorado River

Aqueduct.[9]

Despite the Navy's clear culpability in creating the community's water deficit, Roosevelt's intent quickly bogged down in bureaucratic cement. The War Production Board asked for a year's construction delay due to manpower shortages. Some in Washington believed the Navy could escape the project by citing the war's impending end, while others lumped it within war contracts to be canceled.

Vice Adm. J. B. Oldendorf, the Eleventh Naval District commandant, weighed in heavily, citing the emergency nature of the construction. After extensive Washington negotiations, Oldendorf won a compromise where the Navy would complete pipeline construction while the city would reimburse costs (about $14.1 million). The Navy awarded the first con-

Congressman Bob Wilson represented the San Diego area in Congress from 1952 to 1980 and was a member of the House Armed Services Committee for most of his career. Eleanor Ring, daughter of Wells and Belle Reynolds, was chairperson of Wilson's reelection campaign in Coronado, an elected city councilmember, and a delegate to the Republican National Convention. *Susan Ring Keith*

Forge (CV-45) was the only American aircraft carrier in action. Less than four years old, *Valley Forge* raced northward from Hong Kong harbor with news of the North Korean invasion across the Korean thirty-eighth parallel. Her airmen launched the first carrier raids of the war, engaged in bitter battles around the Pusan perimeter, supported the Inchon landings, and bagged the first enemy MiG of the war.[12]

Back in San Diego, carriers *Philippine Sea, Boxer, Sicily,* and *Badoeng Strait* rushed to the front with their accompanying escorts and a dozen amphibious attack transports. Eleven naval reserve aircraft squadrons were activated and began training at North Island, Brown, and Ream Fields, and the carriers *Essex, Princeton, Bon Homme Richard,* and *Antietam* were taken from mothballs and would steam to San Diego for shakedown.

Valley Forge returned to a tumultuous San Diego welcome on 1 December 1950 but, prophetically, she shared headlines that day with news that waves of Communist Chinese troops were swarming south across the Yalu River. Two days later emotions aboard *Valley Forge* abruptly swung from the comforts

struction contract in May 1945 and in 1946 San Diego voters endorsed project bonds and established an expanded water authority to manage it. On 26 November 1947 Navy construction was completed and on 11 December the new aqueduct was dedicated and put into operation.[10]

The Navy's actions did far more than simply construct pipes and flues; it cemented nothing less than San Diego's civic prosperity and economic expansion well into the next decade. Without the Navy's intervention, massive public works water projects might have taken years to maneuver through approval channels, effectively holding economic expansion hostage to the results. Today, over two-thirds of San Diego County's water flows through aqueducts from the Colorado River.

The realities of the Korean War had, again, placed San Diego in its accustomed position as the primary West Coast training, logistics, and research hub for a distant Pacific campaign. During August 1950 sixteen thousand Marines and thirty-four thousand tons of their equipment were shipped from San Diego. Between 1950 and 1952 the number of ships homeported in San Diego increased from 42 to 146, while shore-based naval personnel increased by 500 percent.[11]

For the first two months of the conflict San Diego's *Valley*

Naval aviators at NAS San Diego count the 107 combat missions racked up in Korea by this Navy F4U Corsair, May 1951. *National Archives*

of a well-deserved homecoming to the tight-jawed realities of war when new sailing orders arrived to return immediately to the front. *Valley Forge* embarked a new air group, replenished, and sailed for Korea on 6 December. In three further months on the line, she contributed some twenty-five hundred additional sorties to the war effort. In December 1951 she returned to Korea for her third deployment in less than two years and would deploy for her fourth of the war before the end of 1952, leading Rear Adm. John "Pegleg" Hoskins of Carrier Division 3 to comment: "I can't conceive of modern warfare fought without carriers"—San Diego carriers.

The advent of the Korean War also saw many ships of the South Bay "Mothball Fleet" ordered back into service. By 1946 the wartime 32nd Street Repair Base was largely back into the business of laying up ships and caring for an extensive reserve fleet—its primary prewar activity. As the base had also grown to represent the primary San Diego warship base, the secretary

of the Navy returned its designation to Naval Station, San Diego on 15 September 1946. By December 1946, 340 ships had been mothballed and assigned to the Naval Station's Reserve Fleet, rising to 450 ships by 1949. Most reserve ships concentrated along new piers to the south of the main station taken over after the war.[13]

The primary industrial facilities of the Naval Station, which had served the Navy so well during the Second World War, were combined into the Naval Repair Facility (NRF) on 1 April 1954. NRF's 2,270 employees repaired and maintained active and reserve fleet vessels, performed extensive alterations to *Essex*-class carriers and, even, battery exchanges for San Diego–based submarines.[14]

Yarnall (DD-541) and *O'Brien* (DD-725) were typical of the destroyer activations undertaken at the Naval Station. *Yarnall* had earned seven battle stars during World War II campaigns before entering the San Diego Reserve Fleet in early 1947. With

Philippine Sea (CV-47) returns to North Island after a Korean War deployment in August 1952 with young Ricky Neudek ready to greet his father. *National Archives*

Navy blimps were frequently sighted over the San Diego skyline between World War II and 1959. *U.S. Naval Institute*

the outbreak of Korean hostilities *Yarnall* was ordered back into active service on 31 August 1950 and recommissioned six months later. By 15 May, after shakedown training, she headed west on the first of two Korean War cruises, returning after each to her homeport of San Diego.[15]

O'Brien had been the victim of a Japanese kamikaze attack late in the Second World War. Repaired, she operated out of San Diego until entering the reserve fleet in October 1947. Three years later she was recommissioned, with Comdr. Chester W. Nimitz Jr. in command, and joined the fleet off Korea in March 1951 for the first of two war deployments.[16]

Naval historian Norman Friedman has characterized the decade after World War II as a "Revolution in Naval Affairs," with technology breakthroughs in high-performance jet aircraft operating from "supercarriers," guided missiles, and fast nuclear submarines (and in the advanced techniques of anti-submarine warfare to counter them). This "revolution" re-shaped the face of the world's navies and could easily have left San Diego or other World War II–era naval bases in its wake. But San Diego had the good fortune and the intelligence (just as it had in the 1920s and '30s) to change with the times and remain perfectly aligned with evolving naval trends. Advanced jet aircraft would begin to operate from improved airfields at North Island and from the new Master Jet Base at Miramar; new supercarriers would be homeported in Coronado; new breakthroughs in radar, communications, and sonar would pour from Point Loma naval laboratories; guided missile tech-

nologies would be perfected in operating areas off the coast; and a new nuclear submarine base would rise at the harbor's mouth. Each of these advances would guarantee its own self-fulfilling promise of continued Navy interest in San Diego. Each technological innovation would spawn a host of associated endeavors; each operational advance would solidify San Diego's coveted standing among naval leadership.

Although each of these events may have proceeded naturally and unimpeded, for twenty years each was aided immeasurably by the guiding hands of Congressman Bob Wilson. In stories reminiscent of the energetic William Kettner, Bob Wilson pragmatically orchestrated the power of his congressional station to both the Navy's and San Diego's benefit.

The Navy's drive to establish a master jet base on Kearny Mesa followed no preordained path. The wartime airfield site at Miramar had survived the first major round of postwar cuts in February 1946 when an investigative board led by Adm. F. J. Horne recommended that North Island and Marine Corps Air Station Miramar remain in full commission, Ream Field be placed in reduced commission, and Brown and San Clemente Fields be retained in a maintenance status. All other auxiliary fields in San Diego County were to be deactivated and declared surplus.[17]

But with reduced operations and the need to consolidate, the Marines decided to concentrate their airbase operations in Orange County and began to leave Miramar during June 1947. Miramar reverted to the Navy as an auxiliary air station that supported patrol squadrons and an occasional photographic squadron.

With Miramar underutilized and with its buildings falling into disrepair, the Navy and the city entered discussions on how best to use the field. Some in the Navy wanted to sell the field outright but the city hesitated (some in city government commenting that Miramar was too far from downtown to be useful). Finally, agreement was reached to operate Miramar as a joint-use airport to handle air cargo and to serve as an alternative passenger terminal to Lindbergh Field. A formal agreement was signed on 18 September 1947, giving the city the right to use the south side of the field. Soon thereafter a United Airlines DC-3 with eighteen passengers aboard became the first of forty-four other commercial aircraft that would use the field in the ensuing year.[18] The city budgeted for the construction of a terminal building, a small ramp, and taxiways connecting to the Navy runway.

In 1949, with the introduction of high-performance jet aircraft into its inventory, the Navy began studying the concept of a master jet base, where air groups and squadrons

F8U Crusaders fly over North Island in July 1958 with NAS Miramar still in relatively open country at the top of the picture. *U.S. Naval Institute*

could be assigned to a home field with central office, hangar, and maintenance facilities. Miramar was chosen as one of several sites earmarked for conversion and, with the Korean War in full swing, that development was rapid. The base won designation as Naval Air Station, Miramar on 1 April 1952, and the Navy canceled the embryonic joint-use agreement with the city that same year. To handle the increased flight tempo of the Korean War, a small outlying field, called Hour-glass Field, was established three miles north of the main air station. Its two-year life began in 1954 on a site now occupied by Miramar College.[19]

By the mid-fifties, increasing Cold War tensions and talk of a "bomber gap" were making their mark on San Diego naval aviation. Navy jet fighters at North Island were placed under Air Force control as one means to enhance continental air defenses. VF(AW)-3, initially flying the Douglas F3D-1 Skynight (and

later the delta wing Douglas F4D Skyray), assumed these duties in December 1955, protecting the seaward approaches to Southern California.[20]

When unidentified air contacts were detected approaching the Southern California coast, an Air Force early warning site on Mount Laguna, code-named "Anderson," would sound the scramble alarm at North Island. Within three minutes a pair of Navy fighters would launch on afterburner, "rattling windows of homes in Coronado," and would be vectored to intercept by Anderson. One or two actual scrambles and two to three training scrambles were expected each day.[21]

Miramar would expand throughout the fifties by absorbing many of the wartime Navy and Marine facilities that had spread across Kearny Mesa. The largest of these was the old Marine base at Camp Elliott, a 28,700-acre government reservation originally known in 1934 as Camp Holcomb, a Marine rifle range. At its height during the war, Camp Elliott was home to fifteen thousand personnel and nearly thirty Marine schools ranging from Rifleman to Tanker and Cook.[22] Elliott was transferred to the Navy on 30 June 1944 as a training and distribution center (and, later, a separation center). In 1946 the camp and its 542 buildings were turned over to the War Assets Administration for disposal as surplus.

The Navy briefly reactivated Camp Elliott on 15 January 1951 to meet a sudden surge of Korean War recruits flooding the Naval Training Center. During Camp Elliott's two-year run as an adjunct training facility, more than fifteen thousand recruits attended boot camp there.[23]

A portion of Camp Elliott in Sycamore Canyon was first transferred to the Air Force as a missile test facility and later transferred to NASA for Atlas and Centaur missile testing by San Diego's General Dynamics. Another Marine training site on Kearny Mesa, Jacques Farm Camp (located on the north side of San Diego River), was converted to the Admiral Baker Recreation Center in 1955.[24]

The dream of using Miramar as a city airport did not end with the loss of the joint-use agreement in 1952. In 1955 the first of many city-sponsored airport studies recommended that Lindbergh Field be augmented with a new field of "intercontinental" capacity. If Miramar could not be used, the study

Converted *Essex* carriers, some as attack carriers, others outfitted as ASW carriers, dominated the North Island quay in the 1950s and 1960s. *U.S. Navy*

Bon Homme Richard (CVA-31) spells out "Hello San Diego" upon returning from a six-month WESTPAC deployment in 1963. *U.S. Naval Institute*

recommended Montgomery Field, a new dredge-fill site on the Silver Strand, or joint use of North Island with the Navy. With its usual audacity the Navy objected to all three, suggesting alternative sites at Torrey Pines, the southeast corner of Mission Bay, or Brown Field.[25]

In January 1956 the Navy solidified its grasp on Miramar by requesting to buy all land within a six-mile radius of the jet flight pattern.[26] According to Vice Adm. Ed Martin, Congressman Wilson became further involved with Miramar later in the fifties when the Navy completed a new jet base at Lemoore, California, and planned to move all San Diego fighter squadrons there (including those flying the new F-4 Phantom). Under the Navy's original plan, jet attack aircraft (primarily flying the A-4 Skyhawk) would replace the fighters and concentrate at Miramar. When Wilson discovered those fighter squadrons generally included more pilots and ground-support personnel, he arranged for fighters to stay at Miramar while attack aircraft were transferred to Lemoore.

Bob Wilson's dabbling in the naval aviation priorities of San Diego did not always prove successful. In the late forties the Navy pushed for a new "naval mobile base" concept, where high-performance seaplanes would rapidly deploy and operate from temporary bases supported by naval vessels anchored nearby. Key to this concept was the Navy's main long-range seaplane, the Martin P5M; a new jet-powered seaplane, the Martin P6M Seamaster; and a radical new supersonic jet fighter that could take off from water.

In January 1951 San Diego's Convair received an order for the development of two XF2Y Sea Dart aircraft with retractable twin hydro-skis as a prototype of a water-based fighter. Experimental flight testing began in December 1952 on the waters of North San Diego Bay between the Convair plant at Lindbergh Field and North Island.[27]

Concurrent with the Sea Dart tests in 1953, the Navy began confidential planning for a huge new seaplane base in South San Diego Bay. Twice before the Navy had eyed the South Bay for its seaplane base. In 1941 the Silver Strand was enlarged for a seaplane base by dredge fill (at the site of today's Navy housing) but became an amphibious small-boat training area instead. Later, in March 1945, the CNO approved a new seaplane base concept for the Imperial Beach saltponds at the extreme end of the bay. The South Bay was also used late in the war for classified testing of new air-dropped torpedoes designed for shallow water operations, especially "against hydro-electric installation dams and other facilities." The Navy's ambitious plans for new South Bay bases collapsed with the end of the war.[28]

Five different options for a South Bay seaplane base surfaced anew in 1953, citing San Diego Bay as "the most suitable location for seaplane operations on the entire West Coast," and noting that the Navy already controlled a huge restricted access

The Convair YF2Y-1 Sea Dart, developed, built, and tested in San Diego, could reach supersonic speeds in the air and land and take off from the water on twin hydroskis. A total of five Sea Dart aircraft were built and three flown in a flight-test series that included more than three hundred tests (including open-ocean sea tests several miles south of Point Loma). *U.S. Navy*

area (amounting to roughly half of the bay south of the amphibious base) for seaplane operations.[29] Of the five different plans, the Navy favored sites at either the current Coronado Cays or between the amphibious base and the current location of Navy housing (where the width of the Silver Strand would be doubled through dredging). The three less desirable plans included purchasing Silver Strand State Park area and filling in the bayside, filling the shoreline south of Coronado Cays at Coronado Heights, or filling in all the saltponds of Imperial Beach to build on a site stretching across the lower end of the bay from Coronado Heights to Chula Vista.[30]

In 1954 the Navy made its plans for the hangars, control towers, ramps, and concrete aprons of the new "seadrome" public. Public criticism was unexpectedly light and Bob Wilson speedily introduced legislation to dredge portions of the South Bay to improve seaplane-landing areas. But by September 1956 support was noticeably weakening and the Coronado City Council voted to have the Navy clarify its plans for a new South Bay seadrome. In the fall of 1957 the Navy abandoned its scheme to develop the base when problems developed with the Seamaster seaplane program.[31]

Beaten but not bowed, Wilson looked for ways to shift the already approved South Bay dredging funds for another of his prime projects, the homeporting of the Navy's new large aircraft carriers. Shortly after his first election, Wilson had proposed the construction of a massive outer harbor for large carriers on the ocean side of North Island. The harbor would be protected by a mammoth new breakwater that would be built from Zuniga Point to Imperial Beach, conceptually very similar to the outer Los Angeles/Long Beach harbor.

The *Evening Tribune* favored the plan, suggesting that without the harbor large carriers would never be based here: "A breakwater south from North Island would offer space for large ships that now can stop here only with difficulty or not at all. They would be in position to disperse quickly in an emergency and more room would be available for commercial vessels in the inner harbor." The CNO supported the plan (but thought it expensive) and, not surprisingly, the plan was vigorously opposed by Coronado mayor W. A. Vestal on the logical grounds that it would irreversibly harm Coronado's beaches.[32]

The plan had paralleled a similar (but much smaller) effort advanced by the Navy in 1923 when Rear Adm. George Williams, U.S. Fleet Chief of Staff, suggested that "San Diego missed a golden opportunity of getting the Battle Fleet when it failed to erect a small breakwater on the sea side of Coronado, and connect this breakwater with Coronado's streetcar

The stately gull-winged Martin P5M Marlin was the last of the Navy's long line of operational seaplanes stretching back to the Curtiss A-1. San Diego was long the Navy's premier seaplane base, with seaplanes a common sight taxiing up and down the bay between North Island and their takeoff areas. The last P5M flew out of San Diego in November 1967. *U.S. Navy*

system to accommodate the thousands of bluejackets landed daily from capital ships [at anchor in the Roads]."[33]

Propitiously for San Diego, the outer harbor breakwater plan never gained consensus and Wilson's energy turned toward the more conventional initiative of a deeper turning basin and improved berthing area at North Island. The issue was not insignificant, as the *Union* warned: "Unless this larger dock is provided, San Diego eventually will lose the Pacific Fleet's attack carrier forces, which will be rebuilt around the big flattops." The days of the smaller aircraft carrier were nearing an end and, despite North Island's historic reciprocity with carrier aviation, if San Diego could not capture new supercarriers its hard-fought position as the West Coast's premier naval base might be threatened.[34]

Wrangling and bartering continued for a year, until July 1958 when Wilson successfully inserted a line into the military construction authorization bill for a new supercarrier wharf. Turning basin dredging began almost immediately with two million cubic yards of dredged material helping to form Harbor Island.[35] Harbor dredging was completed just in time in September 1961 to greet the arriving *Kitty Hawk* (CVA-63), which would open the door to an era of carrier homeporting at North Island.

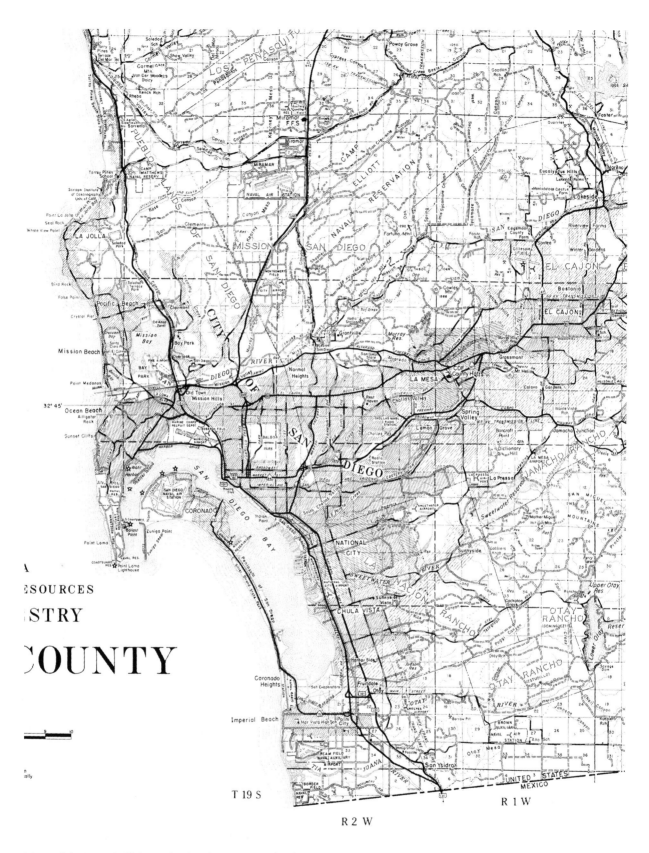

Many of the Navy facilities anchoring the San Diego landscape in 1954 (especially North Island and the Naval Station) would be familiar to most residents today, but others like Ream Field, Border Field, Brown Field, Camp Matthews, and Camp Elliott have felt the impact of history. NAS Miramar stands alone, miles from any city encroachment. *San Diego Historical Society*

San Diego's ability to focus the technological might of its naval laboratories had a profound impact on keeping it "in the game" during the 1950s. Throughout the Cold War technological innovation and technical wizardry were prized military pursuits and San Diego's expanding role as a center of defense and aerospace research and development placed the city at the forefront of these high-tech trends.

Although naval activity in San Diego scaled down immediately after the Second World War, activities at the Point Loma laboratories grew, incubated in many ways by Roger Revelle. NRSL was renamed the Navy Electronics Laboratory (NEL) on 29 November 1945 and by June 1946 UCDWR's remaining contracts and projects had been absorbed within the new lab. In August 1947 NEL gained eleven acres from the Navy's Fuel Facility and the Small Craft Facility and in June 1949 the Quarantine Station property was formally transferred from the Public Health Service (today this area is called Bayside). On 28 April 1949 the property of the Navy Radio Station Point Loma was transferred to NEL to form part of today's "Topside" area.[36]

Unwilling to dissolve the war-tested team of naval operators and civilian and academic researchers in underwater acoustics and ocean physics, the Navy and the University of California entered into a partnership to form the Marine Physical Laboratory (MPL). Managed by Scripps but sponsored by the Navy, MPL was established in 1946 at NEL to continue classified research on underwater acoustics started by UCDWR. To complete this rearchitecture of San Diego underwater research, the Navy named Roger Revelle to head the geophysics branch of the newly established Office of Research and Inventions (later the Office of Naval Research) in Washington, D.C. From this position, Revelle helped direct prized resources toward underwater naval research and, in short order, the Navy became Scripps's primary customer as many classified wartime projects were transferred to San Diego.[37]

With the foundations of NEL, MPL, and Scripps, San Diego instantly became a recognized world leader in oceanography and a centerpiece of Navy research, development, testing, and evaluation. It was the perfect match of needs: the Navy gained tactical advantages through breakthroughs in classified underwater research, San Diego benefited through a continuous flow of resources, the attraction of premier talent, and even the Navy's willingness to repair and partially man Scripps research vessels. When congressional support was needed, there was always Bob Wilson, whose interest in oceanography on behalf of San Diego was legend.

San Diego also soon became a world leader in the area of arctic underwater research led by Dr. Waldo Lyon. In 1950 Lyon approached the NEL Scientific Council with the idea of establishing a lab to support Navy submarines in the Arctic, an expanding operational requirement with important Cold War ramifications. "You couldn't do everything in the field, you couldn't do everything by just taking a submarine and trying

Six carriers lie alongside North Island in this 1955 aerial. *San Diego Historical Society*

The huge Wullenweber direction-finding radio antenna became a landmark for a whole generation of navymen at Coronado Heights north of Imperial Beach. *U.S. Navy*

things. You had to have laboratory work," Lyon argued. Initially rebuffed, Lyon went ahead anyway, specializing the activities of NEL's Submarine Research Facility toward ice operations and "almost single-handedly trying to convince the Navy of the importance of the Arctic."[38]

Despite years of disappointments, Lyon's valuable arctic experience on both diesel submarines and icebreakers contributed mightily to *Nautilus*'s (SSN-571) success during its

first arctic explorations. In 1967 the name of the Submarine Research Facility was changed to Arctic Submarine Laboratory with Lyon as its director. Research focused on sound acoustics, hull strengthening, navigation, and weapons use. For over forty years, it was said, San Diego's Waldo Lyon dominated the field of naval arctic operations as no one has before or since.[39]

Bob Wilson recognized, as did many others, that the coming of the nuclear submarine would reshape the Navy's submarine service much as new supercarriers were redefining carrier aviation. In the 1950s submarines in San Diego were either moored alongside piers at the destroyer base or were tied up alongside tenders anchored near the main shipping channel. In 1950 the Navy named a submarine flotilla commander for San Diego to help coordinate the activities of an increasing number of ships and, by 1958, San Diego stood as the only West Coast submarine homeport with two squadrons, each with twelve submarines assigned.[40]

In August 1958 Wilson cornered the secretary of the Navy on a plane returning to Washington to press for the need for a new San Diego nuclear submarine base. Although submarines had been stationed at 32nd Street for years and recommendations had been floated for a new South Bay submarine base, most opinion favored a base site near the harbor's mouth, in part to remove any potential nuclear threat from

Summit County (LST-1146) and four other LSTs conduct landing practice on the Silver Strand during the early 1960s. *Naval Historical Center*

directly in front of downtown.[41] Through Wilson's efforts, a broad consensus between the Navy and city slowly began to jell, built upon the desire to keep "current" with the modern Navy and remove submarines from their mid-channel moorings (thus making the harbor freer for commercial shipping).[42] San Diego newspapers strongly favored Wilson's initiative: "There is no time to lose in swinging San Diego's support behind the Ballast Point project. In seven to ten years, the nuclear submarine will have replaced the conventional undersea craft. San Diego must keep pace with the atomic age Navy. It must look ahead."[43] There was even the suggestion that San Diego might become a submarine construction base for General Dynamics and General Atomic.

The first supercarrier to call San Diego home, *Kitty Hawk* (CVA-63), arrives to a tumultuous San Diego welcome in 1961. *San Diego Historical Society*

Eighteen submarines nestle alongside tenders *Nereus* (AS-17) and *Sperry* (AS-12) in January 1958. One of the primary arguments in favor of developing a new submarine base at Ballast Point was that it would remove submarines from clogging the channel where they impeded large commercial vessels and were susceptible to collisions or other damage. *U.S. Naval Institute*

Recruit "training" extended far beyond classroom instruction and drill at the Naval Training Center. Here, three recruits practice the finer points of peeling potatoes. *National Archives*

Throughout the debate Congressman Wilson consistently and shrewdly "whipped up the lather of the Cold War" to find strategic logic to underpin the argument and to balance the political and economic ambitions of San Diego advocates. "The present uneasy international situation, in my opinion, demands a speeding up of ASW training," warned Wilson. Since the Pacific Fleet's "ASW forces which train in the San Diego area are to be trained with nuclear submarines," the city must have the piers. Otherwise the nuclear subs would be based in Hawaii and they and the ASW forces would lose training time and "nuclear power core life" sailing to their rendezvous.[44]

The Ballast Point site was officially transferred from the Army to the Navy on 2 July 1959, with the Navy subtly designating it only as an extension of NEL. In June 1960 Congress approved $1.7 million for construction of the first submarine pier at Ballast Point. In August 1962 *Scamp* (SSN-588) became the first nuclear submarine to dock at the new pier. Wilson, in characteristic fashion, stumped for even more during the pier's formal dedication: "We hope eventually to have more piers so the entire Pacific Submarine Fleet can be stationed here."[45]

A year later the base was supporting four nuclear submarines, twenty-two diesel submarines, two submarine tenders, and two submarine rescue ships and was formally broken off from NEL and redesignated as a Naval Submarine Support Facility on 23 October 1963.[46]

On 1 October 1981 the Naval Submarine Support Facility designation was changed to Naval Submarine Base, San Diego, and by the mid-1980s the base was supporting over twenty submarines, two submarine tenders, various submarine rescue vessels (including the deep submergence rescue vessels *Avalon* and *Mystic*), deep submergence vessels, and an array of training simulators. A floating drydock capable of accommodating large attack submarines became operational in 1984.[47] The Navy has restored many of the old Army post buildings—including at least one said to be haunted, built over the site of a sailor's burial ground.

Vice Adm. Hyman Rickover remembered the assistance that Bob Wilson had provided in garnering support for a Ballast Point nuclear submarine base and in 1978 asked Wilson to select a name for a new *Los Angeles*–class submarine. Wilson selected "La Jolla" and Secretary of the Navy J. William Middendorf quickly agreed. Several years later Wilson was told a story that the CNO had once been asked way the Navy named a submarine *La Jolla*, pointing out that most of the class had been named for major U.S. cities and that La Jolla was anything but. The CNO was reputed to have answered: "We named it the USS *La Jolla* because Congressman Wilson wanted it named La Jolla. If Bob Wilson had wanted to name it the USS *La Brea Tar Pits* that's what we would've called it."[48]

The Vietnam War was not the first conflict that the Navy had relied upon San Diego as its chief West Coast support base, but it turned out to be the longest and, in many ways, the most painful. As such, during the years of San Diego's involvement there were rarely peaks of triumph and excitement or depths

A chief boatswain instructs recruits in safely handling mooring lines aboard USS *Recruit* at the Naval Training Center in 1951. *National Archives*

A common sight at 32nd Street during the Vietnam era. All-gun destroyers built for World War II—but still useful for many fleet missions—are tied up alongside *Dixie* (AD-14) in 1969. *Dixie* had been commissioned in April 1940 and by the time she was stricken in June 1982 flew the coveted "Don't Tread on Me" commemorative jack as the oldest commissioned ship in the Navy. *U.S. Naval Institute*

of dread and fear—rather, the war would play out in unending and sobering vignettes as hundreds of thousands would be exposed to the war's fury even at twelve thousand miles' distance. Nary a month would go by without a major deployment of ships, aircraft, and personnel from North Island's docks and Miramar's flightline. Nary a week would go by without an enthusiastic rallying announcement of progress or ceremonial recognition of intrepidity or achievement. Nary an hour would go by when some San Diego family did not feel the loss from a combat death, the uncertainty from a POW's plight, or the pain from an untimely draft notice. San Diegans lived the campaigns, breathed the strategies, prepared the op-plans, and tested the next technological invention.

Faced with projections for a lengthy campaign, the Navy did not surge its forces forward as it had done in every previous major conflict but rather metered them to the war zone in an unbroken series of half-year deployments or one-year in-country assignments. This most fundamental of planning decisions ultimately would define the entire tone of San Diego's side of the war. For San Diego's Navy, Vietnam would be reduced to a war of cycles—and, as the conflict lengthened, a war of cycles built upon cycles, with a host of accompanying rhythms and harmonics like a high school physics project run amuck. San Diego's portion of the equation hinged on the support that it would provide to deploying naval forces and

those ships and squadrons inevitably were locked into rigid deployment cycles. Training advanced in phases of simple to hard to harder. Readiness for combat drove schedules, repairs, maintenance, testing, installations, and exercises. Servicemen and servicewomen arrived to fulfill three- to four-year tours of duty, industrial workers labored in extended shifts. Cycles rode upon cycles with dizzying regularity.

Vietnam stood as an occasion for noble service but as the war lengthened and many questioned the direction and the correctness of the struggle, most in the Navy would agree with Adm. Leighton "Snuffy" Smith's description of one attack squadron's deployment:

> We kind of thought that our mission was moralistically right. We'd all been trained to do what we were told to do. And in those days, we didn't do a lot of questioning of "what was America doing there" or "are we winning this war." If you agreed with the policy, that was fine, you just went and did your job; if you didn't agree with the policy, it was just fine and you went and did your job. . . . The thing I guess, that I admire the most about that generation, is that even if we didn't agree with the policy, we did what we were told to do. And in some cases, at great personal danger.[49]

San Diego's Navy was in motion throughout the entire war. Naval aviators trained in Southern California skies and at live fire ranges, surface sailors bombarded San Clemente Island,

Sporting a "homeward bound" pennant from her aft mast (its length proportional to the number of personnel aboard), hospital ship *Repose* rounds Point Loma on the final hour of her deployment as excited sailors begin to gather at the rail. *National Archives*

Navy SEALs practiced their craft on the Silver Strand, doctors at Balboa Hospital treated the war's gritty survivors, and technicians at Point Loma labs propelled a steady stream of masterworks into inventory. San Diego's *Constellation* and *Ticonderoga* would fly some of the first naval air strikes against North Vietnam and over half of the ships standing off Saigon during its final evacuation were San Diego–based.

Large-scale amphibious operations early in the war required innovative tactics, plans inevitably developed in San Diego and tested on San Diego beaches.[50] Training for PCF (patrol craft, fast) "Swift Boat," PBR (patrol boat, river), and PTF (patrol boat, fast) crews was conducted in San Diego Bay. Naval Amphibious Base planners supported the "Tonkin Gulf Yacht Club" craft of Operation Game Warden along the Vietnamese coast and Brown Water Navy sailors engaged in riverine warfare.[51]

One of the better known Navy specialty schools in the sixties was SERE School (Survival-Evasion-Resistance-Escape) or, officially, the Fleet Airborne Electronics Training Unit, Pacific—Detachment Warner Springs. SERE was officially established in June 1964 as one means to train naval aviators for survival and evasion if forced down behind enemy lines. Tales of brutally realistic prison camp conditions, arduous interrogations, and living off the land in the worst of weather conditions soon filtered through the San Diego Navy community from SERE participants (some would say "survivors"). In 1965 the SERE detachment was moved to a new location eight miles north of the Warner Springs Resort, and in 1972 its title

was further changed to Fleet Aviation Specialized Operational Training Group, Pacific.[52]

By early 1968 San Diego hosted another specialized training effort that grew out the brutal lessons of Southeast Asia combat. Navy combat kill ratios in Vietnam were the worst in U.S. aerial warfare history, maintaining a ratio of just a little over 2 to 1. No Navy pilot had more than one MiG kill and the MiG threat, helped by training provided by Russian regulars, was increasing ominously.

The Navy commissioned a study by Capt. Frank Ault that resulted in the celebrated 480-page "Air-to-Air Missile Capability Review." The Ault Report advocated over two hundred changes and improvements to the Navy's fighter weapons systems, including the call for a dedicated Fighter Weapons School to be established at the Fightertown complex at Miramar. The launch of the Fighter Weapons School (known universally as TOPGUN) and the adoption of other Ault recommendations ultimately improved the Navy fighter kill ratio to more than twelve to one.[53] A class for F-4 crews was begun in March 1969 and TOPGUN was established as an independent command three years later. Comdr. Randy "Duke" Cunningham, a graduate of the first Phantom class, became naval aviation's leading ace in Vietnam with five MiG kills.

Bob Wilson's imprint was felt everywhere across the San Diego–Navy marriage. He was once quoted as saying, "I represent the most militaristic district in the country. We've got more ships docked, more personnel, twenty-one different installations. I'm the product of my area, I fight for a military point of view."[54] Wilson's impact was universally felt in San Diego from consistent appropriations for military construction to consistent support for naval personnel and their families. He always appeared anxious to be quoted on virtually any issue impacting the Navy and his play within the many years of debate swirling around the need for a bridge to span the bay was no exception.

For eighty-three years, in the shadow of nine separate attempts to span the bay with a bridge or tunnel, ferries plied between San Diego and Coronado. During these years, the Navy (with the steadfast backing of its supporters in office) had consistently opposed any bridge-building—usually with the argument that its fleet berthed in South Bay would be impossibly bottled up if the bridge were destroyed through attack, sabotage, or earthquake. In 1935 Rear Admiral Tarrant claimed that a proposed bridge across the harbor would interfere with North Island operations and he threatened to take the

Navy out of San Diego entirely if a bridge was built. In 1951 an engineering study commissioned by the city councils of both Coronado and San Diego recommended construction of a tube between the San Diego ferry landing and the corner of Pomona and Fourth Street in Coronado, but the proposal failed for lack of funds. Ensuing, and cheaper, proposals in the fifties for a bridge were universally opposed by the Navy and by its new stringent voice in Washington, Bob Wilson. Time and again, Wilson warned of the loss of hundreds of millions of dollars if a bridge forced the pullout of the Navy.[55]

Across all these years no consensus of political will and resources materialized, until 1964 when the Navy agreed to removed its objections as long as a suitable clearance for their largest ships—about two hundred feet—could be guaranteed under the bridge. After many years of opposing the bridge, Wilson—like the Navy—fell uncharacteristically quiet as plans for the bridge solidified. Unfortunately for Coronado, the Navy's requirement for a bridge with high clearance worked to their disadvantage as the alignment of San Diego's freeways required that the bridge be constructed south of downtown, necessitating that North Island traffic traverse the entire breadth of Coronado.

Many "San Diegans were nostalgic and many Coronadoans were embittered. But the bridge, 2.12 miles long and supported by 27 of the longest, pre-cast concrete girders ever made, was completed in two-and-a-half years at a cost of $48 million. Its sky-blue color, its graceful 90-degree arc and its sleek profile made it an instant hallmark of San Diego."[56] The bridge finally opened on 3 August 1969.

The final years of Bob Wilson's aggressive guardianship of all Navy activity in San Diego was dominated by a single subject, one that may stand as his greatest legacy—the reconstruction of Balboa Naval Hospital. For years Balboa Hospital had served the Navy and the San Diego community in equal measure, not only as a premier medical facility but also as a magnet attracting generations of medical specialists from around the country to San Diego. At one point in the 1950s two-thirds of the physicians in the San Diego County Medical Society had come to San Diego originally through service with the Navy. "That ratio has declined as the city and its universities have grown," wrote commentator Neil Morgan in 1993, "but a heritage and a culture remain, sensed most keenly within the walls of the massive San Diego Naval Hospital in Balboa Park."[57]

However, by 1972, the existing Balboa Naval Hospital was nearing fifty years of age and had deteriorated into a sprawling and inefficient maze of over seventy buildings. A Navy master plan study concluded that the hospital complex suf-

A site familiar to every tin-can and carrier sailor. *Ranger* (CVA-61) operates with plane guard tucked astern in the SOCAL operating areas. *U.S. Naval Institute*

At the height of the Cold War *Dixon* (AS-37) and twelve nuclear-attack submarines crowd every inch of available pier space at Ballast Point. *U.S. Naval Institute*

fered from functional obsolescence and chronic overcrowding, the structure lacked seismic resistance, and hospital accreditations were under attack.

The Navy began what would become an eight-year search for a suitable expansion site—a search colored by two citywide votes, lawsuits, congressional debate, and presidential decisions. An expansion at or near the erstwhile hospital was favored by Navy planners and Congress to save money by using some existing facilities. But significant public opposition arose to expanding the hospital on city parkland and the first public vote on the hospital in 1979 failed to gain the necessary two-thirds approval to donate land to the Navy. The city offered several competing ideas while the Navy resisted all attempts to split the facility into smaller "specialty" centers.

Bob Wilson stepped into the debate to break the logjam between the city and the Navy and steer them toward a compromise that all parties could accept—ultimately building a new hospital on a parcel of land in Balboa Park's Florida Canyon adjacent to the original hospital. The site could not be seen from downtown, was too steep for easy development, and was characterized by Wilson as "a brush and weed-covered burial ground for dead horses that had worked in the park."

Wilson's logic won the day. "Since the original hospital was on the border of the park," he reasoned, "it seemed logical to build the new hospital on adjacent land to the north on hundreds of acres between the Park and Florida Canyon Road." In a 1983 court-approved settlement, a shift of property was arranged, with the Navy gaining thirty-six acres in Florida Canyon for its new hospital and the city obtaining the original Inspiration Point site, plus fifteen additional acres of a parking lot and $6.8 million.[58]

Following the settlement, the Navy broke ground on its new $308-million medical center that was touted as the largest and most expensive facility of its kind in the world. With Rear Adm. James Sears describing it as "a hospital for the 21st century," Naval Hospital, San Diego was finally dedicated on 23 January 1988.[59]

Bob Wilson retired from Congress in January 1981 after twenty-eight years in office. At the time of his retirement he was the ranking minority member of the House Armed Services Committee. Reflecting both his untiring support for the Navy in San Diego and his specific accomplishments in making the new Balboa Hospital a reality, the main entry road up the steep sides of Florida Canyon to the hospital was named "Bob Wilson Drive." In 2000 Congress proposed that the Naval Hospital facility be named Bob Wilson Naval Hospital.

1990

San Diego Bay was placid today, translucent beneath a softening sheen of oil near the piers, like Vaseline smeared over a camera lens. Beyond it lay the Silver Strand, the line of peninsula leading to North Island and Coronado, and past that, distant and blue as Gibraltar, Point Loma, like a great ship headed out to sea. . . . He followed up the laddered brow onto the [cruiser's] fantail. The feel of hollow steel beneath his feet and the familiar whoosh of blowers told him that even though he wasn't, in a strange way he was home again.

David Poyer, *Tomahawk*

The 1990s would begin with the Navy in San Diego balancing a pound of triumph with an ounce of uncertainty. Well-deserved jubilation swept from Fightertown to the submarine base as navymen stood justly proud of triumphs garnered across the fifty years of the Cold War and the one hundred hours of Desert Storm. The Navy's stock rose to new highs as a supportive citizenry shared in a collective glow with those so recently returned from the landing zones, patrol boxes, screening sectors, and CAP stations of America's faraway wars. But in a democracy the decisiveness of victory always quickly leads to the certainty of retrenchment, and soon San Diego's Navy would be described in the vocabulary of change: BRAC, downsizing, right-sizing, realignment, regionalization, base closure. Many of these concerns, so ominous at the beginning of the decade, would melt to collective sighs of relief as the Navy diligently and intelligently redefined San Diego into a self-described "megaport" by the turn of the millennium.

It was not, though, a decade without tumult, as many San Diego Navy icons that had stood for as long as three-quarters of a century passed out of sight and new faces appeared in their stead. Despite the elimination of its Naval District/Naval Base title, the closure of the venerable Naval Training Center, the departure of droves of surface ships and submarines, the

abandonment of communications facilities from Chollas Heights to Coronado Heights, and the loss of a master jet base with its accompanying fighter squadrons and the famous TOPGUN, the vitality of the Navy in San Diego appeared secure. Large new aircraft carriers moor at North Island docks, stealth surface ships navigate the channel, SEALs prepare for the uncertain challenges of a newly hostile world, a renewed Bob Wilson Naval Hospital stands as a world standard in health care, and SPAWAR (Space and Naval Warfare Systems Command) spins its magic as a world leader in high-tech information technology.

The Navy moved through the 1990s guided by a sense that it had to be ready for change. Its institutions in San Diego had to slim down, and become fast on their feet, ready to absorb the mandates of rapidly changing technology.

Some slimming-down started right at the top. San Diego's Eleventh Naval District, long the overall coordinator of naval activities in San Diego, emerged from the nineties recast and refreshed. It had first expanded on 1 January 1978 to absorb the Twelfth Naval District and then had been abolished in name on 1 October 1978 with the district's commandant becoming Commander, Naval Base, San Diego. Then, on 1 February 1999, that structure too was altered with the Naval Base remodeled as Navy Region–Southwest, a realignment of responsibilities for its commander that would span all Navy installations in the American Southwest.[1]

Within the San Diego Navy complex overseen by the new Navy Region–Southwest, bases were broadly restructured to combine and consolidate many common services in an initiative labeled "regionalization." Regionalization accented common services and best business practice while deemphasizing strict base boundaries. Many San Diego naval activities were amalgamated into three primary facility clusters geographically centered in Point Loma, Coronado, and San Diego proper.

Even with these consolidations, the city's vibrant links with the Navy have remained strong. The Navy League, Armed Forces YMCA, the San Diego USO, and other organizations have been consistently supported by prominent local busi-

nessmen such as Morris Wax and Cushman Dow. An annual salute to the military that was originally launched as an event called "Accolades" in the early 1990s blossomed into the annual Fleet Week celebration that includes a Parade of Ships, air shows, concerts, luncheons, golf tourneys, and ship tours. Continuing a tradition that began at the turn of the century, savvy members of the city's Convention and Visitors' Bureau use Fleet Week as a venue to attract extra tourists San Diego's way.

Another important custom that has long stood within the framework of San Diego's Navy has been the incorporation of capable retired navymen within the fabric of city and county government and industry. Former navymen have served as U.S. congressmen, county public works directors, county tax

San Clemente Island stands sixty miles off the California coast and is the centerpiece of an elaborate system of training and testing areas that directly services the fleet in tasks as diverse as live-fire exercises to advanced laboratory testing of promising new weaponry. Ecologically fragile, the island also boasts sophisticated programs to balance the protection of endangered species with its operational mission. *U.S. Navy*

Constellation (CV-64), homeported in San Diego for nearly forty years, has become a familiar site maneuvering in the channel en route to its accustomed berth at North Island. *U.S. Naval Institute*

collectors, maritime services directors for the port, and port commissioners. Even the San Diego Padres baseball club drew within its executive ranks a retiring senior naval officer, Capt. Jack Ensch, and now can boast the closest relationship in the country between the Navy and professional sports.

Floating in splendid isolation some sixty miles off the coast, San Clemente Island lies at the center of the Navy's efforts to tap the advantages of rapidly improving technology. Hidden from view just over the lip of the far horizon but linked within a San Diego web of datalinks and microwave relays, San Clemente Island is the crown jewel of the San Diego Navy, providing convenient instrumented test ranges above, upon, and underneath the sea—a resource unmatched anywhere in the world.

Great Pacific swells rise with deceptive laziness to crash onto the battered rocks and pinnacles of the island's western coast while formidable bluffs with precipitous drops dominate the east. Yawning chasms and deep gullies scrubbed by infrequent flash floods give the interior a washboard texture. In the truest sense San Clemente represents a wilderness where at times the only sounds heard are the pounding of the surf or the steady ocean breeze rustling through swaying grasses. Sea lions honk and bellow, seagulls screech, and hawks hover effortlessly in the thermals. But it is also a landscape where an explorer is just as likely to come across abandoned slabs of concrete on picturesque heights or meadows littered with the

mangled remains of aerial drones. The low pass of a high-performance jet, the "whoosh" of a cruise missile, or the rumble of naval artillery frequently breaks the silence of wilderness.

The story of San Clemente Island is one filled with the fascination of paradox. This enigmatic island features a naval bombardment training range but also protected species of plants and animals. Those constructing high-bandwidth microwave stations must be careful not to disturb ancient Indian burial grounds. Native California grasses thrive in an environment separated from the crush of the California metropolis, while air sampling still picks up the curse of smog from distant freeways.

Travel to this federally owned and Navy-administered island has been restricted since the late 1930s. Behind a heavy veil of secrecy the island has witnessed some of the century's most dramatic leaps in naval technology from the earliest amphibious assault landings to Tomahawk missile test flights.

The U.S. government claimed ownership of the island in 1848 but allowed leases to sheep herders, who along with seal hunters, whalers, abalone fishermen, bootleggers, and smugglers, composed the majority of the island's inhabitants until the 1930s. Western novelist Zane Grey was said to have written from a lonesome seaside hut on the island's eastern coast.

The Navy began limited use of the island in 1924 and in 1934 closed the island to the public for fleet training. Beginning in 1935 Navy and Marine units began experimenting with new amphibious doctrine through a series of full dress

A formation of the E-1 Tracer air early warning aircraft over North Island in 1963. Built on the airframe of the versatile S-2 Tracker, these aircraft held a powerful airborne radar within their distinctive radome that inspired nicknames of "Willy Fudd" or "Stoof with a Roof." *U.S. Navy*

amphibious landings. The first of these Fleet Landing Exercises (FLEX) was held in the Caribbean but FLEX 2 was conducted along San Clemente's beaches, followed by FLEX 3 during 30 January–16 February 1937.[2] Here Marine, Army, and fleet units practiced new tactics of amphibious assault and coordinated shore bombardment. Since they lacked specialty landing craft, landings were conducted by conventional whaleboats and launches. "We came in on a night approach [to the island]," wrote one observer. "We used smoke to protect us from simulated fire from ashore. On San Clemente, we fired live ammunition from destroyers, cruisers, and battleships. There was a strong surf running on San Clemente when we sent in the first troops in whaleboats. In perfect line abreast, the whaleboats hit the surf together and just like an act, they all turned over in unison. We had a bunch of wet men. So the rest of the landing was called off."[3]

The primary buildings of Fleet Training Base, San Clemente Island were established at Camp Tarrant, now called Wilson Cove.[4] Befitting a training base, target ranges dotted the meadows, gun emplacements marked bluffs, and target balloons floated skyward from the shore. The Marines occupied an earthen landing strip built across the waist of the island in 1937–39 that later became a Naval Auxiliary Air Station.[5] In the years prior to and during World War II carrier aircraft used San Clemente for weapons practice, and ships from San Diego

and San Pedro were frequent visitors to the shore bombardment range at Pyramid Cove.

After the war the island was deactivated but by 1949 had become a favorite site for weapons evaluations by the new Naval Ordnance Test Station (NOTS). High cliffs and deep water close to shore were particularly well suited for the filming and evaluation of underwater launches and air drops of weapons. This topography, coupled with the island's isolation from the public and nearness to both Navy laboratories and fleet units, convinced NOTS in 1951 to establish the Navy's first underwater test range close to the island.[6]

During the fifties and sixties, an impressive parade of the Navy's primary frontline weapons were tested, retested, and perfected in the island's waters and from firing pads erected along its blufflines. Mark 13, 32, 43, 44, and 46 torpedoes, Weapon ALFA, SUBROC, ASROC, submarine-launched Harpoon, advanced 5-inch projectiles, Redeye and Chaparral missiles were all put through their paces by NOTS. There were even tests of the Navy's remote-controlled DASH antisubmarine helicopter and the first secret "pop-up" tests of the submarine-launched Polaris missile.

During the 1960s SEALAB and America's Man-in-the-Sea Program were based off the island's eastern coast. San Clemente also hosted deep submergence vehicles such as *Trieste* and *Trieste II* (many stationed at Ballast Point) and early deep submergence rescue vehicle prototypes.[7] The Navy's first Fleet Operational Ranging Accuracy Calibration Site (FORACS) range was established for acoustic measurements of ship and submarines, and an early three-dimensional underwater range was later enlarged into the Southern California Offshore Range (SCORE) for underwater tests and antisubmarine training.[8]

During the 1970s San Clemente's isolation again proved an asset as it became the test site for the development of America's classified over-the-horizon (OTH) radar that could detect environmental conditions and aircraft at thousands of miles. The first of these projects, known as NONESUCH, began in 1971 and by 1973 a series of "Bogle" antennas were operating from the island's northwest shore "aimed" at the Gulf of Alaska in Project Sea Echo.[9]

Beginning in July 1984 San Clemente Island became the Navy's nucleus for the flight testing and development of the new Tomahawk cruise missile. Live warhead tests were conducted against targets on the island and antiship profiles against target ships offshore. The Navy's Tomahawk test ship, *Merrill* (DD-976), was stationed in San Diego and was a frequent visitor to San Clemente's ranges. These activities and breakthroughs in integrated strike planning were critical for the successful introduction of the single most revolutionary naval weapon system of the second half of the century, one that redefined American national defense and international diplomacy.

UDT (underwater demolition team) frogmen and today's Navy SEALs have maintained an almost continuous presence on San Clemente Island since the Second World War.[10] Both basic and advanced training take place at the SEAL training facility in a cove below the island's airstrip. Night assault training is stressed as well as live-fire sessions, explosives training, over-the-beach operations, and small unit tactics. Foreign special operations teams frequently join the training and the island provides a secure area for the testing and operational evaluation of new SEAL weapons and equipment. San Clemente provides the only site in the world where all of these SEAL support operations can be conducted in a coordinated and, many times, simultaneous manner.

Coronado forms the heart of the SEAL Special Operations community. Neither underwater swimmer training nor special operations training began at Coronado, but the need for underwater beach reconnaissance in amphibious warfare brought some of the first underwater swimmers to Naval Amphibious Base both during and immediately after World War II.

SEAL teams trace their history back to the joint Army-Navy Scouts and Raiders reconnaissance units who were trained in amphibious warfare early in the Second World War and to the Naval Combat Demolition Units (NDCUs) formed in 1943 to clear obstacles from landing beaches. These teams were consolidated into underwater demolition teams (UDTs) that assumed the important missions of beach reconnaissance and underwater obstacle demolition in advance of landings. Many current SEAL missions were first performed by the Operational Swimmers of the Office of Strategic Services (OSS) during World War II. Early training for OSS swimmers (who pioneered the use of flexible swim fins and closed-circuit breathing equipment) was conducted at Camp Pendleton and Oceanside harbor in November 1943.

Navy UDT frogmen, armed many times only with knife and swim fins, cleared the way for landings from Normandy to the Pacific theater. UDTs were also active during the Korean War in clearing amphibious landing areas, beach reconnaissance, guerrilla landings, and minesweeping support.

The long quay wall at North Island shows its versatility by berthing three supercarriers, *Kitty Hawk* (CV-63), *Constellation* (CV-64), and *Independence* (CV-62). *U.S. Naval Institute*

When World War II ended some thirty UDTs were reduced to two teams on each coast and many remembered the piles of fins and facemasks that were consigned to surplus at the amphibious base. UDT-1 and UDT-3 were assigned to Coronado. In the rapid response to Korean War requirements UDT-5 stood up in 1952 and in February 1954 these teams were redesignated as UDT-11, -12, and -13. Formal frogman training, begun in 1950, was conducted in conjunction with other coordinated amphibious training by the Naval Beach Group School.[11]

In January 1962 the first SEAL teams were established to conduct unconventional warfare, counterguerrilla warfare, and clandestine operations in maritime and riverine environments with SEAL Team 1 in Coronado formed from other West Coast UDTs. Team 1 concentrated on expanding the team's counterinsurgency and commando skills, building on the underwater demolition and diving techniques that were the norm for UDT. Lt. David Del Giudice was Team 1's first commanding officer and, forsaking room at the UDT headquarters on the beach, he requisitioned an old warehouse on the Naval Amphibious Base for his headquarters and an unused building owned by the base fire department as his parachute loft.[12] With no resources for such basics as command vehicles or maintenance, stories were told of SEALs driving their official trucks until they dropped and then going to the nearby naval station to "requisition" new Navy vehicles in the dead of night.

Almost immediately after Team 1's founding, two officers flew to Vietnam to "get the lay of the land and see what the SEALs might do" in the new environment of antiguerrilla

Merrill (DD-976) served as the test ship for Tomahawk cruise-missile testing in the early 1980s. Here she fires a land-attack version of the missile from a position off the west coast of San Clemente Island. *U.S. Naval Institute*

warfare.[13] The first recommendation of this month-long survey stimulated in-country training for Vietnamese in clandestine military operations, jungle warfare, and related skills by a series of SEAL Mobile Training Teams. For the next ten years the focus of the UDT/SEAL Teams was the war in Vietnam. Forty-nine UDT/SEALs were killed in Vietnam with many more wounded while three Congressional Medals of Honor and seven Navy Crosses were awarded to UDT/SEAL team members.

In 1983 the teams reorganized, dropped the name "Underwater Demolition Team," and added two SEAL delivery vehicle teams and two new SEAL teams. SEAL Teams 1, 3, and 5 are based in Coronado, with geographic areas of concentration of Southeast Asia, Southwest Asia, and the Northern Pacific respectively. SEAL operations in Grenada, Panama, Desert Storm, and the Balkans point to their continuing viability in maintaining the Navy's global reach. Frogmen have always controlled and operated their own boats and those organizations have now evolved to Special Boat Units.

The Naval Special Warfare Command—the Navy component of the U.S. Special Operations Command—was commissioned on 16 April 1987. Rear Adm. Irve Charles LeMoyne was sent as its first commander and established his headquarters of nine people, a trailer, and a flag on the beach at the Naval Amphibious Base. At first the Navy was reluctant to assign its SEAL teams to the command, fearing the loss of operational control to a unified command. LeMoyne started by pulling the Naval Special Warfare Center and the Basic Underwater Demolition/SEAL (BUD/S) Training Unit under the command and within eleven months had all SEAL teams organized under his banner. In the years that followed LeMoyne would help shape the SEALs with new missions and new equipment, ranging from the aiming of portable lasers for smart bombs to the use of advanced submarine delivery vehicles, and the conversion of submarines to support near-shore SEAL operations.[14]

Although formal training for new frogmen was begun in both Coronado and Little Creek in 1950, by 1968 all accession training was centralized in Coronado and given the name Basic Underwater Demolition/SEAL (BUD/S) Training.[15] Before becoming a full-fledged SEAL, candidates must survive a rigorous year-long training regimen that includes both basic training and six months of further apprentice training with a team. Under intense physical and mental conditioning (considered by some as the world's toughest military training) each prospective SEAL undergoes three phases of BUD/S over six months, involving basic conditioning, diving, and land warfare. The first four weeks of training culminate in a demanding "Hell Week"—a rugged test of physical and mental motivation across nonstop ordeals that run the gamut from swimming and rowing to obstacle courses and visits to the mud.

For years the rocks at the Hotel del Coronado have been a night-swim training destination where trainees learn to master their algae-slick sides and dangerous footing in the midst of a frequently pounding surf and, occasionally, wandering hotel guests. Lengthy underwater swims off the Strand are a frequent training requirement, as are familiarization training with the team's wide assortment of underwater swimmer delivery vehicles. The long stretch of the Strand has made an excellent covert training ground for night insertions and residents of Coronado can frequently hear the sound of small arms in the still night air.

The 1990s proved to be a period of downsizing and mission redefinition for many in San Diego's Navy. Although the high-technology pursuits on San Clemente Island and the down-and-dirty basics of the SEALs would fare well during the ensuing transformations, others in San Diego would face sudden turmoil.

During the nineties the Department of Defense used strict procedures laid down by the Base Realignment and Closure (BRAC) Act to reduce the size of shore bases to match the need for a smaller Navy at the end of the Cold War. With the overall fleet being cut almost in half, reasoning went that naval shore stations serving the fleet should be reduced in kind. Although San Diego would not go unscathed in the process, it would—just as it had done at the end of World War II, the Korean War, and the Vietnam War—be largely shielded from large cuts in bases that would impact other cities.

One of the most debated of the BRAC recommendations was the decision to close the seventy-five-year-old Naval Training Center, formally effected during a tear-filled ceremony on a clear warm afternoon on 21 March 1997. By that date Navy presence on the station had been reduced to a bare caretaker staff after recruit training and many of its service schools had been transferred to the Great Lakes Naval Training Center outside Chicago. Although few agreed with the Navy's questionable logic in ordering the move, nearly everyone present at NTC's closing ceremony could take heart in the training center's history of distinguished graduates. Vice Adm. Pat Tracey, facing an audience of veterans spanning four generations, concluded with emotion: "In this final moment of honor, we know that this place lives on in the faces of thousands of sailors who trained here and are now serving this country and in the millions who have served and

The Tomahawk was largely perfected in tests off the San Diego coast including these tests against a reinforced concrete structure, the size of a warehouse, set up on San Clemente Island in July 1984. *U.S. Naval Institute*

trained here and are now civilians." More than 1.75 million recruits and more than a million "A" and "C" school personnel graduated from NTC during its reign.[16]

Nostalgic as the ceremony was, no one could ignore NTC's stunning future promise, for San Diego would not just close a base but would gain title to a remarkable corner of its central core. What had once been mudflats and undeveloped land in a tidal estuary had survived as a relatively open area while the city grew densely around it. The result was an immensely valuable prize for the city, almost half the size of San Diego's downtown.

The transfer has sparked a cascade of promises and stirring rhetoric. NTC has been called "Balboa Park West," a "civic plum," and "the most dominant central acquisition since Alonzo Horton founded New Town."[17] New plans included creation of an arts and culture center, an office and research park, market-rate housing, two hotels, a short golf course, and a naval museum along the boat channel. The ninety-acre historic core, with its arched Spanish Colonial Revival buildings

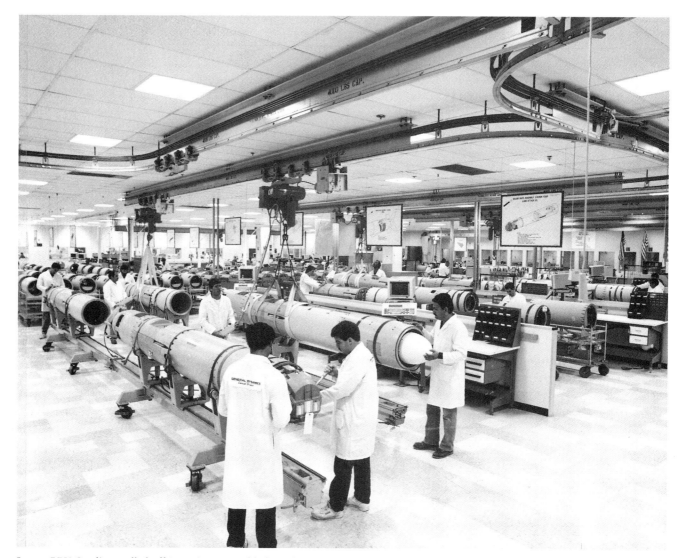

Just as PBY Catalinas rolled off San Diego assembly lines directly into Navy operation in the 1940s, Tomahawk cruise missiles rolled off decidedly higher-tech San Diego assembly lines directly into Navy operation fifty years later. *U.S. Naval Institute*

faced with fine ceramic tiles and rooflines softened in terra cotta, will be restored.

Standing literally in the midst of these vibrant plans for grand redevelopment, new parks, and energizing industries stands what once was a commissioned vessel of the United States and now is a solitary symbol of NTC's tenure, the USS *Recruit*. Securely grounded upon a cement foundation, *Recruit* has played host to untold thousands of raw Navy recruits who have looked to her as a form of introduction to the mystic ways of shipboard routine. "She was the first of its kind—not quite a building, not quite a ship . . . the Navy's first non-ship," ran one description.[18]

Recruit was formally commissioned on 27 July 1949 by the Eleventh Naval District Commandant and proudly merited a commissioning pennant, ensign, and Union Jack. At 225 feet in length and featuring a forty-one-foot mast, *Recruit* featured the accoutrements of an actual warship, including bridge, forecastle, main deck, brow, quarterdeck, lines to a "pier," and—even—an official designation, "TDE-1." She was the *Bluejackets Manual* come alive. Recruits could learn everything from marlinespike seamanship to watchstanding from her decks and hidden classrooms.[19]

Once the center of attention, *Recruit* stands today forlorn and untended, an anachronism representing another age in San Diego history. As the distinguishing nautical timbre of NTC fades in the light of redevelopment, *Recruit* remains as a shining link to a golden past where farm boys first haltingly pronounced, "Request permission to come aboard," where city boys learned the mysteries of a clove hitch, and where some of the saltiest chiefs in the Navy daily held court.

The year 1997 also served as the end of the line for Naval Air Station, Miramar. BRAC recommendations had tabbed the airfield for transfer to the Marine Corps and the first step in this transition began in 1994 with the arrival of the first Marine squadron, the "Green Knights" of VMFA-121 (who had flown Wildcat fighters from MCAB Camp Kearny during the Second World War). By 1996 all San Diego Tomcat fighter squadrons had been transferred to Virginia, while one of the mainstays of Fightertown, TOPGUN, relocated to the Naval Strike and Air Warfare Center in Fallon, Nevada.

On 1 October 1997, fifty years after Marine squadrons had left Miramar for Orange County, the air station officially changed hands back to the custody of the Marine Corps. As nostalgic as NTC's ceremony had been, "the [Miramar] transition ceremony had the planning of an invasion, the pomp of a parade and the seating of a wedding—sailors on the left, Marines on the right," read the newspaper account.[20] But as the ceremony ended, and as the commandant of Marines and the Marine Corps Band took center stage, many paused to remember what had been as sailors filed off in trim marching formation and two F-14 fighters rose on afterburner into San Diego skies for the last time.

The last Navy planes to leave Miramar were four E-2 Hawkeyes of VAW-117 who waited until their deployment on *Carl Vinson* in November 1998 to change home fields. "As the last one out, it's kind of sad," said Comdr. Joseph Kupcha, who had spent his entire Hawkeye career at Miramar.[21] Most think that Lt. Pete "Maverick" Mitchell would say much the same thing.

Even the submarine base was not immune to rumors of closure. The Pacific Fleet's submarine force would be reduced by half during the 1990s and moves to concentrate its remaining boats in Pearl Harbor were under consideration. There was talk of turning Ballast Point into a training base, an adjunct to the naval station, or a base for SPAWAR testing of new technologies aboard ship.

In the end, the logic of having submarines based in San Diego near fleet training facilities and the homebase of the Pacific Fleet's Surface Force, the argument originally posed by Congressman Bob Wilson forty years before, prevailed. Although the number of nuclear attack submarines based in San Diego was reduced and the presence of submarine tenders (a fixture in San Diego since World War I) was eliminated, the base would stay in place with its primary mission clearly pointed toward submarines.

What the Navy might have been losing on 1 October 1997 on the scrubgrass fields of Kearny Mesa it was regaining in spades on that same day at a small ceremony at old Air Force Plant no. 19 at Pacific Highway and Barnett. There the Space and Naval Warfare Systems Command, more widely known by its acronym, SPAWAR (universally mispronounced, with roughly half of those pronouncing its name with a long *a* as in "space," the other half of officialdom slurring the pronunciation with a soft *a* as in "spa," and each camp maligning the other as never getting it right), officially established its headquarters after a move from the Washington, D.C., suburbs.

The move of SPAWAR headquarters to San Diego was widely seen as another victory for San Diego business boosters such as the Chamber of Commerce who caught SPAWAR's attention by stressing San Diego's high-technology attributes. During the thirty years leading to SPAWAR's arrival in San Diego, the naval laboratory complex on Point Loma amassed an unbroken history of technological and laboratory achievement especially in the sensors and communications fields that was SPAWAR's forte. These thirty years also bore witness to yet another area of unique achievement for the Point Loma laboratory complex—the growth in the use of complex alphabet-soup acronyms that only the most hardened government bureaucrat or professional signmaker would enjoy.

Prior to 1967 the lab complex was generally known as the Navy Electronics Laboratory (NEL), the postwar descendant of the venerable Navy Radio and Sound Laboratory (NRSL). Although several labs conducted their business within this loose command structure, "NEL" had a certain clarity and simplicity associated with it that made it, especially in light of the Navy's follow-on activities, a nostalgic favorite among San Diegans.

In 1967 NEL was renamed, imposingly, as the Naval Command Control Communications Laboratory Center (NCC-CLC). With absolutely no hope of anyone writing, pronouncing, or remembering this cumbersome acronym, the name was altered within a year's time to the Naval Electronics Center (NELC). At that same time the undersea weapons components of the Naval Ordnance Test Station at Inyokern and Pasadena merged with NEL's undersea technology element to form the Naval Undersea Warfare Center (NUWC) in San Diego. This reorganization brought focus to the important disciplines of ASW and ocean engineering but it quickly became clear that the word "warfare" within the laboratory's title proved a significant liability in the political climate of the late 1960s. Finding invitations to conferences drying up and campus recruitment declining, NUWC renamed itself in 1969 to the more politically correct Naval Undersea Research and Development Center (NURDC).[22]

No one, though, had apparently pronounced the NURDC acronym in mixed company prior to approving the lab's name change. With the paint hardly dry on NURDC signs, Capt. Charles Bishop spoke the obvious when he assumed command of the lab in 1968: "I'm not going to be the head of a bunch of nerds." Without going through lengthy paperwork, Bishop simply changed the name to the Naval Undersea Center (NUC) and reported such to Washington.[23]

Across the 1970s NELC and NUC propelled a host of cutting-edge naval warfare projects such as Fleet Satellite Communications (FLTSATCOM), the Inverse Synthetic Aperture Radar (ISAR) imaging radar, fixed undersea surveillance systems such as SOSUS, towed array sonars such as SURTASS, Mk 46 and Mk 50 torpedoes, and experiments with trained Marine mammals. In 1972 NUC was chartered as the Navy's principal research and development center for undersea surveillance, ocean technology, and advanced undersea weapons systems.[24]

On 1 March 1977 NELC and NUC were consolidated and yet another new name was in the offing—the Naval Ocean Systems Center (NOSC). NOSC's mission was to be the principal Navy center for command, control, communications, ocean surveillance, surface- and air-launched undersea weapons, and supporting technologies. Many of the linchpin systems of the fleet today had their foundation at NOSC: satellite communications systems, command and control systems ashore and afloat, lightweight torpedoes, underwater fire-control systems, undersea vehicles, and undersea surveillance systems. NOSC also continued its leadership in advanced technology disciplines such as microelectronics, acoustics, radar applications, signal and image processing, and computer science. During the 1980s NOSC filed over four hundred patent applications.[25]

In February 1986 the secretary of the Navy transferred the management of the Navy's R&D centers from Chief of Navy Research to Commander, Space and Naval Warfare Systems Command to align laboratories more appropriately with SPAWAR's material and technical support organization and to streamline administration.[26]

Twenty-three LCACs (landing craft air cushion) are visible on the apron at the Assault Craft Unit-5 facility along Interstate 5 on Camp Pendleton. ACU-5 was formed specifically to operate LCACs on 1 October 1983 and the Camp Pendleton facility opened in August 1986. The largest deployment of LCACs came during Desert Storm when four detachments of eleven craft operated in the Persian Gulf. *U.S. Navy*

The easily pronounceable acronym NOSC (and, in the information technology era, an easily written web address!) was summarily executed in January 1992 when yet another realignment established the Naval Command, Control and Ocean Surveillance Center (NCCOSC). Responsive as ever to "nameology" changes, the San Diego laboratory broke new ground by inventing a site name for its primary lab organization with acronyms *within* acronyms, calling its lab NRaD where the *N* represents NCCOSC and *RaD* the Research, Development, Test and Engineering (RDT&E) Division. Again, San Diego retained its focus on the command and control and information technology specialties.

Cunning as this nomenclature innovation was, NRaD failed to survive the test of time and was retired to the taxonomy graveyard after a mere five years, although the clever novelty of acronym-within-acronym was retained. In the latest version of the SPAWAR "corporate" organization, a SPAWAR headquarters component (in San Diego) oversees several engineering, research, and development support laboratory subsidiaries around the country. In San Diego this laboratory element was renamed SSC–San Diego, significant for its diligence in retaining the purism of the acronym-within-acronym creativity as the "SPAWAR Systems Center–San Diego." Thus SSC-SD employees can look back today and with a great deal of pride in their long and distinguished terminology record: SSC-SD = NraD = NCCOSCRDT&E = NOSC = NELC = NUC = NURDC = NUWC = NELC = NCCCLC = NEL = NRSL.

When it arrived in 1997 SPAWAR assumed many of the offices assigned to NCCOSC and concentrated most of its headquarters component within Air Force Plant 19 at Pacific Highway and Barnett. That huge, drab corrugated-steel building had started as Consolidated Aircraft's Plant No. 2 in 1941, a government-financed plant on a seventy-one-acre site that would supply production parts to the main Consolidated assembly lines at Lindbergh Field. B-24 wings (each over fifty feet long) as well as other aircraft assemblies took shape on a moving assembly line going from north to south within Plant No. 2. The final stop on the assembly line was at the plant's far southern building, where all aircraft fuselage assemblies were painted before being shipped for final assembly to the Lindbergh Field plant by Consolidated's own rail line.[27]

The Air Force obtained the site in the 1950s and leased space to General Dynamics Convair for the manufacture of missile assemblies. As such, the Intermediate Nuclear Force Treaty identified it as a "strategic site" and trailers were maintained on site for visiting Soviet inspection teams during the Cold War. The Air Force transferred title to the Navy in 1994

Sea Shadow began to operate regularly from San Diego in the late 1990s to test advanced features of ship design that reduce detectability to radar and other sensors. Many ship design concepts pioneered aboard *Sea Shadow* when she was part of a top-secret stealth program in the mid-1980s have found their way into today's warship designs. *U.S. Naval Institute*

and, today, multistory office subbuildings have risen within the building's huge volume and multimillion-dollar antenna farms dot its saw-toothed roofline.[28]

SPAWAR Systems Center is important to the Navy as it provides the product of information and the cutting-edge technology to collect, transmit, process, display, and manage information as it ebbs and flows to support essential naval operations. More than four thousand employees working within disciplines as diverse as atmospheric physics, electrooptics, underwater acoustics, engineering psychology, artificial intelligence, microelectronics, and biological sciences have converged to offer products similarly as diverse: universal information access, distributed collaboration, high-speed internets, new antennas, submarine communications, information operations assurance, intelligent displays, and others.

SSC–San Diego is important to San Diego as it provides part of the fuel that powers the city's high-tech growth. "Because of San Diego's history as a Navy town and naval research center, thousands of military technicians and engineers, both active and retired, continue to call it home, amounting to a vast and persistent contribution by the federal government to the city's intellectual growth."[29]

No discipline is changing as fast as information technology and San Diego Navy laboratories are among the nation's leaders in the cutting-edge science and technology research that supports it. As Neil Morgan wrote, "There is no tighter military security in San Diego than at the complex of gray buildings above the surf on the outer tip of Point Loma, no better view of migrating gray whales and golden sunsets, and no workplace more reassuring of the San Diego future."[30]

Rear Adm. George Wagner, SPAWAR's first San Diego commander, has said, "SPAWAR's move to San Diego benefits the Navy's fleet because SPAWAR's engineers and scientists will be able to see firsthand how their ideas, designs and equipment function aboard ship." This close interrelationship between SPAWAR and the fleet can be seen daily aboard *Coronado* (AGF-11), flagship of the San Diego–based U.S. Third Fleet.[31] Three decks have been constructed within the ship's well deck for an advanced command center, masts bristle with advanced antennae, and SSC-SD technicians bustle everywhere. In this realm of global command and control, *Coronado* is the most advanced ship in the world. From her berth at Ballast Point,

Coronado has been named as a sea-based battle lab and has been at the hub of a series of fleet battle experiments during the nineties that have honed modern military operations to meet the demands of the information age. In many ways these innovative naval exercises resembled the successful series of fleet problems in the 1930s that helped the fleet harness the technologies of that era to tactical merit—but instead of perfecting aircraft carrier operations, dive-bombing, or shore strikes that would prove so critical to success in World War II, these new exercises focused on database transmission, video teleconferencing, and long-range strike planning, harbingers of the future naval warfare challenge.[32]

The sponsor of *Coronado,* this "most advanced" of warships, and the person who christened her on the building ways and

By the early 1970s the original Naval Hospital in Balboa Park had outgrown its facilities and Congressman Bob Wilson led an effort to build a new state-of-the-art Naval Medical Center in Florida Canyon adjacent to the original site. The Navy and the city negotiated an exchange of properties that allowed continued efficient operation of the hospital while restoring Inspiration Point to park and recreation purposes. *U.S. Navy*

sent her into the water with a spray of champagne, was Eleanor Reynolds Ring.

Vice Adm. Stanhope Ring had retired from the Navy in late 1955 and he and Eleanor returned to Coronado. With their service time behind them, Eleanor became a dynamo in local civic, community, and political organizations. Her work with local Republican women's groups brought her to the attention of Congressman Bob Wilson and for years she assisted in his runs for reelection, including work as his reelection chairperson in Coronado. Eleanor would staunchly represent local issues, and she served for a time as an elected Coronado City councilmember. Her work helped continue the enduring and positive links between San Diego and its Navy. Upon Admiral Ring's death, Eleanor would later marry another notable in San Diego history, Rear Adm. Putnam "Put" Storrs.

Eleanor Ring Storrs's three children would help perpetuate her remarkable family association across San Diego's Navy. Eldest son Stewart Ring would rise to flag rank with service aboard *Yarnall, Bridget* (DE-1024), Destroyer Squadron 5, and *Harry E. Yarnell* (CG-17), based in San Diego. He would marry Frances McCampbell, daughter of World War II ace and Medal of Honor winner Capt. David McCampbell. Eleanor's son William served aboard *Bausell* (DD-845) and *Tulare* (AKA-112) in San Diego before succumbing to leukemia while a lieutenant on active duty. Daughter Susan would marry R. Taylor S. Keith Jr., who would rise to the rank of captain and see service aboard *Parsons* (DDG-33) and command of *Henry B. Wilson* (DDG-7) and Destroyer Squadron 7 in San Diego. Captain Keith's father, Vice Adm. Robert T. S. Keith, who came first to San Diego as gunnery officer of *Aylwin* (DD-355) just before the Second World War, would command the Pacific Fleet Cruiser-Destroyer Force and the U.S. First Fleet, both from

headquarters in San Diego. Susan followed her mother's political precedent and was elected to the Coronado City Council, while her son, R. Taylor S. Keith III ("Ty"), would graduate from Annapolis with the class of 1987 and later serve aboard *Halsey* (CG-23) in San Diego.

In many ways, Eleanor represented the best the Navy had to offer San Diego. As Neil Morgan has observed: "The least understood merit of our military population may be the skills that they bring to their jobs as they become civilian San Diegans. San Diego and the Navy have always had a symbolic relationship, each helping the other, not out of financial motivation but because of friendship, patriotic duty and mutual benefit."[33]

Across a hundred years from father to grandson, the men Eleanor knew best contributed mightily to an enduring framework of the Navy within the San Diego metropolis. Their service would span uninterrupted from sail power to computer power, would include some of the most important naval victories of America's wars, and would enrich the triumph of deterrence during the Cold War.

Across these same hundred years, the San Diego spied to starboard as stalwart warships headed to sea would grow from 17,000 to 1.7 million, while the support and warmth shown by San Diego for its Navy would grow in kind. Dramatic as the contribution of Eleanor Ring's dynamic Navy family was, their story is but one among the millions that have added depth and color to the San Diego cityscape. These many men and women of the Navy and their families share a common bond made stronger by life in a remarkable corner of a great land—and their unflagging energies focused on both their service and their community have polished the San Diego–Navy essence to a brilliant luster.

CONCLUSION

To best grasp the indelible maritime character of San Diego, one must approach from seaward in the fresh light of early morning. Viewed from main channel, the city rises in a semicircle of grandeur from beach toward mountain much as an open amphitheater ascends from lighted stage to flag-topped pavilion. Distant jagged ridgelines encircle the scene—Palomar, Laguna, Otay—focusing San Diego's attention toward the sea while forming a comfortable distant boundary for the eye. The metallic and crystal spires of downtown rise Oz-like from the bayshore and form the nexus of this maritime amphitheater's central stage.

Anchoring the left-hand sweep of view from the channel are the sharp greens and tans of stoic Point Loma, the stately headland that has greeted San Diego sailors from time immemorial. The drumming surf, the broad leaves of ocean kelp, the pulsing light at the tip of the point—all lead the eye toward whitewashed homes with red-tiled roofs and Spanish archways that terrace up surrounding slopes.

In foreground view, the crisp new light slowly transforms the water's murky blue to aquamarine; an unblemished arc of gleaming sand curves gently toward the right from the Silver Strand toward Mexico. Formations of pelicans trace this tranquil beach in search of a breakfast treat while a gray hint of haze floats south of the border.

Even from the channel's outer reaches, San Diego's awakening heartbeat is easily discernible. The early morning tempo bubbling across the metropolis is fueled largely by the aroma of black coffee—black Navy coffee—wafting up from mugs in tugboat wheelhouses, aircraft carrier ready rooms, maintenance shops, and admirals' offices. As the sun moves higher into the sky, the city rises to greet its Navy neighbor, a partner and consort who has already been on deck for hours.

Approaching from seaward early in the morning, one can hear the rhythmic chop of helicopters and vacuum cleaner–like whine of jet aircraft as they rise from the flat expanse of North Island. In the main shipping channel the eighty thousand–ton bulk of a nuclear-powered aircraft carrier maneuvers ponderously, surrounded by a calliope of toots and whistles from a harem of brightly colored tugs. Along the Silver Strand a team of SEALs jogs to a singsong cadence in deep sand. At Balboa Hospital loudspeaker announcements blend with the beeps and pings of high-tech consoles that scrupulously guard the health of the ailing.

Separately, each harmonic represents a distinctive action by skilled, highly educated, and dedicated servicemen and servicewomen. Together, these individual activities form a symphony that captures the special essence of San Diego's Navy. This symphony is far more subtle than dramatic, emphasizing the silk of strings over the clang of percussion as it drifts and flows to nearly every corner of the city: morning traffic cuing up on Catalina Boulevard, leather flight jackets in bagel shops, white pickup trucks "For Official Use Only," blue ballcaps with gold lettered ship names at Home Depot, a black Porsche with a FLY FTRS license plate, company offices with three-letter names in Mission Valley, a city park with antique naval cannon, Pearl Harbor survivors carrying the flag on the Fourth of July, the after-work crowd at McP's.

The Navy's footprint in San Diego is startling in its breadth. Most obvious are the eighty warships, hundreds of aircraft, and 240,000 men and women who call San Diego home. However, Navy activity reaches far beyond the piers of 32nd Street and the runways at North Island. For the world at large, San Diego is, above all, a Navy town. One could no more imagine San Diego without the Navy than Honolulu without Diamond Head.

From Neil Morgan's perspective:

What is too easy for us to forget is that this remains a Navy city in every positive and cheerful sense of the phrase. Their bands and crisp color guards brighten public events, but beyond that they are a mainstay of the economy. Because there are so many of us in San Diego who understand a little of such life, we will always be a Navy city. No matter how much we talk about Mexican trade or biotech or higher education as the San Diego future, we will always be a Navy city. Not because of those billions of dollars in tied-down shore bases, but because San Diego grew up with the Navy.... The military is part of the San Diego economy, but it's more than that. Unlike many cities, San Diego has never been afraid to be called a Navy town.[1]

For over 150 years, San Diego and its Navy have mutually traveled a path of shared goals and expectations. From the very first days of California's independence from Mexican rule, San Diego's destiny has been guided by an unshakable association with the men, women, ships, and aircraft of the U.S. Navy. At times its protector, at times its cushion against economic travail, at times its largest employer—the Navy has provided San Diego with a foundation for growth characterized above all else by a synergy of spirit that has blended two distinct cultures into one.

As the Navy has redefined itself from the days of sail, through the coal-fired days of the Great White Fleet and into the nuclear age, so too has San Diego refined its relationship with its service neighbor. As the Navy has progressed from biplanes to vast carrier armadas to high-precision cruise missiles, San Diego has kept in step technologically and philosophically.

Generations of Navy men and women have entered through San Diego's many portals—many to stay, enthralled by the city's special mix of lifestyle and weather. Thousands of Navy veterans, whetted to San Diego's allure, have settled for life. Thousands more sons and daughters of Navy veterans, once comfortable with San Diego's lifestyle, have stayed to enrich its culture.

A special relationship, a marriage, a splendid match. San Diego's Navy has, many times, been that and more. It has been a glue holding the elements of a dynamic multicultural society together at the same time it has been the dynamo the city requires for continued growth and prosperity.

The Navy in San Diego is more than a mere count of warships and invested dollars. The San Diego in the Navy is more than talk of midwinter warmth and international diversity. This joint relationship holds a mystique as directly definable as it is indistinct, as obvious as it is subtle. It may be enough to say that if there had never been a Navy, San Diego would not exist as it does today. And if there had never been a San Diego to train, house, and renew its operating forces, the Navy of today would be vastly different as well.

APPENDIX A
Ships That Have Held San Diego–Area Names

San Diego (**AFS-6**). Combat stores ship, 1969–97. *San Diego,* a 15,900-ton stores ship of the *Mars* class, specializing in underway replenishment of battle groups, was laid down on 11 March 1967 by National Steel and Shipbuilding of San Diego and commissioned 24 May 1969 with Mrs. Frank Curran (wife of the mayor of San Diego) as her sponsor. She served primarily in the Atlantic and the Mediterranean during her years of service and participated in Operation Desert Storm in 1991. *San Diego* transferred to the Military Sealift Command and was redesignated T-AFS-6 on 11 August 1993 and was laid up in reserve on 10 December 1997.

San Diego (**ACR-6**). Armored cruiser, 1907–18. Originally built as *California.* An armored cruiser of the *Pennsylvania* class, *California* displaced 13,680 tons and was armed with four 8-inch guns and fourteen 6-inch guns. Armored cruisers of the *Pennsylvania* class were the most powerful of their kind in the pre-dreadnought era. She was assigned to the Pacific Fleet along the West Coast at the time of her commissioning, was renamed *San Diego* on 1 September 1914, and frequently served as flagship for Commander in Chief, Pacific Fleet. On 18 July 1917 she was ordered to the Atlantic Fleet, reaching Hampton Roads on 4 August, where she was assigned to escort duty for European convoys en route to the war front. On 19 July 1918, bound from Portsmouth, New Hampshire, to New York, *San Diego* struck a mine laid by the German submarine *U-156* southeast of Fire Island. The cruiser sank in twenty-eight minutes but with the loss of only six lives, the only major warship lost by the United States in World War I. She serves today, still, as a popular dive site for recreational divers.

San Diego (**CL-53**). Antiaircraft light cruiser, 1942–46. *San Diego* was laid down on 27 March 1940 by Bethlehem Steel of Quincy, Massachusetts, sponsored by Mrs. Percy J. Benbough (the wife of the mayor of San Diego), and commissioned on 10 January 1942—a cruiser of six thousand tons armed with sixteen 5-inch guns. After commissioning she transited the Panama Canal and arrived in San Diego on 16 May 1942. Escorting the carrier *Saratoga* she barely missed the Battle of Midway. She later served in the Battles of Guadalcanal, Tarawa, Saipan, Peleliu, Philippine Sea, Iwo Jima, and Okinawa. On 27 August 1945 *San Diego* was the first major Allied warship to enter Tokyo Bay and occupy the Yokosuka Naval Base at the end of hostilities. After having steamed over three hundred thousand miles in the Pacific, she returned to San Francisco on 14 September 1945 and visited her namesake city on Navy Day in October. She was decommissioned and placed in reserve on 4 November 1946 and struck from the Navy list on 1 March 1959. *San Diego* received fifteen battle stars for service in World War II.

Mission Bay (**CVE-59**). Escort aircraft carrier, 1943–45. *Mission Bay* was a member of the mass-produced *Casablanca* class of small aircraft carrier built by Kaiser in Vancouver, Washington. She participated in shakedown training in San Diego in late 1943 and initially was assigned to convoy and antisubmarine duty between the East Coast and North Africa. *Mission Bay* later ferried a load of Army planes to India, participated in antisubmarine patrols in the South Atlantic, and conducted training for pilots off both Quonset Point, Rhode Island, and New York City. On 19 December 1945 she was placed into a reserve status and was ultimately struck from the Navy's rolls on 1 September 1958.

San Onofre (**ARD-30**). Auxiliary repair drydock, 1944–present. Completed in 1944, *San Onofre* has a capacity of 4,500 tons.

Point Loma (**AGDS-2**). Deep submergence support vessel, 1958–93. Originally built as *Point Barrow* (AKD-1), a 9,400-ton dock cargo ship, and commissioned on 28 February 1958. As originally configured she had roll-on-roll-off cargo handling capability and was "Arcticized" for polar operations. *Point Loma* was converted to the role of a deep submergence support vessel and placed into commission as AGDS-2 on 30 April 1975. One of her key roles was supporting the deep submergence vessel *Trieste II*. In 1982 she completed a second conversion to support the Trident missile test program. On 30 September 1986 she was turned over to the Military Sealift Command and redesignated T-AGDS-2. Stricken 1993.

La Jolla (**SSN-701**). Nuclear attack submarine, 1981–present. *La Jolla*, a member of the *Los Angeles* class of nuclear attack submarines, was commissioned on 24 October 1981 after being sponsored and christened by Mrs. Bob Wilson, the wife of the U.S. congressman representing San Diego. *La Jolla* was the first *Los Angeles*–class submarine homeported in San Diego, the first Pacific Fleet submarine in the Tomahawk cruise missile program, and the first *Los Angeles* submarine to be fitted as a mother submarine for deep submergence rescue vehicles (DSRVs). By 1998 she had completed seven overseas deployments.

Escondido (**PCC-1169**). Control submarine chaser, 1943–45. Commissioned 16 October 1943 with a displacement of 280 tons and an armament of two 3-inch guns.

Oceanside (**LSM-175**). Medium landing ship, 1944–61. LSM-175 was laid down at the Charleston Naval Shipyard and commissioned 25 September 1944. During World War II she participated in the Okinawa landings and in cargo literage among Pacific bases. Following a period of inactivation she was recommissioned September 1950, homeported at San Diego, and assigned to the training of Marines and SeaBees in amphibious operations and was used in the logistics support between the islands of the Eleventh Naval District being officially renamed *Oceanside* in October 1959. On 1 February 1961 she was transferred to the Republic of Vietnam Navy. *Oceanside* received one battle star for World War II service and is credited with downing one enemy aircraft.

Ramona (**IX-76**). Steel-hulled schooner, 1942–43. Built in 1920 she was acquired by the Navy under bareboat charter and was placed in service 5 August 1942. Homeported at San Diego during her eight months in service, she patrolled off the California coast until placed out of service 1 April 1943. She was returned to her owner on 5 August 1944.

San Clemente (**AG-79**). Aircraft tender, 1920–46. Originally built as *Wright. Wright* had an illustrious career supporting all kinds of naval aircraft from the fledgling days of aviation. The first ship to carry the designation "lighter than air" aircraft tender AZ-1, and then aircraft tender AV-1, *Wright* was based in San Diego for extended periods in the 1920s and 1930s and acted as flagship for Commander, Air Squadrons. By 1940 *Wright* was engaged in establishing advanced seaplane bases and missed the attack on Pearl Harbor by a day returning from Wake and Midway Islands. She acted as a transport and tended seaplane squadrons in the South Pacific for the duration of the war. While serving as flagship for Service Squadron 7, Service Force Pacific Fleet, *Wright* was reclassified as headquarters ship effective 1 October 1944, with her designation changed from AV-1 to AG-79. On 1 February 1945 *Wright* was renamed *San Clemente* to clear the name Wright for the light fleet carrier CVL-49, then under construction. *San Clemente* remained as flagship for ServRon 7 and the nerve center of the Pacific Fleet Service Force based in the Philippines and, after the Japanese surrender, along the China Coast. She returned to San Francisco on 2 May 1946 and was decommissioned on 21 June 1946. *Wright/San Clemente* earned two battle stars for World War II service.

Coronado (**AGF-11**). Command ship, 1970–present. Originally built as an amphibious transport dock of the *Austin* class, *Coronado* was commissioned on 23 May 1970 with Mrs. Eleanor Ring Storrs as her sponsor. *Coronado* was converted in 1980 as a flagship for the Middle East Force, then as flagship of the Sixth Fleet and then the Third Fleet. She completed an eighteen-month conversion in 1997 to serve as Joint Force Command Ship with the conversion of her well deck to a three-story command facility.

Coronado (**PF-38**). Patrol frigate, 1943–45. A patrol frigate of 1,296 tons, *Coronado* sailed from San Diego on her maiden combat cruise on 8 February 1944 and received four battle stars for World War II service in the southwest Pacific and the Philippines. She later saw service in both the Russian and Japanese navies.

APPENDIX B
Major San Diego–Area Bases

Lineage of Major San Diego Navy Commands, 1900 – 2001

Command					
Commander, Navy Region Southwest: Feb 1999	Commander, Naval Base, San Diego: Oct 1980	Commandant, ELEVENTH Naval District: Jan 1921	Commandant, Naval Base San Diego: Dec 1919		
Naval Station, San Diego: Sep 1946	US Naval Repair Base: Oct 1943	US Destroyer Base: Feb 1922	US Shipping Board, Emergency Fleet Corporation: 1918		
Naval Base, Coronado: 2000	Naval Air Station, North Island: 1955	Naval Air Station, San Diego: Jun 1918	Camp Howard (Marines): Jul-Dec 1914	Camp Trouble: Jan-May 1912	Camp Thomas (Marines): Mar-Jul 1911
			Rockwell Field (Army): 1917	Signal Corps Aviation School (Army): Dec 1913	Fort Pio Pico (Army): 1901
Naval Base, Coronado: 2000	Naval Amphibious Base, Coronado: Jan 1946	Naval Amphibious Training Base: Jan 1944	Landing Craft Det, Destroyer Base: Sep 1942		
Marine Corps Air Station, Miramar: Oct 1997	Naval Air Station, Miramar: Apr 1952 (note 1)	Naval Aux Air Station, Miramar: Jul 1947	Marine Corps Air Station, Miramar: May 1946	Marine Corps Air Depot, Miramar: Sep 1943	Marine Corps Air Base Kearny Mesa: Mar 1943
				Naval Aux Air Station, Camp Kearny: Feb 1943	Camp Kearny (Army): 1917-1920
Naval Base, Point Loma: 2000	Naval Submarine Base, San Diego: Oct 1981	Naval Submarine Support Facility: Oct 1963	Naval Electronics Lab Ballast Point: Jul 1959	Battery Wilkeson, Fort Rosecrans (Army): 1898	

Naval Medical Center, San Diego Aug 1993	Naval Hospital, San Diego: Oct 1982	Naval Regional Medical Center: July 1972	Naval Hospital, San Diego: May 1919	War Dispensary: May 1917	4th Regiment Field Hospital: 1914
Naval Training Center, San Diego: Apr 1944 - Mar 1997	US Naval Training Station, San Diego: Jun 1923	US Naval Training Station, SD (Balboa Park): May 1917			
Naval Special Warfare Command: Apr 1987 (note 2)	Seal Teams ONE, THREE, FIVE: 1983	Seal Team ONE: Jan 1962	UDT-11, UDT-12, UDT-13: Feb 1954	UDT-1, UDT-3, UDT-5: 1952	UDT-1, UDT-3: May 1946
Naval Special Warfare Command: Apr 1987 (note 2)	Naval Special Warfare Group ONE: Jul 1975	Naval Inshore Warfare Group ONE: 1973	Naval Special Warfare Group ONE: 1967	Naval Operations Support Group ONE: Oct 1963	UDU-1: Aug 1950
Naval Special Warfare Command: Apr 1987 (note 2)	Special Boat Squadron ONE: Oct 1978	Coastal River Squadron ONE: July 1971	Boat Support Unit ONE: Feb 1964		
SPAWAR Systems Center, San Diego: Oct 1997 (note 3)	NCCOSC RDT&E Division (NRaD): Jan 1992	Naval Ocean Systems Center: 1977	Naval Electronics Laboratory Center: 1968	Naval Command, Control & Communications Laboratory Center: 1967	Naval Electronics Laboratory: 1945
				Univ. of Calif. Div of War Research: 1941	US Navy Radio & Sound Laboratory: 1940
Naval Undersea Center: 1972-1977 (note 4)	Naval Undersea Research & Dev. Center: 1969	Naval Undersea Warfare Center: 1967	Naval Ordnance Test Station (Inyokern): 1943		
Fleet & Industrial Supply Center: 1992	Naval Supply Center: Sep 1959	Naval Supply Depot: Aug 1922	Naval Fuel Depot: c1916	Naval Coaling Station: 1904	

Southwest Div, Naval Facilities Eng Command: Oct 1989	Engineering Field Activity, Southwest: Dec 1988	Officer in Charge of Construction, Southwest: Aug 1987	Resident Officer in Charge of Construction, San Diego: Jun 1970	Southwest Div, Naval Facilities Eng Command: May 1966	Southwest Div, Bureau of Yards & Docks: Jun 1961
				Public Works Officer, ELEVENTH ND: Jan 1921	Public Works Officer, TWELFTH ND: Oct 1917
Naval Aviation Depot: May 1987	Naval Air Rework Facility: Apr 1967	Overhaul & Repair Department: Jul 1948	NAS San Diego, Assembly & Repair Dept.: Jul 1919		
Shore Intermediate Maintenance Act. (SIMA), SD: Oct 1978	Inactive Ships Maint Facility: 1946-1975	DATC-Fleet Maint. Assistance Group (FMAG): Aug 1972	Development and Training Center (DATC): Dec 1967	Naval Repair Facility, San Diego: Apr 1954	Naval Repair Base, Industrial Command: Oct 1943
Naval Aux. Landing Field (Brown Field): Jun 1961-62	Naval Auxiliary Air Station, Brown Field: Jul 1954	Naval Auxiliary Air Station, Brown Field: Jun 1943-46	Naval Auxiliary Air Station, Otay Mesa: Mar 1943	Navy Landing Field: 1923	East Field (Army): Apr 1918
Outlying Landing Field, Imperial Beach: Dec 1974	Naval Air Station, Imperial Beach: Jan 1968	Naval Aux. Air Station, Ream Field: July 1955	Naval Aux. Landing Field, San Ysidro: 1950	Naval Aux. Air Station, Ream Field: 1943 -46	Naval Aux. Landing Field, Imperial Beach: 1920's
			Ream Field (Army): 1918	Oneonta Flying Fld. (Army): 1918	Camp Hearn (Army): 1916
Naval Computer and Telecommunications Station, SD 1990	US Navy Communications Station, SD: 1953	US Navy Communications Station, 11th ND: 1947	Naval Radio Transmitting Facility, Chollas Heights: 1916-1992	Naval Radio Station, Pt. Loma: May 1906	
Naval Radio Receiving Facility, Imperial Beach: 1972 (note 5)	US Naval Radio Station (R), Imperial Beach: 1960	Naval Communication Training Center: 1957	US Naval Radio Station (R)(S), Imperial Beach: 1950	US Navy Communications Station, Imperial Beach: 1947	Fort Emory (Army): Dec 1942

Camp Hearn (Army): 1916	Naval Radio Compass Station, Imperial Beach: 1920	Navy Direction Finder Station, Imperial Beach: 1932	Supplementary Radio Station, Imperial Beach: 1941	Battery Imperial (Army): Dec 1941	
Commander, Air Squadrons, Pacific Fleet: Oct 1921	Commander, Air Squadrons, Battle Fleet: Jun 1922	Commander, Air Squadrons, Battle Force: 1931	Commander, Aircraft, Battle Force: Apr 1933	Commander, Naval Air Force, Pacific Fleet: Sep 1942 (Pearl Harbor) (note 6)	Commander, Naval Air Force, Pacific Fleet: May 1949 (San Diego)
Commander, Air Detachment, Pacific Fleet: Oct 1919	Commander, Air Forces, Pacific Fleet: Jul 1920				
Commander, Destroyer Squadrons, Battle Fleet: 1922	Commander, Destroyers, Battle Force: 1931	Commander, Destroyer Force, Pacific: Apr 1942 (Pearl Harbor)	Commander, Destroyers, US Pacific Fleet: 1946 (San Diego)	Commander, Cruiser-Destroyer Force. US Pacific Fleet: Oct 1949	Naval Surface Force, US Pacific Fleet: Mar 1975 (note 7)
Commander, Destroyer Squadrons, US Pacific Fleet: 1919					
Commander, Cruiser Squadrons, Battle Fleet: 1922	Commander, Cruisers, Battle Force: 1931	Commander, Cruiser Force, Pacific: Apr 1942 (Pearl Harbor)	Commander, Battleships-Cruisers, US Pacific Fleet: 1946 (Pearl Harbor)	Commander, Cruiser-Destroyer Force. US Pacific Fleet: Oct 1949	Naval Surface Force, US Pacific Fleet: Mar 1975 (note 7)
Commander, Cruiser Squadrons, US Pacific Fleet: 1919					
		Commander, Task Force THREE: Sep 1941	Commander, Amphibious Force, US Pacific Fleet: Mar 1942 (Pearl Harbor)	Commander, Amphibious Force, US Pacific Fleet: Apr 1946 (San Diego)	Naval Surface Force, US Pacific Fleet: Mar 1975 (note 7)

Training Command. US Pacific Fleet: Aug 1945 - Oct 1997	Fleet Operational Training Command: Jan 1943				Destroyer Division NINETEEN: 1936
Fleet Anti-Submarine Warfare Training Center: Sep 1995	Fleet Anti-Submarine Warfare Training Center, Pacific: July 1973	US Fleet Anti-Submarine Warfare School: Mar 1960	US Fleet Sonar School, San Diego: Sep 1945	West Coast Sound School (Harbor Drive): Mar 1943	West Coast Sound School (Destroyer Base): 1941
Fleet Combat Training Center, Pacific: 1976	Fleet Anti-Air Warfare Training Center: 1960	U.S. Fleet Air Defense Training Center: 1954	Combat Information Center Group Training Center: 1946	Combat Information Center Indoctrination School: Feb 1945	Radar Operators School: 1942

Notes:

1. NAS Miramar also included the grounds of Camp Elliott that had originally been established in 1934 as Camp Holcomb for the Marine Corps.

2. The Naval Special Warfare Command in Coronado integrated the activities of several San Diego-based commands including Seal Teams ONE, THREE, FIVE, Naval Special Warfare Group ONE, Swimmer Delivery Vehicle Team ONE, Special Boat Squadron ONE and the Naval Special Warfare Center.

3. The headquarters of the Space and Naval Warfare Systems Command (SPAWAR) was established in San Diego in October 1997.

4. The Naval Undersea Center joined with the Naval Electronics Laboratory on Point Loma to form the Naval Ocean Systems Center in 1977.

5. Naval Radio Receiving Facility, Imperial Beach ultimately merged with Naval Computer and Telecommunications Station, San Diego.

6. When the Naval Air Forces, Pacific Fleet staff was established in Pearl Harbor in September 1942, it also included Commander, Patrol Wings, Pacific Fleet (established in May 1942 from Commander, Aircraft, Base Force) and Commander, Carriers, Pacific Fleet (established in April 1942 from Commander, Carrier Divisions, US Fleet).

7. Naval Surface Force, U.S. Pacific Fleet was formed from San Diego-based Cruiser-Destroyer Force, Pacific Fleet and Amphibious Force, Pacific Fleet as well as Service Force, Pacific Fleet and Mine Force, Pacific Fleet.

NOTES

Prologue

1. As late as 1793, British captain George Vancouver, in his *Voyage of Discovery,* mentioned Point Loma being cut off from the rest of San Diego during periods of high tide or high river levels.

2. During recorded times, the river generally flowed into San Diego Bay from 1769 to 1825, Mission Bay 1825–1855, San Diego Bay 1855–1876, and Mission Bay in years thereafter. During rainy seasons or during high spring tides, the river would frequently change its path for short duration.

3. John Winterhouse, "The Historical Geography of San Diego—Some Aspects of Landscape Change Prior to 1850," thesis, San Diego State University, San Diego, 1972, 59.

4. Eugene K. Chamberlain, *Old LaPlaya and LaPlaya Trail* (San Diego: Naval Ocean Systems Center, 1989), 7.

5. George Vancouver, *Voyage of Discovery* (1793), 1111.

6. Richard Henry Dana Jr., *Two Years Before the Mast* (New York: Mead and Co., 1946), 100.

Chapter 1. 1846

1. Commander Samuel Francis DuPont, letters to Sophie DuPont, 31 July 1846, Papers of Samuel Francis DuPont, 1803–1865, Hagley Museum and Library, Greenville, Del. (hereafter DuPont papers).

2. Elizabeth Douglass VanDenburgh, *My Voyage in the U.S. Frigate Congress* (New York: Desmond Fitzgerald, 1913), 74.

3. Donald L. Canney, *The Old Steam Navy: Frigates, Sloops, and Gunboats, 1815–1885* (Annapolis, Md.: Naval Institute Press, 1990), 43; Robert Erwin Johnson, *Thence Round Cape Horn* (Annapolis, Md.: Naval Institute Press, 1963), 88–89.

4. K. Jack Bauer, *Surfboats and Horse Marines* (Annapolis, Md.: Naval Institute Press, 1969), 149–54. The razee *Independence* had originally been built in 1814 as a 74-gun ship-of-the-line with three decks of guns. Her topmost deck was "razeed" (removed) in 1836 and her rating reduced to that of a 54-gun frigate. As a frigate she was known as one of the best ships in the Navy, a "smart sailer" and relatively fast with her large canvas size and reduced weight. She was finally sold for scrap in 1914, a hundred years after her commissioning.

5. *Cyane* and her sister ship *Levant* were originally rated as 18-gun sloops, but by 1846 were armed with 22 guns (18 carronades, 32 pounders, and four long 24 pounders, they themselves were later replaced with four 8-inch shell guns). In the clever appropriations techniques of the day to authorize new ships for the Navy in Congress, *Cyane* was actually considered a "rebuilt" ship, replacing the original *Cyane,* a sloop captured from the British in the War of 1812. No rebuilding ever took place, though; *Cyane* was built as a new ship and the older *Cyane* destroyed.

6. Stephen C. Rowan, "Recollections of the Mexican War," *U.S. Naval Institute Proceedings* 34, no. 3 (1888): 539–58. In early 1846, Capt. Joseph Snook, a British mariner who had settled in San Diego, assumed master of the schooner *Juanita,* owned by James Scott and John Wilson. He took the ship to Mazatlan in February, embarked a cargo worth $40,000, and was back in Santa Barbara by the middle of July. Trying to avoid the American squadron he returned to San Diego and was in port for about ten days before *Cyane* arrived. After DuPont had seized the ship, owner Scott asked U.S. Consul Thomas Larkin to use his influence to procure the *Juanita*'s release and pledged her neutrality. Snook and the crew gave their parole, and after receiving a safe conduct license the captain took the schooner back to San Diego from San Pedro. It was later rumored that *Juanita* delivered munitions to the Californios headquartered at San Luis Obispo despite her parole.

7. Ibid., 540.

8. The Delaware chief, Jim Staniox, told Captain DuPont as they left Monterey for the voyage to San Diego (and headed into giant Pacific rollers) that "I frightened now, first time in my life."

9. Walton Colton, *Deck and Port* (New York: A. S. Barnest Co., 1854), 390.

10. John Charles Fremont, *Memoirs* (Chicago: Belford, Clarke and Company, 1886), 563.

11. DuPont, orders issued to Lt. G. W. Harrison, U.S. Ship *Cyane,* 3 August 1846, DuPont papers.

12. James M. Merrill, *DuPont: The Making of an Admiral* (New York: Dodd, Mead, 1986), 181; DuPont, letters to Sophie DuPont, 3 August 1846.

13. Theodore W. Fuller, *San Diego Originals* (Pleasant Hill, Calif.: California Profiles Publications, 1987), 198.

14. DuPont, letters to Sophie DuPont, 5 August 1846.

15. DuPont, report to Commo. R. F. Stockton, 31 July 1846, DuPont papers.

16. DuPont, letters to Sophie DuPont, 8 August 1846.

17. C. Dewey Caldwell, *The Port of San Diego, 1846–1890* (Claremont, Calif.: Claremont Graduate School, 1969), 23; Max Miller, *I Cover the Waterfront* (New York: Dutton, 1932), 154. Ezekial Merritt was a frontiersman from Frémont's original topographic survey who had stayed in San Diego as part of the skeleton armed landing party—he was particularly famed for his accuracy with chewing tobacco.

18. Log of the USS *Congress,* 1846, RG 24, National Archives and Records Service, Washington, D.C./Laguna Niguel, Calif. (hereafter NARS).

19. Robert Carson Duvall, "Excerpts from the Log of the USS *Savannah,*" *California Historical Society Quarterly* 3, no. 2 (1924): 71–73.

20. Howard Lamar, *The Cruise of the Portsmouth, 1845–47: A Sailor's View of the Naval Conquest of California* (New Haven: Yale University Press, 1958), 170.

21. Ibid., 172.

22. Ibid., 185.

23. Richard F. Pourade, *The Silver Dons* (San Diego: Union-Tribune Publishing, 1963), 102; DuPont, letters to Sophie DuPont, 2 January 1847.

24. Miller, *I Cover the Waterfront,* 150; DuPont, letters to Sophie DuPont, 23 January 1847.

25. Clark G. Reynolds, *Famous American Admirals* (New York: Van Nostrand-Reinhold, 1978).

26. Lamar, *Cruise of the Portsmouth,* 186.

27. *Dictionary of American Naval Fighting Ships,* 8 vols. (Washington, D.C.: U.S. Government Printing Office, 1959–81).

28. The U.S. steamer *Massachusetts* had been built for commercial service in 1845 but bought by the War Department in 1847 as a troop transport. After the Mexican War she was assigned to the Pacific Squadron and operated along the West Coast through 1852 on surveys of harbors and sites for lighthouses and buoys.

29. Paul M. Callaghan, "Fort Rosecrans, California," thesis, University of San Diego, San Diego, 1980, 4. The formal conveyance of the military reservation by the trustees of the City of San Diego was accomplished in November 1868 (over the protests of local residents who had staked claims in the area). In 1897 the California Legislature ceded to the federal government all lands that were being used for military purposes.

30. Jerry MacMullen, *They Came by Sea* (San Diego: Maritime Museum Association of San Diego, 1988), 56.

31. Chester Lyman, *Around the Horn to the Sandwich Islands and California, 1845–50* (New Haven: Yale University Press, 1925), 307.

32. John E. Pomfret, *California Gold Rush Voyages, 1848–1849* (San Marino, Calif.: Huntington Library, 1954), 234.

Chapter 2. 1893

1. The U.S. Navy Pay Corps at the turn of the century was the rough equivalent of today's Navy Supply Corps. From its earliest days of sail, the American Navy had employed pursers aboard its warships to handle matters of supply and finance. In 1860, pursers were retitled "paymasters" and a professional Pay Corps was established to oversee their worldwide operation. Entry into the Corps was highly selective and the passing of a rigorous entry examination was required.

2. Frank M. Bennett, *The Steam Navy of the United States* (Westport, Conn.: Greenwood Press, 1896), 708. For the Greely rescue mission, the Navy fitted out *Thetis* with a star-studded crew that included Comdr. Winfield S. Schley, later victor over the Spanish at Santiago, as her commanding officer and George W. Melville, later Engineer-in-Chief of the Navy, as her engineer.

3. Log of USS *Thetis,* 1893, RG 24, NARS.

4. Yates Stirling, *Sea Duty: The Memoirs of a Fighting Admiral* (New York: Putnam and Sons, 1939), 42.

5. The years after 1893 were not kind to faithful *Thetis.* She continued her resolute surveys of the Baja coast until 1897, returning periodically to San Diego for repairs and supplies. In 1899 she was transferred to the Revenue Cutter Service, the precursor of today's Coast Guard, and for the next sixteen years alternated patrol duty in Hawaiian and Alaskan waters. She was sold in 1916 for commercial service but her rugged Scottish construction served her all the way until finally grounding in 1950.

6. James E. Moss, *San Diego Pioneer Families* (San Diego: San Diego Historical Society, 1978), 83.

7. Katherine E. Carlin and Ray Brandes, *Coronado, the Enchanted Island* (Coronado, Calif.: Coronado Historical Association, 1987), 112; Jerry MacMullen, "North Island's First Shipyard," *San Diego Union,* 5 January 1969, G-1.

8. "Prominent Wedding," *San Diego Union,* 22 August 1895.

9. Johnson, *Thence Round Cape Horn,* 135.

10. W. L. Field, Report on the value of a coaling station at San Diego, 1900, General Records, 1799–1947, RG 80, NARA.

11. Barry A. Joyce, "James Alden: Naval Officer, Scientist and Explorer," thesis, San Diego State University, San Diego, 1990, 83; Donald R. Craig, "Annotated Bibliography of the History of the U.S. Naval Training Center," thesis, University of San Diego, San Diego, 1969, 7.

12. Editorial, *San Diego Herald,* 17 May 1856, 2; Corps of Engineers, *The Ports of San Diego and San Luis Obispo, California* (Washington D.C.: U.S. Printing Office, 1936), 4. On 15 April 1893 the U.S. government condemned through the courts eighteen acres on the extreme southwesterly tip of North Island and the Corps of Army Engineers awarded a contract to build the first unit of Zuniga Jetty.

13. Johnson, *Thence Round Cape Horn,* 142.

14. Charles A. Bencik, "The Strange Affair of the *Itata,*" *Mains'l Haul* (Spring 1997): 29.

15. "Long Stern Chase," *San Diego Union,* 12 May 1891, 1.

16. "Now for the *Itata,*" *San Diego Union,* 10 June 1891, 1.

17. Bennett, *Steam Navy of the United States,* 796.

18. "The *Itata,*" *San Diego Union,* 5 July 1891, 1. *Itata* stayed in San Diego Bay during lengthy court proceedings until she was finally released in March 1892.

19. H. P. Wood, *The Port of San Diego* (San Diego: Frye, Garrett and Smith Printers, 1900), 1–4.

20. "Cabrillo Activities," *San Diego Union,* 30 September 1892.

21. John D. Alden, *The American Steel Navy* (Annapolis, Md.: Naval Institute Press, 1972), 39.

22. William R. Braisted, *The United States Navy in the Pacific, 1897–1909* (Austin: University of Texas Press, 1958), 15.

23. Ships of the Pacific Squadron included: *Monadnock, Monterey, Philadelphia, Marion, Adams, Corwin,* and *Albatross,* accompanied by the ship-rigged British ironclad HMS *Comus.*

24. Craig, "Annotated Bibliography of the History of the U.S. Naval Training Center," 9; "A Memorable Night," *San Diego Union,* 23 February 1897, 2.

25. "Coronado Beach: A Unique Corner of the Earth," pamphlet, E. S. Babcock, Manager of Coronado Beach Company, Coronado, Calif., 1898, 3.

26. "Patriots Enlisting," *San Diego Union,* 26 April 1898, 2.

27. Johnson, *Thence Round Cape Horn,* 152; Miller, letter to SecNav John D. Long, 15 April 1898, Rear Adm. Joseph Miller, Area Nine File, 1814–1910, Navy Section, War Records Branch, NARA.

28. "Harbor Notes," *San Diego Union,* 29 April 1898, 6; Barry Alan Joyce, *A Harbor Worth Defending: A Military History of Point Loma* (San Diego: Cabrillo Historical Association, 1995), 17.

29. U.S. Corps of Engineers (Los Angeles Office) letter, 9 February 1905, General Correspondence, Naval Coaling Station, NARA Laguna; Diane Cooper, "Remember the *Maine* and Mine the Harbors," *Mains'l Haul* (Spring 1998): 30.

30. Charles A. Bencik, "The San Diego Naval Militia," *Mains'l Haul* (Fall 1993): 15.

31. Braisted, *United States Navy in the Pacific, 1897–1909,* 53.

32. Arnold Klaus, *History of the San Diego Chamber of Commerce* (San Diego: San Diego Chamber of Commerce, 1967), 396.

33. William E. Smythe, *History of San Diego, 1542–1908* (San Diego: The History Co., 1908), 110; Joyce, *Harbor Worth Defending,* 17. San Diego Bay had perennially been a seasonal calving area for the migrating California grey whale, much as the lagoons of Baja California are today, and as late as 1872 whales were found in numbers within the bay. San Diego whaling was shore-based, different from the better-known Nantucket industry. Whalers would depart from La Playa in small boats, round Point Loma, and search for their catch in the kelp beds. One estimate figured that between fifteen hundred and two thousand whales were towed back to La Playa for rendering during this period.

34. Herbert J. Nelson, "The Port of San Diego: Development of Terminal Facilities for Water-borne Commerce by Federal and Municipal Agencies," thesis, San Diego State University, San Diego, 1956, 59.

35. Abraham Shragge, "Radio and Real Estate: The U.S. Navy's First Land Purchase in San Diego." *Journal of San Diego History* 42 (Fall 1996): 243.

36. Bureau of Yards and Docks, Report to the Secretary of the Navy on Yards and Stations on the Pacific Coast, 1898, RG 71, NARA.

37. Sen. George Perkins, letter to the Asst. SecNav, 27 April 1900; Minutes of the Board of Directors, San Diego Chamber of Commerce, 6 April 1900, San Diego Chamber of Commerce files, San Diego (hereafter SDCOC files); SDCOC, letter to the SecNav, 7 April 1900, SDCOC files.

38. BuEquip, response to SDCOC letter, 26 April 1900, SDCOC files.

39. Needham, letter to H. P. Wood, SDCOC, 8 May 1900, SDCOC files.

40. "Survey of Harbor Has Commenced," *San Diego Union,* 25 May 1900, 6.

41. SDCOC, Minutes of the Board of Directors, SDCOC, 4 May and 25 May 1900, SDCOC files.

42. Field, Report on coaling station.

43. "A Flotilla of Torpedo Boats," *San Diego Union,* 21 June 1900, 6; BuEquip, letter to the SecNav, 31 July 1900.

44. Abraham J. Shragge, "Boosters and Bluejackets: The Civic Culture of Militarism in San Diego, California, 1900–1945," diss., University of California–San Diego, 1998, 125.

45. "Admiral Bradford Here to Select a Coaling Station," *San Diego Union,* 2 December 1900, 6.

46. Wood, letter to Board of Directors, SDCOC, 8 February 1901, SDCOC files.

47. SecNav, Annual Report, 1900, 297.

48. "Ready to Build Coaling Station," *San Diego Union,* 20 April 1901, 8.

49. SecNav, Endorsement on BuEquip recommendation, 10 January 1901, Secretary of the Navy, General Correspondence, RG 80, NARA. The land was transferred from the War Department on 11 May 1901. The La Playa Coaling Depot was formally established in 1904. The original Army Torpedo Station was transferred to the Navy Department in 1909.

50. SecNav, Annual Report, 1901, 366.

51. SecNav, Annual Report, 1902, 351.

52. SecNav, Annual Report, 357.

53. Minutes of the Board of Directors, SDCOC, 7 November 1902; Ed Fletcher, letter to President Roosevelt, 16 September 1902, SDCOC files.

54. Minutes of the Board of Directors, SDCOC, 15 May 1903; Shragge, "Boosters and Bluejackets," 123.

55. Minutes of the Board of Directors, SDCOC, 12 January 1900; "Will Ratify Treaty Tomorrow Evening," *San Diego Union,* 19 March 1903, 6; Minutes of the Board of Directors, SDCOC, 13 November 1903; Daniels, letter to H. P. Wood, 21 January 1904, SDCOC files.

56. MacMullen, *They Came by Sea,* 57.

57. Dewey, letter to SecNav, 26 October 1904, General Board letters, vol. 3, RG 80, NARA.

58. Department of the Navy, *The U.S. Naval Hospital Complex in Balboa Park, San Diego, California: A Report for the Historical American Buildings Survey* (San Diego: Department of the Navy, July 1987), 6; "Most Important Harbor on the Pacific Coast," *San Diego Union*, 30 November 1904, 1.

59. Wood, letter to Board of Directors, SDCOC, 23 January 1905.

60. Minutes of the Board of Directors, SDCOC, 3 August 1904.

61. Comdr. Lucien Young (1852–1912) graduated from the Naval Academy in 1873 and by 1905 had amassed five medals and five battle bars, including commendations for gallantry during the Spanish-American War and heroism.

62. Port Harford is now Port San Luis, located just north of Pismo Beach on the California central coast.

63. Several reports in the media also had Commander Young visiting a downtown bar to quaff down a few last-minute beers before departing port.

64. Asa N. Bushnell, "There Came Upon Me a Day of Trouble," *San Diego Historical Society Quarterly* 7, no. 4 (1961): 45.

65. Leonard Ash, "The Death of the *Bennington*," *Mains'l Haul*, pt. 1 (Summer 1992): 24.

66. Eugene K. Chamberlain, *Fort Rosecrans National Cemetery, California Registered Historical Landmark #55* (1990), 12; RAdm. Thomas J. Senn, "The History of the Navy in San Diego," in *History of San Diego County*, ed. C. H. Heilbron (San Diego: San Diego Press Club, 1936), 57. Gunner's Mate Causey would later serve five years at North Island before retiring in 1929 and in 1932 was elected to the Coronado City Council.

67. "Over Fifty Lives Lost on the *Bennington*," *San Diego Union*, 22 July 1905, 2.

68. Johnson, *Thence Round Cape Horn*, 161.

69. Ensign Perry's casket was immediately shipped home to Massachusetts. When funds became authorized for the Navy to ship the remains home of those killed in the line of duty many coffins were disinterred and sent back to relatives for reburial. The reports of the day indicated forty-seven coffins were placed in a long trench at the military cemetery during the 23 July ceremony.

70. Ash, "Death of the *Bennington*," 26; "Forty-Seven Coffins Placed in a Trench," *San Diego Union*, 24 July 1905, 1.

71. Carney, letter to Rear Adm. C. F. Goodrich, Commanding Pacific Squadron, 23 August 1905, RG 181, NARA.

Chapter 3. 1906

1. *Charleston* was the first of the modern "New Steel Navy" warships the Navy was to lose through either mishap or combat.

2. Edgar Hebert, "San Diego's Naval Militia," *San Diego Historical Society Quarterly* 9, no. 2 (1963): 15. Lt. Thomas Alexis Nerney, formerly captain of Company B, San Diego City Guard, was the first commanding officer of the San Diego "Naval Reserves"—formally Company A, Naval Battalion NGC (National Guard of California). He would later be chosen to command the California Battalion. The San Diego Company was later named the Third Division of the state's militia when the Naval Battalion NGC was renamed the Naval Militia in 1903.

3. Hebert, "San Diego's Naval Militia," 16. The German-American "Turnhalle," a large gymnasium located on 8th St near H, was used extensively by the San Diego Naval Militia company as a meeting area and armory. A new naval militia armory was completed at the foot of 28th Street in 1911.

4. Hebert, "San Diego's Naval Militia," 19. The *Alert* was assigned as the militia's training ship in 1903 as a replacement for *Pinta*.

5. Hebert, "San Diego's Naval Militia," 22. The California Naval Militia existed for over twenty-nine years. Ultimately, the name of the Navy's national militia organization was changed to the National Naval Volunteers and later was supplanted by the U.S. Naval Reserve.

6. James W. Hinds, *San Diego's Military Sites* (San Diego: San Diego Historical Society, 1986), 115.

7. Bencik, "San Diego Naval Militia," 16; Edward D. Stevens, "They Used to Call It Wireless," *San Diego Historical Society Quarterly* 9, no. 1 (1963): 8. Rear Adm. Caspar Goodrich was one of the brightest naval officers of his era and an early proponent of San Diego as a Pacific Squadron base of operations. He graduated first in his class at the Naval Academy and later helped found both the Naval Institute and the Naval War College.

8. "Finished Wireless Installation," *San Diego Union*, 12 May 1906, 3.

9. Department of the Navy, *U.S. Naval Hospital Complex in Balboa Park*, 6. Before the wireless community and the Navy standardized three- and four-letter call signs, Point Loma was known unofficially as "TM."

10. L. S. Howeth, *History of Communications-Electronics in the United States Navy* (Washington, D.C.: Office of Naval History, 1963), 522; "San Diego May Get Wireless Station Second to None," *San Diego Union*, 26 July 1913, 10.

11. Gordon C. O'Gara, *Theodore Roosevelt and the Rise of the Modern Navy* (New York: Greenwood Press, 1943), 10. Members of the General Board in 1907–9 proposed a Pacific Fleet more powerful than the entire Japanese Fleet as part of plans to counter the expanding Japanese threat. Naval officers believed that distances were too far to the West Coast to constitute an actual threat but they used the menace of Japan to counter opposition to their plans for more battleships and shore bases on the West Coast.

12. Minutes of the Board of Directors, SDCOC, 1907, 3.

13. "Officers Urge Bar Deepening," *San Diego Union*, 17 March 1908, 7.

14. E. B. Potter, *Bull Halsey* (Annapolis, Md.: Naval Institute Press, 1985), 86.

15. James R. Reckner, *Teddy Roosevelt's Great White Fleet* (Annapolis, Md.: Naval Institute Press, 1988), 56.

16. Robert D. Jones, *With the American Fleet from the Atlantic to the Pacific* (Seattle: Harrison, 1908), 259.

17. Evan Fleet Celebration Official Program (San Diego, 1908).

18. Jones, *With the American Fleet*, 259; "City's Doors Are Always Open to Tars," *San Diego Union*, 16 April 1908, 2.

19. Jones, *With the American Fleet*, 113–257.

20. "Warships Depart, City Felicitates," *San Diego Union*, 19 April 1908, 14.

21. D. C. Collier, editorial, *San Diego Union*, 21 June 1910.

22. Smythe, *History of San Diego, 1542–1908*, 629.

23. SDCOC, telegram to SecNav Metcalf, 8 December 1907.

24. SecNav, Annual Report, 1908, 298; Pacific Torpedo Fleet, letter to SecNav, 22 February 1910.

25. Alexander D. Bevil, "Remember the *San Diego,*" *Olde San Diego Gazette,* August 1998, 19. *California*'s navigator for this historic transit of the harbor was later five-star admiral William D. Leahy.

Chapter 4. 1911

1. Glenn H. Curtiss, *The Curtiss Aviation Book* (New York: Fred Stokes, c. 1912), 98–101.

2. "Biplane Conquers Air and Sea," *San Diego Union,* 27 January 1911, 11.

3. Gary F. Kurutz, "The Only Safe and Sane Method: The Curtiss School of Aviation," *Journal of San Diego History* 25 (Winter 1979): 58.

4. Ibid.

5. Hinds, *San Diego's Military Sites,* 43.

6. Mary L. Scott, *San Diego, Air Capital of the West* (Virginia Beach, Va.: Donning Company, 1991), 19.

7. Curtiss, letter to the SecNav, 29 November 1910, NAS North Island archives.

8. Jeffrey Charles Brown, "An Historical Geographical Study of North Island," California State University–Long Beach, 1991, 27.

9. Kurutz, "Only Safe and Sane Method," 55; Carlin and Brandes, *Coronado, the Enchanted Island,* 116.

10. Clara Studer, *Sky Storming Yankee: The Life of Glenn Curtiss* (New York: Arno Press, 1972), 252.

11. "Curtiss in Hydroplane Flies to Cruiser in Bay," *San Diego Union,* 18 February 1911, 7.

12. Elretta Sudsbury, ed., *Jackrabbits to Jets: The History of NAS North Island, San Diego, California* (San Diego: San Diego Publishing, 1992), 19.

13. "Curtiss in Hydroplane Flies to Cruiser in Bay," *San Diego Union,* 18 February 1911, 7.

14. "Curtiss Demonstrates His Air-Land and Water Machine," *San Diego Union,* 27 February 1911, 8.

15. Kevin Starr, *The Dream Endures: California Enters the 1940s* (New York: Oxford University Press, 1997), 111.

16. Archibald D. Turnbull and Clifford L. Lord, *History of United States Naval Aviation* (New Haven: Yale University Press, 1949), 15–17.

17. Sudsbury, *Jackrabbits to Jets,* 23.

18. "Aviators Fly Over Coronado Hotel," *San Diego Union,* 31 January 1912, 6.

19. Scott, *San Diego, Air Capital of the West,* 28; Sudsbury, *Jackrabbits to Jets,* 24.

20. Curtiss, *Curtiss Aviation Book,* 103.

21. Edward L. Leiser, "North Island Wings Its Way into History," *Traditions* (November 1994): 3.

22. Brown, "Historical Geographical Study of North Island," 27; Clayton, letter to Commanding Officer, Signal Corps Aviation School, 1 December 1915, NAS North Island archives.

23. Clayton, letter to Commanding Officer, Signal Corps Aviation School, 1 December 1915.

24. U.S. Congress, *Report of the Army Commission (Reber Report),* 64th Cong., 1st sess., 29 December 1915, H. Doc. 687 (Washing-ton, D.C.: U.S. Government Printing Office, 1916). The five sites considered included North Island, Coronado Heights (at the southern end of the Silver Strand), Dutch Flats (the site of Lindbergh Field and the Naval Training Center), Chula Vista just north of the Sweetwater River, and Chula Vista on the bay near the present marina.

25. Hinds, *San Diego's Military Sites,* 43.

26. Ibid., 41.

27. William R. Braisted, *The United States Navy in the Pacific, 1909–1922* (Austin: University of Texas Press, 1971), 230.

28. U.S. Congress, *Preliminary Report of the Navy Yard Commission (Helm Report),* 64th Cong., 2nd sess., 17 January 1917, H. Doc. 1946 (Washington, D.C.: U.S. Government Printing Office, 1918).

29. Turnbull and Lord, *History of United States Naval Aviation,* 78.

30. William Kettner, *Why It Was Done and How* (San Diego: Frye and Smith, 1923), 87.

31. H. H. Arnold, "The History of Rockwell Field," 1924, 36–42; Kettner, *Why It Was Done and How,* 98.

32. Leiser, "North Island Wings Its Way into History," 4; Minutes of the Board of Directors, SDCOC, 3 April 1918. East Field was named for Maj. Whitten J. East, USA.

33. Minutes of the Board of Directors, SDCOC, 19 June 1918. Ream Field was named in honor of Maj. William Roy Ream, the first flying surgeon in American's air service who had been long stationed at Rockwell Field and who had died in a flying accident.

34. James H. Doolittle, *An Autobiography by General James H. Doolittle* (New York: Bantam Books, 1991), 45.

35. SecNav, Annual Report, 1971, 523.

36. Duchess of Windsor, *The Heart Has Its Reasons* (New York: David McKay Co., 1956), 62.

37. Ibid., 54; Bates, letter to Miss Elretta Sudsbury, 6 July 1966, NAS North Island archives.

38. Charles Higham, *The Duchess of Windsor, the Second Life* (New York: McGraw-Hill, 1988), 78; Stephen Birmingham, *Duchess: The Story of Wallis Warfield Windsor* (Boston: Little, Brown, 1981), 101.

39. Sudsbury, *Jackrabbits to Jets,* 51; "Former Air Station Commander Dies Here," *Coronado Journal* (1 June 1950): 3.

40. George R. Pond, *Aviation Review: U.S. Navy in San Diego, California, 1921* (San Diego: Dove and Robinson Printers, 1921), 33. Formal transfer of Army land to the Navy and establishment of Naval Air Station, San Diego were completed on 17 June 1918.

41. Pond, *Aviation Review,* 33; Bates, letter to Miss Elretta Sudsbury, 6 July 1966.

42. Brown, "Historical Geographical Study of North Island," 30.

43. Ibid., 31.

44. Janice Fahey, "The Architectural/Historical Significance of Buildings at Naval Air Station, North Island, San Diego, California," San Diego, May 1988, 23.

45. Scott, *San Diego, Air Capital of the West,* 43.

46. Sudsbury, *Jackrabbits to Jets,* 54; Leiser, "North Island Wings Its Way into History," 4.

47. "Sight of a Lifetime," *San Diego Union,* 28 November 1918, 1.

48. Pond, *Aviation Review,* 49.

49. "New Commander to Take Charge at North Island," *San Diego Union,* 8 December 1919, 6.

50. Clark G. Reynolds, *Admiral John H. Towers* (Annapolis, Md.: Naval Institute Press, 1991), 173; Theodore Taylor, *The Magnificent Mitscher* (New York: Norton, 1954), 33.

51. William F. Trimble, *Admiral William A. Moffett* (Washington, D.C.: Smithsonian Institution Press, 1994), 61; Reynolds, *Admiral John H. Towers,* 174.

52. Reynolds, *Admiral John H. Towers,* 173; Taylor, *The Magnificent Mitscher,* 69.

53. Reynolds, *Admiral John H. Towers,* 175. The Pacific Fleet Air Detachment was upgraded to Air Force, Pacific Fleet in July 1920 and would be further designated in mid-1921 as, first, Air Squadrons—Pacific Fleet and, later, Air Squadrons—Battle Fleet.

Chapter 5. 1912

1. Benjamin Franklin Cooling, *Gray Steel and Blue Water Navy* (Hamden, Conn.: Archon Books, 1979), 185.

2. Joseph P. Lash, *Eleanor and Franklin* (New York: Norton, 1971), 201.

3. "Bruder Bill Surprises Supporters," *San Diego Union,* 12 November 1912, 4.

4. Edward J. P. Davis, *Historical San Diego* (San Diego: Pioneer Printers, 1953), 36.

5. Shragge, "Boosters and Bluejackets," 203.

6. Dewey, letter concerning establishment of a Naval Station in San Diego, 20 December 1907, SecNav General Correspondence File, RG 80, General Records of the Department of the Navy, 1798–1947, National Archives and Records Service, Washington, D.C./Laguna Niguel, Calif. (hereafter RG 80, GRDN).

7. Dewey, General Board, letter 404 to SecNav, 18 March 1909, General Board letters, RG 80, GRDN.

8. Dewey, General Board, letter to SecNav, 19 December 1912, General Board letters, RG 80, GRDN.

9. "Names San Diego a Torpedo Fleet Base," *San Diego Union,* 21 December 1909, 6. The Pacific Torpedo Fleet was a command independent of the Commander-in-Chief, Pacific Fleet from 1909 to 1913. *Iris* served as the parent ship for the Pacific Torpedo Fleet for several years, finally ending her days towing targets for gunnery practice off Point Loma. Torpedo boats favored moorings at the Coronado Ferry Landing and at the Spreckels Company wharf just east of the ferry slips that would later become a Coronado boatyard.

10. "Submarines to Go North Today for Permanent Base," *San Diego Union,* 21 July 1913, 7.

11. "Admiral Manney's Appointment," *San Diego Union,* 25 February 1909, 4; Edward S. Miller, *War Plan Orange* (Annapolis, Md.: Naval Institute Press, 1991), 98. The rich petroleum fields of the Western United States offered Pacific ships the opportunity to operate without reliance on Atlantic coal supplies and the planned conversion of ship's propulsion from coal to oil helped speed the basing of ships to Pacific ports.

12. Dewey, Fuel Supply at San Diego, 6 May 1916, File 10924 (126), RG 80, GRDN.

13. Josephus Daniels, *The Wilson Era: Years of Peace, 1910–1917* (Chapel Hill: University of North Carolina Press, 1944), 313.

After 1908 the Chamber of Commerce was able to obtain lists of retiring naval officers from the Navy and used those as a means of inviting many influential officers to settle in San Diego. Rear Admiral Manney's decision to settle in San Diego was widely applauded including a *Union* article saying he "would be a welcome addition to SD's already large colony of officers active and retired, whose presence here is so agreeable a feature of social life in this city." Manney was later elected a Chamber director and served as chairman of the Chamber's harbor committee. He then served on the city council and was a director of San Diego Securities, the real estate company that later sold hundreds of acres of bayfront property to the Navy Department.

14. "Cheers Sound Loudly as Secretary Promises to Bring Battleships Here," *San Diego Union,* 23 July 1913, 1.

15. Ibid.

16. "Cruiser's Guns Boom Farewell to Daniels," *San Diego Union,* 24 July 1913, 3; E. David Cronon, *The Cabinet Diaries of Josephus Daniels, 1913–1921* (Lincoln: University of Nebraska Press, 1963), 79.

17. Daniels, *The Wilson Era,* 315. The Chamber of Commerce also did not forget the important role that Captain Plunkett had played during the visit. Years later in 1919, the Chamber sent a personal letter of congratulations to Plunkett when he was selected for promotion to flag rank.

18. "To Begin Dredging Harbor Entrance," *San Diego Union,* 23 July 1913, 7.

19. "San Diego May Get Wireless Station Second to None," *San Diego Union,* 26 July 1913, 10.

20. Reflecting the strategic importance the Navy placed on its new high-power wireless network, the existing Point Loma wireless site was dropped from consideration due to its supposed vulnerability to attack from the sea.

21. Shragge, "Radio and Real Estate," 249.

22. SecNav, Annual Report, 1917.

23. Daniels, letter to Congressman William Kettner, 1 August 1914, SDCOC Minutes 1914; Minutes of the Board of Directors, SDCOC, 18 August 1914. Interestingly, *California* was the second of the armored cruisers rechristened, with the renaming of *Pennsylvania* to *Pittsburgh* barely noted in the Pittsburgh press.

24. Starr, *The Dream Endures,* 111; "San Diego to Be Great Navy Base," *San Diego Union,* 13 April 1914, 1.

25. Department of the Navy, *U.S. Naval Hospital Complex in Balboa Park,* 10.

26. "Full Atlantic Fleet Coming to San Diego Says Roosevelt," *San Diego Union,* 29 March 1915, 1. Kettner just missed Roosevelt in San Diego but met him immediately upon his return to Washington. Kettner had had a busy month accompanying two separate parties to the Exposition, one for the members of the Naval Affairs Committee on 13 March and one for the Secretary of the Interior a week later.

27. "First Battleship Squadron to Anchor in Man-o'-War Row Here," *San Diego Union,* 29 July 1915, 1. The battleship squadron was the first ever to enter San Diego harbor and *Missouri* was the first battleship to transit the Panama Canal.

28. Frederick S. Harrod, *Manning the New Navy* (Westport, Conn.: Greenwood Press, 1978), 76.

29. Minutes of the Board of Directors, SDCOC, 24 February 1906 and 3 August 1904.

30. Will H. Holcomb, "Getting a Naval Training School," *San Diego Magazine*, April 1930, 50; Shragge, "Boosters and Bluejackets," 141.

31. Kettner, *Why It Was Done and How*, 60; Daniels, *The Wilson Era*, 308.

32. "Great Base Probably Will Be Established at Exposition," *San Diego Union*, 2 May 1917, 1.

33. Kettner, *Why It Was Done and How*, 60.

34. Shragge, "Radio and Real Estate," 255.

35. Kettner, *Why It Was Done and How*, 63.

36. Minutes of the Board of Directors, SDCOC, 23 October 1918.

37. Annual Report of the SDCOC President, 31 October 1919; Craig, "Annotated Bibliography of the History of the U.S. Naval Training Center," 16.

38. Tom Burgess, "Struggle for Dispensary Recalled," *San Diego Union*, 24 January 1988, A-6. Smith was later assigned in 1922 as the flight surgeon in *Langley* and later served in *Saratoga*. He retired as a captain in 1952.

39. "San Diego Naval Hospital Celebrates Anniversary," *Dry Dock*, 13 August 1948, 2; Ellen B. Holzman, "Hospital Grows in Balboa Park," *Traditions* (Summer 1997): 22. Dr. Farenholt rose to the rank of Rear Admiral returning for his last tour of duty prior to retirement as the District Medical Officer, Eleventh Naval District.

40. Paolo E. Coletta, ed., *United States Navy and Marine Corps Bases, Domestic* (Westport, Conn.: Greenwood Press, 1985), 566.

41. Daniels, *The Wilson Era*, 314.

42. Kettner, *Why It Was Done and How*, 101.

43. Roosevelt, letter to mayor of San Diego, 17 May 1922, SecNav General Correspondence File, RG 80, GRDN.

44. Kettner, *Why It Was Done and How*, 101.

45. Department of the Navy, *U.S. Naval Hospital Complex in Balboa Park*, 58.

46. Ibid., 18; Coletta, ed., *United States Navy and Marine Corps Bases*, 566.

47. Johnson, *Thence Round Cape Horn*, 186.

48. David H. Grover, "Bully of the Pacific Mixes It Up with Huns," *Traditions* (Summer 1997): 16.

49. Don B. Marshall, *California Shipwrecks* (Seattle: Superior Publishing, 1978), 15.

50. Braisted, *United States Navy in the Pacific, 1909–1922*, 465.

51. "Explosion Aboard Navy Craft," *San Diego Union*, 15 April 1919, 1.

52. "Armada in Proud Review," *San Diego Union*, 8 August 1919, 1.

53. "Daniels for Great Harbor," *San Diego Union*, 9 August 1919, 1.

54. SecNav, Annual Report, 1919, 186; James D. Newland, "Admiral Cements Station's Foundation," *Traditions* (November 1995): 8.

55. Turnbull and Lord, *History of United States Naval Aviation*, 162.

56. Gerald D. Nash, *The American West in the Twentieth Century* (Englewood Cliffs, N.J.: Prentice-Hall, 1973), 76.

57. Starr, *The Dream Endures*, 113.

58. "Building a Seaport," *San Diego Union*, 2 August 1920, 4.

59. "Navy Items Carried by Record Vote," *San Diego Union*, 4 August 1920, 1.

60. SecNav, letter to William Kettner, 9 Aug 1920, SecNav General Correspondence File, RG 80, GRDN.

61. Shragge, "Boosters and Bluejackets," 229.

62. Daniels, *The Wilson Era*, 314.

Chapter 6. 1920

1. Roger Welles, letter to Adm. H. B. Wilson, 4 January 1920, Roger Welles Papers, LOC (hereafter Welles Papers). Mrs. Welles had established a career in her own right—somewhat of a social rarity at the time—writing short stories and books for a large national audience. One of her stories appeared, coincidentally, in the December 1919 issue of *Scribner's*.

2. Tomb, letter to Rear Admiral Welles, 14 January 1920, Welles Papers.

3. "Admiral Wants Bigger Port," *San Diego Union*, 31 January 1920, 1.

4. "Welles of the Navy," *Rotator of the Rotary Club*, San Diego, 10 August 1920.

5. Welles, letter to Admiral Coontz, 3 February 1920, Welles Papers. Heretofore, San Diego naval activities fell under the administration of the Commandant of the Twelfth Naval District in San Francisco.

6. Jeffrey W. Farquhar, "The History of Naval Station San Diego," thesis, University of San Diego, San Diego, 1996, 38.

7. Ibid., 34; Newland, "Admiral Cements Station's Foundation," 8.

8. Minutes of the Board of Directors, SDCOC, 17 April 1918. The marine railway of this era consisted of a large metal cage attached to a sliding track on an incline. To extract a ship from the water for repair, the cage would be lowered into the harbor, the ship floated into the cage, and the cage then drawn up the incline by a steam locomotive.

9. Minutes of the Board of Directors, SDCOC, 17 April 1918.

10. Daniels, telegram to CNO Benson, 24 June 1920. The Scofield Brothers, hoping to up the ante for land at 32nd Street (and knowing of the Navy's urgent need for berthing space for its growing number of inactive destroyers), threatened to exercise an option to buy the property, causing Rear Admiral Welles to bluff: "if we are forced outside of San Diego Harbor, we would be obliged to move up to San Pedro, or perhaps Long Beach, after the jetty is extended."

11. Farquhar, "History of Naval Station San Diego," 42; Newland, "Admiral Cements Station's Foundation," 8.

12. Norman Friedman, *U.S. Destroyers* (Annapolis, Md.: Naval Institute Press, 1982), 428–38; Gerald E. Wheeler, *Admiral William Veazie Pratt, USN* (Washington, D.C.: Department of the Navy, 1974), 154.

13. Farquhar, "History of Naval Station San Diego," 43; Newland, "Admiral Cements Station's Foundation," 9. After many years at San Diego, *Rigel* was in overhaul at Pearl Harbor during the 7 December attack and later served in the Southwest Pacific and the Philippines during World War II, earning a total of four battle stars.

14. Wheeler, *Admiral William Veazie Pratt,* 160.

15. Thomas B. Buell, *The Quiet Warrior* (Boston: Little, Brown, 1974), 42; Potter, *Bull Halsey,* 116.

16. Buell, *Quiet Warrior,* 42.

17. Charles A. Lockwood and Hans Christian Adamson, *Tragedy at Honda* (Philadelphia: Chilton, 1960), 11.

18. Destroyers wrecked at Honda included *Delphy* (DD-261), *S. P. Lee* (DD-310), *Young* (DD-312), *Woodbury* (DD-309), *Nicholas* (DD-311), *Fuller* (DD-297), and *Chauncey* (DD-296) with *Sommers* (DD-301) and *Farragut* (DD-300) slightly damaged through grounding. *Percival* (DD-298), *Kennedy* (DD-306), *Paul Hamilton* (DD-307), *Stoddert* (DD-302), and *Thompson* (DD-305) avoided the rocks.

19. "The Destroyer Man," *San Diego Union,* 11 September 1923, 4.

20. "10,000 Pay Reverent Tribute to Honda Dead," *San Diego Union,* 24 September 1923, 1; Lockwood and Adamson, *Tragedy at Honda,* 203.

21. Wheeler, *Admiral William Veazie Pratt,* 225.

22. Lockwood and Adamson, *Tragedy at Honda,* 198.

23. "Back from the Deep," *Los Angeles Times,* 8 March 1986, C-1.

24. Commandant, Annual Report, 1923, Commandant Files, Eleventh Naval District, NARA Laguna; Newland, "Admiral Cements Station's Foundation," 11. The Navy had originally placed its submarine base in San Pedro during World War I as a temporary measure, as recommended by the Helm Commission, and reflecting its preference for operating submarines in the waters off Los Angeles rather than San Diego. The Navy Department had intended to use property to be provided by the city of Los Angeles. Postwar budget constraints prevented this planned action and the Commander-in-Chief of the Pacific Fleet recommended removing the submarines to San Diego, occupying a corner of the destroyer base where they could receive maintenance efficiently. Eighty men were transferred to San Diego with the move.

25. Wheeler, *Admiral William Veazie Pratt,* 162.

26. Coontz, letter to Rear Adm. Roger Welles, 28 January 1921, Welles papers.

27. Welles, memorandum to SecNav, 19 July 1920, Welles papers; Eleventh Naval District, *Administrative History* (San Diego: Department of the Navy, 1946), 8.

28. SecNav, Annual Report, 1920; Commandant, Eleventh Naval District, Annual Report, 1922, RG 80, GRDN.

29. Eleventh Naval District, letter 700-7 of 5 September 1924, SecNav General Correspondence Files, RG 80, GRDN; Coletta, United States Navy and Marine Corps Bases, Domestic, 565.

30. Welles, letter to Admiral Coontz, 23 April 1923, Welles Papers.

31. "San Diego Says Goodbye," *San Diego Union,* 1 August 1923, 4.

32. Kaplan and Associates, "Architectural and Historical Significance of Selected Buildings at the Naval Training Center, San Diego, California," 1989, 28.

33. "San Diego Naval Training Station Commissioned in Brief Ceremony," *San Diego Union,* 2 June 1923, 1; "$4M Naval Training Station Dedicated," *San Diego Union,* 28 October 1923, 1. Captain Sellers had been an auspicious choice as the Naval Training Station's first commanding officer. Sellers arrived in San Diego with an experience base that balanced operational acumen and diplomatic style. He had commanded two battleships, had been awarded the Navy Cross during World War I combat operations, and had served tours of duty on commander-in-chief staffs and as the aide to the secretary of the Navy. In later years he would rise to become Commander-in-Chief, U.S. Fleet, and superintendent of the Naval Academy, and would retire as a full admiral.

34. The term *boot camp* was derived from the white leggings or "boots" that the new recruits were required to wear as a part of their training uniform. "Detention Camp" was a period for initial indoctrination and medical and physical exams, and as a means to rapidly transition recruits from a civilian lifestyle.

35. Mary E. Camacho, *Cradle of the Navy: The History of Naval Training Center San Diego* (San Diego: Jostens, 1997), 52. Capt. Edwin B. Woodworth, the first executive officer of the Naval Training Station, asked to have his ashes spread in his honor under a eucalyptus tree on the Sail Ho Golf Course after his death from cancer in 1932. His wife was similarly remembered and a plaque commemorating the couple still exists in the middle of the course.

36. C. W. Cole, "Training Men at San Diego for America's First Line of Defense," *San Diego Magazine,* November 1927, 8.

Chapter 7. 1924

1. "Deadliest Ship Afloat Arrives Here," *San Diego Union,* 30 November 1924, 1.

2. Norman Friedman, *U.S. Aircraft Carriers* (Annapolis, Md.: Naval Institute Press, 1983), 36. Langley's original design even included an elaborate fantail pigeon house. As radios were still rudimentary, most cross-country aviators carried carrier pigeons in case of emergency. The attempt to train pigeons to return to a moving ship was a great failure, though, and the bird quarters was later converted into the executive officer's quarters, encouraging all nature of tongue-in-cheek humor.

3. Jackson R. Tate, "We Rode the Covered Wagon," *U.S. Naval Institute Proceedings* (October 1978): 69.

4. John Fry, *USS Saratoga CV-3* (Atglen, Pa.: Schiffer Publishing, 1996), 10.

5. Mason also was involved in another San Diego first, when he commanded the division of F-5-L seaplanes in their record-breaking seven thousand–mile Canal Zone flight in 1921.

6. The first night landing was actually accidental and occurred in February 1925 when an aircraft stalled during a practice night approach.

7. Boone T. Guyton, *Air Base* (New York: McGraw-Hill, 1941), 30.

8. Bureau of Aeronautics, *History of the Use of North Island, San Diego, Ca. for Flying Activities of the Army and Navy* (Washington, D.C.: Department of the Navy, 1932), 2.

9. Brown, "An Historical Geographical Study of North Island," 33.

10. Paul Stillwell, *Battleship Arizona* (Annapolis, Md.: Naval Institute Press, 1991), 90.

11. Turnbull and Lord, *History of United States Naval Aviation,* 235.

12. Actually NC-5 departed the next morning, catching up with the flight in Baja California after repairing damage incurred during her attempted 30 December takeoff.

13. "Huge Planes to Fly to Balboa," *San Diego Union,* 30 December 1920, 1.

14. Junius B. Wood, "Seeing America from the Shenandoah," *National Geographic* (January 1925): 37.

15. Douglass H. Robinson and Charles L. Keller, *Up Ship! A History of the U.S. Navy's Rigid Airships, 1919–1935* (Annapolis, Md.: Naval Institute Press, 1982), 96.

16. Sudsbury, *Jackrabbits to Jets,* 122.

17. Charles Lindbergh, *The Spirit of St. Louis* (New York: Scribner's, 1953), 103.

18. Reynolds, *Admiral John H. Towers,* 200.

19. Ibid., 203.

20. Guyton, *Air Base,* 102.

21. Stillwell and Tillman, The Reminiscences of Capt. Daniel Webb Tomlinson IV, 37.

22. Bates, letter to Miss Elretta Sudsbury, 6 July 1966, NAS North Island archives.

23. "Wild Navy Plane Endangers Lives," *San Diego Union,* 28 September 1932, 1.

24. Later, Tomlinson trained his entire squadron in the aerial maneuvers of the Three Seahawks. "To have a little fun, I had 15 planes in V formation. We came in over North Island at about 1500 feet and looped the whole squadron in formation. People still remember that."

25. Stillwell and Tillman, The Reminiscences of Capt. Daniel Webb Tomlinson IV, 113. Sudsbury, *Jackrabbits to Jets,* 128.

26. Sudsbury, *Jackrabbits to Jets,* 133.

27. Bureau of Aeronautics, *History of the Use of North Island,* 1.

28. Sudsbury, *Jackrabbits to Jets,* 206.

29. Thomas Wildenberg, *Destined for Glory* (Annapolis, Md.: Naval Institute Press, 1998), 10.

30. Guyton, *Air Base,* 18; Wildenberg, *Destined for Glory,* 18. Squadron dive-bombing maneuvers ultimately included high-altitude approaches in an echelon V and a split into three sections that would attack a ship's bow and port and starboard sides within seconds on each other.

31. *Lexington* and *Saratoga* were nearly identical in appearance and after friendly forces "sunk" *Lexington* in Fleet Problem IX, mistaking her for *Saratoga,* a vertical stripe was painted down the center of *Saratoga's* massive stack while a horizontal stripe adorned the top of *Lexington's.*

32. Guyton, *Air Base,* 130.

33. Ray Brandes, *Coronado, We Remember* (Coronado, Calif.: Coronado Historical Association, 1993), 200.

34. "*Saratoga* Welcomed in Harbor," *San Diego Union,* 8 November 1931, 1.

35. Schofield, letter to CNO, 15 February 1932, U.S. Fleet Correspondence Files, RG 80, GRDN.

36. Harvey M. Beigel, "The Battle Fleet's Home Port: 1919–1940," *U.S. Naval Institute Proceedings,* Supp. (1985): 61.

37. Scott, *San Diego, Air Capital of the West,* 55.

38. By 1928 Rockwell Field was headquarters to the Army's 7th Bombardment Group, 11th Bombardment Squadron, and 95th Pursuit Squadron, and various air training activities.

39. Sudsbury, *Jackrabbits to Jets,* 150. One of the most noticeable improvements in the 1933 program was the installation of a circular landing and takeoff mat twenty-two hundred feet in diameter. The black-tarred mat was clearly visible from long distances and allowed aviators to take off in several different directions, generally into the wind—a great improvement over the dusty sand and dirt runways that had existed up to that time.

40. Ibid., 177.

41. Bureau of Aeronautics, *History of the Use of North Island,* 78.

42. Turnbull and Lord, *History of United States Naval Aviation,* 287; "Navy Planes Take Possession of Field Evacuated by Army," *San Diego Union,* 26 October 1935, 10. Although Army flying operations ended in 1935 and most squadron equipment was shipped off the station, San Diego historian Ray Brandes states that the last days of Army tendency of Rockwell Field extended until January 1939 when Col. Harold Strauss handed over the final keys to equipment and storage buildings of the Army Air Depot to Capt. Arthur L. Bristol, USN.

43. Coletta, ed., *United States Navy and Marine Corps Bases, Domestic,* 572.

44. Hinds, *San Diego's Military Sites,* 71.

45. T. C. Macaulay, "The Lighter than Air Affair," *San Diego Magazine,* February 1930, 3. Inspection sites for a new lighter-than-air base included Camp Kearny, Otay Mesa, Grossmont, and Coronado Heights.

46. "City Plans Dirigible Plant," *San Diego Union,* 13 September 1928, 1.

47. "A Good Election," *San Diego Union,* 4 April 1929, 4.

48. Arnold Klaus, *History of the San Diego Chamber of Commerce,* 440.

49. Richard K. Smith, *The Airships Akron and Macon* (Annapolis, Md.: Naval Institute Press, 1965), 37.

50. Macaulay, "The Lighter than Air Affair," 5.

51. Smith, *Airships Akron and Macon,* 57.

52. "*Macon* Cruises Over San Diego and Goes North," *San Diego Union,* 17 November 1933, 1.

53. Hinds, *San Diego's Military Sites,* 83.

54. Starr, *The Dream Endures,* 113. San Diegans gloried in their self-declared portrayal of their city as "Aviation Capital of the West" and aviation breakthroughs were reported with stunning regularity—so much so that the *San Diego Union* ran a regular feature on Aviation News.

55. Commandant, Eleventh Naval District, Annual Report, 1923, Eleventh Naval District, NARA Laguna.

56. "Naval Aviation Depot Celebrates Its 80th Anniversary," *Coronado Eagle-Journal,* 21 July 1999, 16; Scott, *San Diego, Air Capital of the West,* 137. One of the biggest days for North Island's Assembly and Repair Department came in August 1942 when a damaged Japanese Mitsubishi Zeke fighter was recovered intact in the Aleutians and was sent to North Island. Assembly and Repair workers prepared the plane for testing and evaluation behind locked doors inside the balloon hangar. Navy pilots then flew the Zeke over North Island and off Point Loma, evaluating its strengths and weaknesses and engaging in mock combat.

57. William Wagner, *Reuben Fleet and the Story of Consolidated Aircraft* (Fallbrook, Calif.: Aero Publishers, 1976), 158.

58. Ibid., 165.

59. Ibid., 182.

60. Ibid., 160.

61. Ibid., 35.

62. Ibid., 38.

63. Roscoe Creed, *PBY: The Catalina Flying Boat* (Annapolis, Md.: Naval Institute Press, 1985), 32–38.

64. J. C. Stovall, *NAVAER 1411 Aviators Flight Log Book ICO RM2 J. C. Stovall* (1938). Stovall, who had enlisted in 1929, would later serve during World War II as Admiral Nimitz's personal radio operator on flights visiting Pacific bases. Stovall's logbook shows that prior to his 18 January mass flight, Stovall had logged flights on seven different dates in January, averaging 6.5 hours per mission, devoted to testing, familiarization, night flying and equipment calibrations, and instrument flying.

65. Andrew Hendrie, *Flying Cats: The Catalina Aircraft in World War II* (Annapolis, Md.: Naval Institute Press, 1988), 212.

66. Guyton, *Air Base*, 27.

67. San Diego navymen were never far from some of the most tumultuous events of our times. During the climactic Battle of Leyte Gulf of World War II, Ralph Alexander's command *Reno* (CL-96) was torpedoed and nearly sunk in furious fighting, while son Dick kept up with events over the tactical circuits from destroyer *Cushing* (DD-797) twenty miles away.

68. Carlin and Brandes, *Coronado, the Enchanted Island*, 182. Shragge, "Boosters and Bluejackets," 423.

Chapter 8. 1935

1. "Commander-in-Chief Views Local Navy, Marine Bases," *San Diego Union*, 3 October 1935, 1.

2. "Chief Executive Commands Fleet in Mimic Fight," *San Diego Union*, 3 October 1935, 9.

3. Starr, *The Dream Endures*, 94.

4. Stephen Roskill, *Naval Policy Between the Wars: The Period of Anglo-American Antagonism, 1910–1929* (New York: Walker and Co., 1968), 354. In 1922 the U.S. Fleet realigned into four major and permanent task forces, with the Battle Fleet (the powerful core of the Fleet) and the Fleet Base Force assigned purposefully to operate in the Pacific. By 1932, largely as a consequence of Japanese aggression in Manchuria, the Scouting Force joined these task forces, leaving only the smallest of the four task forces, the Control Force, in the Atlantic.

5. Ivor D. Spencer, "U.S. Naval Air Bases from 1914 to 1939," *U.S. Naval Institute Proceedings* (November 1949): 1253.

6. Gregg R. Hennessey, "San Diego, the U.S. Navy, and Urban Development," *California History* 72, no. 2 (Summer 1993): 148.

7. "Centenarians Share Their Memories," *San Diego Union-Tribune*, 11 November 1999.

8. C. M. Tozer, "The Navy's Relationship to San Diego's Business," *San Diego Magazine*, February 1930, 9; Jay L. Kerley, *California and the Navy* (San Diego, 1935), 1.

9. "Thousands Thrilled by Vast Array," *San Diego Union*, 13 March 1925, 1; Richard F. Pourade, *The Rising Tide* (San Diego: Union-Tribune Publishing, 1967), 32.

10. Eddie Fredericks, "Early Naval History in San Diego," *Mains'l Haul* (Winter 1985): 7.

11. Judith Morgan, "Old Ironsides Captured Hearts of San Diegans," *San Diego Union*, 1 January 1969.

12. Tozer, "Navy's Relationship to San Diego's Business," 9.

13. Commandant, Annual Report, 1923, Commandant Eleventh Naval District Files, NARA, Laguna.

14. Brown, "An Historical Geographical Study of North Island," 23; Joseph W. Brennan, "What a Dime Can Do," *San Diego Magazine*, June 1931, 6.

15. Hennessey, "San Diego, the U.S. Navy, and Urban Development," 144.

16. Coletta, ed., *United States Navy and Marine Corps Bases, Domestic*, 556; Stephen Roskill, *Naval Policy Between the Wars, The Period of Reluctant Rearmament, 1930–39* (Annapolis, Md.: Naval Institute Press, 1976), 161; Minutes of the Executive Committee, SDCOC, 18 July 1935.

17. Stillwell, *Battleship Arizona*, 73.

18. Guyton, *Air Base*, 130; Buell, *The Quiet Warrior*, 58. Depression economics could still alter carefully wrought schedules as future five-star admiral William Leahy (who commanded Destroyers-Battle Force) discovered during the summer of 1933, when so little money was available for operations that he ordered his destroyers to spend most of their time in San Diego hoarding fuel and ammunition.

19. *Administrative Study of the Commander Destroyers/Cruisers Pacific Fleet during World War II* (Department of the Navy, 1946), 13.

20. "Navy Day," *San Diego Union*, 27 October 1934, 4.

21. "San Diego Welcomes the Men of the Fleet," *San Diego Union*, 13 March 1925, 1.

22. Shragge, "Boosters and Bluejackets," 412.

23. Stillwell, *Battleship Arizona*, 144.

24. Shragge, "Boosters and Bluejackets," 423.

25. Stillwell, The Reminiscences of Chief Warrant Officer Cecil S. King, Jr., USN (ret.), 15; Stillwell, The Reminiscences of Lieutenant Commander Richard A. Harralson, USN (ret.), 41.

26. Brandes, "San Diego's Chinatown and Stingaree District," University of San Diego Copley Library, San Diego, 53. The Stingaree district has a long history of bawdy entertainment that was easily available both by proximity and inclination to visiting mariners to San Diego. "Stingaree" took its name from a ray-like fish with a long thin tail that contained sharp barbs. From the late nineteenth century, the district lay at the shoreline of the harbor where stingarees were plentiful.

27. Guyton, *Air Base*, 125.

28. "Dangerous Good News," *San Diego Union*, 12 August 1923, 4.

29. John Nolen, *A Comprehensive City Plan for San Diego, California* (Cambridge, Mass.: Walker-Hartzog Associates, 1926), 24; Shragge, "Boosters and Bluejackets," 542.

30. Shragge, "Boosters and Bluejackets," 441. The 750,000 gallons of sewage the Navy emptied into the bay each day was not quite as bad as it sounded, but still an act that the Navy should not be proud of. The city, during this era, dumped as much as eight million gallons of its own sewage in the bay per day.

31. Camacho, *Cradle of the Navy,* 62.

32. Stillwell, The Reminiscences of Lieutenant Commander Richard A. Harralson, USN (ret), 30.

33. Kaplan and Associates, "Architectural and Historical Significance of Selected Buildings," 19.

34. Holzman, "Hospital Grows in Balboa Park," 23.

35. Department of the Navy, *U.S. Naval Hospital Complex in Balboa Park,* 59.

36. Ibid., 60.

37. "San Diego Naval Hospital Celebrates Anniversary," *Dry Dock,* 13 August 1948, 5; Department of the Navy, *U.S. Naval Hospital Complex in Balboa Park,* 52. On 27 February 1926 the city deeded 5.46 acres to the Navy for a hospital expansion, in July 1940 deeded another 32.93 acres, and in May 1941 a final 21.32 acres.

38. Department of the Navy, *U.S. Naval Hospital Complex in Balboa Park,* 54; Holzman, "Hospital Grows in Balboa Park," 23.

39. Newland, "Admiral Cements Station's Foundation," 11.

40. John D. Alden, *Flush Decks and Four Pipes* (Annapolis, Md.: Naval Institute Press, 1965), 13; D. P. Moon, "Recommissioning the Destroyers," *U.S. Naval Institute Proceedings* (February 1931): 162.

41. Moon, "Recommissioning the Destroyers," 164.

42. Alden, *Flush Decks and Four Pipes,* 14.

43. Jeffrey W. Farquhar, "The History of Naval Station San Diego," thesis, University of San Diego, San Diego, 1996, 59; E. B. Potter, *Nimitz* (Annapolis, Md.: Naval Institute Press, 1976), 150.

44. Potter, *Nimitz,* 150.

45. Buell, *The Quiet Warrior,* 57. Nimitz commanded 32nd Street until the summer of 1933 when ordered to command of the new heavy cruiser *Augusta* (CA-31).

46. Farquhar, "History of Naval Station San Diego," 61; Coletta, ed., *United States Navy and Marine Corps Bases, Domestic,* 555.

47. The National City property included Olivewood, a beautiful Victorian home of Warren and Flora Kimball, that was a favorite tourist attraction of the city. It was razed in 1942 for a six hundred–unit military housing project.

48. Donald I. Thomas, "Recommissioning Destroyers, 1939 Style," *U.S. Naval Institute Proceedings* (September 1979): 72.

49. Ibid., 70; Farquhar, "History of Naval Station San Diego," 66.

50. Kinderman, *USS Ward Fires First Shot of World War II* (St. Paul, Minn.: Leeward Publications, 1983). *Ward* held a hidden advantage by being the last four-stacked commissioned; as *Ward* needed equipment that had been "borrowed" by the crews of other ships, it all had to be replaced with newly manufactured equipment. Coincidentally, *Ward* was sunk by a kamikaze on 7 December 1944, three years to the day after her brief moment of glory at Pearl Harbor.

51. Fry, *USS Saratoga CV-3,* 96.

52. Richard F. Pourade, *City of the Dream* (La Jolla, Calif.: Copley Books, 1977), 15.

53. Ellis M. Zacharias, *Secret Missions* (New York: G. P. Putnam, 1946), 220; Mason and Stillwell, The Reminiscences of Rear Admiral Odale D. Waters, Jr., 37.

Chapter 9. 1941

1. Fry, *USS Saratoga CV-3,* 109.

2. Steve Ewing and John B. Lundstrom, *Fateful Rendezvous* (Annapolis, Md.: Naval Institute Press, 1997), 106.

3. Kitchen, The Reminiscences of Vice Admiral Paul D. Stroop, 68.

4. Alvin H. Grobmeier, "Radio Station Alerts Nation to 'Day That Will Live in Infamy,'" *Traditions* 1, no. 4 (1994): 5; Joyce, *A Harbor Worth Defending,* 44.

5. Stovall, letter to author, 14 September 1999.

6. Max Miller, *Harbor of the Sun: The Story of the Port of San Diego* (New York: Doubleday, 1940), 247.

7. Lee Dye, "San Diego Rises to Pearl Harbor Challenge," *San Diego Evening Tribune,* 7 December 1966, A-10.

8. Charles R. Witherspoon, "Navy Training a Shock to System," *Traditions* (July–August 1996): 30.

9. "SD Folk Tense as They Listen for War News," *San Diego Union,* 8 December 1941, A.

10. *Administrative History of the Western Sea Frontier,* 7 vols. (Department of the Navy, 1946), 3:31.

11. Scott, *San Diego, Air Capital of the West,* 54. Although originally ordered for the defense of Wake Island, these Marine aircraft were diverted to Oahu.

12. Kitchen, The Reminiscences of Vice Admiral Paul D. Stroop, 68. *Saratoga* would be back in Bremerton only twelve months later for repairs after an attack by a Japanese submarine. Once repaired, she would retrace her December 1941 Bremerton–San Diego–Hawaii track, departing San Diego on 1 June 1942 and barely missing the Battle of Midway.

13. Pourade, *City of the Dream,* 17; Potter, *Nimitz,* 15.

14. Clark G. Reynolds, "Submarine Attacks on the Pacific Coast, 1942," *Pacific Historical Review* 33, no. 2 (1964): 186; Joyce, *Harbor Worth Defending,* 49; Bert Webber, *Retaliation: Japanese Attacks and Allied Countermeasures on the Pacific Coast in World War II* (Corvallis: Oregon State University Press, 1975), 15.

15. W. W. Lowery, "An Enemy Sub Off S.D.: Saved by the Bombardier's Rules," *San Diego Union,* 4 December 1966, C-1.

16. Reynolds, "Submarine Attacks on the Pacific Coast, 1942," 188.

17. Brandes, *Coronado, We Remember,* 300.

18. Eleventh Naval District, *Administrative History,* 32.

19. *Administrative History of the Western Sea Frontier,* 69.

20. Pourade, *City of the Dream,* 16.

21. Hinds, *San Diego's Military Sites,* 110.

22. Howard B. Overton, Oral Histories of Cabrillo National Monument, San Diego; Joyce, *Harbor Worth Defending,* 53. Although one set of submarine nets was normally used at the harbor entrance, when tensions were highest two antisubmarine nets were deployed, where one would open while the other remained closed.

23. Shragge, "Boosters and Bluejackets," 551.

24. Wagner, *Reuben Fleet and the Story of Consolidated Aircraft,* 253; James Steinberg, "SD Warrior Nears 60," *San Diego Union-Tribune,* 31 May 1999, 1.

25. Shragge, "Boosters and Bluejackets," 553; "Boom Town: San Diego," *Life,* July 28, 1941, 65.

26. Welton Jones, "A Decade Divided," *San Diego Union-Tribune*, 27 June 1999, E-7.

27. U.S. Naval Training Station, "Ashore in San Diego" (pamphlet), San Diego, 1942.

28. Ewing and Lundstrom, *Fateful Rendezvous*, 104.

29. Miller, *Harbor of the Sun*, 287.

30. Sudsbury, *Jackrabbits to Jets*, 241.

31. Chief of Naval Operations, letter of 15 July 1940, "Aviation Shore Facilities to Support the 10,000 Plane Program," and letters of 4 March 1941 and 10 December 1942, Bureau of Aeronautics, *World War II Administrative History*, Navy Historical Center.

32. Frederic Wakeman, *Shore Leave* (New York: Farrar and Rinehart, 1944), 243.

33. Eleventh Naval District, *Administrative History*, 271.

34. Ibid., 283.

35. Hotel del Coronado Room leases, Hotel del Coronado Land Booklet No. 501, Coronado, Calif., 1941.

36. Larry Creaghe, Hotel del Coronado Oral History Collection, 4 February 2000.

37. Elwood Meyer, Hotel del Coronado Oral History Collection, 2 February 2000.

38. Warren Goodman, letter with attached article c. 1995 entitled "Way to Go!" that appeared in *The Intercom* newsletter, 12 September 1995; Abele, Hotel del Coronado Oral History Collection, 4 February 2000; Meyer, Hotel del Coronado Oral History Collection.

39. Denise Draper Croft, "Hotel del Coronado: An Architectural and Social History," University of California–Riverside, 1975.

40. Eleventh Naval District, *Administrative History*, 300. The fourth Coronado ferry entered service in early 1945.

41. Eleventh Naval District, *Administrative History*, 288.

42. SecNav, General Order 181, 12 October 1942; *World War II Administrative History: Bureau of Aeronautics*, volume 11, *Aviation Shore Establishments* (Department of the Navy, 1947), 111. The first four wartime Naval Air Centers were located at San Diego, Seattle, Wash., Hampton Roads, Va., and Hawaii.

43. Eleventh Naval District, *Administrative History*, 307.

44. Hinds, *San Diego's Military Sites*, 86.

45. Eleventh Naval District, *Administrative History*, 308. Comdr. Melville S. Brown was the victim of a Descanso plane crash in 1936 and is buried at Fort Rosecrans Cemetery.

46. Guyton, *Air Base*, 17; Chambers, Consultants and Planners, "The Cultural Resources of Naval Air Station, North Island and Outlying Field, Imperial Beach, San Diego County, California," April 1982, 4–25.

47. Hinds, *San Diego's Military Sites*, 35.

48. Eleventh Naval District, *Administrative History*, 384.

49. Alvin H. Grobmeier, "Blimps Found Fair Grounds for Mooring," *Traditions* (December 1994): 7.

50. Eleventh Naval District, *Administrative History*, 312, 315 (emphasis added). Before the final selection of Holtville, two additional sites were under serious consideration for construction of the new NAAS in 1942, Lake Henshaw and Ramona. "The potential combat zone" here referred to San Diego Bay from fear of enemy landings on the coast.

51. Hinds, *San Diego's Military Sites*, 36; Scott, *San Diego, Air Capital of the West*, 140. *Long Island* was the Navy's first "jeep carrier," converted from the freighter *Mormacmail*.

52. Alvin H. Grobmeier, "Chronological History of U.S. Navy Radio Activities, Imperial Beach, California," *NCVA Cryptolog* (May 1995): 2. Radio Compass Station, Imperial Beach shared Point Loma's NPL call sign for a time, then received its own: NPZ.

53. Lockwood and Adamson, *Tragedy at Honda*, 34. Imperial Beach was one of three radio direction finder stations established by the Navy along the California coast—the others were located at Point Arguello (that would feature prominently in the Honda disaster) and at the Farallon Islands off San Francisco.

54. Eleventh Naval District, letter ser G-2 to CNO, 27 February 1939, Commandant Files, Eleventh Naval District, NARA Laguna. The Army's Military Reservation on the Silver Strand extended for some forty acres from south of Coronado's Tent City to the approximate present position of Silver Strand State Park. It was sold to the state before World War II.

55. CNO, letter ser 2786 to Chief of the Bureau of Engineering, 5 July 1939; BuShips, Supplementary Radio Station Properties, method of acquiring and status of acquisition, 15 February 1945, NAVCOMMSTA Imperial Beach files, Naval Security Group Archives, Washington, D.C.

56. CNO, letter ser 01520 to Commandant, Eleventh Naval District, 11 January 1942, NAVCOMMSTA Imperial Beach files, Naval Security Group Archives, Washington, D.C.

57. BuShips, letter ser 3754 to CNO, 9 February 1943.

58. Grayton A. Lewis, *A History of Communications Intelligence in the United States* (Eugene, Ore.: Naval Cryptologic Veterans Association, 1982), 37.

59. Hinds, *San Diego's Military Sites*, 24.

60. Fleet ASW School, *Command History* (Department of the Navy, 3 June 1965), 3. The earliest prototype echo-ranging or underwater sound gear in the U.S. Navy, designated QA, was tested at sea in 1927. An improved QC set went into much wider production with nine U.S. destroyers fitted with the echo-ranging gear in 1934.

61. *History of the Fleet Operational Training Command, Pacific*, 2 vols. (Department of the Navy, 1946), 1:417.

62. Ibid., 423.

63. Naval Ocean Systems Center, *Fifty Years of Research and Development on Point Loma, 1940–1990* (San Diego: NOSC, 1990), 4.

64. Ibid., 6. Dr. Vern Knudsen came from UCLA to be the first head of UCDWR. The famed Dr. Harald Sverdrup, then director of Scripps, left there to work at UCDWR.

65. Neil Morgan and Judith Morgan, *Roger: A Biography of Roger Revelle* (San Diego: University of California–San Diego, 1996), 22.

66. Ibid., 30.

67. NOSC, *Fifty Years of Research and Development on Point Loma*, 14.

68. Ibid., 8.

69. Completion Report, 26 April 1941 to 30 June 1946, University of California Division of War Research, San Diego, 1946, 196.

70. *History of the Fleet Operational Training Command, Pacific*, 1:65.

71. Completion Report, 230.

72. Lease, *Lease of Property to the U.S. Navy*, 9 August 1949. In 1999 the Navy exercised its option to continue its lease, an action that was disputed by the San Diego Unified Port District. When brought to court, a federal judge ruled in the Navy's favor.

73. NOSC, *Fifty Years of Research and Development on Point Loma*, 12.

74. *History of the Fleet Operational Training Command, Pacific*, 107.

75. Ibid., 100.

76. Ibid., 324.

77. Ibid, 289.

78. "Training Command, U.S. Pacific Fleet," *U.S. Naval Training Bulletin* (January 1949): 6; "Pacific Beach Gunners Get Cease Fire Orders," *San Diego Union*, 4 November 1945.

79. *History of the Fleet Operational Training Command, Pacific*, 174.

80. Hinds, *San Diego's Military Sites*, 115.

81. "Training in the San Diego Area," *Naval Training Bulletin* (May 1951): 12.

82. *Building the Navy's Bases in World War II* (Washington, D.C.: U.S. Government Printing Office, 1947), 206; Farquhar, "History of Naval Station San Diego," 84.

83. Meredith Vezina, "Fire . . . fire . . . fire," *Traditions* (November 1995): 27.

84. Eleventh Naval District, *Administrative History*, 110; *Building the Navy's Bases in World War II*, 350.

85. Eleventh Naval District, *Administrative History*, 188.

86. EDAW-Inc., *Master Plan for Naval Amphibious Base, Coronado* (Coronado: Naval Base Coronado, 1998), 35

87. Coletta, ed., *United States Navy and Marine Corps Bases, Domestic*, 573. By November 1955 the federal government had obtained clear title to all packets of land that formed the original Naval Amphibious Base, including land outright obtained and some leased under a long-term lease.

88. John Curtis, "Paradise Revisted by German POW," *The Amphibian*, c. 1974; Chris Cote, *German Prisoners of War in San Diego during World War II* (1963).

89. "Coronado—Pacific Fleet Amphib Center," *Navy Times*, 16 January 1954, 24; Coletta, ed., *United States Navy and Marine Corps Bases, Domestic*, 574.

90. "The Amphibious Base, Still Bustling after 30 Years," *Coronado Journal*, 26 September 1974, 8; Eleventh Naval District, Brochure of Activities, 1945. The 11th Naval District Commandant reported proudly that the amphibious base also contained twenty toilet and shower buildings in 1945 with each containing forty-three bowls, ten urinals, fifty washbasins, and twenty-two showerheads.

91. Camacho, *Cradle of the Navy*, 87.

92. Abe Hollandersky, *The Life Story of Abe the Newsboy: Hero of a Thousand Fights* (Los Angeles: Abe the Newsboy, 1930).

93. Hinds, *San Diego's Military Sites*, 60.

94. Michelle Poncia, "Dinosaurs Retired as Hospital Evolves," *Traditions* (Summer 1997): 30.

95. Charlie George, *U.S. Naval Hospital, San Diego, 1919–1958* (1958), 22.

96. Jim Hinds, "Officers Convalesce in Rural Area," *Traditions* (Summer 1997): 29; Coletta, ed., *United States Navy and Marine Corps Bases, Domestic*, 557. The city used the money provided by the Navy to refurbish the badly deteriorated original Exposition buildings after the war.

97. Even ten years later, Vice Adm. Ed Martin, USN (ret.), remembers following Fourth Street in Coronado to line up and land on the interfield area of North Island between the runways.

98. "City Explodes in Exuberance Over Victory," *San Diego Union*, 15 August 1945, 3A; Melody Hyde Morgan, Hotel del Coronado Oral History Collection, Hotel del Coronado, Coronado, Calif., 28 February 2000.

99. Jack Smith, "Only a Jukebox," *Westways* (January 1999): 33.

100. Fred Whitmore, "USS *San Diego*: The Unbeatable Ship That Nobody Ever Heard Of," *Mains'l Haul* (Spring 1997): 8. The USS *San Diego* CL53 Memorial Association is active in San Diego, sponsoring a campaign for a permanent ship's memorial and displays of USS *San Diego* memorabilia.

101. Craig, "Annotated Bibliography of the History of the U.S. Naval Training Center," 31.

Chapter 10. 1953

1. Bob Wilson had served in the Coast Guard Reserve (Port Security Force) and was drafted for a brief stint in the Army but never saw combat.

2. Bob Wilson, *Confessions of a Kinetic Congressman* (San Diego: San Diego State University Foundation, 1996), 32; Alec C. Schiller, "Congressman Bob Wilson's Contribution to the Navy and San Diego 1952–62," thesis, San Diego State University, San Diego, 1990.

3. Glenn C. Erickson, "The Effect of the Military Establishment and the Aviation Industry on the Need for a More Balanced Economy in San Diego," Stanford University Graduate School of Business, Palo Alto, 1954, 37.

4. Nash, *American West in the Twentieth Century*, 197.

5. Abraham Shragge, "A New Federal City: San Diego during World War II," *Pacific Historical Review* 63, no. 3 (1994): 360.

6. Citizens' Aqueduct Celebration Committee, *San Diego's Quest for Water* (San Diego, 1947).

7. Pourade, *The Rising Tide*, 246.

8. Citizens' Aqueduct Celebration Committee, *San Diego's Quest for Water*.

9. Steve LaRue, "Pipeline Brought Water, Prosperity," *San Diego Union-Tribune*, 23 November 1997.

10. Ibid.; Citizens' Aqueduct Celebration Committee, *San Diego's Quest for Water*.

11. Pourade, *City of the Dream*, 88; Ray Tarbuck, *Analysis of the Transfer of Naval Vessels from San Diego* (San Diego: San Diego Chamber of Commerce, 1952), 3.

12. *Dictionary of American Naval Fighting Ships*. San Diego's *Valley Forge* would carry designations as an attack carrier, antisubmarine carrier, and amphibious assault ship in her quarter-century of service and would earn eight battle stars for Korean War actions, nine battle stars for Vietnam service, and three Navy Unit Commendations.

13. James Newland, "Ups and Downs from Korea to Gulf War," *Traditions* (November 1995): 23; Farquhar, "History of Naval Station San Diego," 93.

14. "U.S. Naval Ship Repair Facility, San Diego," *Bureau of Ships Journal* 6, no. 6 (1957): 13. Cost reductions by 1964 forced the Navy to consolidate its shipyard facilities and on 1 January 1965 NRF was disestablished and ship repair work directed to Long Beach Naval Shipyard until political pressures forced its reactivation. In the years that followed, ship repair at the Naval Station remained a key industrial activity organized at various times under Navy commands such as the Ship Repair Facility (SRF) and the Shore Intermediate Maintenance Activity (SIMA). In recent years, purely Navy ship repair activities have been deemphasized in favor of commercial alternatives managed by the Supervisor of Shipbuilding, Conversion and Repair (SUPSHIP).

15. *Dictionary of American Naval Fighting Ships.*

16. Ibid. *Yarnall* was later transferred to the Taiwan navy where she lived out her days until 1991 as *Kuen Yang* (DD-19); *O'Brien* would serve until 1972, earning three battle stars for Vietnam service.

17. Department of the Navy, *Senior Member Board to Survey the Continental Naval Shore Establishments* (Washington, D.C.: Department of the Navy, 1 June 1946).

18. Floyd R. Moore, "San Diego Airport Development," thesis, San Diego State University, San Diego, 1960, 44.

19. Comprehensive Planning Organization, San Diego County Government, "Aviation in San Diego, 1917–1971," San Diego, 17 November 1971, 7; Hinds, *San Diego's Military Sites,* 97.

20. Joseph F. Bouchard, "Guarding the Cold War Ramparts," *Naval War College Review* 52, no. 3 (1999): 116. Central to the belief in a "gap" was the identification of powerful new Soviet bombers capable of delivering nuclear weapons at intercontinental ranges. VF(AW)-3 was the only Navy squadron permanently under Air Force operational control for air defense and it twice won Air Defense Command's Best Unit award.

21. Ibid., 124.

22. Ellen B. Holzman, "General Defends Marine Readiness," *Traditions* (January/February 1996): 27.

23. Coletta, ed., *United States Navy and Marine Corps Bases, Domestic,* 558. Elliott Annex recruits spent their first three weeks of training at the main Naval Training Center, then the next three weeks at the annex, and then returned to the main center for their final three weeks.

24. Hinds, *San Diego's Military Sites,* 80. In 1969 NASA transferred the Sycamore Canyon missile test site to the General Services Administration, and they in turn turned it back to the Navy, who incorporated it back into Miramar on 6 December 1972. It later served as a Tomahawk missile assembly and test site.

25. Comprehensive Planning Organization, "Aviation in San Diego," 8. Brown Field was declared as surplus and leased to the county in 1946 for intended air-freight operations. The Navy repossessed the facility as a carrier practice facility during the Korean War and formally recommissioned it as a Naval Auxiliary Air Station on 1 July 1954. Brown Field was downgraded to an Auxiliary Landing Field on 30 June 1961 and surrendered back to the city in 1962.

26. Schiller, "Congressman Bob Wilson's Contribution to the Navy and San Diego," 83.

27. Comdr. B. J. Long, "Sea Dart," *Foundation* 19, no. 2 (1998): 97.

28. Naval Air Station North Island, Report of Shallow Water Torpedo Drops, 26 June 1945; Commander, Planning for Shore Station Development, Seaplane Base, South San Diego Bay, 20 November 1953, Navy Security Group Archives, Washington, D.C.

29. Presidential Proclamation no. 34-12, dated 27 January 1940, set aside special anchorages for seaplanes in South Bay.

30. Commander, Naval Air Bases, 11th and 12th Naval Districts, Planning for Shore Station Development, Seaplane Base, South San Diego Bay, 20 November 1953; U.S. Army Corps of Engineers, *The Port of San Diego, California* (Washington, D.C.: U.S. Government Printing Office, 1956), 8. As a salve to local interests, the Navy also recommended building a golf course on seaplane base land for the "joint use" of the City of Coronado and the Navy.

31. Schiller, "Congressman Bob Wilson's Contribution to the Navy and San Diego," 59.

32. "Will the Forrestal Come Here? Yes, If We Have Outer Harbor," *San Diego Evening Tribune,* 18 November 1954, C-2; Schiller, "Congressman Bob Wilson's Contribution to the Navy and San Diego," 52.

33. Pourade, *The Rising Tide,* 32.

34. Shragge, "Boosters and Bluejackets," 565; "San Diego Needs to Keep Close Tie with Navy," *San Diego Union,* 14 July 1957, C-2.

35. Schiller, "Congressman Bob Wilson's Contribution to the Navy and San Diego," 67. The Navy's first plans for a twelve hundred–foot supercarrier wharf placed it along the southwestern edge of North Island parallel to the channel. When it was discovered that it would be cheaper to improve existing piers on the southeastern side of North Island to accept the new and larger carriers, the original plans were scrapped.

36. NOSC, *Fifty Years of Research and Development on Point Loma,* 24; Completion Report, 228.

37. Morgan and Morgan, *Roger,* 33. Revelle returned to Scripps in 1948 and was named its associate director, rising to acting director in 1950 and director in 1951.

38. Kitchen, The Reminiscenses of Dr. Waldo K. Lyon, 92; William M. Leary, *Under Ice: Waldo Lyon and the Development of the Arctic Submarine* (College Station: Texas A&M University Press, 1999), xi.

39. Leary, *Under Ice,* xi. Waldo Lyon retired from civil service in 1996 with 55 years of service to the Navy.

40. Stillwell, The Reminiscences of Rear Admiral Norvell G. Ward, USN (ret), 257.

41. Schiller, "Congressman Bob Wilson's Contribution to the Navy and San Diego," 100; Mason, The Reminscences of Rear Admiral Roy S. Benson, USN (ret).

42. Shragge, "Boosters and Bluejackets," 568; Wilson, *Confessions of a Kinetic Congressman,* 57.

43. "Keep Pace with Atomic Navy," *San Diego Union,* 15 July 1959, B-2.

44. Roger W. Lotchin, *Fortress California, 1910–1961* (New York: Oxford University Press, 1992), 304, from a statement before the House Armed Services Committee, 31 May 1960.

45. Schiller, "Congressman Bob Wilson's Contribution to the Navy and San Diego," 108; "A-Sub Pier Is Dedicated," *San Diego Union,* 30 September 1962, A-23.

46. Lester Bell, "New Sub Base Gets Key Role," *San Diego Union,* 18 November 1963.

47. Coletta, ed., *United States Navy and Marine Corps Bases, Domestic,* 571.

48. Wilson, *Confessions of a Kinetic Congressman,* 220.

49. Leighton W. Smith, interview, 11 May 1999, *Frontline.* WGBH, Boston.

50. Landings at Camp Pendleton and Coronado perfected new tactics for LVT tracked amphibian craft to allow them to be dropped off from the wet wells of amphibious transports along the beach while the ship was at 15 knots.

51. A PBR, featured in Francis Ford Coppola's *Apocalypse Now,* has been restored and is on display at the Amphibious Base's CISM Field along with a restored PCF as part of the planned Navy/Coast Guard Vietnam Unit Memorial Monument.

52. Hinds, *San Diego's Military Sites,* 124. SERE School during the Vietnam era was an outgrowth of survival training near Warner Springs that had originally been established in 1953 by the Fleet Airborne Electronics Training Unit, Pacific.

53. Frank Ault, "The Father of Top Gun," *Shipmate* (March 1999): 5.

54. Shragge, "Boosters and Bluejackets," 564.

55. George W. Mahnke, "The Urban Impact on Coronado of the San Diego–Coronado Bay Bridge," thesis, San Diego State University, San Diego, 1970, 8; Neil Morgan, "Like an Airport, the Blue Bridge Took 50 Years," *San Diego Union,* 14 July 1994, A-2. The owners of the Coronado ferry system, J. D. and A. B. Spreckles Securities Company, filed the first formal bridge application on 9 October 1926.

56. Morgan, "Like an Airport, the Blue Bridge Took 50 Years," A-2.

57. Neil Morgan, "S.D.: World Center of Alcoholism Research?" *San Diego Union-Tribune,* 24 January 1993, A-2.

58. Wilson, *Confessions of a Kinetic Congressman,* 223; Department of the Navy, *U.S. Naval Hospital Complex in Balboa Park,* 70.

59. Tom Burgess, "21st Century Hospital Is Dedicated by Navy," *San Diego Union,* 24 January 1988, 1.

Chapter 11. 1990

1. Coletta, ed., *United States Navy and Marine Corps Bases, Domestic,* 554.

2. William J. Sturgeon, "San Clemente Island, Chronological Military History, 1934–2000" (1999; http://www.scisland.org).

3. Stillwell, The Reminiscences of Admiral Ernest M. Eller, USN (ret), 307.

4. Sturgeon, *San Clemente Island.* Named for Rear Adm. W. T. Tarrant, Commandant of the Eleventh Naval District June 1933–June 1936.

5. Spencer, "U.S. Naval Air Bases from 1914 to 1939," 1253.

6. NOSC, *Fifty Years of Research and Development on Point Loma,* 50.

7. Between 1958 and 1963, the deep-diving submersible *Trieste* under NEL control made 78 deep dives, including the record-breaking dive to 35,800 feet in the Marianas Trench.

8. Sturgeon, *San Clemente Island.* The SCORE range was later enlarged to encompass 670 square miles.

9. Sturgeon, *San Clemente Island.*

10. SEAL = Navy Sea-Air-Land Special Operations community.

11. Bill Kreh, "Coronado, Pacific Fleet Amphibious Center," *Navy Times,* 16 January 1954, 24.

12. Orr Kelly, *Brave Men, Dark Waters* (Notovo, Calif.: Presidio Press, 1992), 80.

13. Ibid., 101.

14. Tom Hawkins, "Some Thoughts about Chuck LeMoyne," *The Blast* (First Quarter 1997): 29.

15. When BUD/S training was created in 1968, the term correctly referred to the goal of training new members for both UDT and SEAL teams. With the amalgamation of all UDTs into SEAL teams, the logical and lexicologically correct temptation to change BUD/S training to BS training was avoided.

16. Patricia Dibsie, "A Final Drill: NTC Fades Away," *San Diego Union-Tribune,* 22 March 1997, B-1; Disestablishment Ceremony, Naval Training Center San Diego.

17. Neil Morgan, "Dream Site for Civic Park at NTC Base Up for Bids," *San Diego Union-Tribune,* 8 December 1998, A-2.

18. Camacho, *Cradle of the Navy,* 127.

19. *Recruit* lost her "commissioned" status in 1967 (some say through an edict filed by distant bureaucrats who couldn't fathom a "high and dry" vessel) but had so proved her worth that she was refitted and "modernized" in 1982.

20. James W. Crawley, "Marines Mark Their Return Home to Miramar," *San Diego Union-Tribune,* 2 October 1997, B-1.

21. James W. Crawley, "Carrier Departure Closes Books on Naval Aviation at Miramar," *San Diego Union-Tribune,* 10 November 1998, B-1.

22. NOSC, *Fifty Years of Research and Development on Point Loma,* 68.

23. Ibid., 94.

24. Ibid., 95.

25. Ibid., 125.

26. Ibid., 112.

27. Steinberg, "SD Warrior Nears 60," 1.

28. Miriam Raftery, "Navy Work at Historic Plant 19 Is Remodel Job on Mammoth Scale," *San Diego Union-Tribune,* 16 October 1994, H-2.

29. Joel Kotkin, "Role Model," *San Diego Union-Tribune,* 9 March 1997, G-1.

30. Neil Morgan, "It's Secret, but Our Future's on Point Loma," *San Diego Union-Tribune,* 9 January 1994, A-2.

31. James W. Crawley, "Navy's SPAWAR Brings Personnel, Big Budget," *San Diego Union-Tribune,* 2 October 1997, B-1.

32. James W. Crawley, "Navy's High-tech Command Center Tests Its Sea Legs," *San Diego Union-Tribune,* 6 November 1997, B-1.

33. Neil Morgan, "Easy to Forget," *San Diego Union-Tribune,* 29 June 1995, A-2.

Conclusion

1. Neil Morgan, "Easy to Forget," A-2.

BIBLIOGRAPHY

Archival Sources and Government Documents

Bureau of Aeronautics. *History of the Use of North Island, San Diego, Ca., for Flying Activities of the Army and Navy.* Washington, D.C.: Department of the Navy, 1932.

——. *World War II Administrative History,* vol. 11, *Aviation Shore Establishments.* Washington, D.C.: Department of the Navy, 1947.

Bureau of Yards and Docks. RG 71, National Archives and Records Service, Washington, D.C.

——. *Building the Navy's Bases in World War II.* Washington, D.C.: U.S. Government Printing Office, 1947.

Completion Report, 26 April 1941 to 30 June 1946. University of California Division of War Research, San Diego, 1946.

Deck logs of U.S. naval vessels, RG 24, National Archives and Records Service, Washington, D.C.

Department of the Navy. *Administrative History of the Western Sea Frontier.* 7 vols. Washington, D.C.: Department of the Navy, 1946.

——. *Administrative Study of the Commander Destroyers/Cruisers Pacific Fleet during World War II.* Washington, D.C.: Department of the Navy. 1946.

——. General records, 1798–1947. RG 80. National Archives and Records Service, Washington, D.C., and Laguna Niguel, Calif.

——. *History of the Fleet Operational Training Command, Pacific.* 2 vols. Washington, D.C.: Department of the Navy, 1946.

——. *Senior Member Board to Survey the Continental Naval Shore Establishments.* Naval Historical Center Archives. Washington, D.C.: Department of the Navy, 1 June 1946.

——. *The U.S. Naval Hospital Complex in Balboa Park, San Diego, California: A Report for the Historical American Buildings Survey.* San Diego: Department of the Navy, July 1987.

DuPont, Samuel Francis. Papers of Samuel Francis DuPont, 1803–1865. Hagley Museum and Library, Greenville, Del.

EDAW-Inc. Master Plan for Naval Amphibious Base, Coronado. Naval Base Coronado, 1998.

Eleventh Naval District. *Administrative History.* San Diego: Department of the Navy, 1946.

——. Annual Reports of the Commandant. Commandant Files, Eleventh Naval District, NARA-Laguna.

——. "Brochure of Activities." San Diego, 1 January 1945.

Fleet Antisubmarine Warfare School. *Command History.* San Diego: Department of the Navy, 3 June 1965.

Naval Ocean Systems Center. *Fifty Years of Research and Development on Point Loma, 1940–1990.* San Diego: Naval Ocean Systems Center, 1990.

Office of the Chief of Naval Operations. RG 38, National Archives and Records Service, Washington, D.C.

San Diego Chamber of Commerce. Minutes of the Board of Directors. San Diego, Calif.

Secretary of the Navy. Annual Reports. Department of the Navy, Washington, D.C.

U.S. Congress. House. *Establishment of Naval Bases on the Pacific Coast.* 66th Cong., 3rd sess., H. Rept. 1272. Washington, D.C.: U.S. Government Printing Office, 1921.

——. *Preliminary Report of the Navy Yard Commission (Helm Report).* 64th Cong., 2nd sess., 17 January 1917. H. Doc. 1946. Washington, D.C.: U.S. Government Printing Office, 1918.

——. *Report of the Army Commission (Reber Report).* 64th Cong., 1st sess., 29 December 1915. H. Doc. 687. Washington, D.C.: U.S. Government Printing Office, 1916.

Welles, Roger. Welles Papers. Naval Historical Foundation Collection, Library of Congress, Washington, D.C.

Interviews and Correspondence with Author

Alexander, Capt. Dick, USN (ret.)

Bagley, Adm. Worth, USN (ret.)

Bobczynski, Sigmund A.

Clarey, Rear Adm. Stephen, USN (ret.)

Crawford, Donald C.

Dow, H. Cushman

Dunn, Capt. Ivan, USN (ret.)

Gehl, Capt. Michael, USN

Hammett, Steven A.

Keith, Susan Ring

Larson, Jan

LeMoyne, Mrs. Irve Charles

Martin, Vice Adm. Edward, USN (ret.)

McLaurin, Lynn

Mustin, Vice Adm. Lloyd, USN (ret.)

Reynolds, Capt. Milton L., USN (ret.)

Robinson, Senior Chief Gunner's Mate Keith

Smith, Capt. George, USN (ret.)

Stovall, Howard, letter to author, 14 September 1999.

Sturgeon, Comdr. William J., III, USN (ret.)

Wax, Morris

Weimann, Jeff

Whitmore, Comdr. Fred, USN (ret.)

Yatsko, Andy

Oral Histories

Hotel del Coronado Oral History Collection, Hotel del Coronado, Coronado, Calif.

    Abele, Stan, 4 February 2000

    Clakis, Marguerite, 12 March 2000

    Creaghe, Larry and Betty, 4 February 2000

    Meyer, Elwood and Helen, 2 February 2000

    Morgan, Melody Hyde, 28 February 2000

Naval Institute Oral History Series, U.S. Naval Institute, Annapolis, Md.

    Benson, Rear Adm. Roy S., USN (ret.), interviewed by John T. Mason, 1987.

    Harralson, Lt. Comdr. Richard A., USN (ret.), interviewed by Paul Stillwell, 1998.

    King, Chief Warrant Officer Cecil S., Jr., USN (ret.), interviewed by Paul Stillwell, 1990.

    Lyon, Dr. Waldo K., interviewed by Etta-Belle Kitchen, 1972.

    Sharp, Adm. U.S. Grant Sharp, USN (ret.), interviewed by John T. Mason, 1987.

    Stroop, Vice Admiral Paul D., USN (ret.), interviewed by Etta-Belle Kitchen, 1970.

    Tomlinson, Capt. Daniel W., IV, USN (ret.), interviewed by Paul Stillwell and Barrett Tillman, 1995.

    Ward, Rear Adm. Norvell G., USN (ret.), interviewed by Paul Stillwell, 1996.

    Waters, Rear Adm. Odale D., Jr., USN (ret.), interviewed by John T. Mason and Paul Stillwell, 1994.

Oral Histories of Cabrillo National Monument, San Diego Beights, Voyd H.

Books and Articles

Alden, John D. *The American Steel Navy.* Annapolis, Md.: Naval Institute Press, 1972.

——. *Flush Decks and Four Pipes.* Annapolis, Md.: Naval Institute Press, 1965.

Arnold, H. H. "The History of Rockwell Field." NAS North Island Archives. 1924.

Ash, Leonard. "The Death of the *Bennington.*" 2 parts. *Mains'l Haul* (Summer 1992): 21–27, and (Fall 1992): 23–28.

Ault, Frank. "The Father of Top Gun." *Shipmate* (March 1999): 12.

Bauer, K. Jack. *Surfboats and Horse Marines.* Annapolis, Md.: Naval Institute Press, 1969.

Beigel, Harvey M. "The Battle Fleet's Home Port: 1919–1940." *U.S. Naval Institute Proceedings,* Supp. (1985): 54–59.

Bencik, Charles A. "The San Diego Naval Militia." *Mains'l Haul* (Fall 1993): 15–22.

——. "The Strange Affair of the *Itata.*" *Mains'l Haul* (Spring 1997): 20–31.

Bennett, Frank M. *The Steam Navy of the United States.* Westport, Conn.: Greenwood Press, 1896.

Bevil, Alexander D. "Remember the San Diego." *Olde San Diego Gazette,* August 1998, 19.

Birmingham, Stephen. *Duchess: The Story of Wallis Warfield Windsor.* Boston: Little, Brown, 1981.

"Boom Town: San Diego." *Life,* July 28, 1941, 64–69.

Bouchard, Joseph F. "Guarding the Cold War Ramparts." *Naval War College Review* 52, no. 3 (1999): 111–31.

Braisted, William R. *The United States Navy in the Pacific, 1897–1909.* Austin: University of Texas Press, 1958.

——. *The United States Navy in the Pacific, 1909–1922.* Austin: University of Texas Press, 1971.

Brandes, Ray. *Coronado, We Remember.* Coronado, Calif.: Coronado Historical Association, 1993.

Brennan, Joseph W. "What a Dime Can Do." *San Diego Magazine,* June 1931, 5–7.

Buell, Thomas B. *The Quiet Warrior.* Boston: Little, Brown, 1974.

Bushnell, Asa N. "There Came Upon Me a Day of Trouble." *San Diego Historical Society Quarterly* 7, no. 4 (1961): 45–49.

Camacho, Mary E. *Cradle of the Navy: The History of Naval Training Center San Diego.* San Diego: Jostens, 1997.

Canney, Donald L. *The Old Steam Navy, Frigates, Sloops, and Gunboats, 1815–1885.* Annapolis, Md.: Naval Institute Press, 1990.

Carlin, Katherine E., and Ray Brandes. *Coronado, the Enchanted Island.* Coronado, Calif.: Coronado Historical Association, 1987.

Chamberlain, Eugene K. Fort Rosecrans National Cemetery, California Registered Historical Landmark, no. 55. 1990.

——. *Old LaPlaya and LaPlaya Trail.* San Diego: Naval Ocean Systems Center, 1989.

Citizens' Aqueduct Celebration Committee. "San Diego's Quest for Water." Citizens' Aqueduct Celebration Committee, San Diego, 1947.

Cole, C. W. "Training Men at San Diego for America's First Line of Defense." *San Diego Magazine,* November 1927, 8.

Coletta, Paolo E., ed. *United States Navy and Marine Corps Bases, Domestic.* Westport, Conn.: Greenwood Press, 1985.

Colton, Walton. *Deck and Port.* New York: A. S. Barnest Co., 1854.

Cooling, Benjamin Franklin. *Gray Steel and Blue Water Navy.* Hamden, Conn.: Archon Books, 1979.

Cooper, Diane. "Remember the *Maine* and Mine the Harbors." *Mains'l Haul* (Spring 1998): 24–33.

"Coronado—Pacific Fleet Amphib Center." *Navy Times,* 16 January 1954.

"Coronado Beach: A Unique Corner of the Earth" (Pamphlet). Coronado: E. S. Babcock, Manager, Coronado Beach Company, 1898.

Corps of Engineers, U.S. Army. *The Port of San Diego, California.* Washington, D.C.: U.S. Government Printing Office, 1956.

———. *The Ports of San Diego and San Luis Obispo, California.* Washington, D.C.: U.S. Printing Office, 1936.

Cote, Chris. "German Prisoners of War in San Diego during World War II." Coronado, 1963.

Creed, Roscoe. *PBY: The Catalina Flying Boat.* Annapolis, Md.: Naval Institute Press, 1985.

Cronon, E. David. *The Cabinet Diaries of Josephus Daniels, 1913–1921.* Lincoln: University of Nebraska Press, 1963.

Curtis, John. "Paradise Revisited by German POW." *The Amphibian,* c. 1974.

Curtiss, Glenn H. *The Curtiss Aviation Book.* New York: Fred Stokes, c. 1912.

Dana, Richard Henry, Jr. *Two Years Before the Mast.* New York: Mead and Co., 1946.

Daniels, Josephus. *The Wilson Era: Years of Peace, 1910–1917.* Chapel Hill: University of North Carolina Press, 1944.

Davis, Edward J. P. *Historical San Diego.* San Diego: Pioneer Printers, 1953.

Dictionary of American Naval Fighting Ships. 8 vols. Washington, D.C.: U.S. Government Printing Office, 1959–81.

Doolittle, James H. *An Autobiography by General James H. Doolittle.* New York: Bantam Books, 1991.

Duvall, Robert Carson. "Excerpts from the Log of the USS *Savannah.*" *California Historical Society Quarterly* 3, no. 2 (1924): 70–79.

Evan Fleet Celebration Official Program (Pamphlet). San Diego, 1908.

Ewing, Steve, and John B. Lundstrom. *Fateful Rendezvous.* Annapolis, Md.: Naval Institute Press, 1997.

Fahey, Janice. "The Architectural/Historical Significance of Buildings at Naval Air Station, North Island, San Diego, California." San Diego, May 1988.

Fredericks, Eddie. "Early Naval History in San Diego." *Mains'l Haul* (Winter 1985): 6–8.

Fremont, John Charles. *Memoirs.* Chicago: Belford, Clarke and Company, 1886.

Friedman, Norman. *U.S. Aircraft Carriers.* Annapolis, Md.: Naval Institute Press, 1983.

———. *U.S. Destroyers.* Annapolis, Md.: Naval Institute Press, 1982.

Fry, John. *USS Saratoga CV-3.* Atglen, Pa.: Schiffer Publishing, 1996.

Fuller, Theodore W. *San Diego Originals.* Pleasant Hill, Calif.: California Profiles Publications, 1987.

George, Charlie. "U.S. Naval Hospital, San Diego, 1919–1958." 1958.

Grant, Wendy M., ed. *Fightertown USA: A Tribute to NAS Miramar.* San Diego: MWR Department, NAS Miramar, 1997.

Grobmeier, Alvin H. "Blimps Found Fair Grounds for Mooring." *Traditions* (December 1994): 5–7.

———. "Chronological History of U.S. Navy Radio Activities, Imperial Beach, California." *NCVA Cryptolog* (May 1995): 2–3.

———. "Radio Station Alerts Nation to 'Day That Will Live in Infamy.'" *Traditions* 1, no. 4 (1994): 5–13.

Grover, David H. "Bully of the Pacific Mixes It Up with Huns." *Traditions* (Summer 1997): 13–17.

Guyton, Boone T. *Air Base.* New York: McGraw-Hill, 1941.

Harrod, Frederick S. *Manning the New Navy.* Westport, Conn.: Greenwood Press, 1978.

Hebert, Edgar. "San Diego's Naval Militia." *San Diego Historical Society Quarterly* 9, no. 2 (1963): 15–22.

Hendrie, Andrew. *Flying Cats: The Catalina Aircraft in World War II.* Annapolis, Md.: Naval Institute Press, 1988.

Hennessey, Gregg R. "San Diego, the U.S. Navy, and Urban Development." *California History* 72, no. 2 (Summer 1993): 128–49.

Higham, Charles. *The Duchess of Windsor, the Second Life.* New York: McGraw-Hill, 1988.

Hinds, James W. "Officers Convalesce in Rural Area." *Traditions* (Summer 1997): 29.

———. *San Diego's Military Sites.* San Diego: San Diego Historical Society, 1986.

Holcomb, Will H. "Getting a Naval Training School." *San Diego Magazine,* April 1930, 50.

Hollandersky, Abe. *The Life Story of Abe the Newsboy: Hero of a Thousand Fights.* Los Angeles: Abe the Newsboy, 1930.

Holzman, Ellen B. "General Defends Marine Readiness." *Traditions* (January/February 1996): 4–27.

———. "Hospital Grows in Balboa Park." *Traditions* (Summer 1997): 21–25.

Howeth, L. S. *History of Communications-Electronics in the United States Navy.* Washington, D.C.: Office of Naval History, 1963.

Johnson, Robert Erwin. *Thence Round Cape Horn.* Annapolis, Md.: Naval Institute Press, 1963.

Jones, Robert D. *With the American Fleet from the Atlantic to the Pacific.* Seattle: Harrison, 1908.

Joyce, Barry Alan. *A Harbor Worth Defending: A Military History of Point Loma.* San Diego: Cabrillo Historical Association, 1995.

Kerley, Jay L. *California and the Navy.* San Diego: California Pacific International Exposition, 1935.

Kettner, William. *Why It Was Done and How.* San Diego: Frye and Smith, 1923.

Kinderman, Bernard J. *USS Ward Fires First Shot of World War II.* St. Paul, Minn.: Leeward Publications, 1983.

Klaus, Arnold. *History of the San Diego Chamber of Commerce.* San Diego: San Diego Chamber of Commerce, 1967.

Kurutz, Gary F. "The Only Safe and Sane Method: The Curtiss School of Aviation." *Journal of San Diego History* 25 (Winter 1979): 26–59.

Lamar, Howard. *The Cruise of the Portsmouth, 1845–47: A Sailor's View of the Naval Conquest of California.* New Haven: Yale University Press, 1958.

LaRue, Steve. "Pipeline Brought Water, Prosperity." *San Diego Union-Tribune,* 23 November 1997, B-1, B-2.

Lash, Joseph P. *Eleanor and Franklin.* New York: Norton, 1971.

Leary, William M. *Under Ice: Waldo Lyon and the Development of the Arctic Submarine.* College Station: Texas A&M University Press, 1999.

Leiser, Edward L. "North Island Wings Its Way into History." *Traditions* (November 1994): 3–4.

Lewis, Grayton A. *A History of Communications Intelligence in the United States.* Eugene, Ore.: Naval Cryptologic Veterans Association, 1982.

Lindbergh, Charles. *The Spirit of St. Louis.* New York: Scribner's, 1953.

Lockwood, Charles A., and Hans Christian Adamson. *Tragedy at Honda.* Philadelphia: Chilton, 1960.

Long, Comdr. B. J. "Sea Dart." *Foundation* 19, no. 2 (1998): 96–99.

Lotchin, Roger W. *Fortress California, 1910–1961.* New York: Oxford University Press, 1992.

Lyman, Chester. *Around the Horn to the Sandwich Islands and California, 1845–50.* New Haven: Yale University Press, 1925.

Macaulay, T. C. "The Lighter than Air Affair." *San Diego Magazine,* February 1930, 3–21.

MacMullen, Jerry. *They Came by Sea.* San Diego: Maritime Museum Association of San Diego, 1988.

Marshall, Don B. *California Shipwrecks.* Seattle: Superior Publishing, 1978.

Merrill, James M. *DuPont: The Making of an Admiral.* New York: Dodd, Mead, 1986.

Miller, Edward S. *War Plan Orange.* Annapolis, Md.: Naval Institute Press, 1991.

Miller, Max. *Harbor of the Sun: The Story of the Port of San Diego.* New York: Doubleday, 1940.

——. *I Cover the Waterfront.* New York: Dutton, 1932.

Moon, D. P. "Recommissioning the Destroyers." *U.S. Naval Institute Proceedings* (February 1931): 162–74.

Morgan, Neil, and Judith Morgan. *Roger: A Biography of Roger Revelle.* San Diego: University of California–San Diego, 1996.

Moss, James E. *San Diego Pioneer Families.* San Diego: San Diego Historical Society, 1978.

Nash, Gerald D. *The American West in the Twentieth Century.* Englewood Cliffs, N.J.: Prentice-Hall, 1973.

Nelson, Herbert J. *The Port of San Diego: Development of Terminal Facilities for Water-borne Commerce by Federal and Municipal Agencies.* San Diego: San Diego State University, 1956.

Newland, James D. "Admiral Cements Station's Foundation." *Traditions* (November 1995): 3–11.

Nolen, John. *A Comprehensive City Plan for San Diego, California.* Cambridge, Mass.: Walker-Hartzog Associates, 1926.

O'Gara, Gordon C. *Theodore Roosevelt and the Rise of the Modern Navy.* New York: Greenwood Press, 1943.

Pomfret, John E. *California Gold Rush Voyages, 1848–1849.* San Marino, Calif.: Huntington Library, 1954.

Poncia, Michelle. "Dinosaurs Retired as Hospital Evolves." *Traditions* (Summer 1997): 26–32.

Pond, George R. *Aviation Review: U.S. Navy in San Diego, California, 1921.* San Diego: Dove and Robinson Printers, 1921.

Potter, E. B. *Bull Halsey.* Annapolis, Md.: Naval Institute Press, 1985.

——. *Nimitz.* Annapolis, Md.: Naval Institute Press, 1976.

Pourade, Richard F. *City of the Dream.* La Jolla, Calif.: Copley Books, 1977.

——. *The Glory Years.* San Diego: Union-Tribune Publishing, 1964.

——. *Gold in the Sun.* San Diego: Union-Tribune Publishing, 1965.

——. *The Rising Tide.* San Diego: Union-Tribune Publishing, 1967.

——. *The Silver Dons.* San Diego: Union-Tribune Publishing, 1963.

Reckner, James R. *Teddy Roosevelt's Great White Fleet.* Annapolis, Md.: Naval Institute Press, 1988.

Reynolds, Clark G. *Admiral John H. Towers.* Annapolis, Md.: Naval Institute Press, 1991.

——. *Famous American Admirals.* New York: Van Nostrand Reinhold, 1978.

——. "Submarine Attacks on the Pacific Coast, 1942." *Pacific Historical Review* 33, no. 2 (1964): 183–93.

Robinson, Douglass H., and Charles L. Keller. *Up Ship! A History of the U.S. Navy's Rigid Airships, 1919–1935.* Annapolis, Md.: Naval Institute Press, 1982.

Roskill, Stephen. *Naval Policy Between the Wars: The Period of Anglo-American Antagonism, 1910–1929.* New York: Walker and Co., 1968.

——. *Naval Policy Between the Wars: The Period of Reluctant Rearmament, 1930–39.* Annapolis, Md.: Naval Institute Press, 1976.

Rowan, Stephen C. "Recollections of the Mexican War." *U.S. Naval Institute Proceedings* 34, no. 3 (1888): 539–59.

Scott, Mary L. *San Diego, Air Capital of the West.* Virginia Beach, Va.: Donning Company, 1991.

Senn, RADM Thomas J. "The History of the Navy in San Diego." In *History of San Diego County,* ed. C. H. Heilbron. San Diego: San Diego Press Club, 1936.

Shragge, Abraham. "A New Federal City: San Diego during World War II." *Pacific Historical Review* 63, no. 3 (1994): 333–61.

——. "Radio and Real Estate: The U.S. Navy's First Land Purchase in San Diego." *Journal of San Diego History* 42 (Fall 1996): 240–59.

Smith, Jack. "Only a Jukebox." *Westways* (January 1999): 30–33.

Smith, Leighton W. Interview, 11 May 1999. *Frontline.* WGBH, Boston.

Smith, Richard K. *The Airships Akron and Macon.* Annapolis, Md.: Naval Institute Press, 1965.

Smythe, William E. *History of San Diego, 1542–1908.* San Diego: The History Co., 1908.

Spencer, Ivor D. "U.S. Naval Air Bases from 1914 to 1939." *U.S. Naval Institute Proceedings* (November 1949): 1243–55.

Starr, Kevin. *The Dream Endures: California Enters the 1940s.* New York: Oxford University Press, 1997.

Stevens, Edward D. "They Used to Call It Wireless." *San Diego Historical Society Quarterly* 9, no. 1 (1963): 712.

Stillwell, Paul. *Battleship Arizona.* Annapolis, Md.: Naval Institute Press, 1991.

Stirling, Yates. *Sea Duty: The Memoirs of a Fighting Admiral.* New York: Putnam and Sons, 1939.

Stovall, J. C. *NAVAER 1411 Aviators Flight Log Book ICO RM2 J. C. Stovall.* Washington, D.C.: Department of the Navy, 1938.

Studer, Clara. *Sky Storming Yankee: The Life of Glenn Curtiss.* New York: Arno Press, 1972.

Sudsbury, Elretta, ed. *Jackrabbits to Jets: The History of NAS North Island, San Diego, California.* San Diego: San Diego Publishing, 1992.

Tarbuck, Ray. *Analysis of the Transfer of Naval Vessels from San Diego.* San Diego: San Diego Chamber of Commerce, 1952.

Tate, Jackson R. "We Rode the Covered Wagon." *U.S. Naval Institute Proceedings* (October 1978): 62–69.

Taylor, Theodore. *The Magnificent Mitscher.* New York: Norton, 1954.

Thomas, Donald I. "Recommissioning Destroyers, 1939 Style." *U.S. Naval Institute Proceedings* (September 1979): 70–72.

Tozer, C. M. "The Navy's Relationship to San Diego's Business." *San Diego Magazine,* February 1930, 7–11.

"Training Command, U.S. Pacific Fleet." *U.S. Naval Training Bulletin* (January 1949): 2–7.

"Training in the San Diego Area." *U.S. Naval Training Bulletin* (May 1951): 10–14.

Trimble, William F. *Admiral William A. Moffett.* Washington, D.C.: Smithsonian Institution Press, 1994.

Turnbull, Archibald D., and Clifford L. Lord. *History of United States Naval Aviation.* New Haven: Yale University Press, 1949.

"U.S. Naval Ship Repair Facility, San Diego." *Bureau of Ships Journal* 6, no. 6 (1957): 2–13.

U.S. Naval Training Station. "Ashore in San Diego" (pamphlet). San Diego, 1942.

Vancouver, George. *Voyage of Discovery.* New York: Da Capo Press, 1798.

VanDenburgh, Elizabeth Douglass. *My Voyage in the U.S. Frigate Congress.* New York: Desmond Fitzgerald, 1913.

Vezina, Meredith. "Fire . . . fire . . . fire." *Traditions* (November 1995): 26–29.

Wagner, William. *Reuben Fleet and the Story of Consolidated Aircraft.* Fallbrook, Calif.: Aero Publishers, 1976.

Wakeman, Frederic. *Shore Leave.* New York: Farrar and Rinehart, 1944.

Webber, Bert. *Retaliation: Japanese Attacks and Allied Countermeasures on the Pacific Coast in World War II.* Corvallis: Oregon State University Press, 1975.

Wheeler, Gerald E. *Admiral William Veazie Pratt, USN.* Washington, D.C.: Department of the Navy, 1974.

Whitmore, Fred. "USS *San Diego:* The Unbeatable Ship That Nobody Ever Heard Of." *Mains'l Haul* (Spring 1997): 6–19.

Wildenberg, Thomas. *Destined for Glory.* Annapolis, Md.: Naval Institute Press, 1998.

Wilson, Bob. *Confessions of a Kinetic Congressman.* San Diego: San Diego State University Foundation, 1996.

Windsor, Duchess of. *The Heart Has Its Reasons.* New York: David McKay Co., 1956.

Witherspoon, Charles R. "Navy Training a Shock to System." *Traditions* (July–August 1996): 30–35.

Wood, H. P. *The Port of San Diego.* San Diego: Frye, Garrett and Smith Printers, 1900.

Wood, Junius B. "Seeing America from the Shenandoah." *National Geographic* (January 1925): 36–51.

Zacharias, Ellis M. *Secret Missions.* New York: G. P. Putnam, 1946.

Unpublished Sources

Brandes, Ray. "San Diego's Chinatown and Stingaree District." University of San Diego Copley Library, San Diego.

Brown, Jeffrey Charles. "An Historical Geographical Study of North Island." California State University–Long Beach, 1991.

Caldwell, C. Dewey. "The Port of San Diego, 1846–1890." Master's thesis, Claremont Graduate School, Claremont, Calif., 1969.

Callaghan, Paul M. "Fort Rosecrans, California." Thesis, University of San Diego, San Diego, 1980.

Chambers, Consultants and Planners. "The Cultural Resources of Naval Air Station, North Island and Outlying Field, Imperial Beach, San Diego County, California." Navy Region Southwest Environmental Resources Office, April 1982.

Comprehensive Planning Organization, San Diego County Government. "Aviation in San Diego, 1917–1971." University of San Diego Law Library, San Diego, 17 November 1971.

Craig, Donald R. "Annotated Bibliography of the History of the U.S. Naval Training Center." Master's thesis, University of San Diego, San Diego, 1969.

Croft, Denise Draper. "Hotel del Coronado: An Architectural and Social History." Master's thesis, University of California–Riverside, 1975.

Erickson, Glenn C. "The Effect of the Military Establishment and the Aviation Industry on the Need for a More Balanced Economy in San Diego." Master's thesis, Stanford University Graduate School of Business, Palo Alto, 1954.

Farquhar, Jeffrey W. "The History of Naval Station San Diego." Thesis, University of San Diego, San Diego, 1996.

"Hotel del Coronado Land Booklet No. 501, Hotel del Coronado Room Leases." Hotel del Coronado archives, Coronado, 1944.

Joyce, Barry A. "James Alden: Naval Officer, Scientist and Explorer." Master's thesis, San Diego State University, San Diego, 1990.

Kaplan and Associates. "Architectural and Historical Significance of Selected Buildings at the Naval Training Center, San Diego, California." Fleet ASW Training Center Library, San Diego, 1989.

Mahnke, George W. "The Urban Impact on Coronado of the San Diego–Coronado Bay Bridge." Master's thesis, San Diego State University, San Diego, 1970.

Moore, Floyd R. "San Diego Airport Development." Master's thesis, San Diego State University, San Diego, 1960.

Nelson, Herbert J. "The Port of San Diego: Development of Terminal Facilities for Water-borne Commerce by Federal and Municipal Agencies." Master's thesis, San Diego State University, San Diego, 1956.

Schiller, Alec C. "Congressman Bob Wilson's Contribution to the Navy and San Diego, 1952–62." Master's thesis, San Diego State University, San Diego, 1990.

Shragge, Abraham J. "Boosters and Bluejackets: The Civic Culture of Militarism in San Diego, California, 1900–1945." Diss., University of California–San Diego, 1998.

Winterhouse, John. "The Historical Geography of San Diego—Some Aspects of Landscape Change Prior to 1850." Master's thesis, San Diego State University, San Diego, 1972.

INDEX

About the Author

Bruce Linder is a former U.S. Navy captain who has commanded a guided missile frigate and two large bases in San Diego during a career of more than twenty-six years. A past winner of the Naval Institute's Arleigh Burke Literary Award, he has been published in a variety of magazines and journals in the United States, Europe, and Japan.

Captain Linder and his wife reside in Coronado, California, where he is employed as a defense and technology consultant. The Linders have two grown daughters.